PENGUIN BOOKS

The World Turned Upside Down

Christopher Hill (1912–2003) was educated at St Peter's School, York, and at Balliol College, Oxford, and in 1934 was made a fellow of All Souls College, Oxford. In 1936 he became lecturer in modern history at University College, Cardiff, and two years later fellow and tutor in modern history at Balliol. After war service, which included two years in the Russian department of the Foreign Office, he returned to Oxford in 1945. From 1958 until 1965 he was university lecturer in sixteenth- and seventeenth-century history, and from 1965 to 1978 he was Master of Balliol College.

His publications include *Lenin and the Russian Revolution*; *Puritanism and Revolution*; *God's Englishman: Oliver Cromwell and the English Revolution*; *The World Turned Upside Down*; *Milton and the English Revolution*, which won the Royal Society of Literature Award; *A Turbulent, Seditious and Factious People: John Bunyan and His Church*, which won the 1989 W. H. Smith Literary Award and *The English Bible and the Seventeenth-Century Revolution*, which was shortlisted for the 1993 NCR Book Award.

CHRISTOPHER HILL

The World Turned
Upside Down

*Radical Ideas During
the English Revolution*

PENGUIN BOOKS

PENGUIN BOOKS

UK | USA | Canada | Ireland | Australia
India | New Zealand | South Africa

Penguin Books is part of the Penguin Random House group of companies whose
addresses can be found at global.penguinrandomhouse.com.

First published by Maurice Temple Smith 1972
Published in Pelican Books 1975
Reprinted in Peregrine Books 1984
Reprinted in Penguin Books 1991
This edition published 2019
002

Set in 9.25/12.5 pt Sabon LT Std
Typeset by Jouve (UK), Milton Keynes
Printed and bound in Great Britain by Clays Ltd, Elcograf S.p.A.

A CIP catalogue record for this book is available from the British Library

978-0-141-99313-3

www.greenpenguin.co.uk

In gratitude to Rodney for suggesting it, and to B, A, D, without whose cooperation and understanding this book would never have got written.

Contents

CONTENTS

Preface

There are few activities more cooperative than the writing of history. The author puts his name brashly on the title-page and the reviewers rightly attack him for his errors and misinterpretations; but none knows better than he how much his whole enterprise depends on the preceding labours of others. I should like to single out three scholars to whom I am most conscious of indebtedness – Mr A. L. Morton, who has published the only serious book on the Ranters, and whose study of Blake in relation to seventeenth-century radicals is equally important; Dr G. F. Nuttall, whose meticulous scholarship ranges over all the obscure by-ways of seventeenth-century religious history; and Mr K. V. Thomas, whose majestic *Religion and the Decline of Magic* has made us all re-think our ideas about seventeenth-century England. I benefited very greatly from supervising Mr Frank McGregor's thesis on the Ranters, and from reading Professor W. A. Cole's unpublished dissertation on the Quakers and discussing it with him. Many more debts are recorded in the footnotes. Dr Bernard Capp, Mr Peter Clark, Mrs K. R. Firth, Dr A. M. Johnson, Dr R. C. Richardson and Professor Austin Woolrych all allowed me to read and quote from material in advance of publication. Dr Robin Clifton, Professor G. H. George, Dr P. J. R. Phizackerley, Mrs Joan Thirsk and Professor C. M. Williams were generous in answering questions. Professor Rodney Hilton saved me from many errors, and did what he could to make the book more readable. My colleagues at Balliol allowed me a sabbatical term during which most of the writing was done: I am most grateful to them for their forbearance and to the protective vigilance of the College Secretary, Mrs Bridget

Page. Especial thanks are due to Miss Pat Lloyd, who typed the whole book and corrected many of my spelling mistakes. She also helped generously and skilfully with proof-reading. My wife always comes last among those to be thanked and should always come first.

16 October 1971

Note to the Penguin Edition

I am grateful to many friends for suggesting corrections and improvements to the first edition of this book, especially to Dr Bernard Capp, Mr John Dunn, Mr Charles Hobday, Professor Ivan Roots and Mr Keith Thomas. I should have explained in my original Preface that seventeenth-century spelling and capitalization have been modernized in quotations. I have not altered the grammar when – for instance – Winstanley uses a plural subject with a singular verb. Readers of this book may be interested in *The Law of Freedom and Other Writings*, by Gerrard Winstanley, published as a Pelican Classic in 1973.

Abbreviations

The following abbreviations have been used in the notes:

A.H.R.	*Agricultural History Review*
Braithwaite	W. C. Braithwaite, *The First Period of Quakerism* (1912)
C.J.	*Commons' Journals*
C.S.P.D.	*Calendar of State Papers (Domestic)*
E.H.R.	*English Historical Review*
Fenstanton Records	Ed. E. B. Underhill, *Records of the Churches of Christ gathered at Fenstanton, Warboys and Hexham, 1644–1720* (Hanserd Knollys Soc., 1854)
H. and D.	Ed. W. Haller and G. Davies, *The Leveller Tracts, 1647–1653* (Columbia U.P., 1944)
H.M.C.	Historical Manuscripts Commission
I.O.E.R.	C. Hill, *Intellectual Origins of the English Revolution* (Oxford U.P., 1965)
J.M.H.	*Journal of Modern History*
L.J.	*Lords' Journals*
P. and P.	*Past and Present*
P. and R.	C. Hill, *Puritanism and Revolution* (Panther edn)
Sabine	Ed. G. H. Sabine, *The Works of Gerrard Winstanley* (Cornell U.P., 1941)
S. and P.	C. Hill, *Society and Puritanism in Pre-Revolutionary England* (Panther edn)
T.R.H.S.	*Transactions of the Royal Historical Society*
U.P.	University Press

V.C.H.	*Victoria County History*
Wolfe	Ed. D. M. Wolfe, *Leveller Manifestoes of the Puritan Revolution* (1944)
Woodhouse	Ed. A. S. P. Woodhouse, *Puritanism and Liberty* (1938)

The Lord preserveth the strangers; he relieveth the fatherless and the widow: but the way of the wicked he turneth upside down.

Psalm 146, 9

The Lord maketh the earth . . . waste, and turneth it upside down . . . And it shall be, as with the people, so with the priest; as with the servant, so with his master; as with the maid, so with her mistress . . . The earth shall reel to and fro like a drunkard, and shall be removed like a cottage . . . The Lord shall punish the host of the high ones . . . and the kings of the earth upon the earth.

Isaiah xxiv, 1–2, 20–21

They came to Thessalonica . . . and Paul . . . reasoned with them out of the Scriptures . . . And some of them believed . . . and of the chief women not a few. But the Jews which believed not, moved with envy, took unto them certain lewd fellows of the baser sort, and gathered a company, and set all the city on an uproar . . . crying, These that have turned the world upside down are come hither also.

The Acts of the Apostles xvii, 1–6

I
Introduction

It hath been ... mine endeavour ... to give unto every limb and part not only his due proportion but also his due place, and not to set the head where the foot should be, or the foot where the head. I may peradventure to many seem guilty of that crime which was laid against the Apostle, to turn the world upside down, and to set that in the bottom which others make the top of the building, and to set that upon the roof which others lay for a foundation.

HENRY DENNE, *Grace, Mercy and Peace*
(1645) in *Fenstanton Records*, p. 422.

Popular revolt was for many centuries an essential feature of the English tradition, and the middle decades of the seventeenth century saw the greatest upheaval that has yet occurred in Britain. The present book does not attempt to tell again the story of how the Army of the Long Parliament overcame Charles I and his supporters, executed the King and established a short-lived republic. Although there was considerable popular support for Parliament in the 1640s, the long-term consequences of the Revolution were all to the advantage of the gentry and merchants, not of the lower fifty per cent of the population on whom I try to focus attention.

This book deals with what from one point of view are subsidiary episodes and ideas in the English Revolution, the attempts of various groups of the common people to impose their own solutions to the problems of their time, in opposition to the wishes of their betters who had called them into political action. The reader who wishes to restore his perspective might with advantage read the valuable book recently published by Professor David Underdown: *Pride's Purge* (Oxford U.P., 1971). This deals with almost exactly the same period as I do, but from an entirely different angle. His is the view from the top, from Whitehall, mine the worm's eye view. His index and mine contain totally different lists of names.

The revolt within the Revolution which is my subject took many forms, some better known than others. Groups like Levellers, Diggers and Fifth Monarchists offered new political solutions (and in the case of the Diggers, new economic solutions too). The various sects – Baptists, Quakers, Muggletonians – offered new religious solutions. Other groups asked sceptical questions about all the institutions and beliefs of their society – Seekers, Ranters, the Diggers too. Indeed it is perhaps misleading to differentiate too sharply between politics, religion and general scepticism. We know, as a result of hindsight, that some groups – Baptists, Quakers – will survive as religious sects and that most of the others will disappear. In consequence we unconsciously tend to impose too clear outlines on the early history of English sects, to read back later beliefs into the 1640s and 50s. One of the aims of this book will be to suggest that in this period things were much more blurred. From, say, 1645 to 1653, there was a great overturning, questioning, revaluing, of everything in England. Old institutions, old beliefs, old values came in question. Men moved easily from one critical group to another, and a Quaker of the early 1650s had far more in common with a Leveller, a Digger or a Ranter than with a modern member of the Society of Friends.

Our period begins when Parliament seemed to have triumphed over the King, and the gentry and merchants who had supported the Parliamentary cause in the civil war expected to reconstruct the institutions of society as they wished, to impose their values. If they had not been impeded in this, England might have passed straight to something like the political settlement of 1688 – Parliamentary sovereignty, limited monarchy, imperialist foreign policy, a world safe for businessmen to make profits in. But instead there was a period of glorious flux and intellectual excitement, when, as Gerrard Winstanley put it, 'the old world ... is running up like parchment in the fire.'[1] Literally anything seemed possible; not only were the values of the old hierarchical society called in question but also the new values, the protestant ethic itself. Only gradually was control re-established during the Protectorate of Oliver Cromwell, leading to a restoration of the rule of the gentry, and then of King and bishops in 1660.

There were, we may oversimplify, two revolutions in mid-seventeenth-century England. The one which succeeded established the sacred rights of property (abolition of feudal tenures, no arbitrary taxation), gave political power to the propertied (sovereignty of Parliament and common law, abolition of prerogative courts), and removed all impediments to the triumph of the ideology of the men of property – the protestant ethic. There was, however, another revolution which never happened, though from time to time it threatened. This might have established communal property, a far wider democracy in political and legal institutions, might have disestablished the state church and rejected the protestant ethic.

The object of the present book is to look at this revolt within the Revolution and the fascinating flood of radical ideas which it threw up. History has to be rewritten in every generation, because although the past does not change the present does; each generation asks new questions of the past, and finds new areas of sympathy as it re-lives different aspects of the experiences of its predecessors. The Levellers were better understood as political democracy established itself in late nineteenth- and early twentieth-century England; the Diggers have something to say to twentieth-century socialists. Now that the protestant ethic itself, the greatest achievement of European bourgeois society in the sixteenth and seventeenth centuries, is at last being questioned after a rule of three or four centuries, we can study with a new sympathy the Diggers, the Ranters, and the many other daring thinkers who in the seventeenth century refused to bow down and worship it.

The historical narrative, the main outline of events, is given. No amount of detailed working over the evidence is going to change the factual essentials of the story. But the interpretation will vary with our attitudes, with our lives in the present. So reinterpretation is not only possible but necessary. Just as Professor Barraclough has made our generation aware of the narrow provincialism which dominates the outlook of most historians and urges us to extend our geographical area of study, so experience of something approaching democracy makes us realize that most of our history is written about, and from the point of view of, a tiny fragment of the population, and makes us want to extend in depth as well as in breadth.

Each generation, to put it another way, rescues a new area from what its predecessors arrogantly and snobbishly dismissed as 'the lunatic fringe'. Thanks to the admirable work of Messrs Lamont, Toon and Capp, we now see millenarianism as a natural and rational product of the assumptions of this society, shared by John Milton and Sir Henry Vane as well as by Vavasor Powell and John Rogers. Thanks to the admirable work of Dr Frances Yates, Professor Rattansi and Messrs Webster and Thomas, alchemy, astrology and natural magic similarly take their place as reasonable subjects for rational men and women to be interested in, from Samuel Hartlib to Sir Isaac Newton. So far only Mr A. L. Morton and Mr Frank McGregor have demonstrated that the Ranters too must be taken seriously, that they perhaps have something to say to our generation.

Historians, in fact, would be well-advised to avoid the loaded phrase, 'lunatic fringe'. Lunacy, like beauty, may be in the eye of the beholder. There were lunatics in the seventeenth century, but modern psychiatry is helping us to understand that madness itself may be a form of protest against social norms, and that the 'lunatic' may in some sense be saner than the society which rejects him. Many writers who were aware that their views would seem intolerably extreme to their respectable contemporaries deliberately exaggerated their eccentricities in order to get a hearing – as, in rather a different way, George Bernard Shaw did in the twentieth century.[2]

Moreover, foolery had had a social function in medieval society. There was a convention that on certain set occasions – Shrove Tuesday, the Feasts of Fools, All Fools Day and others – the social hierarchy and the social decencies could be turned upside down.

It was a safety-valve: social tensions were released by the occasional *bouleversement*; the social order seemed perhaps that much more tolerable.[3] What was new in the seventeenth century was the idea that the world might be *permanently* turned upside down: that the dream world of the Land of Cokayne or the kingdom of heaven might be attainable on earth now.

During the brief years of extensive liberty of the press in England it may have been easier for eccentrics to get into print than ever before or since. Before 1641, and after 1660, there was a strict censorship. In the intervening years of freedom, a printing press was a relatively cheap and portable piece of equipment. Publishing had not yet developed as a capitalist industry. The late Miss Iris Morley noted the natural harmony which existed between Leveller writers, printers and hawkers of pamphlets, at a time when printing was a small man's occupation.[4] Printers like George Calvert were prepared to run considerable risks to get radical works published.[5] It may also have been that in a market flooded with printed matter there were sales advantages in calculated eccentricity. At least it is better for the historian to err on the side of looking for rational significance in any ideas which the men of the seventeenth century took seriously. If we dismiss such ideas because they seem irrational to us, we may be depriving ourselves of valuable insights into the society, as Mr K. V. Thomas's *Religion and the Decline of Magic* has so brilliantly demonstrated. It is no longer necessary to apologize too profusely for taking the common people of the past on their own terms and trying to understand them.

Historians are interested in ideas not only because they influence societies, but because they reveal the societies which give rise to them. Hence the philosophical truth of the ideas is irrelevant to the historian's purpose, though all of us have our preferences: the reader will no doubt soon discover mine.

By studying some of the less conventional ideas which surfaced during the English Revolution the object of this book is to obtain a deeper insight into English society than the evidence permits either before 1640 or after 1660, when the censorship ensured that really subversive ideas were not published. In so far as the attempt is successful it may tell us something not only about English history in this period of unique liberty, but also about the more 'normal' periods which preceded and followed it – normal because we are again ignorant of what the common people were thinking. We may find that the obscure men and women who figure in this book, together with some not so obscure, speak more directly to us than Charles I or Pym or General Monck, who appear as history-makers in the textbooks. This would in itself be a satisfactorily upside-down thought to come away with.

2

The Parchment and the Fire

Enemies of the church ... abuse the precious saints of God with these and other reproaches ... Oh, these are the men that would turn the world upside down, that make the nation full of tumults and uproars, that work all the disturbance in church and state. It is fit such men and congregations should be suppressed, ... that we may have truth and peace and government again.

WILLIAM DELL, *The Building, Beauty, Teaching and Establishment of the Truly Christian and Spiritual Church* (1646) in *Several Sermons* (1709), p. 109.

I   SOCIAL TENSIONS

I have tried elsewhere to suggest that there was a greater background of class hostility in England before 1640 than historians have normally recognized.[1] A Scottish observer indeed commented in 1614 on the 'bitter and distrustful' attitude of English common people towards the gentry and nobility.[2] These sentiments were reciprocated. Only members of the landed ruling class were allowed to carry weapons: 'the meaner sort of people and servants' were normally excluded from serving in the militia, by a quite deliberate policy.[3] When in the exceptional circumstances of 1588 military training was extended to the whole settled population, there were complaints from Herefordshire that once servants were trained as soldiers they would become unruly and unwilling to continue to serve their masters in proper subordination.[4] In the sixteenth and seventeenth centuries, as population rapidly expanded, London, I shall suggest, became the refuge of 'masterless men' – the victims of enclosure, vagabonds, criminals – to an extent that alarmed contemporaries.[5] One of the arguments advanced in propaganda for colonizing Ireland in 1594 was that 'the people poor and seditious, which were a burden to the commonwealth, are drawn forth, whereby the matter of sedition is removed out of the City'.[6] The same argument was often used later to advocate exporting 'the rank multitude' to Virginia. The judicious Hooker, arguing that 'extraordinary motions of the spirit' could be very dangerous, suggested that this was especially true in the case of 'men whose minds are of themselves as dry fuel, apt beforehand unto tumults, seditions and broils'. Such men, he thought, were to be found among the lower orders of society.[7] They were certainly to be found in Newcastle-upon-Tyne, where we are told in 1633 that 'people of mean condition . . . are apt to turn every pretence and colour of grievance into uproar and seditious mutiny'.[8]

Not far below the surface of Stuart society, then, discontent was rife. In 1626 a soldier had thought of assassinating the Duke of Buckingham, and perhaps the King too, so as to establish a republic or put the King of Bohemia on the throne.[9] When Felton actually did assassinate Buckingham two years later, his popularity was so great that other men pretended they were Felton. 'The devil go with the King and all the proud pack of them,' said a Yorkshire village blacksmith in 1633. 'What care I?'[10]

This class antagonism was exacerbated by the financial hardships of the years from 1620 to 1650, which Professor Bowden has described as economically among the most terrible in English history.[11] The government was held to blame for its mismanagement of the economy and for monopolies and other fiscal devices of the 1630s which visibly added to the cost of living. Looking back at one of these schemes, a pamphlet of 1649 spoke of 'pilling and polling the nation by oppression', and asked, 'How many poor apple-women and broom-men, rag-merchants and people of all sorts, sold and pawned their bedding and their clothes' to buy themselves the freedom of the new royal incorporation of the suburbs of London? 'And when all was done, it proved a cheat: thus was the king's coffers filled with oppression.'[12]

That of course is propaganda, not to be taken too literally. But there can be no doubt of the bloody-mindedness of other ranks in the army which Charles collected to oppose the Scottish invasion of 1640. The common people ('men with no shirts', a disgruntled royalist called them)[13] took an unusually active share in elections for the two Parliaments of 1640, on the anti-court side – often introducing an element of class hostility as well. Thus in High Wycombe all four candidates for the Short Parliament were opponents of the court, but two of them represented 'the popular party' against the local ruling oligarchy.[14] In Essex one of 'the rude vulgar people' threatened to 'tear the gentlemen to pieces' if the popular candidate was not elected for the county. At Great Marlow, Buckinghamshire, bargemen, labourers, shopkeepers – 'the ordinary sort of townsmen', led by 'a country fellow in a plain and mean habit' – put up their own candidate against the local landlord who had court connections – and won.[15]

Yet when the Long Parliament found itself faced by a king who refused to surrender to their demands, they were forced to look for support outside the charmed circle of the ruling class. In London crowds of demonstrators used 'to flock unto Westminster' in moments of crisis. They were, 'most of them, men of mean or a middle quality themselves, having no aldermen, merchants or Common-Council men among them . . . They were modest in their apparel but not in their language.' (One waterman indeed told the Lord Mayor in May 1641 that 'it was Parliament time now', and that 'the Lord Mayor was but their slave'.) 'The present hatred of the citizens was such unto gentlemen, especially courtiers, that few durst come into the City, or if they did, they were sure to receive affronts and be abused.'[16] A royalist called the Grand Remonstrance of November 1641 'that appeal to the people',[17] and he was quite right: it was printed and distributed throughout the country. All major speeches by opposition M.P.s were published and widely circulated: we may be sure they were read and discussed in taverns and ale-houses. Carefully organized petitions of support for Parliament poured in from the counties from 1641 onwards: collecting signatures for these must have been a novel and very effective way of drawing ordinary people into political action.

This background of social insubordination naturally influenced men of property when they had to choose for King or Parliament on the outbreak of civil war. The royalism of Richard Dowdeswell, agent to Lionel Cranfield, Earl of Middlesex, Mrs Prestwich tells us, stemmed from a concern for social order, not from positive loyalty to King or church. 'The countenances of men are so altered,' he wrote in October 1642, 'especially of the mean and middle rank of men, that the turning of a straw would set a whole county in a flame and occasion the plundering of any man's house or goods.'[18] 'Whenever necessity shall force us to make use of the multitude,' Sir John Potts wrote to Sir Simonds D'Ewes in August 1642, 'I do not promise myself safety.' So he was still working for a compromise peace.[19] When war came both Potts and D'Ewes chose the side of Parliament, but the latter too reflected that 'all right and property, all *meum et tuum*, must cease in a civil war, and we know not what advantage the meaner sort also may take to divide the spoils of the rich and noble amongst them, who begin already [1642] to allege that all being of one mould there is no reason that some should have so much and others so little'.[20] 'What do you tell me of birth and descent?' cried a Northamptonshire sectary in July 1643. 'I hope within this year to see never a gentleman in England.'[21]

The civil war years saw the breakdown of church courts and the censorship; judges no longer went on circuit. The actual fighting was not very devastating, at least by comparison with what was going on in Germany at the same time. But in some areas law and order broke down completely. In Gloucestershire royalists plundered any clothier; men assumed that 'the clothiers through the whole kingdom were rebels by their trade'.[22] Between 1643 and 1645 the Verneys in Buckinghamshire were collecting less than ten per cent of rents due.[23] In 1644 Richard Dowdeswell, also from Gloucestershire, complained that 'such kind of people as the tenants are do now take no small liberty over their betters. They that see it not cannot believe it.'[24]

Before civil war started Charles I had warned the supporters of Parliament of the danger that 'at last the common people' may 'set up for themselves, call parity and independence liberty, . . . destroy all rights and properties, all distinctions of families and merit.'[25] The Scottish poet Drummond had the same nightmare three years earlier, asking 'whether these great commotions and discords may not dissolve in *bellum servile*, and peasants, clowns, farmers, base people all in arms, may not swallow the nobles and gentry, invest their possessions, adhere together by a new Covenant, and follow our example'.[26] 'And follow our example': the gentry by encouraging revolt in Scotland and England had broken the chain of degree, disrupted the long accepted hierarchy of subordination; they had only themselves to blame for what followed. Many observers feared that the common people, those below the rank of yeoman, would set up for themselves as a third party. This happened in 1645, when groups of countrymen (Clubmen) all over western and southern England took up arms to oppose royalists and parliamentarians alike. They could not be dispersed until they were faced by the New Model Army, with its regular pay and strict discipline. Tinker Fox, the Birmingham blacksmith who had led popular forces against the royalists in the early years of the war, seemed to be setting himself up as an independent third force in the Midlands until the New Model Army pushed him too into the background.[27]

The New Model, the creation of which had been so fiercely opposed by conservatives, seemed to have saved the social order: this no doubt was the calculation of many M.P.s who voted for it. But the New Model, as it was to declare proudly in June 1647, was 'no mere mercenary Army'; it was the common people in uniform, closer to their views than to those of the gentry or Parliament. And the free discussion which was permitted in this unique army led to a fantastically rapid development of political thinking.

II   LOWER-CLASS HERESY

In addition to, or expressing, these class tensions there was a tradition of plebeian anti-clericalism and irreligion. To go no further back, the Lollards carried a popular version of John Wyclif's heresies into the sixteenth century. Professor A. G. Dickens has shown how Lollard influence survived in a popular materialist scepticism which makes one 'feel appreciably nearer to the age of Voltaire than is normal in the 16th century'.[28] A carpenter in 1491 rejected transubstantiation, baptism, confession, and said men would not be damned for sin; in 1512 a Wakefield man said 'that if a calf were upon the altar I would rather worship that than the ... holy sacrament ... The date was past that God determined him to be in form of bread.'[29] The clergy, an earlier Lollard had declared, were worse than Judas, who sold Christ for thirty pence, while priests sold masses for a halfpenny.[30] The commons, said another, 'would never be well until they had stricken off all the priests' heads'. 'There was a saying in the country,' a north Yorkshireman pleaded in 1542, 'that a man might lift up his heart and confess himself to God Almighty and needed not to be confessed at a priest.' A shearman of Dewsbury elaborated on this point: he would not confess his offences with a woman to a priest, 'for the priest would be as ready within two or three days after to use her as he'.[31] Mr K. V. Thomas has collected a number of similar examples under Elizabeth and the first two Stuarts – denial of the resurrection, of the existence of God (very common in the diocese of Exeter at the end of the sixteenth century) or the devil; all things come by nature. He emphasizes how wrong it is to describe all such fifteenth- and early sixteenth-century expressions of irreligion as 'Lollardy', and expostulates with embarrassed historians who dismiss them as the products of drunks or madmen.[32]

Such men tended to be called Anabaptists or Familists by their enemies. These names – familiar enough on the continent – were very loosely applied in England: most of our evidence comes from hostile accounts in the church courts.[33] The essential doctrine of Anabaptism was that infants should not be baptized. Acceptance of baptism – reception into the church – should be the voluntary act of an adult. This clearly subverted the concept of a national church to which every English man and woman belonged: it envisaged instead the formation of voluntary congregations by those who believed themselves to be the elect. An Anabaptist must logically object to payment of tithes, the ten per cent of everyone's earnings which, in theory at least, went to support the ministers of the state church. Many Anabaptists refused to swear oaths, since they objected to a religious ceremony being used for secular judicial purposes; others rejected war and military service. Still more were alleged to carry egalitarianism to the extent of denying a right to private property. The name came to be used in a general pejorative sense to describe those who were believed to oppose the existing social and political order.

Familists, members of the Family of Love, can be defined a little more precisely. They were followers of Henry Niclaes, born in Münster in 1502, who taught that heaven and hell were to be found in this world. Niclaes was alleged to have been a collaborator of Thomas Münzer in insurrection at Amsterdam.[34] The Puritan divine John Knewstub said of him: 'H.N. turns religion upside down. He buildeth heaven here upon earth; he maketh God man and man God.'[35] Like Francis Bacon, Familists believed that men and women might recapture on earth the state of innocence which existed before the Fall: their enemies said they claimed to attain the perfection of Christ. They held their property in common, believed that all things come by nature, and that only the spirit of God within the believer can properly understand Scripture.[36] They turned the Bible into allegories, even the Fall of Man, complained William Perkins.[37] Familism was spread in England by Christopher Vittels, an itinerant joiner of Dutch origin. In the 1570s English Familists were noted to be wayfaring traders, or 'cowherds, clothiers and such-like mean people'. They believed in principle that ministers should be itinerants, like the Apostles. They were increasing daily by 1579, numerous in the diocese of Ely in 1584, also in East Anglia and the North of England. They were particularly difficult for the ecclesiastical authorities to root out because – like many Lollards before them – they were ready to recant when caught, but not to give up their opinions. The Family of the Mount held even more subversive views. They were alleged to reject prayer, to deny the resurrection of the body. They questioned whether any heaven or hell existed apart from this life: heaven was when men laugh and are merry, hell was sorrow, grief and pain.[38]

Familism, developing the lower-class scepticism of the Lollards, was an anti-clerical, layman's creed. In this it fitted the temper of Elizabethan society, when members of many congregations, increasing in wealth and self-confidence, were more and more critical of traditional clerical claims. In numerous Elizabethan parishes where there is no reason to suspect anything so subversive as Familism, the minister was pushed on by his congregation to reject the ceremonies and vestments of the state church.[39] For the breach with Rome and especially the radical measures of Edward VI's reign had opened up hopes of a continuing reformation which would totally overthrow the coercive machinery of the state church. The Elizabethan settlement bitterly disappointed expectations that a protestant church would differ from popery in the power which it allowed to bishops and clergy. The episcopal hierarchy came to be seen as the main obstacle to radical reform. Puritan attacks on this hierarchy are sometimes dismissed as propagandist exaggerations, though whenever we can check their statements they prove surprisingly reliable. But the most impressive evidence for the unpopularity of bishops and clergy comes not from their opponents but from their defenders.

The opening words of Bishop Cooper's *Admonition to the People of England* (1589) speak of 'the loathsome contempt, hatred and disdain that *the most part of men* in these days bear ... towards the ministers of the church of God'. He attributed such views especially to the common people, who 'have conceived an heathenish contempt of religion and a disdainful loathing of the ministers thereof'.[40] 'The ministers of the world,' Archbishop Sandys confirmed, 'are become contemptible in the eyes of the basest sort of people.'[41] In 1606 a man was presented to the church courts for saying that he would rather trust a thief than a priest, a lawyer or a Welshman.[42]

'If we maintain things that are established,' complained Richard Hooker, 'we have ... to strive with a number of heavy prejudices deeply rooted in the hearts of men, who think that herein we serve the time and speak in favour of the present state because thereby we either hold or seek preferment.'[43] Thomas Brightman in 1615 confirmed that hostility to the hierarchy 'is now favoured much of the people and multitude'.[44] We recall the oatmeal-maker who, on trial before the High Commission in April 1630, said that he would never take off his hat to bishops. 'But you will to Privy Councillors,' he was urged. 'Then as you are Privy Councillors,' quoth he, 'I put off my hat; but as you are the rags of the beast, lo! I put it on again.'[45] Joan Hoby of Colnbrook, Buckinghamshire, said four years later 'that she did not care a pin nor a fart for my Lord's Grace of Canterbury . . . and she did hope that she should live to see him hanged'.[46] (Laud was in fact executed eleven years later, but we do not know whether Joan Hoby was still alive then.)

Further evidence of the unpopularity of the whole church establishment is to be found in the popular iconoclasm which broke out whenever opportunity offered: in the late 1630s and 40s altar rails were pulled down, altars desecrated, statues on tombs destroyed, ecclesiastical documents burnt, pigs and horses baptized. 'Is it well done of our soldiers,' asked *The Souldiers Catechisme* of 1644, 'to break down crosses and images where they meet with any?' The answer was, rather shamefacedly, 'I confess that nothing ought to be done in a tumultuous manner. But seeing God hath put the sword of reformation into the soldiers' hand, I think it is not amiss that they should cancel and demolish those monuments of superstition and idolatry, especially seeing the magistrate and the minister that should have done it formerly neglected it.'[47] So early was the army rank and file encouraged to usurp the functions of minister and magistrate.

In 1641 there were nine hundred petitions against allegedly 'scandalous' ministers, one from every ten parishes in the land. Since they came mainly from the South and East, the proportion in those areas is far higher. 'If the meanest and most vicious parishioner they had could be brought to prefer a petition to the House of Commons against his minister,' Clarendon tells us, the latter was sure to be prosecuted as scandalous.[48] It was 'the very dregs and scum of every parish' who petitioned against 'the orthodox clergy', a royalist pamphlet of 1643 declared.[49] In 1641, 'when the glad tidings were brought to Chelmsford that episcopacy was voted down by the House of Commons, all usual expressions of an exulting joy were used', and 'bonfires were kindled in every street'.[50] In 1642 we find soldiers plundering *all* ministers, royalist or Parliamentarian, and there was much rabbling of the royalist clergy. From London itself there is a great deal of evidence for unpopularity of bishops and parish clergy in the 1640s.[51] All this throws retrospective light on the relationship of church and common people before the Revolution. It is a matter of the advancing education and self-confidence of congregations – especially urban congregations – at least as much as of the inadequacies of the clergy. 'There is scarce a man that can read English,' grumbled Thomas Adams, 'scarce a woman that can make herself ready to church, but will presume to teach the minister, and either we must preach what you will hear, or you will not hear what we preach.'[52]

There was further complaint of interference by church courts in the private lives of ordinary men and women, to an extent that would be thought quite intolerable today. Looking back in 1653 an ex-officer in the Parliamentary army who had become a parson said that the Laudian 'firebrands of state made the bishops odious to the gentry and commonalty' of England and Scotland. 'The people also generally disliked their rigour in citing them to their courts for working on holidays or marrying without a licence or upon a groundless suspicion of unchastity. Many such poor pretences, merely to drain the people's purses, did their officers make.'[53]

It was thus nothing new when in 1642 the Rev. Edmund Calamy told the House of Commons that 'the people complain of their ministers, that they are dumb dogs, greedy dogs, which can never have enough'.[54] They also complained that university-educated divines tended to be members of the ruling class, 'full of all outward necessaries'.[55] The patronage system gave power to 'the greatest of the parish, who were not always the best, to prescribe what religion they pleased to parishioners'.[56] It was 'under pretence of religion', Thomas Hobbes wrote in 1651, that 'the lower sort of citizens . . . do challenge [liberty] to themselves'.[57]

William Tyndale in 1528 had alleged that the hierarchy of his day said to King and lords 'these heretics would have us down first, and then you, to make of all common'.[58] The argument was repeated by the Elizabethan bishop Bancroft, and became a commonplace. 'The title which bishops have to their livings,' said Richard Hooker with unusually crude directness, 'is as good as the title of any sort of men'

to their property; and he warned that by reception of the Presby
ian discipline the world might be 'clean turned upside down'.[59] It w.
a bishop who in the 1650s recorded James I's famous epigram as 'No
bishop, no king, no nobility': 'which, as you see, hath fallen out
according to his prediction'.[60] Oliver Cromwell's first recorded
speech in the Long Parliament attacked the view that parity in the
church must necessarily lead to parity in the state.[61] Most defenders
of episcopacy in the debates of 1641 based their arguments on social
rather than religious grounds.

Both sides were aware of the risks which appealing to the common people involved; but the simple fact remained that the royalists
could not be beaten without arming and taxing ordinary people.
' "The generality of the people must be engaged," ' the Leveller Richard Overton imagined the Parliamentary leaders saying; ' "and how
must this be done? Why," say they, "we must associate with that part
of the clergy that are now made underlings." ' But ' "we must be careful the supreme power fall not into the people's hands" '.[62] John
Selden was almost as cynical as that when he declared 'If men would
say they took up arms for anything but religion, they might be beaten
out of it by reason; out of that they never can, for they will not
believe you whatever you say.' Francis Osborne spoke of religion 'in
which the poor claim no less ample a share than the rich; all being
noted to fight with the greater animosity for the world to come, the
less they find themselves possessed of in this'.[63]

But we need not doubt the sincerity of the great numbers of
preachers who proclaimed that Parliament's cause was God's, and
that – whatever Charles I's subjective intentions – his government
was objectively forwarding the cause of the Roman Antichrist. The
royalists were 'the antichristian party'.[64] Such preachers drew on a
long tradition. Foxe's *Acts and Monuments* established a pedigree
for protestantism among Lollard heretics and Marian martyrs, and
supplied evidence for the idea that it is especially the poor who stand
up against Antichrist. Some English protestants came to see themselves as God's chosen people.[65] The Thirty Years War (1618–48) on
the European continent looked like a death-grapple between protestant and catholic, and had given widespread credence to the view of

an influential group of Bible scholars, that the end of the world was at hand.[66] It was natural for those preachers who genuinely believed that Charles I's government was antichristian to see the civil war as the beginning of cataclysmic events and to call on their congregations to support the cause of Parliament. They encouraged expectations that Christ's kingdom was at hand – expectations which John Milton among many others shared. What turned out to be especially dangerous was the wholly traditional view, repeated by many of the preachers, that the common people had a very special role to play in this crisis, that they were somehow more chosen than the rich and the powerful. 'The voice that will come of Christ's reigning is like to begin from those that are the multitude, that are so contemptible especially in the eyes of Antichrist's spirits and the prelacy.' The words are those of a perfectly respectable Independent divine, by no means an extreme radical, who believed the last times would begin in 1650.[67] There were many similar sermons preached: the doctrine became almost orthodox on the Parliamentary side.

A little imagination will convey to us the effect of this prospect in conditions of economic and political crisis, when Parliament itself was calling the common people to political action for the first time in history, when the accredited preachers of God's word not only proclaimed that the millennium was approaching but told 'you that are of the meaner rank, common people' that they were to take the lead in forwarding Christ's cause.[68] All this at a time when censorship and government control had broken down, when hitherto suppressed sects were able to meet openly, when mechanic preachers could extend and elaborate on the teaching of their betters. 'The vulgar mind,' Sir Edward Dering said in 1642, is 'now fond with imaginary hopes. What will the issue be, when hopes grow still on hopes?'[69] The prospect was enough to bring Sir Edward's own brief period of radicalism to an end. A royalist looking back from 1648 noted that 'heresy is always the forerunner of rebellion'. He spoke of:

> that fatal liberty of the subject, which the profane vulgar in the beginning of these disorders so passionately petitioned the Parliament to

grant them, who intending to save themselves of their blind fury, not only suffered but applauded their violence to their neighbours; but like unskilful conjurors they often raised those spirits which they could [not] lay; for under cover of zeal to the cause, the poor levelled the rich of both parties . . .[70]

'All sorts of people dreamed of an utopia and infinite liberty, especially in matters of religion,' another royalist confirmed in the same year.[71]

'The *vox populi*,' said Stephen Marshall in a sermon preached before the House of Commons in December 1641, 'is that many of the nobles, magistrates, knights and gentlemen, and persons of great quality, are arrant traitors and rebels against God.'[72] A Puritan minister could hardly have put it more strongly than that. It is not surprising that the hint was taken up by many outside Parliament who would not need to be reminded that *vox populi* was also *vox dei*. Nor indeed was this class emphasis new. As long ago as the 1620s that neglected radical thinker Thomas Scott had, in a pamphlet called *Vox Populi*, pointed to great landowners as of the Spanish, i.e. the antichristian, faction.[73] In 1642 preachers were quoting 'When Adam delved and Eve span, Who was then the gentleman?'[74] So it was only a development, not a daring innovation, when Christopher Feake in 1646 declared that there was an 'enmity against Christ' in aristocracy and monarchy.[75]

There was then a long tradition of popular materialist scepticism and anti-clericalism; there was the Familist tradition that Christ was within every believer; there was the sectarian tradition of opposition to a state church, to the tithes which paid for its ministers and to the patronage system which ensured that its clergy were appointed by the ruling class.[76] There were also the millenarian hopes built up by the Puritan preachers. It is hardly surprising that the breakdown of censorship and the establishment of effective religious toleration let loose a flood of speculation that hitherto had only been muttered in secret. In England as in Switzerland 'the lower sort of people being bred in an ancient hatred against superiors', greedily embraced the doctrines of Anabaptism.[77] Anabaptists, William Gouge told his shocked

City congregation in the 1620s, 'teach that all are alike and that there is no difference betwixt masters and servants'.[78]

In the early 1640s attitudes towards the lower-class heresy of Familism were almost the test of radicalism. John Milton defended Familists. The Leveller William Walwyn asked the enemies of the Family of Love, 'What family are you of, I pray?'[79] John Hales of Eton condescendingly observed that 'some time or other those fine notions will take in the world'.[80] Hales was a member of Falkland's set at Great Tew, a collection of intellectuals who discussed liberal theories together in that depopulated parish. But while they were talking, Walwyn and hundreds like him were walking the streets of London, discussing, organizing, canvassing the 'fine notions' with the intention of making them 'take in the world'. They came near to turning it upside down – so near that the members of the Great Tew circle supported the royalists in the civil war.

The sects insisted that ministers should be elected by the congregation and paid by the voluntary contributions of its members; many of them denied the need for a separate clergy at all, and would have had a gifted layman preach on Sunday whilst labouring with his hands the other six days of the week. They advocated toleration for all protestant sects, rejecting ecclesiastical censorship and all forms of ecclesiastical jurisdiction in favour of a congregational discipline with no coercive sanction behind it. They attached little importance to many of the traditional sacraments of the church. Their programme would have destroyed the national church, leaving each congregation responsible for its own affairs with only the loosest contact between congregations; the church would no longer have been able to mould opinion in a single pattern, to punish 'sin' or proscribe 'heresy'. There would have been no control over the thinking of the middle and lower classes.

The attempt in the 1640s to replace church courts by a Presbyterian disciplinary system – later described as 'Egyptian bondage to keep up and maintain the oppression of tithes'[81] – led to fierce hostility against what Lilburne called 'the devil and the clergy his agents', and a later pamphlet called the 'black guard of Satan'.[82] 'Without a powerful compulsive presbytery in the church,' reflected the Leveller

Richard Overton in 1646, 'a compulsive mastership of aristocratical government over the people in the state could never long be maintained.'[83] 'The necks of the people of the world,' thought the Rev. William Dell in 1653, 'have never endured so grievous a yoke from any tyrants as from the doctrine and domination of the clergy.'[84] The demand for separation of church and state was a demand for the subordination of the clergy, for an end to their coercive authority. Inevitably, utterly inevitably, discussions among the separatist congregations spread over from religion to politics. In the intoxicating new freedom of the early 1640s no holds were barred.

The allegations of royalist propagandists should always be used with caution. But Bruno Ryves's account of the principles held by the lower classes of Chelmsford at the beginning of the civil war bears sufficient resemblance to ideas that developed later to be worth summarizing. Kings, these plebeians thought, are burdens. The relation of master and servant has no ground in the New Testament; in Christ there is neither bond nor free. Ranks such as those of the peerage and gentry are 'ethnical and heathenish distinctions'. There is no ground in nature or Scripture why one man should have £1000 *per annum*, another not £1. The common people have been kept under blindness and ignorance, and have remained servants and slaves to the nobility and gentry. 'But God hath now opened their eyes and discovered unto them their Christian liberty.' Gentlemen should be made to work for their living, or else should not eat. Learning has always been an enemy to the Gospel; it were a happy thing if there were no universities, and all books except the Bible were burnt. Any gifted man may be chosen by a congregation as their minister.[85] The presentation is slanted; but ideas very similar to these will recur in our story.

When the Leveller Richard Overton wrote 'I am confident that it must be the poor, the simple and mean things of this earth that must confound the mighty and strong,' he seemed only to be repeating preachers like Thomas Goodwin. But the words occur in *An Appeale from the degenerate Representative Body the Commons of England ... to the Body Represented, the free people in general* (1647).[86] Overton's political appeal was aimed especially at the people in arms in the New Model Army. At Putney in the same year representatives of the rank and file claimed that since 'the poorer and meaner of this kingdom . . . have been the means of the preservation of the kingdom', 'the poorest man in England' had a right to choose his own government.[87] In 1649 Gerrard Winstanley saw that 'the poor must first be picked out and honoured in this work, for they begin to receive the word of righteousness, but the rich generally are enemies to true freedom'. 'The poor are those in whom the blessing lies, for they first receive the gospel.'[88] But again the apparent continuity with the Puritan preachers is deceptive: for Winstanley 'the word of righteousness', 'the gospel', meant communism, subversion of the existing social order. 'If you would find true majesty indeed, go among the poor despised ones of the earth . . . These great ones are too stately houses for Christ to dwell in; he takes up his abode in a manger, in and amongst the poor in spirit and despised ones of the earth.'[89]

3
Masterless Men

Vagabonds ... which do nothing but walk the streets,
wicked men, to be hired for every man's money to do any
mischief, such as we commonly call the rascals and very
sink and dunghill knaves of all towns and cities ... Into
what country and place soever they come, they cause sedition and tumults.

Geneva Bible, marginal comment on *Acts* xvii, 6[1]

I   MOBILITY AND FREEDOM

The essence of feudal society was the bond of loyalty and dependence between lord and man. The society was hierarchical in structure:
some were lords, others were their servants. 'Whose man art thou?'
demanded a character in one of Middleton's plays. The reply, 'I am a
servant, yet a masterless man, sir', at once produced the incredulous
retort, 'How can that be?'[2] The assumptions were those of a relatively static agricultural society, with local loyalties and local
controls: no land and no man without a lord. Reality never corre-
sponded to the model, of course, and by the sixteenth century society
was becoming relatively mobile: masterless men were no longer outlaws but existed in alarming numbers – 13,000, mostly in the North,
a government inquiry calculated in 1569; 30,000 in London alone,
it was guessed more wildly in 1602.[3] Whatever their numbers such
men – servants to nobody – were anomalies, potential dissolvents of
the society.

First, there were rogues, vagabonds and beggars, roaming the countryside, sometimes in search of employment, too often mere unemployable rejects of a society in economic transformation, whose population was expanding rapidly. The necessity to economize led lords to cut down their households; the quest for profit led to eviction of some tenants from their holdings, the buying out of others. The fluctuations of the early capitalist cloth market brought wealth to a fortunate few, ruin to many. The inefficient and the unlucky went to the roads. They caused considerable panic in ruling circles during the sixteenth century, but they were never a serious menace to the social order. Vagabonds attended no church, belonged to no organized social group. For this reason it seemed almost self-evident to Calvinist theologians that they were 'a cursed generation'.[4] Not till 1644 did legislation insist that rogues, vagabonds and beggars should be compelled to attend church every Sunday. Such men were almost by definition ideologically unmotivated: they could steal and plunder, but were incapable of concerted revolt. Until the 1640s there seems to have been little concern in the propertied classes to help vagabonds. They presented a security problem, no more. There is plenty of evidence of popular sympathy for the down-and-outs of society. Ordinary people were reluctant to call upon the full penalties of the law against them, even when they stole. But it was not till the revolutionary decades that we get pamphleteers arguing that houses of correction, so far from curing begging, were more likely to make honest men vagabonds and beggars by destroying their reputation and self-respect.[5]

Secondly there was London, whose population may have increased eight-fold between 1500 and 1650. London was for the sixteenth century vagabond what the greenwood had been for the medieval outlaw – an anonymous refuge. There was more casual labour in London than anywhere else, there was more charity, and there were better prospects for earning a dishonest living. In the late sixteenth and early seventeenth centuries men suddenly became aware of the existence of a criminal underworld. Its apparent novelty perhaps caused it to be over-publicized: it was no doubt far less important than the world of dock labour, watermen, building labourers and journeymen of all sorts who had no hope of becoming masters.

(Non-freeholders had been excluded from skilled crafts by the Statute of Apprentices of 1563.) What matters for our purposes is the existence of a large population, mostly living very near if not below the poverty line,[6] little influenced by religious or political ideology but ready-made material for what began in the later seventeenth century to be called 'the mob'. Pym may or may not have called out such support; forty years later Shaftesbury almost certainly did. But 'the mob' is basically non-political: it could be used by Presbyterians against the Army in 1647,[7] by royalists in 1660, by church and king men under Anne. It was, in the prescient words of the Geneva Bible margin, 'to be hired for every man's money to do any mischief'.[8] Its existence was always a potential threat, especially in times of economic crisis.

A quite different sort of masterless men were the protestant sectaries. These had as it were chosen the condition of masterlessness by opting out of the state church, so closely modelled on the hierarchical structure of society, so tightly controlled by parson and squire. Sects were strongest in the towns, where they created hospitable communities for men, often immigrants, who aspired to keep themselves above the level of casual labour and pauperism: small craftsmen, apprentices, serious-minded laborious men, all could recognize each other as the elect in a godless world. As soon as they were free to function legally, the sects organized social services, poor relief etc., for their members: they provided social insurance in this world as well as in the next.[9] Such men were highly motivated, and they carried to its logical conclusion the principle of individualism which rejects all mediators between man and God. From the circumstances of their life in vast anonymous cities and towns they had escaped from feudal lordship. The bond of their unity was a common acceptance of the sovereignty of God, against whose wishes no earthly loyalty could be weighed.

'He which dwelleth in heaven is mightier,' Archbishop Grindal had told that 'mighty prince' Queen Elizabeth.[10] Sir Henry Slingsby in 1628 told the Earl of Huntingdon that 'he cared not for any lord in England, except the Lord of Hosts'.[11] Martin Marprelate succinctly spoke of those who were 'obedient subjects to the Queen and disobedient traitors to God and the realm'[12] – the last three words giving this remark extra bite, looking forward to the time when Charles I would be executed as a traitor to the commonwealth. In the revolutionary decades the argument and the confidence it gave descended the social scale. *God a Good Master* was the title of a pamphlet published by John Goodwin in 1641. 'He that fears God is free from all other fear; he fears not men of high degree,' said William Dell in 1645.[13] 'We have chosen the Lord God Almighty to be our king and protector,' the Diggers told Fairfax in June 1649.[14] In 1653 a Fenstanton farmer was afraid his landlord would turn him out if he joined the Baptists. Henry Denne told him 'to trust God, and he would be a better landlord than Mr Bendwich'.[15] 'Be not afraid of man,' Margaret Fell urged her husband in the same year. 'Greater is he that is in you than he that is in the world.'[16] 'He that is in you': God has been democratized. He is no longer merely the greatest feudal overlord, a kind of super-king. He is in all his saints, but he is almighty and gives them of his power.

Fourth among our masterless men are the rural equivalents of the London poor – cottagers and squatters on commons, wastes and in forests. Like our first two categories, these were victims of the rapid expansion of England's population in the sixteenth century; sometimes the victims, sometimes the beneficiaries of the rise of new or the growth of old industries. Unlike the relatively stable and docile populations of open arable areas, these men, cliff-hanging in semi-legal insecurity, often had no lords to whom they owed dependence or from whom they could hope for protection. They might exist for long enough to establish a precarious customary claim to continuance. Labourers' cottages erected within a mile of any mineral works, coal mines, quarries, etc., were not regarded as coming within the statute of 1589 which prohibited the erection of any cottage without four acres of land.[17] Such men might form a useful source of additional labour. Clothiers, stocking-knitters, iron-masters, coal-owners, all might have uses for such casual labourers, and so the latter might win a relatively secure position so long as the market held. They were liable to suffer from large-scale schemes for agricultural betterment – disafforestation, fen drainage and the like. Meanwhile they existed, in the interstices of society, but undoubtedly growing in numbers by migration.[18]

Sylvan liberty is idealized in the ballads of Robin Hood, in Shake-speare's Forest of Arden and in the wise 'wild men' who appear in Elizabethan and Jacobean pageants. This may relate to contemporary migration to forests in search of security and independence.[19] Freedom of tenure was traditionally enjoyed in forest clearances; from at least the fourteenth century there had been numbers of free craftsmen in woodland areas, as well as outlaws.[20] In Massinger's *The Guardian* (licensed 1633) the bandits – ostensibly Neapolitan, but explicitly related to 'the courteous English thieves' – were occupants of the woods, opposed to the king and his laws. They specialized in robbing those who ground the faces of the poor, enclosers of commons, usurers foreclosing on land, 'builders of iron mills that grub up forests with timber trees for shipping', cheating shop-keepers and vintners; but not rent-racked farmers, needy market folks, labourers, carriers or women.[21] Firth noted the sympathy for 'spirited crime' in the popular ballads of the period;[22] it continued at least till the eighteenth century.

The Forest of Arden gave shelter to a shifting population of black-smiths and nailers as well as to Shakespeare's artless countrymen; to Tinker Fox and his partisans as well as to Coventry Ranters. Richard Baxter refers to the 'exceeding populousness of the country' round Dudley (Worcestershire), 'where the woods and commons are planted with nailers, scythe-smiths and other iron-labourers, like a continued village'. 'Among weavers, tailors and such-like, there is usually found more knowledge and religion than among the poor enslaved husbandmen.' 'Constant converse and traffic with London doth much promote civility and piety among tradesmen.'[23]

Fifthly, shading off from our fourth category of masterless men, was the itinerant trading population, from pedlars and carters to badgers, merchant middlemen. The number of craftsmen in villages, in those days of restricted markets, was vastly greater than it is today:[24] in bad times they would look for customers over a wider area. Professor Everitt has suggested that these wayfarers, linking heath and forest areas, may have helped to spread radical religious views – as earlier Familists had been weavers, basket-makers, musicians, bottlemakers, joiners, who lived by travelling from place to place.[25] In 1556 a clothier collecting wool acted as liaison man in Dudley's conspiracy. An itinerant cobbler was the principal dispenser of the Marprelate Tracts.[26] Propaganda for the abortive Oxfordshire rising of 1596 was made by a carter and a miller 'travelling the country'.[27] Scottish Covenanters in the 1630s were alleged to have used travelling merchants 'to convey intelligence and gain a party in England'. The same charge was made against the Rye House plotters in 1683.[28] Certainly the Privy Council was worried about carriers in 1637–8.[29] In a sermon deploring *The Growth and Spreading of Haeresie*, preached before the House of Commons on 10 March 1647, Thomas Hodges attributed to 'every . . . vagrant itinerant huckster' such heresies as denial of the Trinity, of the authority of the Bible, of the historicity of Jesus.[30] Country inns and taverns used by itinerants were noted as centres for news and discussion. In the civil war, Professor Everitt observes, troops were normally billeted in the inns of provincial towns.[31]

Dr Thirsk and Professor Everitt, to whom we are indebted for emphasizing the distinction between woodland and pasture areas on the one hand, and champaign arable on the other, remind us that the former was much more extensive in the sixteenth and seventeenth centuries than it is now, including e.g. North Essex, the Weald, the 'cheese' area of Wiltshire, the industrial parts of Yorkshire and Lancashire, as well as forests like Sherwood, Arden, the New Forest, the Northamptonshire forests, and the highland zone generally. Professor Everitt distinguishes between 'a relatively free and mobile society in the heath and wood parishes, and a relatively static and subservient one in the parishes of the fielden plains'.[32] (Just because they were 'relatively static', I say little about the mass of simple husbandmen. This would be wrong if I were analysing the society as a whole, but seems inevitable in a book whose emphasis is on social and intellectual change. The reader should remember that husbandmen in fielden parishes formed a majority of the rural population.) The heath and woodland areas were often outside the parochial system, or their large parishes were left with only a distant chapelry, so there was freedom from parson as well as from squire: here men might, in Winstanley's words, 'live out of sight or out of slavery'.[33] In such areas feudal ties of subordination hardly existed, and there was little obstacle to the intrusion of rural industry in search of cheap part-time labour. The 'mean people' of the woods, Aubrey tells us, 'live lawless, nobody to govern them; they care for nobody, having no dependence on anybody'. These were also the areas in which there was most peasant revolt in the early seventeenth century – Wiltshire and the Forest of Dean, for instance.

Dr Thirsk and Professor Everitt go on to suggest that squatters in forest or pastoral regions, often far from any church, were wide open to radical religious sects – or to witchcraft. (Hostility to the clergy had been a striking element in the Robin Hood ballads.[34] Pendle and Knaresborough forests harboured witches.[35]) The Weald was 'that dark country which is the receptacle of all schism and rebellion' – a view confirmed by Thomas Edwards. The densely populated forests of Northamptonshire were centres of rural puritanism, strange sects, and witchcraft.[36] The 'cheese' district of Wiltshire, the scene of violence resulting from dis-afforestation in the early seventeenth century, was also an area of poorly-paid part-time clothing workers and of religious heresy.[37] Ely, Edwards's 'island of errors and sectaries', had long been a centre of plebeian irreverence and resistance, down to the time when Oliver Cromwell, 'Lord of the Fens', encouraged the commoners. Ely became a Seeker centre in the forties, when it was for some time William Erbery's headquarters. In the Isle of Axholme the inhabitants were said to have been virtual heathens till the draining of the Fens; in 1650–51 they supported the Levellers enthusiastically enough.[38] In Cumberland in the mid-fifties the Quakers met 'in multitudes and upon moors'.[39]

Professor Walzer has suggested that Puritan insistence on inner discipline was unthinkable without the experience of masterlessness. Their object was to find a new master in themselves, a rigid self-control shaping a new personality. Conversion, sainthood, repression, collective discipline, were the answer to the unsettled condition of society, the way to create a new order through creating new men. He compares Jacobins and Bolsheviks in similar circumstances.[40] This runs parallel to the contemporary vogue for gipsies, depicted by Cervantes as critics of society, seen by the French engraver Jacques Callot (1592–1635), and by English poets from 'The raggle-taggle gipsies' to Wordsworth, as offering a freer alternative to the constrictions of society. The comparison is illuminating and helpful; but Professor Walzer takes, I think, a rather one-sided view of the phenomenon of masterlessness. What produced alarm and anxiety in some was an opportunity for others – though not an opportunity for climbing up the normal social ladder. A masterless man was nobody's servant: this could mean freedom for those who prized independence more than security. Richard Brome's *A Joviall Crew* certainly idealizes the beggars' life in seventeenth-century England, which must have been anything but romantic. Nevertheless, the form his romanticization takes is interesting. The beggars are

> The only freemen of a common-wealth;
> Free above scot-free; that observe no law,
> Obey no governor, use no religion,
> But what they draw from their own ancient custom
> Or constitute themselves, yet are no rebels.[41]

Beneath the surface stability of rural England, then, the vast placid open fields which catch the eye, was the seething mobility of forest squatters, itinerant craftsmen and building labourers, unemployed men and women seeking work, strolling players, minstrels and jugglers, pedlars and quack doctors, gipsies, vagabonds, tramps: congregated especially in London and the big cities, but also with footholds wherever newly-squatted areas escaped from the machinery of the parish or in old-squatted areas where labour was in demand. It was from this underworld that armies and ships' crews were recruited, that a proportion at least of the settlers of Ireland and the New World were found, men prepared to run desperate risks in the hope of obtaining the secure freehold land (and with it, status) to which they could never aspire in overcrowded England. In England mobility was taken for granted, at least outside the champaign agricultural areas. (This is, incidentally, another reason for looking sceptically at total population figures based on surviving records from agricultural villages, by definition much more stable than those of the woodland areas. A family which can be reconstituted, Mr Peter Clark suggests, is by this very fact an untypical family.[42])

The eternally unsuccessful quest by J.P.s to suppress unlicensed ale-houses was in part aimed at controlling these mobile masses, which might contain disaffected elements, separatists, itinerant preachers. Given a favourable spiritual environment, itinerant crafts-men could easily become itinerant ministers, underground before 1640, openly in the freedom of the forties. Walter Cradock said there were eight hundred such preachers in Wales by 1648.[43] Itinerant preachers could promote themselves to being itinerant Messiahs. Apart from anything else, there were economic advantages: William Franklin and Mary Gadbury were put up for long periods by their disciples.[44] It was logical, if not unnaturally resented, for J.P.s to use the same procedures against such Messiahs, Quaker missionaries and Baptist tinkers as against vagabonds. The Vagrancy Act of 1656 was directed against 'all wandering persons'; the Quakers com-plained that it would 'have taken hold of Christ' and the Apostles.[45]

Demographers might also pay more attention to the spiritual autobiographies and journals surviving from this period. These confirm the footlooseness of the society, the ease with which men uprooted themselves and managed to live whilst roaming the coun-tryside, alone or with a consort. Money had to be earned every now and then, which might entail returning to a stable base, or settling temporarily in an area where casual labour was in demand. Mrs Clarkson sometimes accompanied her Ranter husband on his wan-derings, sometimes waited at home like a sailor's wife: Lawrence never failed to send her money even while giving his body to other ladies in distant ports. William Franklin used to return to London from time to time in order to earn money, leaving Mary Gadbury in Hampshire to promote his Messiahship in his absence.[46]

II FORESTS AND COMMONS

'The nurseries of beggars are commons, as appears by fens and for-ests,' it was said in 1607.[47] Of cottagers in Rockingham Forest an Elizabethan surveyor said 'so long as they may be permitted to live in such idleness upon their stock of cattle, they will bend themselves to no kind of labour'. 'Common of pasture ... is a ... maintaining of the idlers and beggary of the cottagers', for it and 'the gentleness that is shown ... to the bribers and stealers of woods and hedge-breakers without punishment is the only occasion of the resort of so many naughty and idle persons'.[48] The poor in Northamptonshire 'dwell in woods and deserts and live like drones, devoted to thievery, among whom are bred the very spawn of vagabonds and rogues'. Disafforestation and enclosure were needed to get rid of the 'multi-plicity of beggars'.[49] In the Forest of Dean lived 'people of very lewd lives and conversations, leaving their own and other countries and taking the place for a shelter as a cloak to their villanies'.[50] In 1610 James I suggested that the House of Commons should take action against the multitudes of cottages on waste grounds and commons, especially forests, which were 'nurseries and receptacles of thieves, rogues and beggars' – as well as against itinerant Scots accused of eating the commons bare.[51] 'Mountainous grounds so-called' in Huntingdonshire were not 'properly heaths' because 'few of them have ... much beggary on them'.[52]

Disafforestation and enclosure could thus be regarded as a national duty, a kindness in disguise to the idle poor, as well as of more imme-diate benefit to the rich encloser. James I thought draining Sedgmoor 'a religious work'.[53] 'England had many hundreds of acres of waste and barren lands,' said Samuel Hartlib in September 1649, 'and many thousands of idle hands; if both these might be improved, England by God's blessing would grow to be a richer nation than it now is by far.'[54] By enclosure, it was argued in 1663, people were added to the manufacturing population who previously did not increase the store of the nation but wasted it.[55] But a cottager enjoyed greater freedom in some respects than a living-in servant, who had to have a testimo-nial from his employer before he might change his job.[56] A wage-earner who had lost his common rights would be much more dependent on his employer than one who had not. Enclosure, Adam Moore argued in its favour, 'will give the poor an interest in toiling, whom terror never yet could enure to travail'.[57]

For all these reasons the well-to-do disliked cottagers. The 'new brood of upstart intruders' in unlawful cottages, no doubt increased with the civil war disorders, the uprooting of people and the break-down of authority, were often richer 'than the honest, harmless, modest, painful husbandman', and certainly less docile. 'The poor increase like fleas and lice, and these vermin will eat us up unless we enclose.'[58] Surveyors were notoriously hostile to cottagers, which was one of the reasons for the unpopularity of the profession.[59] Mr Osborne noted a campaign by J.P.s against squatters, and a destruction of cottages, especially in Hertfordshire, Middlesex, Warwickshire and Hampshire in the years 1646–60.[60] It may have been even more wide-spread after 1660.[61] One of the divisive things in the 1650s was that the Army wanted forests to be sold to pay their wages, regardless of protests on behalf of the poor who knew that enclosure would follow sale.[62]

There were thus two completely opposed policies for dealing with forests, commons and wastes. As population grew, as new cottages were erected, so timber was destroyed, commons were over-stocked with animals, often by rich men, 'the new (more covetous) gentry', who bought up cottages in order to profit by their right of common-age.[63] Such men had 'land of their own to keep them in the winter or when the commons are eaten bare, and the poor for want of such winter provision have no benefit at all'.[64] Yet for all this the land was not fertilized. Despite prohibitions, the very poor scraped dung from the commons to use it as fuel.[65] 'There are fewest poor where there are fewest commons,' wrote Samuel Hartlib – not a heartless man.[66]

As long ago as the 1530s Starkey had suggested that the poor should be settled on new holdings carved out of the waste.[67] On the other hand the royal policy of disafforestation and enclosure, or of draining the Fens, as applied before 1640, involved disrupting a way of life, a brutal disregard for the rights of commoners; they and their children were often deprived of old-established playing areas – to the detriment, traditionalists complained, of proficiency in shooting with the long-bow.[68] A consequence of the policy was to force men to sole dependence on wage labour, which many regarded as little bet-ter than slavery. ('Think you that we can advise ourselves no better than to turn off our children to foolish [sweating] trades?') Employ-ment would be increased, but the gap between classes would be widened.[69] There is also evidence of stricter enforcement of the game laws in the 1630s, with severer penalties, as the number of squatters and cottagers increased.[70]

Naturally enough, there was great popular hostility to schemes for disafforestation and enclosure before 1640; and when these schemes collapsed in the forties commoners everywhere resumed their rights. In 1631 the Forest of Dean had been a refuge for rioters against this royal policy in the mid-western counties. In July 1640, bored conscript soldiers occupied themselves in pulling down fences in Needwood Forest in Staffordshire.[71] During the civil war, forest laws broke down and there was much stealing of game and timber.[72] The economic necessity for improving wastes and forests, thus both increasing the food supply and releasing labour, still seemed obvious to agricultural writers of the forties and fifties. 'The principal end' of enclosure of forests, the Council of State was told in 1654, 'is advantage to husbandry and tillage, to which all commons are destructive.'[73] Pamphleteers now realized however that gestures had to be made in the direction of safeguarding the interests of commoners, since though 'the better part' favoured enclosure, 'the greater part' did not.[74]

There were legal problems affecting the rights of commoners. Lawyers held that the Statutes of Merton and Westminster II established the lord's right in the soil of the waste.[75] But a statute of 1550 protected small cottagers building on wastes and commons. It was a judicial decision of 1605 which denied that inhabitants as such had common rights on the waste. The Diggers, for instance, argued that no statute deprived the common people of their rights in the common lands, 'but only an ancient custom bred in the strength of kingly prerogative'.[76] 'The poor have an interest in them already,' said Peter Chamberlen of the commons.[77] Yet this 'interest', whether or not valid in abstract law, could not be enforced before 1640. 'Though the law forbids such enclosure' of commons, said Thomas Adams, yet 'when they are once ditched in, say the law what it will, I see no throwing out.'[78] But after 1640 commoners were able to reassert their rights by direct action. In Lincolnshire, Miss Hipkin showed, men opposing encroachment on rights of common emphasized the fundamental law of the land as the basis of their claim – an emphasis which connects them with the Levellers.[79] Even when the enclosure of the waste had taken place by agreement, it established new relationships, less protected by custom, more open to competitive pressures than what had gone before – especially in the disturbed conditions of the revolutionary decades.[80] All copyhold lands, Winstanley thought, 'are parcels hedged in or taken out of the common waste land since the [Norman] Conquest'.[81]

The radical agrarian programme was defeated with the Levellers and Diggers. After 1649 the Rump of the Long Parliament did nothing to encourage agrarian reform, despite continued protests, as when Colonel John Pyne, radical M.P. for Poole, denounced 'the taking away the right of the poor in their commons'. On the contrary, acts were passed for fen drainage and to protect deer against poachers.[82] The Barebones Parliament appears to have taken no notice of a scheme for nationalizing forests, fens and waste lands throughout England, and letting them with first offer to the poor.[83] J.P.s restricted the right to gather fuel from the waste.[84] The bill introduced into Parliament in 1656, commonly referred to as the last legislative attempt to prevent enclosure, actually proposed to regulate commons and commonable land so as to prevent depopulation whilst improving the waste.[85] When Isaiah depicted the utter instability which would follow when the Lord turned the world upside down, the image which the 1611 translators adopted was 'the earth . . . shall be removed like a cottage'.[86]

4

Agitators and Officers

Time may come . . .
When lies alone shall be adored by
The strange wild faith of its [Albion's] plebeian rout,
Who sooner will believe what soldiers preach
Than what ev'n angels or apostles teach.

JOSEPH BEAUMONT, *Psyche* (1648),
in *Complete Poems*, ed. A. B. Grosart
(Hildesheim, 1968) II, p. 67.

I THE NEW MODEL ARMY

A collection of masterless men whom I did not consider in the last chapter – the most powerful, the most politically motivated, but also the shortest-lived – was the New Model Army. Dr Thirsk and Professor Everitt have speculated whether the heath and forest lands may not have supplied most of the troops of the Parliamentarian armies in the civil war.[1] A group of 'Moorlanders' led by 'a person of low quality' bore the brunt of the early fighting in Staffordshire.[2] In Lancashire in 1642 it was 'those sturdy churls in the two forests of Pendle and Rossendale' who 'have resolved to fight it out'.[3] The fenmen of Holland, 'like those tried and notorious foresters of Dean', were 'ever ready to rise against his Majesty's forces', it was said in 1645; they rallied against Charles II in 1651.[4] The Isle of Ely may well have been Cromwell's mass recruiting base.

There had never been anything like the New Model Army before.

Armies were normally conscripted from gaols and the lowest sort of men. Not all New Model soldiers were volunteers, but the officers and most of the cavalry were. Very little work has so far been done on the social composition of the Army, but it was probably, as many claimed, a more representative cross-section of the people of England than the House of Commons was.[5] Thanks to freedom of organization and discussion the Army became a hothouse of political ideas.[6] In the enforced leisure after the war had been won, the thinking of the rank and file developed apace. In 1646 some in the Army were calling for an upper limit to the landed property that anyone might hold.[7] This was two years after George Wither, himself a captain in the Army, had asked why the royalist gentry should not be made peasants by confiscation of their estates – 'a degree to which honest men are born, and too good for these, some of them being made lords and knights for attempting to enslave freemen'.[8]

The Parliamentarian armies were the supreme example of social mobility in our mobile period. They marched backwards and forwards across the country, mixing up populations in a way previously unknown. Chaplains in the New Model preached to civilian congregations as well as to soldiers. As time progressed, an increasing number of common soldiers took upon themselves preaching functions. All these preachers had much in common with itinerant mechanic preachers. Army chaplains of the period included many radicals who figure in our story, like Hugh Peter, John Saltmarsh, William Erbery, John Webster,[9] Henry Pinnell, Thomas Collier and William Dell. *Mr Peters Last Report of the English Warres* (1646) contained a number of reforming proposals, and suggested that the Army should be used 'to teach peasants to understand liberty'.[10] Saltmarsh held that 'the interest of the people in Christ's kingdom is not only an interest of . . . submission, but of consultation, of debating, counselling, prophesying, voting'.[11] William Erbery relied on the support of other ranks in the Army in a debate at Oxford in 1646, when he argued that 'those that are called ministers' had no 'more authority to preach in public than private Christians who were gifted'.[12] Henry Pinnell in December 1647 defended the Agitators to Oliver Cromwell's face.[13] Thomas Collier was also associated with the Levellers, putting forward most of their programme in a sermon of 1647 as 'this great interest of God'.[14] He, like Erbery, was in favour of toleration for the Jews.[15] Dell was reported, also at Oxford in 1646, as telling his congregation (composed mainly of soldiers) 'the power is in you, the people; keep it, part not with it'. Dell, like Collier and Erbery, thought the ministers of the state church were antichristian.[16]

Presbyterian and Independent preachers had only themselves to blame if theories of the sovereignty of the people arose in the Army and in London. William Bridge preached that in case a prince shall neglect his trust, so as not to preserve his subjects but to expose them to violence, it is no usurpation in them to look to themselves but an exercise of that power which was always their own.[17] Such ideas had seemed necessary to persuade people to support armed rebellion, and not all those who preached them expected the lower orders to take them too seriously. 'I am far from the monster of a democracy,' said Edward Bowles, chaplain successively to the Earl of Manchester, General of the Eastern Association, and to Sir Thomas Fairfax, Commander-in-Chief of the New Model Army; 'that which I call to the people for is but a quick and regular motion in their own sphere'.[18] But alas: the people saw a door opening out of their own sphere, and rushed through it. The common people, Winstanley claimed, are 'part of the nation', and should have equal rights with the gentry and clergy.[19] 'It will never be a good world,' Baxter often heard men say, 'while knights and gentlemen make us laws, that are chosen for fear and do but oppress us, and do not know the people's sores. It will never be well with us till we have Parliaments of countrymen like ourselves, that know our wants.'[20] This was not what Parliament and the preachers had meant when they made their appeal to the people in 1641–3. 'When we mention the people,' Marchamont Nedham wrote with the wisdom of 1652, 'we do not mean the confused promiscuous body of the people.'[21]

Parliament and Presbyterian ministers were naturally worried by the state of affairs in the Army, and furious with those chaplains who seemed to be inflaming the lower classes just when they needed quietening down. But worse was to come when in the spring of 1647

Parliament tried to disband part of the Army (without fully paying arrears of wages) and send the rest off to conquer Ireland. It had not even passed an act of indemnity to protect soldiers from the legal consequences of actions committed under orders in time of war. 'Our fellow soldiers suffer at every assize for acts merely relating to the war,' declared a pamphlet of April 1647, giving fifteen instances. Men were even committed for speaking words against the King.[22]

Faced with this provocation, the rank and file took matters into their own hands at the end of March 1647, calling on their officers 'to go along with us in this business, or at least to let us quietly alone in this our design'.[23] The troops elected Agitators, two for each regiment, starting with the cavalry. By the middle of May, 'every foot soldier gave four pence apiece' towards the expenses of a meeting, so they too were organized by then. The troops wore a red ribbon on their left arm, as a symbol of solidarity till death.[24] 'All or most of the officers sat still like so many drones and snakes,' wrote Lilburne later.[25] But after a good deal of dithering most of the officers followed the lead of the rank and file, in order 'to regulate the soldiers' proceedings and remove as near as we could all occasion of distaste'.[26] The Agitators called on Fairfax to order a general rendezvous, otherwise 'we ... shall be necessitated ... to do such things ourselves'. The Council of War put it upon record that it believed the Agitators would in fact act if the General did not.[27]

This was the moment at which Cornet Joyce and 'a party of horse sent from the committee of troopers of the Army',[28] seized the King on 3 June, the day before the rendezvous at Newmarket. Oliver Cromwell knew in advance that Charles was to be secured, but the initiative for the whole operation seems to have come from the Agitators. A week earlier Fairfax had still been trying vainly to prohibit meetings of the troops. The King's removal from Holmby House by Joyce and his men had no authorization: when Charles demanded to see Joyce's commission to remove him, he could only point to the troops drawn up behind him. 'All commanded,' they had replied the day before when challenged.[29] No general would have sent a mere cornet in command of five hundred horse: Fairfax dispatched a colonel to take charge as soon as he heard what had happened.

Meanwhile Joyce reported, 'Let the Agitators know once more we have done nothing in our own name, but what we have done hath been in the name of the whole Army.'[30]

As Joyce rode with the King to Newmarket, the rendezvous which the Agitators had demanded was taking place there. With the Agitators in total command of the situation, the Engagement of 5 June 1647 set up an Army Council, 'to consist of those general officers of the Army who have concurred with the Army, . . . with two commission officers and two soldiers to be chosen from each regiment'. The officers and soldiers of the Army committed themselves 'not willingly [to] disband nor divide' without a satisfaction and security that their grievances would be met.[31] The troops 'hooted divers officers out of the field, unhorsed some and rent their clothes and beat them . . . Officers at that time being only admitted by mutual consent, they could have no power but what was betrusted to them by the soldiers.'[32]

I have given this account mostly in the words of Agitators or Levellers, not because they are necessarily always accurate but because for our purposes what matters is what men believed to have happened, the Leveller/Agitator myth. Brailsford was quite right when he said, 'there has been nothing like this spontaneous outbreak of democracy in any English or continental army before this year of 1647, nor was there anything like it thereafter till the Workers' and Soldiers' Councils met in 1917 in Russia'.[33] The rank and file organized themselves from below, led by the yeoman cavalry regiments. Petitions were drafted, some of them dealing with political as well as military matters. In the summer of 1647 the Agitators had their own printer, a Leveller, John Harris; at the height of their influence his became an official Army press. And the Army radicals linked up with their civilian counterparts. Petitions calling on the Army to give a radical political lead began to come in from hawkers and pedlars in London,[34] and from the counties. Clement Walker later suggested that these petitions against tithes, enclosure and copyhold fines were 'prompted' by the Agitators 'to encourage them to side with the Army against all the nobility, gentry and clergy of the land . . . and to destroy monarchy itself: since it is impossible for any prince to be a king only of beggars, tinkers and cobblers'.[35] Thus encouraged, the Army began to advance on London. It had entered on a course of decisive political action, and though it was now united under the command of Fairfax and Oliver Cromwell, the initiative for this action had come from the rank and file, in close contact with the London Levellers. The apprentices of London, under Lilburne's influence, had appointed 'agitators' too.[36]

II   LEVELLERS AND THE ARMY

The story of the Levellers has often been told: I do not propose to repeat it. What I want to emphasize is that we should not confine our attention to the organized movement and its leaders, but should think of something much vaster if more inchoate. We have to take scraps of information as we find them. Thus, in August 1645, a royalist newspaper criticized the Parliamentarian *Mercurius Britanicus* because it sided 'with the rout and scum of people ... to make them weekly sport by railing at all that's noble'. *Mercurius Britanicus* thought 'the Army and the mean multitude' would 'act further than some of our pretending ministers in reform'. Cavaliers were anti-patriotic social parasites, who did not know honest labour.[37] 'The nobility and gentry who have continued many generations are now sinking,' declared the astrologer William Lilly in 1645 – a sure barometer; 'and an inferior sort of people ... are ascending'.[38] By August 1647 a pamphleteer could write that the nobility and gentry had lost not only 'the power and command they formerly held over their tenants' but also the respect of all, 'no man in these days valuing his lord of whom he holds his lands (his free rent being paid) more than another man, scarce anything at all'.[39]

So when Richard Overton in July 1647 declared his confidence that 'it must be the poor, the simple and mean things of this earth that must confound the mighty and strong', he was both drawing on the Foxe tradition which the Puritan preachers had taken over, seeing the lower classes as Christ's most outstanding warriors, and also appealing directly to the other ranks in the Army against their officers.[40] 'The great things that have been done for the Parliament,' the Leveller William Walwyn agreed, 'have been done by the meaner sort of men.' 'It was an unconscionable thing,' Walwyn was reported as saying at about the same time, to 'the indigent and poorer sort of people, . . . that one should have £10,000, and another more deserving and useful to the commonwealth should not be worth 2d.'[41]

The Levellers in London aspired to put themselves at the head of 'the meaner sort of men'. They are often criticized for an excessively rational approach to politics, for neglecting military force, but in the spring of 1647 they established close contact with the Agitators, and they had many friends among all ranks. At this stage some at least of them appreciated that if they were to be politically effective they must capture control of the Army. Overton, for instance, said in July 1647 that the Army is 'the only formal and visible head that is left unto the people for protection and deliverance'.[42] 'It is clearly evident,' Lilburne added two months later, that 'there is now no power executed in England but a power of force; a just and moral act done by a troop of horse being as good law as now I can see executed by any judge in England.'[43] There seems during the summer of 1647 to have been some free-lance recruitment to the Army of politically convinced radicals, notably by the Leveller Captain William Bray.[44] 'There was a third party,' Cromwell said later, 'little dreamed of, that was endeavouring to have no other power rule but the sword.' He referred especially to Major White, whom D. M. Wolfe calls 'an unswerving Leveller'.[45] Walwyn was accused in 1649 of having said that 'a very few diligent and valiant spirits may turn the world upside down', though he denied it.[46]

White, Agitator of Fairfax's own regiment, was expelled from the Army Council on 9 September for maintaining that there was 'now no visible authority in the kingdom but the power and force of the sword'. This can hardly have been a merely personal view: it was shared by Captain Bray. Rainborough, whom Gardiner described as the principal spokesman of this third party among the officers, also expressed anxiety in the Army Council lest he should be 'kicked out'.[47] White did not conclude that *any* act of force was therefore justified – a doctrine held by the cruder Hugh Peter, which greatly shocked Lilburne.[48] White set his views out at length before Fairfax both in 1647 and just over a year later. 'The King and his party being conquered by the sword,' White wrote, 'I believe the sword may justly remove the power from him and settle it in its original fountain next under God – the people.' He held that all laws made since the Norman Conquest which were contrary to equity should be abolished, and told Fairfax that his authority derived less from Parliament than from the Solemn Engagements of the Army. He objected not to Charles I as a person but to the kingly office. William Erbery went even further, and suggested in January 1649 that the Army's authority was as legitimate as would be that of 'other following representatives'. The Levellers thought that the state had broken down in the course of the civil war; until it was legitimately refounded a state of nature existed in which the sword was the only remaining authority. But military force could justly be used only to hand power back to the people. This was the purpose of the Agreement of the People, the Levellers' new social contract refounding the state, which was submitted to the Army Council in October 1647.[49]

The Agreement of the People was discussed by officers and men at Putney in the days after 28 October. There is no need to do more than refer the reader to these fundamental debates about the theory of democracy. If the Agitators had managed to capture control of the Army, a Leveller theory of military dictatorship in the interests of democracy would certainly have emerged: the later Leveller repudiation of military violence sprang from their dislike of the purposes for which this violence was used. But already during the Putney Debates the Agitators had lost the initiative they had so gloriously held from March to August. Agitators of five cavalry regiments had been recalled by their constituents, under suspicion of having been corrupted by their officers; they were replaced by new representatives. It was these new Agitators who presented the Agreement of the People to the Army Council.

We do not know the full story of the debates in the Army Council. At one time agreement seemed to have been reached on a general rendezvous at which the Agitators intended the Agreement of the People to be accepted by the whole Army. The Agreement had been amended so as to include a substantial extension of the franchise – to all soldiers, and all others except servants and beggars. The state of nature was to be ended, and the English commonwealth restored as a democracy. But Cromwell and Ireton made a perfectly-timed counter-attack. The old Agitators repudiated the new programme:[50] somehow the generals reasserted their authority. On 8 November the Agitators were sent back to their regiments, the Army Council was adjourned for over a fortnight, and the general rendezvous was replaced by three separate assemblies.

But now the pattern of June was startlingly reversed. Then the rank and file were united and held the initiative: the Agitators seized the King, and the officers had to accept the situation at the general rendezvous at Newmarket as the only means of preserving the unity of the Army. Now the rank and file were already divided and had lost the initiative, when the shattering news came that Charles I had escaped from Army captivity on 11 November. The radicals had been ineffectively discussing a seizure of the King for some time, and it is possible that the Grandees deliberately encouraged Charles's flight.[51] The threat of a new civil war loomed: Army unity had to be restored, but now this meant submission of the radicals to the generals. The three separate rendezvous were held in place of the single one on which the Agitators had pinned their hopes. Promises of arrears of pay were given, and vague declarations about political reforms. Fairfax threatened to resign if this was not accepted. 'You have been fed with paper too long,' the Agitators cried; 'ye can create new officers,' the Leveller Wildman asserted.[52] But in the prevailing political circumstances nothing but surrender was possible. There was a brief skirmish when two regiments tried, against orders, to attend the first partial rendezvous at Corkbush Field, near Ware: the highest officer allowed to remain with them was Captain Bray. 'There was no visible authority in the Kingdom but the general,' Bray was reported as saying; and 'the general was not infallible'.[53] But discipline was swiftly asserted, and instead of the Agreement of the People being read at the head of each regiment, Private Richard Arnold was shot at the head of his. At another partial rendezvous two days later, near Kingston, the regiments not surprisingly expressed 'a ready compliance and subjection'. Bray was arrested, together with Lt.-Col. William Eyres, William Everard, William Thompson and others.[54]

So ended the Leveller attempt to capture control of the Army. In retrospect it is clear that the recall and replacement of the Agitators of the five cavalry regiments – done apparently on Lilburne's advice[55] – was going much faster than the majority of the rank and file were prepared to follow. They were concerned mostly with wages and indemnity, and royalist sentiments were not unknown among them ('Who knows not that the forces in pay will be at the King's back, whenever he be warm in his throne? Did not many regiments at Ware cry out for the King and Sir Thomas?') The Declarations of the new Agitators show them fairly consistently on the defensive.[56]

The General Council of the Army met intermittently for the next six weeks after Ware, but it had lost its purpose, was dominated by the Grandees and faded out at the beginning of the New Year. There were mutinies in February and September 1648, led by former Agitators. In April Rich's regiment reappointed Agitators, who petitioned for the Agreement of the People: they were forcibly dispersed by their officers. By judicious manoeuvring the generals retained control before and during the second civil war. In the summer of 1648 Henry Marten and the Leveller Lt.-Col. William Eyres raised a regiment of cavalry volunteers 'for the people's freedom against all tyrants whatsoever'. 'The rustics of Berkshire' and other counties, 'the basest and vilest of men', rushed to enlist: they hoped to 'level all sorts of people, even from the highest to the lowest'. But once the second civil war had been won this private force was incorporated in the Army and neutralized.[57]

In the political crisis which followed the second civil war, leading to Pride's Purge and the execution of the King, Ireton used rank-and-file petitions to achieve his own political ends; the Grandees contemptuously exploited and then cast aside the Levellers, 'of whom there is no fear', as Cromwell put it.[58] Some of the forms recommended by the Levellers were adopted – a republic, abolition of the House of Lords – but none of the democratic content which alone, in the Leveller view, could have legitimated military intervention in politics. The Leveller leaders were arrested, the radical regiments provoked into unsuccessful mutiny, which was crushed at Burford in May 1649. Army democracy was finished. So, effectively, were the Levellers.

A myth remained, and a series of martyrs – Richard Arnold, shot at Corkbush Field; Robert Lockier, shot on 27 April 1649, whose funeral in London was one of the greatest political demonstrations of the Revolution; Cornet Thompson, Corporals Church and Perkins, shot at Burford on 15 May; William Thompson, brother of the Burford martyr, killed near Wellingborough three days later. Bray was kept in prison until 1651. We last hear of Agitators in May 1649 – until they reappear in 1659–60.[59] There were also villains like Cromwell and Ireton, White, who seems to have played a treacherous role in negotiations at Burford, and 'Judas Denne', one of the leaders of the rebellious regiments, who saved his life by grovelling and preached a sermon of repentance to his fellow-prisoners in Burford church. We shall meet him again as a Baptist minister.

The myth was that of the people's army, which had pledged itself never to disband or divide until its democratic objectives were obtained, treacherously overcome by Machiavellian generals who regarded it as a mere professional military machine which they used to further their own selfish aims and ambitions. And in betraying the people the generals had also betrayed God. The former army chaplain John Saltmarsh wrote on 28 October 1647 that 'ye have not discharged yourselves to the people in such things as they justly expected from ye ... The wisdom of the flesh hath deceived and enticed'.[60] A few weeks later he rose from his deathbed and rode from Ilford to Army Headquarters at Windsor, in the depth of winter, to tell Fairfax (with his hat on) 'the Lord had now forsaken them and would not prosper them, because they had forsaken him, their first principle'.[61] A great number of the characters in this book served their apprenticeship in the New Model Army: William Dell, William Erbery, John Webster, Henry Pinnell, Thomas Collier as Army chaplains; John Spittlehouse the Fifth Monarchist, Everard the Digger, Bauthumley, Clarkson, Coppe and Salmon the Ranters, James Nayler and William Deusbury and many other Quakers, probably John

Bunyan.[62] Thousands of their followers must have shared similar experiences, similar loyalties, similar hopes. These common memories would remain even when Cornet Joyce had become a Colonel and a land speculator and Sexby a conspirator in touch with royalists.

The idea that the Army represented the people of England, or more frequently the people of God in England, was still from time to time put forward;[63] but after 1649 this now expressed the views of millenarians, not democrats. For the latter, political defeat was total and irreversible. 'The ground of the late war between the King and you [Parliament] was a contest whether he or you should exercise the supreme power over us,' declared a Leveller petition a week after the rendezvous at Ware; 'so it's vain to expect a settlement of peace amongst us until that point be clearly and justly determined, that there can be no liberty in any nation where the law-giving power is not solely in the people or their representatives.' 'Is not all the controversy, whose slaves the poor shall be?' asked the Leveller pamphlet, *The Mournfull Cries of Many Thousand Poore Trades-men*, in January 1648.[64] The experiment of democratic politics had been tried, in the most favourable possible forum, the Army, that cross-section of politically-conscious men of goodwill; and even there it had failed. It had failed, the myth said, not because the ideas were wrong but because the generals were too wicked, the radical leaders too trusting, the mass of those whom they aspired to lead too little impressed with the importance of the issues. Sin, in seventeenth-century parlance, was too powerful.

This is the essential background to bear in mind when we consider later attempts to achieve democratic political objectives – the Diggers by quiet infiltration, by contracting in, by appeal to Oliver Cromwell; the Fifth Monarchists, who expected the direct intervention of King Jesus in English politics to bring about the effects which democratic political methods had failed to achieve; the Seekers and Ranters, less directly political, but deeply concerned, as were the Quakers, with the problem of 'sin' and how to escape from its all-pervasiveness. What strikes the historian is how many political objectives all these groups have in common – abolition of tithes and

47

a state church, reform of the law, of the educational system, hostility to class distinctions. They differ profoundly in the means they advocated to achieve these common ends as they thrash around in the confining pool of their society, from which, in the last resort, there is no escape. 'Sin' is the reflection in the minds of men of the realities of this society.

The Army radicals had one great achievement. It shall be expressed in the words of their enemy, Clement Walker:

> They have cast all the mysteries and secrets of government ... before the vulgar (like pearls before swine), and have taught both the soldiery and people to look so far into them as to ravel back all governments to the first principles of nature ... They have made the people thereby so curious and so arrogant that they will never find humility enough to submit to a civil rule.[65]

5

The North and West

O thou North of England, who art counted as desolate
and barren, and reckoned the least of the nations, yet out
of thee did the branch spring and the star arise which
gives light unto all the region round about.

> EDWARD BURROUGH, *To the Camp of the Lord in
> England* (1655) in *The Memorable Works of a Son of
> Thunder and Consolation* (1672), p. 66.

I   THE DARK CORNERS OF THE LAND

The familiar civil war division between royalist North and West,
Parliamentarian South and East, is also a division between the relatively backward North and West, and the economically advanced
South and East. The North and West were regarded by Parliamentarians as the 'dark corners of the land', in which preaching was
totally inadequate, despite the efforts of many Puritans to subsidize
it.[1] In 1641 Lord Brooke observed that there was 'scarce any minister
in some whole shires, as in Cumberland, Westmorland, Northumberland and especially in Wales'.[2] Eighteen years later Baxter argued
that 'multitudes in England, and more in Wales, Cornwall, Ireland,
the Highlands, are scarce able to talk reason about common things'.
Are these, he asked, 'fit to have the sovereign power, to rule the
commonwealth?'[3]

Yet one of the paradoxes of the period is that, of the most radical
sectarian groups, the Quakers started almost exclusively in the

North of England, the Baptists were very strong in Wales. The new English Independency was overthrown by the Welsh, said Erbery; 'baptized churches have the greatest fall from the northern saints both in England and Wales ... John's spirit is in the North of England and the spirit of Jesus rising in North Wales is for the fall of all the churches in the South ... The whirlwind comes from the North.'[4] From the early 1650s there was a rapid expansion of Particular Baptists in Wales[5] and of Quakers all over the North of England. The light of God risen in the North, Burrough said, discovers the abomination of England's teachers and worship, and shall not only shine throughout the nation but 'shall spread over kingdoms'.[6] Their enemies agreed in speaking of 'the Northern Quakers'; Ephraim Pagitt in 1654 said the Quakers were 'made up out of the dregs of common people' and were 'thickest set in the North Parts'.[7] 'This opinion of free will ... doth increase ... in these north parts,' wrote Paul Hobson in 1655, referring especially to Hull.[8] Earlier, Hugh Peter and others had noticed that the Welsh border counties, Herefordshire and Worcestershire, were 'ripe for the gospel', and emissaries were sent from Glamorgan to London in 1649 asking for preachers.[9] When the Quakers turned south in 1654 they made great progress among 'that dark people' of the dark county of Cornwall, as well as in Wales, and among weavers generally, notably in Gloucestershire.[10]

The paradox is increased by the fact that such Puritan ministers as there were in the North had mostly been cleared out by Archbishop Neile in the 1630s.[11] Others had fled from their parishes in the North and in Wales during the civil war, when royalist forces occupied their areas. Erbery gives a different reason for the absence of episcopally-ordained ministers in the North and in Wales: 'they are gone to fat parsonages from whence malignants have been thrown out'. Erbery prophesied that 'the saints shall build those old waste places, ... not men who call themselves ministers, but those whom the people shall call ministers'.[12] In fact as early as 1646 the sharp eye of Thomas Edwards noted that 'emissaries out of the sectaries' churches are sent to infect and poison ... Yorkshire and those northern parts, ... Bristol and Wales'. 'Sects begin to grow fast in these northern parts, for want of a settlement in discipline.' An Independent congregation was already gathered at Halifax. Thomas Collier helped to establish a Baptist congregation in the Taunton area. Army chaplains like Collier had a special interest in such work. Edwards comments 'Truly 'tis a sad thing that in all the towns and cities (for the most part) taken by the Parliament's forces, this should be the fruit of it, that errors and heresies should abound there, and that sectaries of all sorts get places of profit and power.'[13] In this struggle for positions of influence the Army was on the spot: Parliament and the Presbyterian clergy were far away. It was in vain that Herbert Palmer in 1646 urged the House of Commons to fill the deserted pulpits in the North: 'Churches ... will be your strongest castles, if you furnish them with ministers.' But, as he ruefully pointed out, in agreement with Erbery, larger maintenance was necessary to persuade 'spiritual commanders' to fight the Lord's battle in the North.[14] One of *Mercurius Politicus*'s correspondents was still saying in November 1650 that preachers in the North 'would do as much good service to the state as a regiment of soldiers in a shire'.[15]

It was to remedy this defect that the Commissions for Propagating the Gospel in the North and in Wales were set up. But the itinerant propagators were often unordained mechanics, and the whole atmosphere of the operation was too radical to be acceptable to the Presbyterian clergy or the gentry. The object, Clement Walker said, was 'to preach anti-monarchical seditious doctrine to the people (suitable to that they call the present government), to raise the rascal multitude and schismatical rabble against all men of best quality in the kingdom, to draw them into associations and combinations with one another in every county and with the Army, against all lords, gentry, ministers, lawyers, rich and peaceable men'.[16] Anthony Ashley Cooper observed in 1654 that he had passed through Wales and found 'churches all unsupplied, except a few grocers or such persons that have formerly served for two years'.[17]

Professor Stone suggests, moreover, that there were far fewer small private schools, run by clergymen, in the North and West than in the South and East, which must in itself have widened the cultural gap between the two regions.[18] We therefore have to look for other explanations than the influence of southern Puritanism for the sudden burgeoning of radical religious ideas in the outlying areas of the North, West and South-west of England, and in Wales. Traditional southern English middle-class Puritanism of the Presbyterian variety had a hold only in isolated areas of the North (Lancashire, Newcastle, the West Riding) and hardly at all in Wales, except for the area of Harley influence in Worcestershire and Herefordshire along the Welsh border. Here Sir Thomas's 'planting of godly ministers and then backing them with his authority made religion famous in his little corner of the world'.[19] But this absence of traditional Presbyterianism does not mean that there were no popular religious movements in these parts, still less that there were no traditions of popular revolt.

Professor Dickens and Mr Thomson have demonstrated the existence of a powerful Lollard tradition, especially in the West Riding of Yorkshire. Professor Barbour has pointed out that the Quakers were initially strongest in areas which contributed the popular element to the Pilgrimage of Grace in 1536–7. The Robin Hood ballads were of northern provenance.[20] Familists were said to have been strong in the North, and there were the Grindletonians in the West Riding whom I shall be considering in a moment: they may bridge the gap between Familism and Quakerism.[21] But we hear of such groups only by accident, when they get into trouble, as with the group of Antinomians which met secretly in private houses in Barnstaple in the early 1620s. This group was drawn from serving men and women and other members of the lower classes.[22] What we may call the English Middle West was the scene of anti-enclosure risings at the end of the 1620s – Dorset, Gloucestershire, Worcestershire, Shropshire, Wiltshire. This was also the area of the Clubman movement in 1645. Clarendon testifies to the existence of support for the Parliamentary cause among the common people of Yorkshire, Lancashire, Shropshire, Cheshire and North Wales, the Forest of Dean and the south-western counties.[23] There is plenty of confirmation from other sources.[24] Even in distant Carlisle the 'rascal rout' tried to seize the town for Parliament in 1643 and 'set beggars on horseback'.[25]

All these considerations may help to explain why the New Model Army, 'having marched up and down the kingdom, to do the work of God and the state, ... met with many Christians who have much gospel-light ... in such places where there hath been no gospel-ministry'.[26] Dr Richardson, the most learned authority on Puritanism in Lancashire and Cheshire, notes that it was strongest in market towns and in pastoral areas, as Dr Thirsk would have anticipated. He also observed that where before 1642 Puritanism had grown up around a particular incumbent or town lecturer, it increasingly involved the laity, who often proved much more radical than their ministers; often indeed such Puritanism developed in an anticlerical direction. Similarly in the many large parishes, the curates in the outlying chapelries became financially dependent on their congregations. Here too the laity tended to push them in a radical direction.[27]

Traditional middle-class Presbyterian Puritanism never took deep hold in the North, still less in Wales and south-western England. In the North there were pockets of Puritanism in the pastoral-industrial districts of eastern Lancashire and the West Riding of Yorkshire, as well as in the area around Newcastle.[28] In these parts the congregation often took the lead; we can see how this might develop into 'mechanic preaching', separatism, as soon as liberty of conscience was established. The defeat of the royalist armies in the civil war, the bankruptcy of the traditional clergy, created an even greater spiritual void than in the more traditional Puritan centres of the South and East. Yet the period was one of much greater prosperity in the pasture and farming areas. Blith in 1652 singled out 'the woodland parts in Worcestershire, Warwickshire, Staffordshire, Shropshire, Wales-ward and North-ward' for their improved pasture farming combined with industry. This prosperity is confirmed by a shift of population to the North and West of England, by the rebuilding of peasant houses in stone, in the North, South-west, and in Wales.[29]

The Quakers, whose original leaders were almost exclusively northern yeomen and craftsmen, came from this background. Lancashire Quakers included former victims and opponents of oppressive royalist landlords, who had gained experience of cooperative action in resisting increases in rents, labour-services and tithe payments.[30] Levellers were active in Lancashire throughout 1649.[31] But such men could also draw on pre-existing underground traditions which were suddenly enabled to flourish after Parliament's victory. When George Fox rode into the North in 1651 he found congregations of Seekers or 'shattered Baptists' waiting for him everywhere among the yeomen farmers of the Yorkshire dales, the Lancashire and Cumberland pastoral-industrial areas. By 1656 Quakerism 'began to spread mightily' in the south-western counties of England.[32] In Wales and the Marches it was the Particular Baptists who initially filled the spiritual gap, though in some parts they were superseded by Quakers.[33] The Fifth Monarchists never had much influence in the North, and only superficially in Wales, though they were stronger in Devon and Cornwall. Mr Capp suggests that Fifth Monarchism was a specifically urban movement: he found little connection between Fifth Monarchy and forest areas before the 1670s.[34] It seems to have been mainly in response to this radical challenge that the traditional clergy in the outlying regions joined in the movement led by Richard Baxter to build up voluntary county associations of ministers, a 'Presbyterianism from below'.[35]

'Those that come out of the North are the greatest pests of the nation,' said the M.P. for Southwark in 1656; 'the Diggers came thence.'[36] Samuel Highland was thinking primarily about James Nayler and the Quakers, and he was wrong about most of the Diggers, so far as we know. But he was right about their leading theorist, Gerrard Winstanley, born in Wigan; and he might, had he taken the trouble, have added the Ranter Lawrence Clarkson, born in Preston; the Yorkshiremen John Saltmarsh (described in 1648 as 'now the chief Familist in England'[37]), John Webster and Henry Jessey; the Northumbrian John Lilburne. Had he extended his coverage to Wales and the Welsh Border he might have added Vavasor Powell, Morgan Lloyd, Walter Cradock, William Erbery; John Bidle, Socinian, from Gloucestershire; Thomas Harrison and Henry Danvers, Fifth Monarchists from Staffordshire; the Leveller William Walwyn from Worcestershire; Hugh Peter and John Carew from Cornwall.

Even that is not the whole story of the cultural impact of the North and West upon the more advanced South and East. Who are the greatest metaphysical poets? John Donne is separated by at least one generation from the Welsh forebear who sent his younger son to London to be apprenticed.[38] But George Herbert and Henry Vaughan are Welshmen, Marvell a Yorkshireman, Crashaw son of one; Traherne came from the Welsh marches. In the second rank we may add Lord Herbert of Cherbury, John Davies of Hereford. Inigo Jones was of Welsh descent. Turning to the field of mathematics and science, and especially that twilight world of alchemy and magic which historians are more and more coming to recognize as of crucial importance in the origins of modern science, we find Robert Recorde, John Dee, Robert Fludd, Matthew Gwynne, Edmund Gunter, Thomas Vaughan and Edward Somerset, Marquis of Worcester, all Welsh or of Welsh descent;[39] Jeremiah Horrocks of Lancashire, William Turner of Northumberland, Henry Briggs and Henry Power of Halifax, the Towneley group of scientists just over the border in Lancashire, who carried barometers up George Fox's Pendle Hill.[40] It would be interesting to make a serious study of the cultural consequences of the union of Great Britain, begun by Henry VII and VIII, extended by James I, completed by the New Model Army.

II   THE GRINDLETONIANS

Grindletonianism is the only English sect which takes its name from a place rather than a person or a set of beliefs,[41] and there is significance in this. For although Roger Brearley, curate at Grindleton from 1615 to 1622, is very important in the history of the movement, it probably antedates him and certainly survived him. The Pennine valleys and Cleveland dales, extending from Bradford to the extreme north-west of Yorkshire, provided safe refuges for religious unorthodoxy. Familism probably got a hold here in Elizabeth's reign, and interest in it extended over most of the area. During Brearley's curacy, 'many go to Grindleton [from Giggleswick, seven miles away] and neglect their own parish church'. Brearley often preached outside his own parish. By 1627 opinions 'tending to the sect called Grindletonians' were detected within a few miles of York.[42] Brearley moved to Kildwick in 1622, ten miles east of Grindleton. He left the diocese altogether in 1631, but in 1634 John Webster became curate of Kildwick, only a few miles from John Lambert's residence at Kirby Malham. Webster was in trouble with the church courts as a Grindletonian about 1635.[43] He quotes Brearley in his *Examen Academiarum*.[44] In the 1650s he was a schoolmaster at Clitheroe, just across the Lancashire border, and preached occasionally at Grindleton.[45] What is interesting about Grindleton is the share of the congregation in the making of the heresy – recalling Dr Richardson's observations about congregations forcing the pace in Lancashire. A traditional independence is suggested by the agreement of 1587 between freeholders and copyholders of Grindleton to enclose and divide a common.[46] There was no resident rector or vicar, only the curate, presumably hired by the congregation and therefore likely to hold views acceptable to them. In 1617 fifty charges were drawn up against Roger Brearley *and his congregation*. Some of them seem much more radical than the views which the curate published in his sermons, or than are to be found in writings printed after his death. It is probable that they represent developments made by lay members of his congregation; in 1627 at least three laymen were involved in further accusations, including that of holding private meetings.[47]

Among the fifty charges of 1617 were the following beliefs:

(1) a motion rising from the spirit is more to be rested in than the Word itself; (2) it is a sin to believe the Word . . . without a motion of the spirit; (3) the child of God in the power of grace doth perform every duty so well, that to ask pardon for failing in matter or manner is a sin; (7) the Christian assured can never commit a gross sin; (14) a soul sanctified must so aim at God's glory, as he must never think of salvation; (33) a man having the spirit may read, pray or preach without any other calling whatsoever; (38) neither the preacher nor they pray for the King . . . They know not whether he be elected or not; (46) they cannot have more joy in heaven than they have in this life by the spirit.

Brearley himself speaks of mastering sin, which sets believers free from hell and death.[48]

Belief in the priority of the spirit over the letter of the Bible, denial of the significance of ordination, the possibility of living without sin and attaining heaven in this life – we shall often meet such views again. They represented a grave challenge to traditional Calvinism, which could be very daunting in moments of depression. In 1622, when Thomas Shepard was about seventeen years old and in deep despair, he 'heard of Grindleton' and asked himself 'whether that glorious estate of perfection might not be the truth?' and whether the preachers whose doctrines had so frightened him 'were not all legal men, and their books so?'[49] A sudden conversion saved him for Calvinism, and he went on to be a successful minister in New England. But Governor Winthrop attributed the heresies of Mistress Anne Hutchinson to Grindletonian doctrines.[50] When in the 1640s Calvin and the Eternal Decrees were under attack from all sides in England, the voices of 'the Grindletonian Familists'[51] were listened to again – especially by the laity. John Webster was closely associated with the Welshman William Erbery; Robert Towne, curate of various parishes in west Yorkshire and east Lancashire from the 1630s to 1664, had been accused of Grindletonianism in 1640.[52] Roger Williams called the Quaker leaders John Camm and Francis Howgill Grindletonians, though they are usually spoken of as Seekers; we have a description by Thomas Bancroft (1657) of his own conversion from the Grindletonians to the Quakers.[53]

Finally, though I suggested that Brearley's own congregation may have outstripped him, he himself points forward to the 1640s and 50s. What could be more relevant than his only good poem, *Self civil war*?

> Unto myself I do myself betray . . .
> Myself agrees not with myself a jot . . .
> I trust myself, and I myself distrust . . .
> I cannot live, with nor without myself.[54]

There we have the 'double heart' of Brearley's fellow Yorkshireman, Andrew Marvell, which is central to the whole of metaphysical poetry; linked with the spiritual turmoil and dissatisfaction which prepared so many congregations of Seekers in Yorkshire, Lanca-shire, Cumberland and Westmorland for the message of George Fox and James Nayler. In a similar way John Webster was to link the Grindletonian distrust of an educated and ordained clergy with an advanced programme for the reform of higher education. Grindle-ton, lying at the foot of Pendle Hill, George Fox's Mount of Vision,[55] should perhaps have a more prominent place on maps of seventeenth-century England than is usually accorded to it.

III   SUMMARY SO FAR

Historians of science distinguish between 'internal' and 'external' causes of advance in scientific knowledge; between the logical devel-opment of structures of ideas on the one hand, and response to social pressures and technical needs on the other. Both clearly are import-ant in the history of science. I attempt in this book to look at the external and internal causes of the florescence of radical ideas of all kinds in the decade after the end of the English civil war.

In chapters 3, 4 and 5 I have stressed the social background – the isolation and freedom which permitted radical ideas to develop among some communities in woodland and pasture areas; the mobile society of early capitalism, serviced by itinerant merchants, crafts-men, pedlars; the crowds of masterless men, vagabonds and urban poor, who no longer fitted into the categories of a hierarchical agrar-ian society. The great shake-up of the civil war suddenly and remarkably increased social and physical mobility. The New Model Army itself can be regarded as a body of masterless men on the move. Just as – given religious freedom – itinerant craftsmen and merchants could become itinerant ministers, so the New Model Army – the main protagonist in the fight for religious liberty – contained mech-anic preachers and gathered churches. It linked up the hitherto obscure radical groups scattered up and down the kingdom, and gave them new confidence, especially in the lonely North and West. It was also itself an outstanding example of social mobility.

The New Model was the match which fired the gunpowder. But once the conflagration started, there was plenty of combustible material lying around. To appreciate this we must look at the development of radical and heretical ideas in England, some religious, others secular; some inherited from the Lollards, some imported from the continent, all modified in the rapidly changing society of sixteenth- and early seventeenth-century England. Chapter 2 attempted to survey some of these traditions; chapters 6, 7 and 8 pick out others. In the hectic and exhilarating freedom of the 1640s and 50s all these elements were cast into a melting pot from which unprecedented new compounds were to emerge.

6

A Nation of Prophets

[I wrote *Gangraena*] out of the pride and vanity of my own mind, out of disdain that plain unlearned men should seek for knowledge any other way than as they were directed by us that are learned; out of base fear, if they should fall to teach one another, that we should ... lose our domination in being sole judges of doctrine and discipline, whereby our predecessors have over-ruled states and kingdoms: or lastly that we should lose our profits and plenteous maintenance by tithes ... All this I saw coming with that liberty which plain men took to try and examine all things ...

WILLIAM WALWYN, *A Prediction of Mr Edwards His Conversion and Recantation* (1646) in Haller, *Tracts on Liberty*, III, p. 343.

I ASTROLOGERS AND MILLENARIANS

Most men and women in seventeenth-century Britain still lived in a world of magic, in which God and the devil intervened daily, a world of witches, fairies and charms. If they failed, the royal touch would cure scrofula. Arise Evans, born in 1607 in Merionethshire, said it was usual for thieves to go to cunning men or astrologers to find out whether they would be hanged or not.[1] Most villages had their 'cunning man', their white witch: they were cheaper than doctors or lawyers. If we think about the world in which men lived, it is easy to see why miraculous interventions in daily life were taken for granted. We believe in a law-abiding universe because in fact 'acts of God' are rarer than in the seventeenth century. Universal insurance, including social insurance, better medical services and especially anaesthetics, no plague, houses made of bricks and therefore far less inflammable, winter feed for cattle, so that spring is no longer starvation time – all this has transformed ordinary existence. The traditional insecurity of medieval life had been intensified by the new insecurity of the capitalist market. Nation-wide slumps like that in the clothing industry during the 1620s led to intensified competition; the new attitudes – 'a man may do what he will with his own', and 'the devil take the hindmost' – disrupted the low-level social security of the medieval village. Dr Macfarlane and Mr Thomas have argued that persecution of witches *increased* in the sixteenth and seventeenth centuries as men blamed the victims of their anti-social actions rather than blaming themselves.[2]

Dr Thomas Beard, Oliver Cromwell's schoolmaster and friend, contributed to a vast literature describing God's providences against Sabbath breakers and other sinners, when the Almighty intervened directly and drastically to manifest his disapproval of some human action. Sir Walter Ralegh, Sir Francis Bacon, Sir Kenelm Digby and many other future Fellows of the Royal Society, believed in sympathetic magic: that bleeding could be stopped at a distance by applying *to the weapon* a handkerchief dipped in the blood of the injured party: John Locke believed in it too.[3] We cannot separate the early history of science from the history of magic, cannot give prizes to good rationalists as against bad magicians, astrologers, alchemists. 'In those dark times,' said John Aubrey of the days before the civil war, 'astrologer, mathematician and conjuror were accounted the same things.'[4] Giordano Bruno, John Dee, John Kepler, Tycho Brahe were all magi. John Wilkins, future secretary of the Royal Society, in 1648 still quoted Dee and Fludd as authorities on 'mathematical magic'. If an Elizabethan wanted gold, he could raid the Spanish Main, or he could practise alchemy: Sir Walter Ralegh tried the one, John Dee the other: Sir William Cecil invested in both.

It is true that in the long run protestantism worked against all magic, black or white, against charms, spells, incantations and love potions. Countless sermons denouncing transubstantiation helped to produce a materialist and sceptical attitude towards the miracle of the mass: miracles generally were pushed back into the past. But it was a long time before these things affected ordinary men and women. Meanwhile cunning men took over many of the jobs previously performed by Roman Catholic priests and neglected by their successors. The Duke of Buckingham, favourite of James and Charles I, had his astrologer, Dr Lambe: serious politicians sought astrological advice – Oliver Cromwell, Whitelocke, Richard Overton.[5] The Puritan divine John Preston took astrology seriously;[6] Elias Ashmole, F.R.S., practised it. It is significant that there was a Society of Astrologers in London more than a decade before there was a Royal Society. At the popular level, 'the malice of the clergy' could no longer prevent the publication of astrological books after 1640 as it had done before,[7] and they appeared in abundant profusion, together with a number of prophecies, old and new. Almanacs became at once more numerous, more polemical and propagandist, and appealed to a wider public at twopence a time. They also became more profitable, as almanac-makers took sides in the civil war: 1800 copies of William Lilly's *Prophecy of the White King* sold within three days of publication in 1644.[8] Astrological almanacs sold even better than the Bible; they were alleged by many contemporaries to have done greater harm to the royal cause than anything else.[9] It is only from our modern vantage point that we can separate what is 'rational' in seventeenth-century science from what is not. We must not allow this wisdom after the event to make us condescending about beliefs held by men like Bacon, Boyle and Newton. Only in the course of the century did the laws of nature harden and congeal; meanwhile scientists were of all men the most anxious to demonstrate that science proves the existence of God.[10]

The English, wrote Fuller in the mid-seventeenth century, are said always to carry 'an old prophecy about with them in their pockets, which they can produce at pleasure to promote their designs, though oft mistaken in the application of such equivocating predictions'. Bishop Hacket agreed that 'we English are observed to be too credulous of vain prophecies such as are fathered upon Merlin and no better authors'.[11] The prophecies of Merlin, Mother Shipton and many others probably circulated far more than we have evidence to demonstrate. Fifth Monarchists in the 1650s cited them as well as the Sibylline prophecies, Nostradamus, Paracelsus and astrologers.[12]

Lilly specialized in applying old predictions to the circumstances of the revolutionary decades. His *Prophecy of the White King* elaborated on a prediction attributed to Merlin.[13] Lilly's repeated prophecies of 'a restraint on monarchical power', his call, on strictly astrological grounds, for Charles I and the Oxford Parliament to return to Westminster, his repeated predictions of defeat and a violent end for the King, may have contributed to bring about these effects.[14] It was a fortunate coincidence for Lilly that his prophecy of disaster for Charles was published on the day of the Battle of Naseby. 'His writings have kept up the spirits of the soldiery, the honest people of this realm, and many of us Parliament men,' said an M.P. in 1651.[15] Three years earlier Parliament had voted him a gift of £50 and a pension of £100 *per annum*. Lilly, Arise Evans wrote in 1655, 'knows nothing, nor ever did know anything, but as the Parliament directed him to write'.[16] But then Evans was a rival, and less successful, prophet. Lilly must have done much to make, or keep, astrology acceptable to the radicals. He himself had, or wrote as though he had, strong anti-clerical and anti-aristocratic convictions, speaking up in 1644 for the yeomen of England and for the private soldiers.[17] His enthusiasm led him in 1652 to predict 'a cessation of all taxes, and all things governed by love'.[18]

The Reformation, for all its hostility to magic, had stimulated the spirit of prophecy. The abolition of mediators, the stress on the individual conscience, left God speaking direct to his elect. It was incumbent on them to make public his message. And God was no respecter of persons: he spoke to John Knox rather than to Mary Queen of Scots. Knox himself thanked God for his gift of prophecy, which established his [Knox's] *bona fides*.[19] The common man, Luther, Calvin and Knox showed, could remake history if kings and princes did not.

In England the revolutionary decades gave wide publicity to what was almost a new profession – the prophet, whether as interpreter of the stars, or of traditional popular myths, or of the Bible. It is therefore very important for us to grasp the role of prophecies in popular psychology. 'Dreams and prophecies do thus much good,' Selden observed; 'they make a man to go on with boldness upon a danger or a mistress. If he obtains, he attributes much to them; if he miscarries, he thinks no more of them, or is no more thought of himself.'[20] Hobbes too in his history of the civil war noted that prophecy was 'many times the principal cause of the event foretold'.[21] Dr Leff has suggested that the appeal to the Bible as history or prophecy was one of the most momentous developments of the later Middle Ages. Eschatological prophecy became a major part of protestant controversial literature, aided especially by the invention of printing.[22]

Protestant scholarship exposed many Catholic superstitions, and popularized the vernacular Bible. Similarly, protestant study of the prophetical books of the Bible was intended to put the science of prophecy on a rational basis. Other prophecies, unless positively assisted by devils,[23] always fooled those who trusted them: Birnam wood did come to Dunsinane in a most unfair manner.[24] The invention of printing, by putting prophecies on permanent record, perhaps helped to expose their ambiguities and fallacies.[25] The feeling of freedom which reliance on such prophecies had given was illusory. But the Bible, if properly understood, really would liberate men from destiny, from predestination. By understanding and cooperating with God's purposes men believed they could escape from the blind forces which seemed to rule their world, from time itself; they could become free.[26]

It was in a *scientific* spirit that scholars approached Biblical prophecy. It was the job of mathematicians and chronologers, like Napier, Brightman, Mede, Ussher and Newton. Such men believed in the possibility of establishing a science of prophecy, just as Hobbes believed in the possibility of establishing a science of politics. Both hopes proved unrealizable: neither is therefore to be despised. By the mid-seventeenth century a consensus seemed to have been reached, indicating the advent of remarkable events in the mid-1650s: the fall of Antichrist, perhaps the second coming and the millennium. This underlay the confident energy, the utopian enthusiasm, of the Puritan preachers in the early 1640s. With what subsequently seemed to them naïve optimism, they called the common man to fight the Lord's battles against Antichrist.[27]

Bacon and others urged scientists to study the techniques of craftsmen, their mysteries, handed on verbally from master to apprentice. The idea that there was a secret traditional wisdom, Egyptian or Hermetic, to be wrung from nature, died very hard. From the time of the Gnostics there had been a similar tradition that there were secret meanings behind the sacred text of the Scriptures, known only to the initiates, to scholars. Ordinary Bible-readers in the sixteenth and seventeenth centuries wanted to democratize these mysteries; to abolish mumbo-jumbo men, whether priests, lawyers or scholars.[28] They believed, on good protestant authority, that *anyone* could understand God's Word if he studied it carefully enough, and if the grace of God was in him. And then the Bible could be made to reveal the key to events of his own time.

Bibles were not expensive as book prices then went. Josselin mentions 3s. 2d. as the price in 1649; later it was 2s.[29] The Geneva Bible was published in pocketable editions, so that men could study it in the privacy of their homes, or could produce it in a church or an alehouse to knock down an argument with a text. Men coming to the Bible with no historical sense but with the highest expectations found in it a message of direct contemporary relevance. Take a young Welshman like Arise Evans, who came to London in 1629. He tells us how his attitude towards the Bible changed in the decade before the Revolution. 'Afore I looked upon the Scripture as a history of things that passed in other countries, pertaining to other persons; but now I looked upon it as a mystery to be opened at this time, belonging also to us.'[30] This attitude must have been shared by many of the victims of economic and political crisis who turned to the Bible for guidance in those perplexing years. The 1640s and 50s were indeed the great age of 'mechanick preachers' – laymen like Bunyan interpreting the Bible according to their untutored lights with all the confidence and excitement of a new discovery. 'I am as the Paul of this time,' Evans exclaimed; 'he was a mechanic, a tent-maker, Acts

18.3. I am a tailor.'[31] 'Poor, illiterate, mechanic men,' said William Dell of the Apostles, 'turned the world upside down.'[32]

The Bible was the accepted source of all true knowledge. Everybody cited its texts to prove an argument, including men like Hobbes and Winstanley, who *illustrated* from the Bible conclusions at which they had arrived by rational means. The difference in the case of simpler men like Arise Evans is that they believed the Bible to be divinely inspired, and applied its texts directly to problems of their own world and time, with no idea of the difficulties of translation, nor of the historical understanding required. So Arise Evans thought that Revelation 8 and 11 gave an account of the civil war, that chapters 8 and 9 of Amos set down all that came to pass since the beginning of the Long Parliament. In Amos 9.1 the lintel at the door, which is to be smitten that the posts may shake, must refer to Speaker Lenthall.[33] But these untrained minds included a George Fox and a John Bunyan. They were grappling with the problems of their society, problems which called urgently for solution, and they were using the best tools they knew of. More solid Puritan divines had cited the Bible against bishops, against persecution, against tithes. The Evanses studied it very carefully, if less skilfully and more selectively, in order to understand and so be able to control what was going to happen.

If we add to this the Familist belief taken over by the Quakers, that only the spirit of God within the believer can properly understand the Scriptures, we get an intense sense of the immediate personal relevance of the Bible's message. Men came to know the Bible so well that their relationship to it was almost passive. In *Grace Abounding* texts are hurled at Bunyan's head like thunderbolts of God. The Bible spoke direct, outside history, to men who believed passionately that the day of the Lord was imminent: they only understood what the Lord meant. The appeal to the past, to documents (whether the Bible or Magna Carta), becomes a criticism of existing institutions, of certain types of rule. If they do not conform to the sacred text, they are to be rejected. Priests and scholars would have liked to keep interpretation of the Bible the monopoly of an educated élite, as it had been in the days before the vernacular Bible existed. The radical reply was to assert the possibility of any individual

receiving the spirit, the inner experience which enabled him to understand God's Word as well as, better than, mere scholars who lacked
this inner grace. Luther, who invented the priesthood of all believers,
had been able to beat the theologians at their own game. But for
seventeenth-century English radicals the religion of the heart was the
answer to the pretensions of the academic divinity of ruling-class
universities.

Emphasis on private interpretation was not however mere absolute individualism. The congregation was the place in which
interpretations were tested and approved. George Fox's trip to the
North of England in 1651 was overwhelmingly successful because
his message was acceptable to pre-existing congregations of Seekers
or Grindletonians. The congregation guaranteed the validity of the
interpretation for the given social unit, was a check on individualist
absurdities.[34]

Any careful reading of the Bible gives rise to thoughts about the
end of the world. In the highly-charged atmosphere of the 1640s,
many people expected it in the near future. This, as Mr Lamont has
shown, was not a view peculiar to the radicals. It was held, among
others, by King James, Sir Walter Ralegh and William Chillingworth.[35] 'The most of the chief divines,' the Scot Robert Baillie
reported from London in 1645, 'not only Independents but others, . . .
are express Chiliasts.' As soon as the censorship broke down,
Foxe's Book of Martyrs, which Laud had forbidden to be reprinted,
circulated again; English translations and popular summaries of the
works of Napier, Brightman, Mede and Alsted were published, all
seeming to underpin the utopian hopes of less scholarly readers of
the Bible.[36] Preachers on the Parliamentary side called on ordinary
people to fight for God's cause, and got ultimately rather more enthusiasm than they bargained for. But millenarianism existed at both
levels: we must see the eccentricities of popular Fifth Monarchists in
the 1650s against this scholarly background, which led Milton to
speak of Christ as 'shortly-expected King'.[37]

It is difficult to exaggerate the extent and strength of millenarian
expectations among ordinary people in the 1640s and early 50s: I
have tried to give the evidence elsewhere.[38] They affected Levellers

like Lt.-Col. John Jubbes, Major Francis White and Captain William Bray no less than a poet like George Wither. Mr Toon suggests that these expectations reached their zenith in the late 1640s: the Fifth Monarchist movement marked a decline.[39]

To many men the execution of Charles I in 1649 seemed to make sense only as clearing the way for King Jesus, as the prelude to greater international events. John Spittlehouse in 1650 warned Rome to 'beware of Nol Cromwell's army, lest Hugh Peter come to preach in Peter's chair'. In the same year Arise Evans had a vision in which he went through France to Rome, where 'a voice came to me saying, So far as thou art come, so far shall Cromwell come'.[40] A Bristol Baptist in 1654, hearing that two Frenchmen had been imprisoned for fore-telling the end of the world for 1656, was worried because he was not prepared for that event.[41] Between 1648 and 1657 Ralph Josselin was reading millenarian tracts, one of which suggested that Oliver Cromwell would conquer the Turk and the Pope. He was continually thinking and dreaming about the millennium. He noted in his Diary that men expected the world to end in 1655 or 1656, though he did not share the belief. 'This generation shall not pass,' declared John Tillinghast in 1654, until the millennium has arrived.[42] John Bunyan announced in 1658 that 'the judgment day is at hand'.[43]

Dr Capp has shown that the strength of the Fifth Monarchist movement in the fifties was among cloth workers and other craftsmen. He stresses their class consciousness, their hostility to aristocracy. John Rogers attacked 'naughty nobles' and 'profane and swaggering gentry'.[44] Their programme was in many points similar to that of the Levellers, attacking tithing priests and lawyers as well as the rich. It seems to have been their associations with the clothing industry rather than their study of the Bible which made them favour war against the Netherlands and peace with Spain. Dr Nuttall and others believe that the spread of Quakerism would have been impossible in the 1650s without the antecedent millenarian excitement, of which the Fifth Monarchist movement was only part.[45] With his usual good sense George Fox rebuked a Quaker who set a specific and very imminent date for the day of judgment.[46] But Quakers, like Fifth Monarchists, helped to fill the vacuum left by the execution of

Charles I. They believed that Christ had come to reign in all men. It was a more republican and democratic even if less directly political doctrine.

II RELIGIOUS TOLERATION

Religious toleration is the greatest of all evils, thought Thomas Edwards in 1646. It will bring in first scepticism in doctrine and looseness of life, then atheism. If a toleration be granted, all preaching will not keep heresies out. 'No man knows where these sectaries will stop or stay, or to what principles they will keep.' Later he wrote the considered words: 'We are in a far worse condition than when the enemy was in the height of his success and victories at the taking of Bristol, or ever since the Parliament began.'[47] We are now perhaps in a position to see why he felt so strongly.

'Religion is the only firm foundation of all power,' Charles I had said. 'The church and state do mutually support and give assistance to each other,' wrote Bishop Goodman. 'The state pays them [the clergy], and thus they have dependence upon the state,' as Hugh Peter more brutally put it.[48] The function of a state church was not merely to guide men to heaven: it was also to keep them in subordination here on earth. Different societies, different churches: but to want no state church at all seemed to traditionalists a denial of all good order.

Those M.P.s who in 1641 had defended the established church as the buttress of the existing social order had been proved correct. Ecclesiastical authority, the functioning of church courts, had utterly broken down; the attempt to replace them by a Presbyterian disciplinary system enjoyed a very limited success. The lower orders were freer than they had ever been – free from prosecution for 'sin', free to assemble and discuss in their own congregations, free (if they wished to be) from the supervision and control of a university-educated ministry, free to choose their own lay preachers, mechanics like the rest of the congregation. The attack on tithes, common to all the radicals, undermined the whole concept of a state church, since if parishioners could not be legally compelled to pay tithes there would be no 'livings' for the clergy to occupy, no impropriated tithes for the gentry to collect in the forty per cent of livings which were lay fees. Disestablishment of the church would deprive the gentry of another property right – the right of presentation to a living, a right for which they or their ancestors had paid hard cash and which gave them useful opportunities of providing for a younger son or a poor relation. If there were no ready-made livings for the clergy, then what would happen to the universities, whose main function was training ministers and whose own finances depended largely on impropriations?

If ministers were dependent on the voluntary contributions of their congregations, as was made explicit by the church covenant in Independent churches, they would also have to reflect the theological and political outlook of these congregations, and so the church as an organ for imposing and maintaining a single consistent outlook would cease to exist. In the even more democratic churches of Baptists and other sectaries, the distinction between clergy and laity ceased to exist.[49] 'Mechanick preachers', labouring six days a week, would cost their congregations nothing, and would be closer to the views of their hearers in urban congregations and in many pastoral-industrial areas. The Baptist principle of adult baptism meant that each individual must choose or be chosen by a congregation after he was grown up: it too disrupted the very idea of a national church. 'Once give over christening the whole parish infancy,' wrote Samuel Fisher in his Baptist days, 'and then farewell that parish posture which the Pope set up in all Christendom some six hundred years ago, yea then down falls the parochial-church-steeple-house, priest-hood, pay and all. Amen, so be it.'[50]

William Dell, New Model Army chaplain, argued in 1645 and 1646 that 'unity is Christian, uniformity antichristian'; that no magistrates may forbid preaching of the gospel by gifted laymen; that 'the variety of forms in the world is the beauty of the world'.[51] He told M.P.s to their faces that it was not Parliament's job to reform the church: that was for members of congregations, among whom 'a poor plain countryman, by the spirit which he hath received, is better able to judge of truth and error touching the things of God than the greatest philosopher, scholar or doctor in the world that is destitute of it'.[52] In 1641 Sir Edward Dering 'started with wonder and anger' when 'a bold mechanical' said 'I hope your worship is too wise to believe that which you call your creed.'[53] It took some getting used to.

There is overwhelming contemporary evidence that the strength of the sectaries lay with what Lilburne called 'the base and obscure fellows of the world'.[54] Their contribution to the theory and practice of religious toleration has often been analysed.[55] I am concerned here principally with the political and social overtones which necessarily hung around the question in the 1640s. If liberty be granted to sectaries, Thomas Case had told the House of Commons in May 1647,

> they may in good time come to know also ... that it is their birthright to be free from the power of Parliaments and ... of kings, and to take up arms against both when they shall not vote and act according to their humours. Liberty of conscience, falsely so called, may in good time improve itself into liberty of estates and liberty of houses and liberty of wives.[56]

The words 'heretics' and 'schismatics' are 'but nicknames for any that oppose tyrants and oppressors', said a pamphlet of the following month.[57] The point was often made in one way or another. One of the three things Philip Henry did not like about 'the Independent way' was that 'they pluck up the hedge of parish order'.[58] Winstanley equated not only a state church but also the Independent congregations themselves with private property: 'all your particular churches are like the enclosures of land, which hedges in some to be heirs of life and hedges out others'.[59]

Another familiar economic analogy, used by Milton in *Areopagitica*, was between freedom of trade and religious toleration – 'free trading of truth'.[60] Roger Williams's famous comparison between 'the church or company of worshippers' and 'a corporation, society or company of East India or Turkey merchants'[61] was criticized by Dell as insufficiently radical, since the true Church, unlike 'the Society of Mercers or Drapers or the like' cannot be known by 'the help of any outward sense'. Being 'the freest society under heaven' the church must of course choose its own officers, and not have them thrust upon it, as in parish churches.[62]

To the argument that individual interpretation of the Scriptures and congregational autonomy would lead to religious anarchy, radicals retorted that the inner light is one, and can be recognized by the children of the light. *Areopagitica* assumes that, given freedom of debate, all men's reason must naturally lead them, sooner or later, to recognize the same truths. This is the kind of view likely to appeal to men whose economic life demands freedom of trade from monopolies. It did not seem so self-evident to the big City merchants who read *Gangraena* or *The Holy Commonwealth*.

The hatred of the established clergy which we noted earlier[63] did not cease with the disappearance of bishops and church courts, despite the triumphant cry of a pamphleteer in 1641: 'no more prying into people's actions'.[64] In 1646 a trooper in Northamptonshire 'laid his hand on his sword and said "This sword should never be laid down, nor many thousands more, whilst there was a priest left in England."' In the following April troopers in Suffolk were saying they would never disband 'till we have cut all the priests' throats'.[65] Three months earlier, when a group of Presbyterian ministers visited the New Model Army at Oxford, 'the multitude of soldiers in a violent manner called upon us to prove our calling, . . . whether those that are called ministers had any more authority to preach in public than private Christians which were gifted'. The soldiers were supported in this by William Erbery, who had himself renounced the title of minister – though not, Francis Cheynell sourly alleged, the pay and salary. 'The very name of Presbytery is hateful to the people,' declared the Independent John Goodwin. But already Erbery had denied that the Independent churches were true churches,[66] and a mere two years later Walwyn was writing that the Independent clergy 'pray, preach, and do all for money; and without it they do nothing'. His opposition, in fact, like Lilburne's, extended to 'all these pretended churches of God, either Independent or Anabaptistical'.[67]

In the Leveller Petition of March 1647 and in the Third Agreement of the People (May 1649) tithes were to be abolished, and not replaced by any system of compulsory maintenance; parishioners were to have complete liberty to choose such ministers as themselves should approve.[68] At least one critic of the radicals suggested that their incitement to refuse payment of tithes 'is one of the chiefest inducements that the . . . sectaries have to encourage the silly people and to poison them with their other errors'.[69] 'Clergymen and lawyers are the chiefest oppressors in the land,' Erbery declared. 'Our preachers of the gospel take up the fifth or fourth part of men's lands and labours.' 'How many men are made poor by making a few ministers rich?' There are no true ministers in the church: the magistrate is the only true minister now. Nor indeed is there any need now of churches or ministers: anyone may preach.[70] It was a great triumph for the radicals when, in the flush of excitement after the victory of Dunbar, Army pressure succeeded in abolishing the obligation on every Englishman to attend his parish church each Sunday.[71]

Professor Jordan found strong evidence of 'dark hostility to clerical leadership' in this period, and suggests that the poorer and normally less articulate classes of society were more tolerant than their betters.[72] 'By the end of the first revolutionary decade,' wrote Mr Maclear, 'a militant anti-clericalism was taken as axiomatic in the popular outlook.'[73] 'As for these men called ministers in this nation,' declared the Quaker Edward Burrough, 'the way of their setting up and sending forth, and the way of their maintenance, . . . they are the greatest and most woeful oppression in the nation. The earth is oppressed by them, the inhabitants groan under them.'[74] The profane multitude, the rabble, Richard Baxter recognized, was hostile to ministers and to religion. It confirmed his low view of the multitude.[75]

'The people are brethren and saints in Christ's church,' said John Saltmarsh; in the state church they were 'parishioners and servants'.[76] Winstanley agreed that 'the Beast will have a whole parish, a whole kingdom, and so the world to be his church'.[77] Ministers are 'very fountains of atheism and antichristianism,' said John Spittlehouse five years later.[78] Men like Winstanley, Erbery and Dell opened the door wide to the Quaker assertion that it was antichristian for 'such as are men of learning and have been at the university and have tongues' to 'be masters and bear rule in every parish, and none shall reprove or contradict what they say in public'.[79]

'Reprove or contradict what they say in public.' One of the essentials of the sectarian position was that the sermon should be followed by discussion: that worship was not a matter of passively hearing the Word preached by a learned minister, but participation by the congregation after a gifted member had opened up a subject for discussion. John Robinson, pastor to the Pilgrim Fathers in the Netherlands, said that after public ministry the elders should exhort anyone who had a gift of speaking to the edification of hearers to make use of it.[80] In 1634 John Cotton included in the order of public worship in the church of Boston prophesying by gifted members of the congregation and discussion of questions addressed to the minister.[81] Meaningful discussion had hardly been possible in the pre-1640 parish church, with the parson safely in control, protected by the traditional ritual and ceremony, with squire and churchwardens to enforce decency and order. Things were quite different in a gathered church, non-hierarchical in structure and social composition, with an elected minister who might himself be a mechanic, with no ritual, no squire or churchwardens. In conditions of social upheaval like those of the 1640s, with the squire perhaps absent from the parish, with irreverent soldiers in the neighbourhood fortifying the lower classes against ruling oligarchies and the parson – in these circumstances it might be possible for a parishioner or an intruder to intervene with an effective contribution of his own. Prophesying, said William Dell, was a 'notable means to keep error out of the church'. One man preaching may err and be left uncorrected; but when the right of prophesying is allowed to the whole church, 'the minister can no sooner vent any error but there is some believer or other . . . ready to convince it by the Word of God'.[82]

In the Baptist churches discussion was institutionalized. Mrs Attaway used to call for objections after her sermons, 'for it was their custom to give liberty in that kind'. Henry Denne had a similar practice. At the Bell Alley Baptist church public debates were held at which all might voice their opinions.[83] It was a rule among the General Baptists 'that it shall be lawful for any person to improve their gifts in the presence of the congregation'. In 1648 the General Baptist Edward Barber was invited by the parishioners of St Benet Fink, London, to come to the parish church and add to what the minister (Edmund Calamy) should say, or contradict him if erroneous.[84] Hanserd Knollys created 'several riots and tumults' by going around churches and speaking after the sermon.[85] One can imagine the irritation this practice might cause when, as time went on, the parson himself became the main target of itinerant interrupters, professionally skilled hecklers, denouncing his self-righteousness and his greed in taking tithes.

Disrupting services had been made a secular offence by an Act of Parliament in Mary's reign, 'by which the priests of England till the last Parliament were guarded'.[86] The Quakers always claimed a legal right to speak after the sermon was over. Thus in July 1653 George Fox sat through a sermon at Booth, Cumberland, but when the minister had done

> I began to speak to him . . . and he began to oppose me. I told him
> his glass [hour-glass] was gone, his time was out; the place was as
> free for me as for him; and he accused me that I had broken the law
> in speaking to him in his time in the morning, and I told him he had
> broken the law in speaking in my time.[87]

This continued until the Lord's Day Act of 1656 (cap. 15) strengthened the law against intruders.[88]

7
Levellers and True Levellers

All men have stood for freedom, ... and those of the
richer sort of you that see it are ashamed and afraid to
own it, because it comes clothed in a clownish garment ...
Freedom is the man that will turn the world upside down,
therefore no wonder he hath enemies ... True freedom lies
in the community in spirit and community in the earthly
treasury, and this is Christ the true man-child spread
abroad in the creation, restoring all things unto himself.

G. WINSTANLEY, *A Watch-Word to the
City of London* (1649), Sabine, pp. 316–17.

I   ST GEORGE'S HILL

The years from 1620 to 1650 were bad;[1] the 1640s were much the
worst decade of the period. On top of the disruption caused by the
civil war came a series of disastrous harvests. Between 1647 and
1650 food prices rose steeply above the pre-war level; money wages
lagged badly behind, and the cost of living rose significantly.[2] Taxation was unprecedentedly heavy, and Pym's new tax, the excise, fell
especially severely on articles of popular consumption like beer and
tobacco. These were the years when sales of church, crown and
royalists' lands were breaking traditional landlord/tenant relations,
whilst disbanded soldiers were trying to pick up a living again. The
city of York's special fund for the assistance of lame soldiers was
doubled in 1649 because of increased calls upon it.[3] 'The poor,'

Wildman tells us in January 1648, 'did gather in troops of ten, twenty, thirty, in the roads and seized upon corn as it was carrying to market, and divided it among themselves before the owners' faces, telling them they could not starve.' 'Necessity dissolves all laws and government, and hunger will break through stone walls,' *The Mournfull Cries of Many Thousand Poore Tradesmen* warned Parliament and the Army in the same month.[4] 'The common vote of the giddy multitude,' a pamphleteer admitted in October 1648, would be for the King if it were allowed to express itself freely.[5] Rents had risen so much, cavalry troopers in Northumberland complained in December 1648, that copyholders had to hire themselves out as wage-labourers or shepherds.[6]

The economic and political situation in the early months of 1649 was particularly explosive. Levellers and Army radicals felt that they had been fooled in the negotiations which led up to the trial and execution of the King in January; and that the Independent Grandees had taken over republican reforms from their programme without making any real concessions to their democratic content. The abysmal harvest of 1648 led to widespread hunger and unemployment, especially among disbanded soldiers. In March 1649 the poor of London were being supplied with free corn and coal. On 3 April Peter Chamberlen announced that many were starving for want of bread: he feared they would proceed to direct action unless something was done for them.[7] Clubmen reappeared in the Severn valley, seizing corn. Whilst food prices reached famine levels, the Levellers demanded re-election of Agitators and recall of the General Council of the Army. 'We were before ruled by King, Lords and Commons, now by a General, a Court Martial and House of Commons; and we pray you what is the difference?'[8] At the end of March Lilburne, Overton, Walwyn and Prince were arrested. A Leveller pamphlet, *More Light Shining in Buckinghamshire*, appealed to the soldiers 'to stand everyone in his place, to oppose all tyranny whatsoever', particularly that of lawyers, enclosing lords of manors and the Army Grandees who have rejected social reform and have done nothing for the poor.[9]

Next month mutinies broke out in the Army when men who

refused to volunteer for service in Ireland were demobilized without payment of arrears – exactly what had driven the Army to revolt two years earlier, though then with the acquiescence of the generals. In May more serious revolts broke out among troops in Oxfordshire, Wiltshire and Buckinghamshire, and there were rumours of civilian support from the South-west, the old Clubman area. Cromwell and Fairfax, acting with great vigour and determination, overwhelmingly defeated the mutinous regiments at Burford on 14 May. The period of crisis for the military régime was over. Frightened conservatives rallied to its support, as the lesser evil. Oxford University and the City of London hastened to honour Fairfax and Cromwell. The sermon preached on the latter occasion appropriately denounced those who aspired to remove their neighbour's landmark.[10] Leveller conspiracies continued, soon to be joined by Fifth Monarchist plots: but none of them offered a serious threat to the régime so long as the repeatedly purged Army remained securely under the control of its generals.

Nevertheless, the early months of 1649 had been a terrifying time for the men of property. It was for some time not so obvious to contemporaries as it is to us that the defeat at Burford had been final and decisive. As late as November 1649 Ralph Josselin tells us that men feared to travel because of danger from robbers, and the rich even felt insecure in their own houses. Poor people, he added the following month, 'were never more regardless of God than nowadays'.[11] This was the background against which not only the Levellers but also Peter Chamberlen, John Cook, Hugh Peter and very many others called for drastic social reform on behalf of the poor. It was also the background to the activities of the Ranter Abiezer Coppe, and to the Digger or True Leveller movement.[12]

One Sunday in March or April 1649 the congregation of the parish church of Walton-on-Thames was startled to see the church invaded by a group of six soldiers after Master Faucet had preached his sermon. The soldiers, in a series of symbolical gestures and amid scenes of some excitement, announced that the Sabbath, tithes, ministers, magistrates and the Bible were all abolished.[13] On Sunday 1 April – quite possibly the same Sunday – a group of poor men (described as labourers in a legal action three months later)[14] collected on St George's Hill in the same parish and began to dig the waste land there. It was a symbolic assumption of ownership of the common lands. It was a further symbolic rejection of conventional pieties, which may link up with the soldiers' demonstration in the parish church, that the digging began on a Sunday.[15] One of the Diggers followed up the soldiers' demonstration in Walton Church by 'getting up a great burden of thorns and briars ... into the pulpit of the church at Walton to stop out the parson'.[16] The numbers of the Diggers soon rose to twenty or thirty. 'They invite all to come in and help them,' an observer noted, 'and promise them meat, drink and clothes ... They give out, they will be four or five thousand within ten days ... It is feared they have some design in hand.'[17]

Consider for a moment the area affected. St George's Hill was just outside London, within easy reach of any poor man there who might be interested in the colony. It lay on the edge of Windsor Great Forest, where in 1641 'scores and hundreds set upon the King's deer'.[18] It was unpromising agricultural land, the improver Walter Blith sniffed ('thousands of places more capable of improvement than this'. Winstanley agreed that it was 'in view of flesh ... very barren'.[19]) Kingston, the nearest town, to which the Diggers were taken for trial by the local landlords, was a great corn market. It had a long-standing radical tradition. In 1588 it had been the seat of Martin Marprelate's secret printing press.[20] The town lecturer at that time was the Puritan John Udall, sentenced to death in 1590. He clearly had a strong following. An artisan from Kingston told Bishop Bancroft that the prayer 'Thy kingdom come' was a petition 'that we might have pastors, doctors, elders and deacons in every parish, and so be governed by such eldership as Christ's holy discipline doth require' – the full Presbyterian system, in fact. Another burgess of Kingston hoped to pull the non-preaching clergy 'out of the church by the ears'.[21]

This radical tradition continued. In 1628 it was in Kingston that Buckingham's assassin, Felton, was welcomed by an old woman with the words 'God bless thee, little David!'[22] Seven years later Archbishop Laud's visitor found Kingston a 'very factious town'.[23] It had a Puritan vicar, and from 1642 a Puritan lecturer as well. Kingston, covering the southern approaches to London, with its bridge across the Thames, was a strategically significant centre. Charles sent troops to guard the Surrey magazine there at the time of his attempted arrest of the Five Members. Kingston was the scene of many civil war skirmishes, and after the Parliamentarians took over the area it was the seat of the county committee. When the Army advanced on London in July 1647 Fairfax sent Rainborough over the Thames at Kingston to link up with Army supporters in radical Southwark. The whole region was an Army centre from that time onwards. The Army Council met at Kingston on 18 August 1647 to draw up a Declaration supporting the Agitators' demand for a purge of Parliament.[24]

The area continued to be radical after the ejection of the Diggers. In 1653 it was a Kingston jury which found Lord Chandos guilty of manslaughter (in a duel), notwithstanding his claim to privilege of peerage: he was sentenced to be burnt in the hand.[25] Next year James Nayler told Fox there was a constant Quaker meeting there.[26] In 1657 the Quaker Edward Burrough occupied his leisure time in Kingston gaol by computing the sum total paid in tithes in England and Ireland at £1½ million a year.[27] George Fox frequently resided at Kingston in later life.

This was the area to which Gerrard Winstanley came, not later than 1643. The son (probably) of a Wigan mercer with Puritan sympathies, Gerrard Winstanley came to London as a clothing apprentice in 1630, and set up for himself in 1637. But it was the worst possible time; by 1643 Winstanley had been 'beaten out of both estate and trade'. In 1649 he was described as of Walton-on-Thames. Here he herded cows, apparently as a hired labourer, and wrote religious pamphlets, until he had a vision in a trance telling him to publish it abroad that 'the earth should be made a common treasury of livelihood to whole mankind, without respect of persons'.[28]

Landowners in the area round St George's Hill were more disturbed by the digging than the Council of State or General Fairfax, who had a series of amicable conversations with Winstanley – despite the latter's refusal to remove his hat to a 'fellow-creature'. Nor does Oliver Cromwell seem to have been unduly alarmed when 'a northern prophetess' warned him, à propos the Diggers, that 'if provision be not made for them poor commoners, England will have new troubles'.[29] But Parson Platt and other lords of manors in Surrey organized raids on the colony and an economic boycott: they harassed the Diggers with legal actions. 'If the Digger's cause was good,' an officer of the Kingston court said, 'he would pick out such a jury as should overthrow him.' One of the cases charging the Diggers with riot led to a technical argument about their commitment which got into the law-books. Serjeant Wilde, who always seems to have done his best for radicals, argued that they should have been discharged because the Sheriff was not present at the finding of the riot. The court bailed but did not discharge them.[30] Even after the Diggers moved to Cobham Heath a few miles away the raids continued, and by April 1650 the colony had been forcibly dispersed, huts and furniture burnt, the Diggers chased away from the area. It was a brief episode in English history, involving perhaps a few score men and their families: we know the names of seventy-three of them.

II   TRUE LEVELLERS

But historians are becoming aware that it was not quite so isolated an occurrence as used to be thought. The Diggers called themselves True Levellers, a name which had been used by Lawrence Clarkson, later the Ranter, in 1647.[31] Winstanley's first Digger manifesto, published on the day on which Robert Lockier was sentenced to death, was entitled *The True Levellers Standard Advanced*. The Levellers were never a united, disciplined party or movement, as historians find to their cost when they try to define their doctrines with any precision. 'We were an heterogeneal body,' said Henry Denne, 'consisting of parts very diverse from one another, settled upon principles inconsistent with one another.'[32] In London there must have been large numbers of Leveller sympathizers who never clearly associated themselves with all their views. It has recently been suggested[33] that Lilburne and Wildman led a moderate, constitutional wing of the Levellers and that there was a more radical wing in the Army and among the London populace, with which Walwyn and Overton may have sympathized. The 'physical force Levellers' like Major White and Captain Bray, whom we discussed above,[34] also seem to have been politically more radical than Lilburne and Wildman.

This wing was less concerned with constitutional issues, more with economics, with defending the poor against the rich, the common people against great men – which one suspects were the chief issues in the minds of the poorer classes in the late 1640s. Its spokesmen may also have reflected agrarian communist ideas which had long circulated in England, reinforced by Anabaptist theories which the Thirty-nine Articles of the Church of England fiercely denounced. The Family of Love and the Family of the Mount had kept such ideas alive in the Elizabethan underworld: both Spenser and Shakespeare had clearly heard communist propaganda.[35] So had Bishop Cooper, though ostensibly he is writing about 1381:

> At the beginning (say they), when God had first made the world, all men were alike, there was no principality, then was no bondage or villeinage: that grew afterwards by violence and cruelty. Therefore why should we live in this miserable slavery under those proud lords and crafty lawyers, etc?[36]

It is difficult to believe that the good bishop invented those sentiments, which he used, rather dishonestly, as an argument for suppressing Presbyterians.

Like so many other underground ideas, communist theories surfaced in the freedom of the 1640s. Thomas Edwards noted in 1646, as the 153rd error of the sectaries, the view that 'all the earth is the saints', and there ought to be a community of goods, and the saints should share in the lands and estates of gentlemen and rich men'.[37] '*Meum et tuum*,' said Peter Chamberlen in 1647, 'divide the world into factions, into atoms; and till the world return to its first simplicity or ... to a Christian utopia, ... covetousness will be the root of all evil'.[38] As early as 1646 we hear of demands in the Army for an agrarian law.[39] A scheme setting an upper limit of one hundred marks a year to the property which any landowner should possess had been put forward, probably by the Commonwealth's Party, in one of Edward VI's Parliaments, though of course unsuccessfully.[40]

In October 1647 soldiers were demanding that no duke, marquis or earl should have more than £2000 a year, and that the income of other classes should be proportionately restricted.[41] The agrarian law was to be made famous by James Harrington's advocacy of it in *Oceana* (1656), from which many other thinkers adopted the idea. But Harrington was only summing up a tradition.

The author of *Tyranipocrit Discovered*, an anonymous pamphlet printed in the Netherlands in August 1649, attacked the government of the English Commonwealth for not having established 'an equality of goods and lands', as God and nature would have, and for taking 'no care to educate all men's children alike'. Echoing Sir Thomas More, the author denounced 'the rich thieves' who 'make a combination and call it a law, to hang a poor man if he do steal, when they have wrongfully taken from him all his maintenance'. 'They make themselves thieves by Act of Parliament.' The property of the rich should be shared among the poor, and redivided at least once a year. 'To give unto every man with discretion so near as may be an equal share of earthly goods,' *Tyranipocrit* continued, is consonant to the law of God and nature. But equality of goods and lands is also desirable 'that so young, strong and able persons might labour, and old, weak and impotent persons might rest'.[42] The Ranter Abiezer Coppe in the same year said that 'it's but yet a little while and the strongest, yea the seemingly purest property, which may mostly plead privilege and prerogative from Scripture and carnal reason, shall be confounded and plagued into community and universality'.[43] In 1650 Lieutenant William Jackson was in trouble for holding, among many other enormities, 'community of all things', including, apparently, wives.[44]

In the Putney Debates of 1647 Rainborough and Sexby made demands for manhood suffrage which seem to conflict with the more moderate proposals of the civilian Levellers, Wildman and Petty, who would have excluded paupers and servants from the vote. The radical wing of the Levellers flourished not only in London and the Army, Professor Barg suggests, but also in the country districts, where traditions of popular revolt no doubt still survived. John Lilburne's favourite phrase to describe his supporters, 'clubs and clouted shoon', occurred in Norfolk during Ket's Revolt of 1549, in Leicester in 1586, and in Shakespeare's *Henry VI*.[45] Fuller in 1655 related the movement to the Revolt of 1381: all the peasants then were 'pure Levellers', their leaders teaching that 'no gentry was *jure divino*, and all equal by nature'.[46] The names 'Leveller' and 'Digger' had been used of participants in the Midlands Revolt of 1607. In Buckinghamshire, county of forests and industry, there were 'tumultuous proceedings' in 1647–9 to throw down enclosures. Ralph Verney, scion of a depopulating family, 'feared they might be resolved to put down all the enclosures in England'. Levellers were foremost in inciting the Buckinghamshire anti-enclosure movement.[47] In December 1648, before Winstanley had announced his communism, a local group of Levellers produced a pamphlet called *Light Shining in Buckinghamshire*, which called for equality of property. 'All men being alike privileged by birth, so all men were to enjoy the creatures alike without property one more than the other.'[48]

The sequel to this pamphlet, *More Light Shining in Buckinghamshire*, appeared on 30 March, two days before digging started on St George's Hill. Similar ideas were arising simultaneously, that is to say, in more or less sophisticated forms, in various parts of the country. Winstanley may have been influenced by the Buckinghamshire pamphlets, and some historians have suggested that he had a hand in drafting them, since he lived only a few miles from the Buckinghamshire border. But their vigorous, rudely boisterous and bellicose style is hardly Winstanley's; the main target of *Light Shining in Buckinghamshire* is monarchy, not Winstanley's more generalized 'kingly power'. *More Light Shining in Buckinghamshire* is also more directly political than Winstanley usually is, appealing specifically to the Army.[49] Whatever is the case with the Buckinghamshire pamphlets, Winstanley could hardly have been associated with the *Humble Representation of the Desires of the Soldiers and Officers in the Regiment of Horse for the County of Northumberland*, which expressed analogous ideas, also at the beginning of December 1648.[50]

We should see the Digger colony on St George's Hill as merely one particularly well-documented example of a trend which was repeated in many other places. Early newspaper accounts of the Diggers invariably treated them as adherents of the Levellers.[51] A pamphlet published in June 1649 reprinted extracts from Winstanley's *Letter to the Lord General* and complained that this paper was being distributed by enemies who were obstructing the relief of Ireland and had deceived even many honest men. If their efforts succeeded, 'we shall be embroiled in anarchy and subjected to strangers and foreigners'.[52] Another pamphlet of the same year, 'published by authority', quoted both Winstanley's *New Law of Righteousness* and *Light Shining in Buckinghamshire* as Leveller pamphlets, in order to show that the Levellers were opposed to religion and property.[53]

Thus unofficial 'Leveller' thought and action went a good deal further than the constitutionalist leaders, and raised the property issue in ways that the latter found embarrassing. Only this can explain Ireton's determination in the Putney Debates to convict the Leveller spokesmen of communism, despite their indignant denials. He got them into considerable difficulties by stressing the 'natural right' basis of their arguments about the franchise: Gerrard Winstanley was to build his communist theories on natural rights, and they were also used by the authors of *Light Shining in Buckinghamshire*. This would also explain Lilburne's excessive concern from February 1648 onwards to disavow communist theories – long before the Digger movement had appeared – as well as his repudiation of 'the erroneous tenets of the poor Diggers at George Hill' in June 1649.[54] The Leveller petition of 11 September 1648 repudiated any idea of abolishing property, levelling estates or making all common, though it declared in favour of laying open recent enclosures of fens and other commons, or of enclosing them chiefly for the benefit of the poor.[55] A Leveller manifesto of 14 April 1649, when digging had been going on for a fortnight on St George's Hill, also asserted that the Levellers themselves 'never had it in our thoughts to level men's estates, it being the utmost of our aim that . . . every man with as much security as may be enjoy his property'.[56] Overton's call in July 1647 for a return of enclosed lands to communal use was quite untypical.[57] Official Leveller pronouncements failed even to take a clear and decisive stand in favour of security of tenure for copyholders and against enclosure – until after the defeat of 1649. It was in the Army that in April 1648 the abolition of base tenures was advocated so as to establish an independent peasantry, 'that by this means persons disaffected to the welfare and freedom of the nation may be prevented from drawing men to a war against themselves by virtue of an awe upon them by such dependent tenures'.[58]

Walwyn was accused of saying, 'It would never be well until all things were common, and ... then there would be no thieves, no covetous persons, no deceiving and abusing of one another, and so no need of government.' Walwyn never very decisively repudiated this charge, though it was often repeated. 'That he is a Leveller and would have all things common,' Walwyn sneered, seemed a more serious accusation to his Independent and clerical enemies than that he was an unbeliever.[59] Both Walwyn and Overton rejected atrocity propaganda levelled against the Münster Anabaptists, allegedly communists. ('That lying story of that injured people ... the Anabaptists of Münster'; 'Who writ the histories of the Anabaptists but their enemies?'[60])

Unlike Lilburne, the Leveller newspaper *The Moderate* laid considerable stress on agrarian reform. It printed *The True Levellers Standard Advanced*, without hostile comment. *The Moderate* stood more consistently for religious toleration, and was more steadily radical in its stand on the franchise: on both these issues the official Leveller leaders were ready on occasion to compromise.[61] (*The Moderate*'s pronouncement that property is 'the original cause of any sin between party and party', and of 'most sins against the heavenly deity', aroused the fury of the Earl of Leicester in the late summer of 1649. The noble lord thought that such sentiments should not be permitted in any Christian state: which tells us a good deal about what such men thought the function of Christianity was.[62]) In 1653, after the constitutionalist leaders had disappeared, and the Levellers were an underground conspiratorial group, the final Agreement of the People firmly called for the abolition of all base tenures.

All this would seem to support Professor Barg's suggestion that the Diggers on St George's Hill were only the visible tip of the iceberg of True Levellerism, that Winstanley spoke for those whom the 'constitutional' Levellers would have disfranchised – servants, labourers, paupers, the economically un-free.[63] Winstanley described himself as a 'servant', though many of the Diggers were householders, born in the parish. Opposition to the digging came, Winstanley tells us, apart from the gentry and parsons, 'only from one or two covetous freeholders, . . . who call the enclosures their own land'.[64] It is interesting that on the eve of their suppression the Levellers were beginning to win support from the North and West, the former royalist areas, from Cornish tin-miners to Northumbrian farmers, from Bristol, Hull, York, Somerset, Lancashire.[65] This may indeed have been a reason for their suppression. The Levellers sent out emissaries, an official pamphlet tells us, 'to raise the servant against the master, the tenant against his landlord, the buyer against the seller, the borrower against the lender, the poor against the rich'.[66] Since this pamphlet deliberately confuses Levellers and Diggers, we are left wondering whether these were Leveller or Digger emissaries.[67]

This explanation would also help to account for the ease with which the Levellers were divided and suppressed after 1649. Lilburne and those who thought like him differed from the Independent Grandees only in degree, since both assumed the immutability of existing property relationships. Professor Macpherson has already insisted that Leveller political theory looks forward to that of Locke.[68] The Grandees stole the Levellers' republican clothes in the early months of 1649, and the constitutional Levellers had no basis on which to appeal to the peasant majority of the population. After Burford had destroyed their political hopes, individual members of the party took up the cause of some of the victims of enclosure, especially in the pasture areas, e.g. in the Isle of Axholme and Hatfield Chase;[69] but by then it was too late for them to become leaders of a specifically anti-landlord party. They simply strengthened the demagogic arguments of Oliver Cromwell, who lumped Levellers and True Levellers together as 'a despicable and contemptible generation of men', 'persons differing little from beasts'. 'Did not the levelling principle tend to reducing all to an equality, . . . to make the tenant as liberal a fortune as the landlord? . . . a pleasing voice to all poor men, and truly not unwelcome to all bad men.'[70]

Even the regiments which revolted in Salisbury in May 1649 had to insist that 'levelling your estates' was no part of their object.[71] The millenarian clergyman Nathanael Homes rejected 'a levelling anarchy'.[72] William Hartley complained in 1651 that sectaries were branded as 'Thompson's party, Levellers'. 'The word Leveller is a term of abuse cast upon many a person for holding forth of righteous principles.' Yet even he felt he had to go out of his way to disavow communism.[73] Blith in 1653 also found it prudent to reject 'the Levelling principle of parity or equality, . . . unless they bring us to the new Jerusalem'.[74] James Harrington spoke of 'robbers or Levellers'.[75] Roger Crab observed that John the Baptist would have been despised if he had called himself Leveller.[76]

Their lack of consistency in relation to the poor peasant majority of the population helps to explain the apparently unprincipled readiness of men like Lilburne, Sexby and Wildman to conspire with royalists against the Independent republic. The True Levellers remained convinced and consistent republicans, since monarchy for them was merely the chief captain of the army of landlordism: the Commonwealth was the lesser evil, offering some hope of further advance in a radical direction.[77] 'God made men,' as the author of *Tyranipocrit Discovered* put it, 'and the devil made kings.'[78]

The constitutional Levellers, then, were not in fundamental disagreement with the type of society that was being set up by the English Revolution. They accepted the sanctity of private property, and their desire to extend democracy was within the limits of a capitalist society. The present book concentrates on those of the English radicals who in one way or another called in question the institutions and ideology of that society, and so the constitutional Levellers play a smaller part in my story than their historical importance would suggest. One must insist, to restore the balance, that the constitutional Levellers were a very radical left wing of the revolutionary party. Some of those who loom larger in this book were much less intellectually consistent and principled than the Levellers: their rejection of capitalism was often backward-looking, negative and unrealistic. The group of whom this is least true, I shall argue, was the True Levellers. It is important to see them in this historical perspective.

III   OTHER DIGGER COMMUNITIES

In the years 1649–50 Winstanley issued a series of pamphlets, appealing to various sections of the population, and some at least seem to have borne fruit. Other Digger colonies appeared at Wellingborough in Northamptonshire, Cox Hall in Kent,[79] Iver in Buckinghamshire, Barnet in Hertfordshire, Enfield in Middlesex, Dunstable in Bedfordshire, Bosworth in Leicestershire, and at unknown places in Gloucestershire and Nottinghamshire.[80] Not enough local work has yet been done on most of these places, but we know something about Wellingborough. It had a long-standing Puritan tradition, the living being in the presentation of the Brooke family.[81] Its lower orders got badly out of hand in 1642–3. Three years later Edwards reported that troopers were preaching there.[82] In May 1649, after the Leveller defeat at Burford, William Thompson made for Wellingborough, but was caught and killed just outside the town.

Ten months later the Wellingborough Diggers produced a *Declaration* which tells us very precisely what sort of people supported their movement. There were 1169 persons in receipt of alms in the parish. Trade was decayed, there was no work; 'rich men's hearts are hardened, they will not give us if we beg at their doors. If we steal, the law will end our lives, divers of the poor are starved to death already, and it were better for us that are living to die by the sword than by the famine.' So they, like the Surrey Diggers, had begun to 'dig up, manure and sow corn upon the common waste ground called Bareshank'. They said they had had much encouragement: 'those that we find most against us are such as have been constant enemies to the Parliament's cause from first to last'. But this colony seems to have been suppressed at the same time as that in Surrey.[83] It is hardly surprising that Wellingborough was one of the earliest places outside the North in which Quakerism was preached. There were hysterical fits in the parish church in 1654, and Wellingborough remained a Quaker centre from that year onwards.[84] But either these were very Ranter-like Quakers, or there were Ranters in Wellingborough as well. In 1657 Francis Ellington was indicted under the Blasphemy Act for saying 'confounded be thee and thy God, and I trample thee and thy God under my feet'. The language is Quaker, and Ellington appears in Besse's *Sufferings of the Quakers*; but the sentiment seems more Ranter than Quaker.[85]

It has been suggested that the unknown Digger colony in Gloucestershire may have been at Slimbridge, where in 1631, during the civil war, and again in 1650, 'rude multitudes' were 'levelling enclosures'. The waste of Slimbridge, John Smyth of Nibley had said in 1639, could yield £1500 a year but was not worth one-fifth of that sum now. On the contrary, it draws 'many poor people from other places' and burdens the township with 'beggarly cottages . . . and alehouses and idle people'.[86]

The colony at Iver, like that at Wellingborough, produced a pamphlet of its own, in May 1650, fiercer and more desperate than those produced before the suppressions in Surrey and Northamptonshire.[87] The Iver Diggers may have had a hand in the two *Light Shining in Buckinghamshire* pamphlets and *A Declaration of the Wel-Affected in the County of Buckinghamshire*, which sprang from a meeting of Levellers at Aylesbury in the first week of May 1649, on the eve of the defeat at Burford.[88] From Kent in 1653 came the anonymous pamphlet *No Age like unto this Age*, in which Digger influence is clear. Enfield, a manor purchased by the third Earl of Essex, had been the scene of riots in June 1649, and was to be again in 1659 on the enclosure of Enfield Chase. This led to the publication by William Covell of a scheme for setting up collective farms on Enfield Chase, which again owed a good deal to Digger influence.[89] Enfield too became a Quaker centre.[90]

In the spring of 1650, as money and food ran short on Cobham Heath, two emissaries were sent out by the colony with a letter signed by Winstanley and twenty-one other Diggers asking for financial help. They went backwards and forwards through the Home Counties and the Midlands, visiting existing colonies and groups of sympathizers. The counties covered were Buckinghamshire, Surrey, Middlesex, Hertfordshire, Bedfordshire, Berkshire, Huntingdonshire, Northamptonshire. The thirty-four places named included the colonies at Dunstable and Wellingborough, Hounslow – a heath, where together with New-market and Hampstead the Diggers had planned a colony[91] – Colnbrook and Harrow-on-the-Hill, with which Winstanley may have had some connection.[92] They went to Fenstanton and Warboys, where Baptist churches had been founded by Henry Denne, the Leveller leader at Burford who recanted to avoid being shot. The Warboys church book recorded not only the Diggers' activities in Surrey but also that there was 'a people called Levellers in these times, of whom one George Foster declares himself to be a prophet', saying that the rich would share their wealth with the poor.[93]

The Digger emissaries also passed near Pirton, Hertfordshire, where Henry Denne had been curate for ten years starting about 1633, and to which Winstanley was to retreat in the autumn of 1650 with a group of Diggers who hired themselves to Lady Eleanor Davies.[94] So from Nottinghamshire and Northamptonshire to Gloucestershire and Kent, Digger influence spread all over southern and central England. They had some influence in intensifying ill-feeling between landlords and tenants, it has been suggested; they may have contributed to the class consciousness of Fifth Monarchists and early Quakers. They must have had a great deal to do with the 'shattering' of Baptist and Independent churches from which ultimately the Quakers were to benefit.[95] It has been pointed out that much of the evidence for early Quaker history from those midland counties in which there were Digger settlements or Digger sympathizers was suppressed or ignored when the Quaker *First Publishers of Truth* was compiled. Mr Hudson speculates that this may have been to remove traces of Digger influence, and that Winstanley may have been on preaching tours through the Midlands in the forties, making contacts which the Diggers of St George's Hill later picked up.[96]

IV FORESTS AND COMMONS

Thus if we see the New Model Army as a short-lived school of political democracy, commons, wastes and forests were longer-lasting though less intensive schools in economic democracy. Winstanley thought that from a half to two-thirds of England was not properly cultivated. One-third of England was barren waste, which lords of manors would not permit the poor to cultivate.[97] 'If the waste land of England were manured by her children, it would become in a few years the richest, the strongest and [most] flourishing land in the world'; the price of corn would fall to 1s. a bushel or less (it was then more like 6s. or 7s.).[98] An increase in the cultivated area, the Digger poet Robert Coster added, would bring down the price of land and therewith the cost of living.[99] The custom by which lords of manors claimed property rights in the commons, and so could prevent their cultivation to the advantage of the poor, argued Winstanley, should have been abolished by the overthrow of kingly power.[100] Communal cultivation could allow for capital investment in improvements without sacrificing the interests of commoners. There was land enough to maintain ten times the present population, abolish begging and crime, and make England 'first of the nations'.[101]

This was the programme which Winstanley conceived in the cruel winter of 1648–9. It seemed to him so novel and so important that he attributed it to a divine command. The vision which he had in a trance told him to declare abroad the message: 'Work together; eat bread together.' 'He that works for another, either for wages or to pay him rent, works unrighteously ... but they that are resolved to work and eat together, making the earth a common treasury, doth join hands with Christ to lift up the creation from bondage, and restores all things from the curse.' After declaring this message both verbally and in print, Winstanley decided he must 'go forth and declare it in my action' by organizing 'us that are called common people to manure and work upon the common lands'.[102]

Winstanley's conclusion, that communal cultivation of the commons was the crucial question, the starting-point from which common people all over England could build up an equal community, was absolutely right. 'The whole Digger movement,' Mr Thomas has written, 'can be plausibly regarded as the culmination of a century of unauthorized encroachment upon the forests and wastes by squatters and local commoners, pushed on by land shortage and pressure of population' – and, Mrs Thirsk adds, by lack of employment for casual labour in the depression of 1648–9.[103] Winstanley had arrived at the one possible democratic solution which was not merely backward-looking, as all other radical proposals during the revolutionary decades – an agrarian law, partible inheritance, stable copyholds – tended to be. The economic arguments against those who merely defended commoners' traditional rights in the waste were overwhelming. England's growing population could be fed only by more intensive cultivation, by bringing marginal land under the plough. Enclosure by men with capital, brutally disregarding the rights of commoners, did at least do the job; in the long run, its advocates rightly claimed, it created more employment. But in the short run it disrupted a way of life, causing intense misery; and the employment which it did ultimately create was not of a sort to attract free commoners.

Collective cultivation of the waste by the poor could have had the advantages of large-scale cultivation, planned development, use of fertilizers, etc. It could have fed the expanding English population without disrupting the traditional way of life to anything like the extent that in fact happened. The Diggers sowed their land with carrots, parsnips and beans – crops of the sort which were to transform English agriculture in the seventeenth century by making it possible to keep cattle alive throughout the winter in order to fertilize the land.[104] 'Manuring' is the crucial word in Winstanley's programme. ('True religion and undefiled is to let every one quietly have earth to manure.') Winstanley had got a solution to his own paradox: 'the bondage the poor complain of, that they are kept poor by their brethren in a land where there is so much plenty for everyone, if covetousness and pride did not rule as king in one brother over another'.[105]

The gentry and parsons around St George's Hill appreciated that the Diggers were doing something different in kind from the traditional squatting of cottagers. Even communal cultivation of the earth, Parson Platt assured Winstanley, was less intolerable than cutting timber that grew on the common. Squatting and cultivating the earth could be deemed to be done by courtesy of the lord of the soil; but cutting wood against his wishes was a direct assertion of a property right which could not be overlooked. And indeed it was intended by the Diggers 'to be a stock for ourselves and our poor brethren through the land of England, . . . to provide us bread to eat till the fruit of our labours in the earth bring forth increase'. The Diggers had ordered the lords of the manor to stop cutting down 'our common woods and trees . . . for your private use'. It was intended, as all the Diggers' actions were, to be a symbolic challenge as well as an economically necessary step.[106]

By 1650 the Diggers had added a demand for confiscated church, crown and royalists' land to be turned over to the poor. In *The Law of Freedom* Winstanley further suggested that the land sales authorized by Parliament should be repudiated, and that all lands confiscated at the dissolution of the monasteries a century earlier should be added to the Commonwealth land fund.[107] These last two proposals would bite deep into existing property relations. The danger from the Diggers was that they called on the poor to organize themselves for practical action. A series of collective communities, if they had lasted, would have overcome the dispersion of forces which bedevilled the Levellers: they would have been for the True Levellers what the New Model Army might have been for the Levellers; and they could have extended all over the country.

Collective manuring of the common lands was a religious act for the Diggers; for Parson Lee 'a hedge in the field is as necessary in its kind as government in the church or commonwealth'. Religion, liberty, property and government were closely linked for both sides in the dispute. 'The very name of reformation' [of the church], Lee added, 'is as much exploded by the vulgar as enclosure; those sacred ordinances of magistracy and ministry . . . are now become offensive to the levelling multitude.'[108]

V   TRUE COMMONWEALTH'S FREEDOM

For Winstanley Jesus Christ was the Head Leveller.[109] Winstanley's thought incorporates many Leveller ideas: it goes beyond them, beyond the vision of the small proprietor, in its hostility to private property as such.

In the beginning of time the great creator, Reason, made the earth to be a common treasury, to preserve beasts, birds, fishes and man, the lord that was to govern this creation ... Not one word was spoken in the beginning that one branch of mankind should rule over another ... But ... selfish imaginations ... did set up one man to teach and rule over another. And thereby ... man was brought into bondage, and became a greater slave to such of his own kind than the beasts of the field were to him. And hereupon the earth ... was hedged into enclosures by the teachers and rulers, and the others were made ... slaves. And that earth that is within this creation made a common storehouse for all, is bought and sold and kept in the hands of a few, whereby the great Creator is mightily dishonoured, as if he were a respecter of persons, delighting in the comfortable livelihood of some and rejoicing in the miserable poverty and straits of others. From the beginning it was not so ...

Winstanley told lords of manors that

the power of enclosing land and owning property was brought into the creation by your ancestors by the sword; which first did murder their fellow creatures, men, and after plunder or steal away their land, and left this land successively to you, their children. And therefore, though you did not kill or thieve, yet you hold that cursed thing in your hand by the power of the sword; and so you justify the wicked deeds of your fathers, and that sin of your fathers shall be visited upon the head of you and your children to the third and fourth generation, and longer too, till your bloody and thieving power be rooted out of the land.[110]

Winstanley extended the Leveller justification of political democracy to economic democracy:

The poorest man hath as true a title and just right to the land as the richest man ... True freedom lies in the free enjoyment of the earth ... If the common people have no more freedom in England but only to live among their elder brothers and work for them for hire, what freedom then have they in England more than we can have in Turkey or France?[111]

Winstanley transcended the Leveller theory of the Norman Yoke, that all we need is to get back to the laws of the free Anglo-Saxons. 'The best laws that England hath,' he declared, 'are yokes and manacles, tying one sort of people to another.' 'All laws that are not grounded upon equity and reason, not giving a universal freedom to all but respecting persons, ought ... to be cut off with the King's head.'[112] But England's rulers had not completed the Revolution:

> While this kingly power reigned in one man called Charles, all sorts of people complained of oppression ... Thereupon you that were the gentry, when you were assembled in Parliament, you called upon the poor common people to come and help you ... That top bough is lopped off the tree of tyranny, and the kingly power in that one particular is cast out. But alas, oppression is a great tree still, and keeps off the sun of freedom from the poor commons still.

Kingly power, clergy, lawyers, and buying and selling were all linked: 'if one truly fall, all must fall'.[113]

Winstanley must have been expressing the opinions of many disappointed radicals when he wrote in 1652:

> Therefore, you Army of England's Commonwealth, look to it! The enemy could not beat you in the field, but they may be too hard for you by policy in counsel if you do not stick close to see common freedom established. For if so be that kingly authority be set up in your laws again, King Charles hath conquered you and your posterity by policy, and won the field of you, though you seemingly have cut off his head.[114]

The Diggers' aim, he had told Fairfax in 1649, was 'not to remove the Norman Yoke only' and restore Saxon laws. 'No, that is not it'; but to restore 'the pure law of righteousness before the Fall'.[115]

In 1652, two years after the collapse of the Digger colony at Cobham, Winstanley published *The Law of Freedom in a Platform*, a draft constitution for a communist commonwealth. 'All men have stood for freedom,' he had written earlier; 'and now the common enemy is gone you are all like men in a mist, seeking for freedom and know not where nor what it is.' Winstanley could tell them. 'True freedom lies where a man receives his nourishment and preservation, that is in the use of the earth . . . A man had better have no body than to have no food for it.' True human dignity would be possible only when communal ownership was established, and buying and selling of land and labour ceased.[116] It is impossible to summarize *The Law of Freedom*: the reader must look at it for himself. Its significance lies not only in the general conception, remarkable enough at that date, but also in the detail with which it is worked out. *The Law of Freedom* seems to have been intended as a 'possibilist' document, dedicated to Oliver Cromwell in the hope that he would implement it. How else in 1652 could it have been realized? This may account for some apparent compromises, but on the whole it is a straightforward statement of Winstanley's ideals as modified by his experience at St George's Hill.

Mr Dell pertinently pointed out some years ago that Winstanley gives two pictures of communist society.[117] The first can be deduced from his critical opposition to the evils of his own times. He depicted by contrast an anarchist society. Magistrates and lawyers would be superfluous when there was no buying or selling, just as a professional clergy would become unnecessary in a society where any mechanic is free to preach.[118] Winstanley then expected the state, in Marxist phrase, to wither away immediately. 'What need have we of imprisonment, whipping or hanging laws to bring one another into bondage?' Only covetousness made theft a sin. Execution even for murder would itself be murder: only God who gives life may take it away.[119] But after the collapse of the Digger colony, when Winstanley came to draft a constitution for his new society, he included laws because he realized that 'offences may arise from the spirit of unreasonable ignorance'. But prisons were abolished, and he insisted that all law must be corrective, not punitive.[120] He emphasized now that an army would be needed to 'restrict and destroy all who endeavour to keep up or bring in kingly bondage again', to protect the community against 'the rudeness of the people', and to enforce the laws; but this army was to be a popular militia, which would not obey any Parliament not representative of the people. Liberty is secured by a right of popular resistance.[121]

Winstanley's experience with 'rude freeholders' at St George's Hill, and perhaps with Ranters among his own ranks,[122] had taught him that some compromises might be required. He now foresaw that a longer process of education and adaptation would be necessary than he had originally envisaged. He proposed to have magistrates, elected annually and responsible to 'their masters, the people, who chose them'. These officials should include planners ('Overseers'). During a transitional period such officers might receive pay and maintenance allowances, in order to ensure that poor men served. The laws for the preservation of the commonwealth were enforced by penalties, including deprivation of civil rights and forced labour. They extended even to the death penalty for murder, buying and selling, rape, or following the trade of lawyer or parson.[123] In 1649 Winstanley had written that 'all punishments that are to be inflicted ... are only such as to make the offender ... to live in the community of the righteous law of love one with another'. He had then postulated forced labour as a punishment for idleness, an offence which he associated with the gentry rather than with the poor.[124] In his ideal commonwealth there would be no lawyers, and prisons would be abolished; accused persons would appear on parole (the breaking of which was another offence punishable by death).

Since Winstanley envisaged no forcible expropriation, there was bound to be a time-lag during which persuasion was used against 'the spirit of unreasonable ignorance', 'the spirit of rudeness'.[125] No doubt for this reason the franchise was extended to all males except supporters of Charles I and those who had been too hasty to buy and sell commonwealth lands – which they were to restore. Officials need not be church members, i.e. universal toleration was instituted. Marriage was to be a civil ceremony, for love not money. Parliament, chosen annually, would be the highest court of equity in the land, overseeing all other courts and officials.[126]

Winstanley, like Harrington, attached great political importance to property in land. Although communal cultivation seemed to him the principal remedy for England's ills, he by no means ignored other aspects of economic life. His list of industries in *The Law of Freedom* illustrates the extent to which in seventeenth-century England virtually all industry was a matter of collecting and processing natural products. Winstanley criticized the way in which tolls in market towns pillaged the country people who used them.[127] This would end when buying and selling were abolished. Winstanley had thought out his problem sufficiently to appreciate that there would have to be a state monopoly for foreign trade, one of the first things the Soviet government established after taking over power in 1917.[128] Abolition of wage labour had as a necessary corollary the preservation of apprenticeship. In general Winstanley thought the system of government in London companies 'very rational and well ordered', provided officials were elected annually.[129]

Education naturally seemed to Winstanley of the greatest importance. It was to continue until a man was 'acquainted with all arts and languages'. Quite exceptionally for the seventeenth century, it was to be universal (for both sexes) and equal: there were to be no specialized scholars living 'merely upon the labours of other men', whose 'show of knowledge rests in reading or contemplating or hearing others speak'. Children should be trained 'in trades and some bodily employment, as well as in learning languages or history'.[130] Girls would learn music and to read, sew, knit and spin. Experiment and invention were to be encouraged and rewarded. Hitherto 'fear of want and care to pay rent to taskmasters hath hindered many rare inventions'. 'Kingly power hath crushed the spirit of knowledge, and would not suffer it to rise up in its beauty and fullness.'[131] Inventions were to be publicized through the two Postmasters who were to be elected in each parish – officers unique to Winstanley, so far as I know. They would collect and report statistical information about the health and welfare of their communities, and would publicize important information from other parts of the country reported to them from regional centres. The idea may owe something to Hartlib's Office of Addresses, but its statistical approach links it with that political arithmetic which William Petty was to make so influential in England in the later seventeenth century. The Postmasters would thus at once make known any new invention or discovery. This was one of the many ways in which Winstanley's communist organization of society would break down internal barriers to national unity. Trade secrets would be abolished. So the commonwealth would be assisted to flourish in peace and plenty, and others would be stirred up 'to employ their reason and industry' in emulation, not merely in order to increase production, as a modern economist would insist, but 'to the beauty of our commonwealth', as Winstanley put it, in words of which William Blake or Herbert Marcuse might have approved.[132]

Winstanley spoke for 'the poor despised ones of the earth',[133] and it was these who formed his colony at St George's Hill. But he thought in terms of society as a whole, of humanity as a whole. 'Alas! you poor blind earth moles,' he cried to 'lords of manors and Norman gentry', 'you strive to take away my livelihood, and the liberty of this poor weak frame my body of flesh, which is my house I dwell in for a time; but I strive to cast down your kingdom of darkness, and to open hell gates, and to break the devil's bonds asunder wherewith you are tied, that you my enemies may live in peace; and that is all the harm I would have you to have.'[134] The Ranter Abiezer Coppe thought there was 'a most glorious design' in the overthrow of property: 'equality, community and universal love shall be in request, to the utter confounding of abominable pride, murder, hypocrisy, tyranny and oppression.'[135] Similarly Winstanley believed that

> wheresoever there is a people . . . united by common community of livelihood into oneness, it will become the strongest land in the world; for then they will be as one man to defend their inheritance . . . Whereas on the other side, pleading for property and single interest divides the people of a land and the whole world into parties, and is the cause of all wars and bloodshed and contention everywhere . . . But when once the earth becomes a common treasury again, as it must, . . . then this enmity of all lands will cease, and none shall dare to seek dominion over others, neither shall any dare to kill another, nor desire more of the earth than another.[136]

VI   GOD AND REASON

The sub-title of *The Law of Freedom* was *True Magistracy Restored*. 'So long as we own landlords' we 'hinder the work of restoration', which is salvation.[137] From his earliest pamphlets Winstanley had argued that reason pervades the whole universe and 'dwells in every creature, but supremely in man'. 'If you subject your flesh to this mighty governor, the spirit of righteousness within yourselves, he will bring you into community with the whole globe.' Then 'you have community with him who is the Father of all things'. 'The spirit within the flesh is Jesus Christ.'[138] In December 1649 Winstanley wrote a preface to a collected edition of his theological pamphlets, which appeared in 1650. This contains a salutary reminder that he did not reject these writings, though his thought had in many respects passed beyond them. He attributed his later ideas to 'the same power' as had carried him forth in his first pamphlets.[139] But the materialistic side of Winstanley's pantheism becomes more explicit in the later, more political, writings.

'The whole creation ... is the clothing of God.' 'The Father is the universal power that hath spread himself in the whole globe; the Son is the same power drawn into and appearing in one single person, making that person subject to one spirit and to know him that dwells everywhere.' All men can become sons in this sense, and attain to this knowledge. 'This is the excellency of the work, when a man shall be made to see Christ in other creatures as well as in himself.' 'Christ or the spreading power of light is drawing the knowledge of himself as he lies in all things into the clear experience of man.' This was an argument for complete Miltonic freedom of enterprise in teaching and reading.[140] Given this spirit of Christ within, man needs no other preachers than 'the objects of the creation', the material world.[141] This idea of God as immanent within the whole material creation compares very interestingly with Traherne's later development of the same theme. In Winstanley, even more than in Traherne, it is connected with a respect for natural science as the means of becoming acquainted with God's works. Winstanley seems to come near an

anticipation of Spinoza's principle: 'the more we understand individual things, the more we understand God.'[142] But this may have been
an application of the Paracelsan magical belief that 'the invisible
things of God ... are seen ... in his works',[143] which appears, cautiously, in Ralegh's *History of the World*.[144]

Winstanley had no use for traditional religion. His anti-clericalism
was much more drastic, surer and more systematic than that of any
other writer during the Revolution – and there were many anti-
clericals among them. 'What is the reason,' Winstanley asked, 'that
most people are so ignorant of their freedoms, and so few fit to be
chosen commonwealth's officers? Because,' he replied, 'the old kingly
clergy ... are continually distilling their blind principles into the
people, and do thereby nurse up ignorance in them.' Many of them
had taught that Charles I was the Lord's Anointed.[145] Priests

> lay claim to heaven after they are dead, and yet they require their
> heaven in this world too, and grumble mightily against the people that
> will not give them a large temporal maintenance. And yet they tell the
> poor people that they must be content with their poverty, and they
> shall have their heaven hereafter. But why may not we have our heaven
> here (that is, a comfortable livelihood in the earth) and heaven hereaf-
> ter too, as well as you? ... While men are gazing up to heaven,
> imagining after a happiness or fearing a hell after they are dead, their
> eyes are put out, that they see not what is their birthrights, and what
> is to be done by them here on earth while they are living.[146]

A traditional Christian, who 'thinks God is in the heavens above
the skies, and so prays to that God which he imagines to be there and
everywhere, ... worships his own imagination, which is the
devil'.[147] 'Your Saviour must be a power within you, to deliver you
from that bondage within; the outward Christ or the outward God
are but men Saviours.'[148] Winstanley himself came to use the word
Reason in preference to God, 'because I have been held under darkness by that word, as I see many people are.' We must be careful 'lest
we dishonour the Lord in making him the author of the creatures'
misery', as hell-fire preachers do.[149] Winstanley spoke of their God in

terms which came near to William Blake's Nobodaddy – unless we are to suppose he held a completely Manichean dualism, which is unlikely. Winstanley told 'priests and zealous professors' that they worshipped the devil.[150] He spoke of 'the God Devil'. 'The outward Christ, or the outward God . . . sometimes proves devils.'[151] He told his opponents in Kingston court that 'that God whom you serve, and which did entitle you lords, knights, gentlemen and landlords, is covetousness.'[152] This God gave men a claim to private property in land. He 'appointed the people to pay tithes to the clergy'.[153] It is this God-Devil that the state church worships. 'We will neither come to church nor serve their God.'[154]

Winstanley's rejection of the deity who justifies the rule of men of property, in whose image he has been created, could hardly have been more complete. To the accusation that his beliefs 'will destroy all government and all our ministry and religion,' Winstanley replied coolly: 'It is very true.' In *The Law of Freedom* he advanced psychological explanations for belief in a personal God and angels, in local places of glory and torment.[155] The philosophy which started with a vision seems to have ended as a kind of materialist pantheism, in which God or abstract Reason can be known only in man or nature; and man is more important than abstractions.

Winstanley pushed this tendency to its logical conclusion. With a nod both towards the magical tradition and towards experimental science, he wrote:

> To know the secrets of nature is to know the works of God . . . And indeed if you would know spiritual things, it is to know how the spirit or power of wisdom and life, causing motion or growth, dwells within and governs both the several bodies of the stars and planets in the heavens above; and the several bodies of the earth below, as grass, plants, fishes, beasts, birds and mankind. For to reach God beyond the creation, or to know what he will be to a man after the man is dead, if any otherwise than to scatter him into his essences of fire, water, earth and air of which he is compounded, is a knowledge beyond the line or capacity of man to attain to while he lives in his compounded body.[156]

VII   NEW MYTHS FOR OLD

One of the most astonishing of the many astonishing things about
Winstanley is his mythological use of Biblical material. There are of
course precedents: the Family of Love was accused of turning the
Bible into allegories, especially the story of the Fall.[157] So did many
Ranters. Joseph Salmon taught that the true Christian was not he
who believed the historical truth of the Bible, 'but he that by the
power of the spirit believes all this history to be verified in the mystery; ... the history is Christ for us, the mystery is Christ in
us'.[158] Abiezer Coppe in an early pamphlet employed the imagery of
the Song of Songs to depict an erotic union between Christ the male
and man the female.[159] Hagar and Ishmael, Sarah and Isaac, were
allegories, Erbery insisted, 'though such persons were'.[160] The Quakers were accused of turning 'all things into allegories, or a Christ
within them'.[161] They mythologized, for example, the story of the
resurrection to such an extent that they were often believed to have
claimed to raise from the dead when they only meant that they had
effected a conversion.[162]

The mental habit was medieval. Calvin too taught that God spoke
to the capacity of his audience. But it was one thing for the clergy to
allegorize a Latin text whose sacredness was accepted on all sides; it
was quite another for mechanic laymen to put their own allegorical
constructions on a vernacular text available for all to read, and to do
this against the background of a critical protestant Biblical scholarship, in conditions of free and unfettered discussion which allowed
popular attitudes free rein, and in an atmosphere charged with millenarian expectations.

In some ways Winstanley looks forward not only to Milton but
also to Vico and Blake. His critical attitude towards the text of the
Scripture is very clear. He noted the contradictions which Walwyn
and Clarkson also saw: the Bible suggested the existence of men
before Adam, for instance. But Winstanley used this not merely neg-
atively, to discredit the Biblical narrative; but to insist that the story
of Adam and Eve must be taken metaphorically, not literally.[163] By

implication Winstanley denied the inspiration of the Bible, as Ranters, Clement Writer and the Quaker Samuel Fisher did.[164] Winstanley was in fact not really interested in the historical truth or otherwise of the Bible: 'Whether there were such outward things or no, it matters not much.' 'The whole Scriptures are but a report of spiritual mysteries, held forth to the eye of flesh in words, but to be seen in the substantial matter of them by the eye of the spirit.' The Bible should be used to illustrate truths of which one was already convinced: Winstanley was prepared to use Acts 4.32 to justify community of property.[165]

The Virgin Birth was an allegory;[166] so was the resurrection. 'Christ lying in the grave, like a corn of wheat buried under the clods of earth for a time, and Christ rising up from the powers of your flesh, above that corruption and above those clouds, treading the curse under his feet, is to be seen within'; Winstanley appears to reject any other resurrection or ascension.[167] The resurrection of the dead occurs during our lives on earth: the day of judgment has already begun and some are already living in the kingdom of heaven.[168] The casting out of covetousness and the establishment of a classless society will be 'a new heaven and a new earth'. Even more remarkably, all the prophecies of the Old and New Testaments regarding the calling of the Jews and the restoration of Israel refer to 'this work of making the earth a common treasury'.[169] Salvation is liberty and peace. The second coming is 'the rising up of Christ in sons and daughters'; the worship of any other Christ but the Christ within man must then cease.[170]

The story of the Garden of Eden Winstanley treated as an idle tale unless taken allegorically. 'The public preachers have cheated the whole world by telling us of a single man called Adam that killed us all by eating a single fruit, called an apple': in fact 'you are the man and woman that hath eaten the forbidden fruit'; Adam symbolizes the power of covetousness in every man.[171] 'The apple that the first man eats is ... the objects of the creation.' 'We may see Adam every day before our eyes walking up and down the street.' The symbolism of the garden has almost as great a significance for Winstanley as for Marvell or Milton. Eden is mankind.[172] In Eden is fought out the conflict between Reason on the one hand and covetous imagination on the other. 'This innocency or plain-heartedness in man was not an estate 6,000 years ago only but every branch of mankind passes through it ... This is the field of heaven wherein Michael and the Dragon fights the great battle of God Almighty.' And this conflict still goes on. 'There is no man or woman needs go to Rome nor to hell below ground, as some talk, to find the Pope, Devil, Beast or power of darkness; neither to go up into heaven above the skies to find Christ the word of life. For both these powers are to be felt within a man, fighting against each other.'[173]

This poetic concern with spiritual meaning rather than with historical truth enabled Winstanley to blend the myth of the Fall with the myth of the Norman Conquest: 'the last enslaving conquest which the enemy got over Israel was the Norman over England.'[174] Equally allegorical is Winstanley's use of the stories of Cain and Abel, of Esau and Jacob: the younger brother being the 'poor oppressed', the elder brother the rich freeholders.[175] 'Cain is still alive in all the great landlords,' said one of the Digger pamphlets which Winstanley probably did not write.[176] But 'the earth is my birthright,' says Winstanley's younger brother: God is no respecter of persons. To this the elder brother replies, like many seventeenth-century clerics, by quoting Scripture. But 'though this Jacob be very low, yet his time is now come'; he will supplant Esau, and 'takes both birthright and blessing from him'.[177] Use of the myth of the two brothers deserves further study. 'Esau is the ending of the old world,' said a pamphlet which circulated in Norfolk in February 1649. 'The reign of Jacob, of the saints ... begins the new world.'[178] The Ranter Abiezer Coppe linked 'the blood of the righteous Abel' with 'the blood of the last Levellers that were shot to death'.[179] George Fox used the myth in 1659.[180] 'Cain's brood,' wrote Bunyan, were 'lords and rulers', while 'Abel and his generation have their necks under oppression.'[181]

Dr Thirsk has shown how actual were the problems of younger brothers in seventeenth-century England.[182] Opposition to primogeniture was perhaps more widespread and more significant than historians have appreciated. It was shared by the Levellers, Hugh

Peter, James Harrington, William Sheppard, Champianus Northto-
nus (1655), Robert Wiseman (1656), William Covell, William Sprigge
and the anonymous author of *Chaos* (1659). Abolition of primogeniture, in order to destroy 'the monopolies of elder brethren', was
one of the objectives of Venner's Fifth Monarchist revolt in 1661.[183]
Quaker converts from landed families after 1662 were mostly
younger sons and daughters[184] – those most opposed to paternal
authority to whom the rough egalitarianism of northern yeomen
would most appeal. But the radicals gave the legend deeper mythological overtones. For men of property, however small their share, a
birthright signified inheritance from ancestors; property was equiva-
lent to freeborn status. Some, like John Bunyan, might be tempted to
sell their birthright.[185] Inheritance was the backbone of seventeenth-
century society. It was the basis of Ireton's defence of property, of the
Levellers' demand for the rights of freeborn Englishmen. The doctrine of original sin assumes transmission of guilt from Adam to all
men living, just as the notion of an original contract assumed that
men in the state of nature could bind their posterity for all time.[186]

Winstanley took over and transformed other popular beliefs. The
myth of the Everlasting Gospel goes back at least to Joachim of Fiore
in the twelfth century. This divided human history into three ages:
that of the Father, from the Fall to the death of Christ, the age of the
Law; followed by that of the Son, the age of the Gospel; the third
age, the age of the Spirit, was always the present age, in which the
Holy Spirit was coming into the hearts of all men to free them from
existing forms and ordinances. It was a heretical doctrine, for it not
only rejected the authority of the institutionalized church, but it put
the spirit within man above the letter of Scripture. This doctrine had
been taken over by the Familists and Jacob Boehme; it was widespread in the England of the 1640s.[187]

Winstanley, by a remarkable imaginative feat, transmuted this
apocalyptic vision into a theory of rationalism and democracy. The
key lies in his equation of God with Reason, and Reason with the
law of the universe. In the third age, now beginning, 'the Lord himself, who is the Eternal Gospel, doth manifest himself to rule in the
flesh of sons and daughters'. Their hearts will be retuned to the

Reason which pervades the cosmos, to 'that spiritual power that guides all men's reasoning in right order to a right end'. Every man subject to Reason's law becomes a Son of God. He no longer 'looks upon a God and a ruler without him, as the beast of the field does'; his ruler is within, whether it be called conscience or love or Reason. This is Christ's second coming, after which 'the ministration of Christ in one single person is to be silent and draw back' before the righteousness and wisdom in every person.[188]

A similar transvaluation took place with the myth of Antichrist. Orthodox divines saw the Pope as Antichrist. More radical Puritans came to regard bishops and indeed the whole Church of England as antichristian, and the civil war as a crusade for Christ against Antichrist. Winstanley again pushed this farther still, seeing property itself as antichristian, embodied in covetousness or self-love.[189] 'The antichristian captivity is expiring,' he thought; but the civil war had not completed Antichrist's overthrow. There was still a conflict of 'Beast against Beast, covetousness and pride against covetousness and pride.'[190] 'That government that gives liberty to the gentry to have all the earth, and shuts out the poor commons from enjoying any part, . . . is the government of imaginary, self-seeking Antichrist', and must be rooted out. Winstanley hoped that England would be the first country to fall off from 'that Beast, kingly property'.[191]

Since the external world is the manifestation of Winstanley's God, our senses are to be valued because by them we know this world. Man must live in himself, not out of himself; in his five senses, not in empty imaginations, books or hearsay doctrines. Then God walks and delights himself in his garden, mankind.[192] We know God by the senses, 'in the clear-sighted experience of one single creature, man, by seeing, hearing, tasting, smelling, feeling'.[193] When the five senses act in their own light, this is 'the state of simple plainheartedness or innocency'. When man places his good in outward objects, imagination 'corrupts the five senses' and this leads to a Hobbist state of nature, a state of competition bordering on war. Man finds no happiness here: only when 'the selfish, imaginary, covetous, murdering power' has been cast out does God become 'all in all, the alone king in that living soul or earth, or the five living senses'.[194] Winstanley passionately asserted the earthly nature of this Paradise of the senses: 'Oh ye hearsay preachers, deceive not the people any longer by telling them that this glory shall not be known and seen till the body is laid in the dust. I tell you, this great mystery is begun to appear, and it must be seen by the material eyes of the flesh: and those five senses that is in man shall partake of this glory.' 'All outward glory that is at a distance from the five senses ... is of a transient nature; and so is the heaven that your preachers tell you of.' Heaven is here in this world. Winstanley made the point with his accustomed epigrammatic vigour by calling on 'proud priests' to 'leave off their trade' and '*stoop* unto our God'.[195] He was literally trying to bring them down to earth, to God in man. The last line of the Diggers' song called for: 'Glory *here*, Diggers all!'[196] But if God is everywhere, if matter is God, then there can be no difference between the sacred and the secular: pantheism leads to secularism.

8
Sin and Hell

Sin and transgression is finished . . . Be no longer so hor-
ridly, hellishly, impudently, arrogantly wicked, as to judge
what is sin, what not.

ABIEZER COPPE, *A Fiery Flying Roll*,
Part I (1649), p. 7.

I   SIN AND SOCIETY

Most religions and most peoples have a legend similar to that of the
Garden of Eden, Arcadia, the Golden Age. There was a state of happiness and innocence in the past, but this has now been lost, and
mankind is at the mercy of an uncontrollable fate. Man is fundamen-
tally sinful, and whatever sacramental means may exist to reconcile
God to him, this reconciliation can never be complete on earth. We
are to expect our happiness in an after-life. In all the great religions
in their prime the after-life is a reflection of society in this world: a
few are in a state of bliss, the vast majority in a state of torment –
although the positions might be reversed after death. Some heretical
movements claimed salvation for all men, or at least for all members
of a given community; but this conception never won acceptance by
any established church so long as it held its monopoly position; in
Europe that is to say until well after the Reformation.

In an unequal agricultural society, with primitive techniques,
where men were at the mercy of nature and starved if the harvest
failed; where plagues and warfare made life uncertain, it was easy to

see famines and epidemics as punishments for human wickedness. As long as the level of technique was too low to liberate men from nature, so long were they prepared to accept their helplessness before a God who was as unpredictable as the weather. Sin, like poverty and social inferiority, was inherited. Magic, an alternative system attempting to control nature, still played a large part in the lives of the common people, and it was used by the priesthood, by those who performed the miracle of the mass. Men conscious of their helplessness, their frustration, could easily be convinced that they were sinful. Because they were sinful they were discouraged from trying to remedy their situation. If they confessed to a priest and paid the appropriate fees, they could be absolved and set free from their sins – until the next time. The medieval church had evolved a workable system of social control, aided by the useful invention of Purgatory.[1] But it over-reached itself in the sale of indulgences, remission of the penalties of sin for cash down. For this commercialization of salvation was recognized as an abuse by those – merchants and artisans especially – whose mastery of more advanced techniques and growing wealth was giving them greater confidence in their ability to stand on their own feet. Such men, whose wealth no doubt initially prompted the sale of indulgences, formed an important part of the popular backing for Luther when he made his protest against the practice.

In protestantism the sense of sin was internalized. Priestly mediators were discarded because each believer had a priest in his own conscience: outward penance and absolution were replaced by inward penitence. This set some men free from the terrors of sin. The elect were those who felt within themselves the power of God. God spoke direct to their consciences, without mediation of priests or sacraments. Luther's doctrine of the priesthood of all believers destroyed the old hierarchical framework of the church, and set men face to face with God. Protestantism emphasizes that some men are predestined to salvation, others to damnation. But it is wrong to stress only the predestinarian aspect of protestantism: for the practical purposes of living in society, its importance is as a doctrine of the *freedom* of the elect, who by divine grace are singled out from the mass of humanity. Most men, like animals and the whole inanimate creation, are subject to and helpless before the forces of nature and society – famine, pestilence, death. They are sunk in sin. The elect alone are free, since to them the forces which govern the world are not blind. The elect understand and cooperate with God's purposes, and this sense of intimacy with the ruler of the universe gives a confidence, an inner assurance, which may enable them to prosper in this world as well as to inherit the next.

It does not give them the exaggerated, unfeeling self-confidence of fatalism: tensions, doubts, always remain. Only God knows his elect. One man's liberation may be another man's despair.[2] But the tensions themselves, in appropriate circumstances, may produce a moral energy, a determination to prove oneself. The theory of justification by faith helped men to live because of the inner hope it gave. It is a *relatively* democratic theory: the elect form a spiritual aristocracy, which bears no relation to the worldly aristocracy of birth. The theory gave a select group of the unprivileged third estate sufficient courage, conviction and sense of unity with each other to be able to force their way towards religious and political freedom by means of a tightly disciplined organization. Necessarily only a select group have the economic status, the education, the leisure, to master this theology; only a minority can be free; only a minority are the elect. They differentiate themselves the more sharply from the remaining mass of the unprivileged third estate (as well as from the godless ruling class) in that they are well aware that their sense of divine grace is all that does distinguish them. It makes them human, as distinct from animals and the unregenerate. It involves a transvaluation of values: for self-respect had been the sin of Lucifer and Prometheus. Tawney was referring especially to Calvinism when he spoke of 'the central paradox of religious ethics – that only those are nerved with the courage needed to turn the world upside down who are convinced that already, in a higher sense, it is disposed for the best by a Power of which they are the humble instruments'.[3]

The spiritual experience of conversion, for a protestant in our period, was a break-through to a new life of freedom. His burden rolled off his back, and he acquired a sense of dignity, of confidence in himself as an individual. Thomas Hooker put it well when he wrote: 'Sound contrition and brokenness of heart brings a strange and a sudden alteration into the world, varies the price and value of things and persons beyond imagination, turns the world upside down, makes the things appear as they be.' 'Such judge not by outward appearance, as it is the guise of men of corrupt minds, but upon experience, that they have found and felt in their own hearts.'[4] Conversion gave a sense of strength too through oneness with a community of like-minded people. The 'collectivist' spirit of early Calvinism has often been noted. The same sense of common interests and beliefs inspired the early sectarian congregations.

This double sense of power – individual self-confidence and strength through unity – produced that remarkable liberation of energy which is typical of Calvinism and the sects during our period. Men felt free: free from hell, free from priests, free from fear of worldly authorities, free from the blind forces of nature, free from magic. The freedom might be illusory: an inner psychological self-deception. Or it might correspond to outer reality, in that it was likely to be felt by men who were economically independent. But even an illusory freedom might give a man the power to win real freedom, just as mimetic magic did help primitive man to grow his crops.

But conversion itself, the leap forward from a world of consciousness of necessity to a world of consciousness of freedom, this *must* come as something arbitrary and external. One could no more wish oneself into a state of grace than one could wish oneself into a higher social class. It was God's intervention in a static universe, the miracle without which one remained among the inert mass of the reprobate, without which freedom was impossible.

Protestantism, as a shrewd commentator puts it, retained medieval sin without the medieval insurance policy – confession and absolution. Men emancipated themselves from priests, but not from the terrors of sin, from the priest internalized in their own consciences.[5] Only very strong characters, or the very fortunate, could stand the strain. Unmodified, it was a doctrine more appropriate to crisis conditions of struggle than to normal living in a stable society.

And it left a problem of social control. Protestant doctrines emphasized the separation of the elect from the unregenerate mass. Confession and absolution were abolished because the elect were their own priests; priestly mediators could do no good to the unregenerate either. But what then was to become of the unregenerate majority of society? Protestant doctrine heavily emphasized the social consequences of the Fall of Man.

If Adam's Fall had not brought sin into the world, men would have been equal, property would have been held in common. But since the Fall, covetousness, pride, anger and all the other sins have been transmitted to his posterity. The mass of mankind is irretrievably damned: a small minority is predestined to eternal life. A coercive state is one consequence of the Fall, necessary to prevent sinful men from destroying one another. Private property is likewise a consequence of sin; but since it inevitably exists, it must be defended against the greedy lusts of the unpropertied, who must be held in subordination. The Tudor state took over many of the functions of the medieval church. These traditional doctrines had not gone unchallenged. The Thirty-nine Articles of the Church of England rely heavily on original sin to defend property and the authority of magistrates against Anabaptists.[6]

So long as church and state were one, the Fall was vital to politics. For if the individual can set up his conscience against priest and church, by the same token he can set himself up against the government with which the church is so intimately associated. Luther said:

> The ungodly out of the Gospel do seek only a carnal freedom, and become worse thereby; therefore not the Gospel but the Law belongeth to them . . . The Gospel is like a fresh, mild and cool air in the extreme heat of summer, that is, a solace and comfort in the anguish of the conscience. But . . . the terrifying of the conscience must proceed from the preaching of the Law, to the end we may know that we have offended against the Laws of God.[7]

Here is a dual standard in religious teaching: Gospel for the godly, Law for the ungodly; and for the later Luther 'the multitude' were the ungodly.

The dualism was all the more necessary because sixteenth-century protestantism was in one sense a revolutionary creed. 'Here I stand, so help me God, I can no other.' Whether Luther actually used the words or not, they express the spirit of his actions. He and those who felt with him would fight or suffer to the death rather than submit to the tyranny of the Pope or a popish secular power. But protestantism was not a democratic creed. It proclaimed *Christian* liberty, liberty for the elect. Calvin turned the dualism into a system, which on the one hand produced a better fighting machine than Lutheranism, and on the other a better disciplinary régime for the lower orders. Solomon, Calvin wrote, 'exhorts the poor to patient endurance, seeing that those who are discontented with their lot endeavour to shake off a burden which God hath imposed on them'.[8] He has imposed it on them because they are sinful. Even slavery, for the Calvinist William Perkins, 'is indeed against the law of entire nature as it was before the Fall; but against the law of corrupted nature since the Fall, it is not'.[9] The godly, Calvin had taught, may use 'the aid of the magistrate for the preservation of their goods, or, from zeal for the public interest, . . . call for the punishment of the wicked and pestilential man, whom they know nothing will reform but death'.[10]

These commonplaces were shared by all except radical protestants. Richard Hooker accepted them no less than did Calvinists.[11] English and Scottish Presbyterians anticipated Hobbes in teaching that it was the function of civil government to restrain the depravity natural to all men. Henry Parker, a political associate of the Presbyterians and a theoretical predecessor of Hobbes, wrote in 1642 that 'man being depraved by the Fall of Adam grew so untame and uncivil a creature that the law of God written in his breast was not sufficient to restrain him from mischief or to make him sociable'.[12] His enemy Sir Robert Filmer asserted that 'a natural freedom of mankind cannot be supposed without a denial of the creation of Adam', and so 'the bringing in of atheism'. Filmer argued indeed that political power existed *before* the Fall of Man.[13] Verbal expressions might vary, but nobody denied the wickedness of the multitude until the multitude began to speak for itself – and then the propertied were all the more convinced of the need for repression. Law protects property, John Pym declared in 1641. 'If you take away the law, all things will fall into a confusion, every man will become a law to himself, which *in the depraved condition of human nature* must needs produce many great enormities.'[14]

For the conservative, the man in possession, the Fall was something which could not be undone. It had permanently affected human nature. To attempt to ignore the sinfulness of man was to fly in the face of facts. He saw evil as something internal, lurking in the heart of every man: not as an external product of society. Sin was an inherited characteristic, transmitted by the sexual act. The idea that it is just to visit the sins of the fathers upon all succeeding generations is part of the primitive complex of ideas which produced the blood feud, and is well suited to a society based on inherited status.

This climate of opinion made possible the (to us) odd assumptions of early political theorists, that heirs are to all eternity bound by contracts made by their remote ancestors. Sir John Davies justified God to men by the parallel of disinheriting not only an erring son but also his (presumably) innocent posterity, and by the privileges won in the past by a corporation.[15] Inherited sin was the obverse of the divine hereditary right of monarchs. There is no damned merit about salvation. Men were redeemed only by the imputed righteousness of Christ, replacing all other mediators. But such arguments were two-edged: Levellers and others claimed that all freeborn Englishmen had a birthright, inherited from their Anglo-Saxon predecessors, of which it was wrong to deprive them.

In a society in which contract was becoming more important than status, such stress on inheritance was beginning to look old-fashioned – as in Filmer's political theory. Hobbes and Locke used the framework of the social contract, but their arguments do not depend in any way on its having occurred in historical fact. Puritan theology in the early seventeenth century was reacting to the new social environment with the covenant theology of Perkins and his successors: God contracted salvation with his elect in a highly legalistic manner.[16] This had one very odd consequence. In the covenant theology Adam (and Christ) became representative figures, in whom the state of all humanity is summed up: public persons. We no longer suffer because we are Adam's heirs, but because Adam was our representative. Christ's imputed righteousness does not wholly come from without but is won for us by our representative.[17] This opened wider doors than the covenant theologians imagined. William Erbery was to suggest that the New Model Army was 'the Army of God, as public persons and not for a particular interest'.[18]

The problem of social control was solved in a makeshift way in Tudor England by retaining church courts which imposed penalties for 'sin'. They continued to be denounced by radical protestants as mere agencies for raising money. The Presbyterian wing among the clergy wished to abolish them altogether, and replace them by a disciplinary system which would have given greatly increased power to themselves. The defeat of the Presbyterian movement within the Church of England in the 1590s created new problems. The Puritan clergy laid ever-increasing stress on preaching, on moral conduct, on building up a convinced body of lay opinion. As Stuart governments came more and more under Arminian influence, so the consolidation of a party of Puritan laymen became increasingly important. As sacramentalism revived within the church, the Puritans won support from many laymen whose motives were anti-clerical rather than theological; and who in the 1640s found Presbyterian clericalism no less distasteful than Arminian. But for the time being the alliance was solid.

There were indeed inherent contradictions in combining a theology which stressed that the elect were a minority with a moral preaching designed to reach all men. All the orthodox would have agreed with William Crashaw's dictum: 'The greater part generally is the worst part.'[19] Thomas Hooker in 1632 could 'speak it by experience that the meaner sort of people, it is incredible what ignorance is among them'.[20] Perkins and other Puritan theologians solved this by teaching that God would accept the will for the deed; that although we cannot save ourselves by our efforts, nevertheless a passionate desire to be saved was strong presumptive evidence that one was in fact among the elect. 'The Lord accepteth the affection and the endeavour for the thing done.'[21] 'He who desires to be righteous, is righteous,' declared John Downame; 'he that would repent, doth repent . . . If there be a willing mind it is accepted.'[22] 'Desire of assurance, and complaint of the want of assurance,' Sir Simonds D'Ewes thought in 1641, amount to 'assurance itself'.[23] This meant that anyone who took the problem of his salvation seriously could have some reasonable confidence that he was saved. The élite were the elect.

When civil war came, the appeal for mass support had to be even more direct, even less discriminating. Anyone who would fight against Antichrist was welcome. How far preachers allowed themselves to be aware of the profound contradiction in their position we do not know. Many of them called the common people into political action, holding out millennial hopes especially to the poor and simple. Yet no Calvinist could logically have any confidence in democracy: his religion was for the elect, by definition a minority. Thomas Goodwin, who appealed to the 'vulgar multitude', still knew it was 'a certain sign of an unregenerate estate, to be carried thus along with the stream, and to be moulded to the same principles the generality of most men are'.[24] To call on the ungodly masses to fight against Antichrist was perhaps no more illogical than appealing to a Duke of Northumberland or Buckingham, an Earl of Leicester or Essex, to reform the church. But it was more dangerous. It staked everything on the clergy retaining control, that is to say retaining the support of those sections of the laity who mattered in politics. They would have had difficulty enough with the Erastians in the Long Parliament; with the rise of the New Model Army they lost control altogether.

So long as the field of debate was circumscribed by a functioning state church, a functioning patronage system, and an effective censorship, the clergy and their Parliamentarian allies were secure. But once all these had been broken down, once the common people had tasted the forbidden delights of liberty, what then? They would certainly not welcome the establishment of a serious disciplinary system, enforcing a stern moral code – Presbyterian scorpions for episcopal whips. Church courts before 1640 had been irritating, but lax and inefficient. Those too poor to be worth fining normally escaped. But Presbyterian discipline meant a different sort of business: it would take seriously the imposition of a code of moral behaviour on the godless multitude. This must not only have reinforced anti-clericalism among the lower classes but also have stimulated that antinomian rejection of the bondage of the moral law which with some Ranters became a rejection of all traditional moral restraints.[25] Presbyterian ministers would have carried the courage of their convictions to the point of persecution. So would the majority in the Long Parliament, indeed in any House of Commons elected on a property franchise, whether in 1640, 1654, 1656, 1660 or 1661. But from 1647 it was the Army, not Parliament, still less the Presbyterian clergy, who decided.

Radical protestants had long waited to complete the Reformation, which they regarded as having got stuck half-way in the Elizabethan settlement. They wanted to abolish church courts and all vestiges of priestly control. Sin was no longer to be the concern of courts, spiritual or secular. It was the internal problem of each believer. In so far as there was to be any social control, it was to be exercised democratically, over their own members, by congregations of the self-selected elect. Their penalties would be purely spiritual. The ungodly would be left to the civil magistrate to keep in order.

But of course matters would not stop there, as sixteenth-century history should have taught the radicals among the clergy. Protestantism began by looking like a great liberation of the human spirit. But within a decade of Luther's protest he was faced by a peasant revolt which attacked property and social subordination, as Luther understood them, altogether; and within another decade the Anabaptists of Münster rose against the whole existing social order. Printing had made protestantism possible because it facilitated the rapid spread of popular theology among the literate, especially in towns. Where the Lollard Bible circulated in tens of copies, Tyndale's New Testament circulated in hundreds and the Geneva Bible in thousands. But printing also ruined protestantism as a single coherent creed because the reading of books is even less possible to control than the reading of manuscripts. The pocketable Geneva Bible could be privately digested and privately interpreted. Once the masses of the population were called into political activity, whether in sixteenth-century Germany or seventeenth-century England, some were bound to demand salvation for themselves. The German and Dutch Anabaptists failed in their attempt to storm heaven. They were bludgeoned back into submission, in this world and the next. Their appearance was for Luther and Calvin clear proof of the inherent wickedness of the mass of fallen humanity. Luther, dependent as he became on German secular princes, reacted by denying to the individual conscience any right of criticism or interference in the sphere of secular government; Calvin, who was the government of Geneva, emphasized the need for discipline, the imposition from above of a rigid code of conduct.

As ordinary people formed their own congregations in the sixteen-forties, free from traditional clerical control, they discussed all aspects of theology and politics in the light of the Bible. Many like Milton proclaimed that the elect could be free from all restraints, including the marriage bond: coercion was to be applied only to the unregenerate. Thus the numbers and identity of the elect became a pressing political problem. In the Putney Debates on the franchise this question was directly relevant. As lower-class sectaries became convinced that they were elect, antinomianism, Calvinism's lower-class alter ego, raised its head. In 1549 a London tradesman had said that a man regenerate could not sin.[26] There were many such in England in the 1640s.

II   ABOLISHING SIN

Insensibly this led on to asking whether the damnation of the majority of mankind was clearly stated in the Bible, or whether the New Testament might not offer salvation to all. What indeed is sin? Is God its author? Or is it a purely subjective concept? Are all things pure to the pure? Milton suggested that 'the greatest burden in the world is superstition . . . of imaginary and scarecrow sins'.[27] Such questions led on to the social function of sin. George Chapman's Bussy d'Ambois had suggested that it was 'the sly charms Of the witch Policy' that exaggerated the horror of sin, making it 'a monster Kept only to show men for servile money'.[28] Chapman was a protégé of Ralegh's; and it was possibly in Ralegh's circle that verses circulated towards the end of Elizabeth's reign suggesting that God, the after-life, heaven and hell were all 'mere fictions', 'only bugbears'. Religion was 'of itself a fable', deliberately invented to 'keep the baser sort in fear' when private property, the family and the state were established.[29]

If sin was an invention, what then justified private property, the division of society into classes, the state which protected property? Nobody could stop such questions being generally discussed in the 1640s. Winstanley reversed the traditional formula: it was not the Fall that caused property, but property that caused the Fall. 'When self-love began to arise in the earth, then man began to fall.'[30] 'When mankind began to quarrel about the earth, and some would have all and shut out others, forcing them to be servants; this was man's fall.' State power, armies, laws and the machinery of 'justice', prisons, the gallows, all exist to protect the property which the rich have stolen from the poor. Exploitation, not labour, is the curse. We must abolish wage labour if we are to restore prelapsarian freedom. Buying and selling, and the laws that regulate the market, are part of the Fall. In a remarkable passage Winstanley suggested that the doctrine of election was a mirror of the unequal social order: 'kingly government . . . hath made the election and rejection of brethren from their birth to their death, or from eternity to eternity'.[31]

Side by side with protestantism, the cult of magic, so popular in the sixteenth and early seventeenth centuries, had also offered man, through mastery of the secrets of nature, liberation from the consequences of the Fall. This liberation was for initiates only, as protestant grace was for the elect only; but there were no theoretical limitations on those who might share the mysteries. Francis Bacon inherited something of this tradition as well as protestantism. For though Bacon accepted a Fall of Man, he rejected the full Calvinist doctrine of human depravity. He shared the hope of alchemists and magical writers, that the abundance of Eden might be recreated on earth, in Bacon's case by experiment, mechanical skill and intense cooperative effort. Sin for him was largely the product of ignorance and poverty. Labour, the curse of fallen man, might be the means whereby he would rise again. George Hakewill held similar views.[32]

The popularization of Bacon's ideas after 1640 thus helped to get rid of the shadow that had dogged humanity for so many centuries: the shadow of original sin. What alchemy and Calvinism had in common was that salvation came from without, from the philosopher's stone or the grace of God. Bacon extracted from the magical-alchemical tradition the novel idea that men could help themselves – mankind, not merely favoured individuals. This together with the dramatic events of the English Revolution helped to transform the backward look to a golden age, a Paradise Lost, into a hope for a better life here on earth, attainable by human effort. Bacon's disciple Comenius hoped 'to restore man to the lost image of God, i.e. to the lost perfection of the free will, which consists in the choice of good and the repudiation of evil'. Comenius wanted men to 'turn over the living book of the world instead of dead papers'. In a free commonwealth, he thought, there ought to be no kings.[33] In 1641 he was invited to England by a group of supporters of Parliament who hoped for a drastic reform of the English educational system.

So by the 1640s there were many converging trends of thought which opposed the orthodox and traditional dogmas of original sin. 'By nature are all alike freemen born,' declared the anonymous *Vox Plebis* in 1646, 'and are since made free in grace by Christ' – an early linking of free grace to the doctrines of political liberty. This pamphlet ignored the Fall altogether.[34] So did Lilburne.[35] A petition of September 1648, alleged to have been signed by forty thousand men, thought that the distinctions of kings and lords were 'the devices of men', and of no use, 'God having made all alike'.[36]

'The corruptness of man's unsanctified nature' was used by Col. John Pyne to justify Pride's Purge.[37] This corruption seemed to the Levellers especially obvious both in the old ruling class and in those (like Pyne himself) who had risen to leading positions during the Revolution: a wider suffrage, annual elections and the fundamentals of the Agreement of the People were intended to preserve rulers from the tendency of power to corrupt. This was a remarkable reversal of hitherto orthodox conclusions about government drawn from the Fall – that the mass of mankind, being wicked, could be restrained only by the law and the magistrate. The tacit assumption was always that laws have been drafted by, and magistrates are, godly men. The process of legislation during the Revolution was carried on too much in public for such views to carry conviction. Overton indeed brushed the whole theological approach to politics aside when he said that what mattered to his neighbour was 'not how great a sinner I am, but how faithful and real to the Common-wealth'.[38] 'It is an hard thing,' Wildman observed, for any man 'by the light of nature to conceive how there can be any sin committed; and therefore the magistrate cannot easily determine what sins are against the light of nature, and what not'.[39] These were very far-reaching arguments indeed.

The Family of Love and the Grindletonians[40] had taught that pre-lapsarian perfection could be attained in this life. But before the 1640s such doctrines had been kept underground. Now nothing could be suppressed. Plebeian materialist scepticism and anti-clericalism could express themselves freely, and fused with theological antinomian-ism. The result was a rejection of clerical control of religious and moral life, and a rejection of the whole concept of sin the great de-terrent. Perfectibility was publicly taught and printed, by Henry Denne and others whom Edwards records.[41] 'I am one that do truly and heartily love all mankind, it being the unfeigned desire of my soul that all men might be saved,' Walwyn assured Edwards in 1646.[42] Winstanley in 1648 declared the salvation of all mankind. To deny Christ to be come in the flesh of the saints was to deny the res-urrection.[43] Richard Coppin argued that the subjects of election and reprobation were not persons but the good and evil qualities in men. In 1655 one of the doctrines he had to repudiate was 'that all men whatsoever should be saved'; but he got his own back by adding that the clergy 'live by telling men of their sins'.[44] The author of *Tyranipo-crit Discovered* believed that all men had the grace to be saved if they only looked for God within them. To seek God elsewhere is in vain.[45] The Socinian John Bidle denied original sin and the doctrine of eter-nal torment. When he got into trouble for this, Levellers spoke up for him.[46] In 1652 an English translation of the Racovian Catechism was ordered by Parliament to be burnt. Next year a *Life of Socinus* was published, and John Owen was commissioned by the Council of State to refute Socinianism. 'There is not a city, a town, scarce a village wherein some of this poison is not poured forth,' Owen declared.[47] Lawrence Clarkson preached free grace even before he became a Ranter. Ranters, like the passage from Greene's *Selimus*, thought sin had been invented by priests and rulers to keep men in subjection.[48] 'If the elect are chosen from all eternity,' Roger Crab asked, 'what do priests take our money for?'[49] George Fox, who in 1648 was renewed 'to the state of Adam, which he was in before he fell', thought God's light was in everyone, really everyone.[50] So the oligarchy of grace was democratized.

Conservatives rallied to the defence of sin. Samuel Purchas had said that at the Fall man passed from freehold to villeinage.[51] If this was to be reversed, what claim might not free men make? It was no longer a mere commonplace when in July 1643 the Westminster Assembly of Divines reminded Parliament of 'the brutal ignorance and palpable darkness possessing the greatest part of the people in all parts of the kingdom'.[52] We should not of course take a remark like that too literally: what seemed brutal ignorance to a Presbyterian divine might be a healthy scepticism about the Eternal Decrees.[53] But the temporary triumph of Calvinism and the establishment of Presbyterianism forced more people (including some of 'the brutally ignorant' themselves) to define their attitudes towards 'brutal ignorance'. 'Remove once the shaking of these rods [the Decalogue] over their heads,' declared a pamphlet of 1647, 'then we open a floodgate to all licentious liberty.'[54] 'We cannot,' Walwyn was told in 1649, 'upon any rational and scriptural ground expect a complete, full, absolute and perfect freedom from all kind of pressures and grievances in the land; surely a natural and complete freedom from all sorrows and troubles was fit for man only before he had sinned, and not since; let them look for their portion in this life that know no better, and their kingdom in this world that believe no other: to what end are the graces of faith, patience and self-denial vouchsafed unto us?'[55] Bishop Goodman agreed: 'If Paradise were to be replanted on earth, God had never expelled man [from] Paradise.'[56] The social function of sin could hardly be more clearly expressed. The Diggers were told in 1649 that they confused cause and effect. 'As men fell before the curse came, so must it follow that (before the earth) man should be restored to the first estate in Adam, and property is but the consequent effect of the first offence.'[57]

Thomas Fuller in his *Church History* is writing of 1254, but clearly thinking of four centuries later:

> Many active spirits, whose minds were above their means, offended that others beneath them (as they thought) in merit were above them in employment, cavilled at many errors in the King's government, being state-Donatists, maintaining the perfection of a Commonwealth might and ought to be attained. A thing easy in the theory, impossible in the practice, to conform the actions of men's corrupted natures to the exact ideas in men's imaginations.[58]

'All this stir of the republicans,' said Richard Baker, 'is but to make the seed of the Serpent to be the sovereign rulers of the earth.'[59] In this hysterical pamphlet, written during the troubled year 1659–60, Baxter with the utmost naïveté equates the godly and the propertied class, the ungodly and the lower orders. This was 'to terrify them with hell fire', as Henry Denne put it.[60] It is difficult not to sympathize with Fox's snort of indignation: 'all professions [i.e. sects] stood in a beastly spirit and nature, pleading for sin and the body of sin and imperfection, as long as they lived'. The preachers 'roar up for sin in their pulpits'. 'It was all their works to plead for it.'[61]

'Their trade is for money to declare against sin,' wrote Samuel Fisher, who always manages to put the commonplace in an engagingly original way, 'yet they must preach it up and talk for it a little too, and do their work not too hastily, all at once, lest there be no more work for them ere long to do, but such as they were never bred up to live by.'[62] 'We have given our money and spent our labour in following them,' wrote Fox of such preachers, 'and now they have gotten our money, they hope we will not look for perfection … while we are upon earth, on this side of the grave, for we must carry a body of sin about us … Oh deceivers!'[63] 'If all the Quakers and Ranters in the world,' was in effect Bunyan's retort, 'were but under the guilt of one sinful thought, it would make them to cry out with Cain, "My punishment is greater than I can bear." '[64] Conviction of sin was the answer to the inner light: the right to exclude from the sacraments the last priestly control left in reformed England. But in the end Coppe's words, quoted as epigraph to this chapter, turned out to be premature. Social pressures ensured that sin survived.

III   HELL

If sin and the Fall were questioned, nothing was sacred, not even God's Eternal Decrees, not even hell itself. Prynne's definition of the former will do for our purposes:

> God from all eternity hath ... predestinated unto life, not all men, ... but only a certain select number; ... others he hath eternally and perpetually reprobated unto death ... The sole ... cause of reprobation ... is the mere free will and pleasure of God, not the pre-vision, the pre-consideration of any actual sin, infidelity or final impenitency in the persons rejected.[65]

There is nothing the majority of us who are so rejected can do about it, however hard we try.

Some accepted this doctrine, and hoped they were themselves among the elect. Others accepted it, and were cast into despair because they thought themselves damned. The protestant abolition of Purgatory left an eternity of bliss or an eternity of torment as the only alternatives facing each individual. Together with the abolition of guardian angels, mediating saints, charms and other protective ecclesiastical magic, this had the effect of imposing a very great strain on those who accepted the doctrine literally.[66] 'The simpler sort,' Bullinger observed in the mid-sixteenth century, 'are greatly tempted and exceedingly troubled with the question of election. For the devil goeth about to throw into their minds the hate of God, as though he envied us our salvation, and had appointed and ordained us to death.'[67] It hardly needed the devil, one would have thought. Predestination, Helwys agreed in 1611, 'makes some despair, as thinking there is no grace for them and that God hath decreed their destruction. And it makes others deeply careless, holding that if God have decreed they shall be saved then they shall be saved, and if God hath decreed they shall be damned they shall be damned.'[68]

Religious melancholy and despair, leading to visions of the devil, were familiar to the Elizabethans and to Caroline doctors, and were anatomized by Robert Burton.[69] We hear much of these feelings in religious biographies and autobiographies of the time, but only because in such cases despair is normally followed by conversion. A few examples: Thomas Shepard around 1622 was in danger of falling into the Grindletonian heresy of perfectibility as a refuge from despair.[70] William Kiffin was in despair about 1632, until he was converted by John Goodwin.[71] Our evidence increases as the revolutionary crisis deepened. The Fifth Monarchist John Rogers was in fear of hell, doubted the existence of God, had thoughts of suicide;[72] John Saltmarsh had temptations to suicide before 1645, and was rescued by conversion to the doctrine of free grace.[73] Sarah Wright was in the grave of deep despair for four years before 1647.[74] Around 1646 William Franklin believed that God had deserted him: his physician recommended blood-letting.[75] Isaac Penington the younger about 1649 was 'broken and dashed to pieces in my religion . . . in a congregational way'; 'everything is darkness, death, emptiness, vanity, a lie,' he declared later.[76] Anna Trapnel, in despair and with thoughts of suicide, was tempted by 'those Familistical ranting tenets'.[77] The Ranters Abiezer Coppe and Jacob Bauthumley claimed to have gone through a similar period of desperation.[78]

In the 1650s Mrs Richard Baxter had doubts of the life to come and of the truth of Scripture: her husband had experienced similar doubts earlier.[79] Thomas Traherne went through a period of general scepticism in the 1650s, including doubts about the Bible.[80] The future Quakers William Deusbury and Edward Burrough were struck with terror at one stage, though in 1654 Burrough was very unsympathetic to Mistress Jane Turner of Newcastle-upon-Tyne, who had questioned the existence of God in her despair.[81] John Crook was in despair in the 1650s, again with temptations to suicide, until he was converted by accidentally hearing William Deusbury preach.[82] Johnston of Wariston in 1654 was discussing temptation to

atheism and suicide.[83] In New England Michael Wigglesworth was
having doubts about the Scripture at about the same time.[84] John
Rogers of Cornwall, some said, committed suicide in 1652 on Helwys's principle: 'if he was born to be damned, he should be damned;
if to be saved, he should be saved.'[85] Walwyn was alleged to have
driven a woman to suicide by 'poisoning her judgment touching the
truth of the Scriptures'.[86]

Gerrard Winstanley in 1648 observed that poverty might lead to
despair.[87] Mr Thomas suggests that religious despair as well as poverty may have driven some of the victims of Matthew Hopkins the
witchfinder in 1645 to turn to the devil for help. Preaching up the
power of the devil might backfire, Hopkins's colleague John Stearne
suggested. 'The devil hath made use of [such-like speeches] to persuade them to witchery'; 'they covenant with the devil to free them
of hell-torment.'[88] The Fifth Monarchist John Rogers was tempted
to resort to magic, necromancy and astrology as remedies against
extreme poverty and hunger.[89] In the 1650s Thomas Goodwin
preached much to encourage those tempted to despair:[90] the author
of *Tyranipocrit Discovered* attacked the doctrine of predestination
because it led to 'the quintessence of hell, I mean despair'.[91] In 1652
Winstanley analysed with some subtlety the way in which 'this doctrine of a God, a Devil, a heaven and hell, salvation and damnation
after a man is dead', could lead either to despair and suicide or to
acceptance of the dominance of priests.[92] Thomas Hobbes indig-
nantly denounced Presbyterian ministers who 'brought young men
into despair and to think themselves damned because they could not
(which no man can, and is contrary to the constitution of nature)
behold a beautiful object without delight'.[93]

So men came to question not only the Eternal Decrees but even
the existence of God. Many of Lodowick Muggleton's acquaintance
about 1650 'did say in their hearts and tongues both, that there is no
God but nature only'. 'I did not so much mind to be saved,' he added
about his own desperation, 'as I did to escape being damned. For I
thought, if I could but lie still in earth for ever, it would be as well
with me as if I were in eternal happiness . . . I cared not for heaven so
I might not go to hell.'[94] We can here see something of the liberating

effect which Overton's *Mans Mortallitie* must have had in 1643. The doctrine was not new: it was known to Lollards in the fifteenth century, to Anabaptists in the sixteenth. In the 1590s in England, Ralegh's protégé Thomas Hariot had questioned the immortality of the soul and suggested that there had been men before Adam; the world might be eternal.[95] Milton accepted the doctrine of soul-sleeping. We can sense too from Muggleton's account how very boring the traditional idea of heaven seemed, how much less attractive than hell was terrifying. This too would prepare men to accept either the idea of a material heaven on earth in an imminent millennium, or the idea that heaven and hell were internal states of mind.

John Bunyan in the early 1650s was terrified by thoughts of hell, and wished that he might be a devil to torment others. But he also asked himself 'whether there was in truth a God or Christ or no? And whether the holy Scriptures were not rather a fable and cunning story?' – 'written by some politicians', he added in 1658, 'on purpose to make poor ignorant people to submit to some religion and government'. 'How can you tell but that the Turks had as good Scriptures to prove their Mahomet the Saviour?' Many tens of thousands lacked knowledge of the right way to heaven, Bunyan reflected: how if all our faith, and Christ and the Scriptures, 'should be but a think-so too?' He was tempted to believe there was no such thing as the day of judgment, that sin was no such grievous thing. As though all that was not enough, Bunyan had many even worse thoughts 'which at this time I may not or dare not utter'.[96] George Fox, who was also tempted to despair on various occasions in 1646 and 1647, thought before 1649 that 'all things come by nature'. In 1651 another Quaker told Fox that 'there was never such a thing' as 'a Christ that died at Jerusalem'.[97]

Popular heresies in the Middle Ages had questioned the existence of hell, or conversely had queried the justness of an omnipotent God who created millions of men and women in order to torment them eternally.[98] The 1552 Articles of the Church of England condemned the belief that hell was only temporary, and that all men would be saved at the last. (This article was dropped in 1562.) The Family of Love believed that heaven and hell are in the world among us; the Family of the Mount that heaven is when we laugh, hell when we are in pain or sorrow.[99] Queen Elizabeth in 1585 went out of her way to denounce those who said there was no hell but a torment of conscience.[100] A shoemaker of Sherborne in 1593 quoted men in his locality (which was also Sir Walter Ralegh's) who said that hell was poverty in this world.[101] With greater sophistication, Marlowe, another dependant of Ralegh's, made Mephistophilis say:

> Hell hath no limits, nor is circumscribed
> In one self place: for where we are is hell.[102]

Milton's Satan repeated the sentiment.

It is clear from Edward's *Gangraena* that as soon as the censorship collapsed many awkward questions began to be asked. Mrs Attaway and others declared that 'it could not stand with the goodness of God to damn his own creatures eternally'. Men taught that Christ died for all, that all men and women shall be reconciled and saved. Others denied the existence of hell and the devil, questioned the immortality of the soul.[103] The new astronomy, more freely popularized in almanacs after 1640, caused speculation about the exact location of heaven and hell.[104] John Boggis of Great Yarmouth asked in January 1646, 'Where is your God, in heaven or in earth, aloft or below, or doth he sit in the clouds, or where doth he sit with his arse?' Others said God was as much in hell as in heaven.[105] Mechanic preachers, another pamphlet declared in 1647, said that all the heaven there is, is here on earth; and that it was antichristian to deny the redemption of the whole creation: there was no original sin.[106] A number of Henry Niclaes's Familist books were reprinted in English translations in the 1640s. So were the works of Jacob Boehme, who taught that every man carries heaven and hell with him in this world, and had prophesied that the lily would bloom in the North.[107] Boehme thought God was in all believers, and preferred the spirit in them to the letter of the Bible. He influenced many of the characters who appear in this book – Erbery, Webster, Lilly, Muggleton and Pordage, for instance.[108] Richard Baxter linked Boehme and the Quakers.[109] George Fox's protector, Judge Hotham, wrote a life of Boehme, and his brother Charles whom Fox also knew, was Boehme's translator. Samuel Hering in 1653 urged

Parliament to set aside two colleges for the teaching of Boehme's doctrines.[110]

William Walwyn was said to have declared that hell was nothing but the bad conscience of evil men in this life. Could God be so cruel as to torment a man for ever 'for a little time of sinning in this world?'[111] Gerrard Winstanley denied the existence of eternal punishment, of any local heaven or hell, or devil.[112] So, it was alleged, did John Bidle, William Erbery, Peter Sterry, Thomas Tany, George Foster, John Reeve, Robert Norwood and Sir Henry Vane.[113] So did Thomas Hobbes in 1651.[114] So did Ranters and Quakers.[115] Nayler denied that God had 'concluded the condemnation of some persons before they come into the world'.[116] John Owen in 1653 was attacking those 'deists' who disbelieve in eternal punishment and talk only of God's goodness; in 1655 he was defending an eternal hell against those who believed that death meant annihilation.[117] Francis Osborne in 1656 reflected that once implicit faith in the creed authoritatively established by a state church was abandoned, 'the unbiassed rabble ... emancipated out of the fetters their former creed confined them to', would question the existence of heaven and hell no less than the Divine Right of Kings of which the Puritan clergy had taught them to be sceptical.[118]

Belief in the existence of hell was one of the strongest props of religious persecution: temporal suffering was insignificant beside an eternity of torment. Hell also seemed, if not to justify, at least to put in perspective the cruelty of the law – what Bunyan called 'those petty judgments among men, as putting in the stocks, whipping or burning in the hand'.[119] Conversely, the greater tolerance which Professor Jordan noted in the lower classes was accompanied by a greater scepticism about the eternal pains of hell. Many of the educated who were themselves doubtful about hell thought it a necessary fiction to keep the lower orders in due subordination. The Fifth Monarchists, Mr D. P. Walker points out, could speak out frankly against hell because they had no alarms about the collapse of society if the deterrent of eternal punishment was removed: they believed traditional society was going to collapse anyway.[120] Winstanley, Ranters and early Quakers had virtually emancipated themselves from the belief altogether.

Winstanley and Coppin believed that all mankind shall be saved at the last, for it does not make sense to believe in an omnipotent and beneficent God who will torment his creatures to all eternity.[121] This doctrine was one of many strands leading to that decline of belief in hell which Mr Walker has shown to have taken place in the seventeenth century. I believe however that he emphasizes insufficiently the contribution of intellectual radicals to this emergence of a more palatable morality. Winstanley carried his theological principles to a logical conclusion by insisting that the Fall was not a pre-social event, but that the corruptions of a propertied society re-enact the Fall in each individual as he grows up. God (i.e. Reason) redeems men from the only true hell, the hell they have created for each other on earth. Winstanley appears to leave open the question of the existence of any other hell: he merely says that nobody knows or can know anything about it, least of all the preachers who emphasize it so much. It exists in men because of the evil organization of society; and the image is then used to perpetuate that society by those who benefit from it. In *A Letter to the Lord Fairfax* Winstanley equated heaven with mankind[122] – an idea of which Blake might have approved.

The view that there is no God but all things come by nature, which attracted George Fox in the 1640s and was familiar to Muggleton and his circle in the early 1650s,[123] was made specific by Lawrence Clarkson, Jacob Bauthumley and other Ranters.[124] In Winstanley and Joseph Salmon it took a more pantheistic form. 'The body of Christ,' Winstanley wrote, 'is where the Father is, in the earth, purifying the earth; and his spirit is entered into the whole creation, which is the heavenly glory where the Father dwells.' Christ returned to the Father 'as a bucket of water first taken out of the sea and standing alone for a time is afterwards poured into the sea again and becomes one with the sea'.[125] Joseph Salmon thought that 'God is that pure and perfect being in whom we all are, move and live; that secret blood, breath and life, that silently courseth through the hidden veins and close arteries of the whole creation'.[126] The content of the doctrine of either Winstanley or Salmon was equally destructive of any personal God.

Religious toleration had indeed produced results which confirmed the gloomy predictions of Thomas Edwards. The Blasphemy Ordinance of May 1648, imposing the death penalty on Mortalists or those who denied the Trinity or that the Scriptures were the word of God, proved unenforceable. Walter Charleton in 1652 said that the present age in England had produced more swarms of 'atheistical monsters' than any age or nation.[127] 'This multiplicity of religions' among 'the giddy multitude,' Robert Boyle thought in the same year, 'will end in none at all'[128] – a disaster he spent much of the rest of his life trying to prevent. Denial of the existence of God or hell, Fuller and the author of *The Whole Duty of Man* agreed, resulted from the diversity and confusion of the Revolution, from liberty of the press and the proliferation of sects.[129] 'God and the magistrate lies blasphemed on every stall,' wrote Francis Osborne in 1659.[130] He had been regarded as a blasphemer himself, and by 1659 his own respect for the magistrate was probably greater than his respect for God. Stillingfleet, looking back from the safety of 1662, said that many had come to 'account it a piece of gentility to despise religion, and a piece of reason to be atheists'.[131] 'It became a common topic of discourse,' Burnet confirmed, 'to treat all mysteries in religion as the contrivances of priests to bring the world into a blind submission to them.' Priestcraft, he admitted, was a fashionable target.[132] If religion is indeed a trade, reflected the author of *The Whole Duty of Man*, ' 'twas sure thought (. . . in all ages but this) a very useful one'. This widely popularized author must have done much to restore belief in the social necessity of hell.[133]

One reaction to the text-swapping of Puritan divines, and to subversive claims to inspiration, was the scepticism of Thomas Hobbes. Anyone who was convinced by *Leviathan* would no longer find it possible to look to the Bible alone for answers to political problems, and would find religious persecution as irrational as resistance in the name of conscience. I suspect it was the influence of Hobbes rather than of religious radicals which caused M.P.s to laugh at excessive reliance on Biblical texts in 1657;[134] they would hardly have done so even ten years earlier.

Another thing that emerged from the widespread discussion of conversion, religious melancholy and despair, was some understanding of the psychology of religious experience. William Walwyn wrote in 1643 that 'many of you may, through sense of sin and of wrath due for sin, walk in a very disconsolate condition: fears and terrors may abound in you'. But these fears are unnecessary, for Christ died for all men. Six years later he had come to appreciate that 'extreme fasting and continuance in prayer (beyond what their bodies could bear)' might make men see visions, hear voices and prophesy.[135] Winstanley recognized that the devils and fearful shapes which a man thinks he sees 'arise from the anguish of his tormenting conscience within', and reflect his own passions and desires.[136]

Even more remarkable is Winstanley's analysis in *The Law of Freedom*:

> Many times when a wise understanding heart is assaulted with this doctrine of a God, a devil, a heaven and a hell, salvation and damnation after a man is dead, his spirit being not strongly grounded in the knowledge of the creation, nor in the temper of his own heart, he strives and stretches his brains to find out the depth of that doctrine and cannot attain to it; for indeed it is not knowledge but imagination: and so by poring and puzzling himself in it, loses that wisdom he had and becomes distracted and mad; and if the passion of joy predominate, then he is merry and sings and laughs, and is ripe in the expression of his words, and will speak strange things: but all by imagination. But if the passion of sorrow predominate, then he is heavy and sad, crying out he is damned, God hath forsaken him and he must go to hell when he dies, he cannot make his calling and election sure. And in that distemper many times a man doth hang, kill or drown himself: so that this divining doctrine, which you call spiritual and heavenly things, torments people always when they are weak, sickly and under any distemper.[137]

Winstanley had moved far in the three years since God spoke to him in a trance.

IV WHAT NEXT?

I have tried to suggest the many trends of thought which led men to question traditional dogmas about original sin and about hell. As the lower classes were set free to discuss what *they* were interested in, the social function of sin and hell was increasingly emphasized. But it was easier to demolish than to reconstruct – to suggest that wicked politicians had invented sin, or that sin was the product of a competitive society, than to agree on how to organize a society in which sin was no longer a plausible concept. Men could give psychological explanations for belief in hell, could expose the crude morality of the carrot and the stick, and pose logical problems about the beneficence and omnipotence of God. But again, without complete revolution, it was easier to internalize hell than to abolish the idea altogether.

In the widespread despair and atheism of the late 1640s and early 50s we can sense the impact of the revolutionary crisis on the certainties of traditional Calvinism. Accepted social categories and hierarchies were upset both in this world and the next. The protestant principle of the priesthood of all believers, carried to its extreme limit in the inner light, together with scholarly protestant textual criticism, destroyed the authority of the Bible. But what should take its place? 'All comes by nature' is not a creed for those who wish to turn the world upside down. Until men had worked out a much stronger sense of history, of evolution, atheism could only be a negative, epicurean creed in a static universe. Atheists could hardly work for a transformation of society: for the revolutionaries God was the principle of change. If they lost belief in God, what remained? This is what made Milton insist on human freedom and responsibility, in his desperate attempt to assert eternal providence and justify the ways of God to men.[138] The backwardness of history and natural science made it impossible to break through to a theory of evolution in which God would become an unnecessary hypothesis.

In the seventeenth century atheism was normally a pose, a revolt, rather than a philosophical system, whether professed by aristocratic rakes or Ranter rank and file.[139] For the latter it justified political passivity, the withdrawal under persecution which the Quakers rejected because of their stronger religious convictions. The historical insights of Marvell, Harrington, Hobbes, Clarendon, significant though they were, remained undeveloped until the Scottish school picked them up in the eighteenth century.[140] Winstanley, who among the radicals came nearest to a sense of evolution, also came nearest to building up a materialism which was neither totally static nor susceptible of only cyclical transformation. For him the abolition of private property would cause a fundamental revolution, and science and invention would continue to keep society in motion. It would have been more difficult for sin and hell to survive in Winstanley's commonwealth.

Nevertheless, there is, it seems to me, great interest in the attempts of the radicals to abolish external constraints in favour of an internal, self-imposed morality, a morality whose sanctions should be human and this-worldly. We can recognize them as being in the modern world. But not wholly. However radical the conclusions, however heretical their theology, their escape-route from theology was theological – even Winstanley's. This paradox will be one of the main themes of the following chapters.

9
Seekers and Ranters

They prate of God; believe it, fellow-creatures,
There's no such bugbear; all was made by Nature.
We know all came of nothing, and shall pass
Into the same condition once it was,
By Nature's power; and that they grossly lie
That say there's hope of immortality.
Let them but tell us what a soul is, then
We will adhere to these mad brain-sick men.

A Ranter Christmas carol, in *The Arraignment and Tryall, with a Declaration of the Ranters* (1650), p. 6.

I   BEFORE THE RANTERS

Familism, so often accused of begetting Seekers and Ranters,[1] had a continuous underground existence from Elizabeth's reign. In 1590 there was a Familist cobbler in Manchester, suspected of having more than one wife.[2] In 1623 John Etherington, a boxmaker of London, was accused of Familism for saying repentance must precede remission of sins, and that the Sabbath was of no force: every day should be a Sabbath.[3] Richard Lane, a London tailor, said in 1631 that perfection may be attained in this life.[4] Seventeen years later Samuel Rutherford accused John Saltmarsh of Familism, for denying the Sabbath among other enormities; and said that Familists teach that an academic education is no help towards understanding the Scriptures, a view which William Dell and many other radicals also held.[5] From 1646 onwards books by Henry Niclaes and many other Familist and antinomian writers were being published.[6]

Mr Thomas has pointed out interesting connections of Familism with Hermetic alchemy and with astrology in the seventeenth century, especially in John Everard (1575–c. 1650).[7] Everard was a perpetual heretic, frequently in prison under James I (who said his name should be 'Never-out'). He was fined under Laud for Familism, Antinomianism and Anabaptism. Everard translated Hermes Tris-megistus and many works of mystical theology, including 'that cursed book', *Theologia Germanica*.[8] He thought God was in man and nature, located heaven and hell in the hearts of men, and allego-rized the Bible. 'The dead letter is not the Word, but Christ is the Word,' he said. 'Sticking in the letter' has been 'the bane of all growth in religion', the cause of controversies and persecution. God's kingdom is come, and his will done, 'when Christ is come into thy flesh'. Miracles have not ceased, 'but our eyes are blinded and we cannot see them'. Everard was warmly praised by John Web-ster.[9] Everard's preaching was aimed especially at 'beggarly fellows', those who were 'mean, poor and despised by the world'; such were 'more welcome to him than so many princes and potentates'.[10] Yet he was for a long time an Anglican clergyman. His friend Roger Brear-ley, the Grindletonian, lived and died one.[11] It would be interesting to know more about the links between them.

There were indeed tendencies even among orthodox Puritans which pointed in the same direction; free grace came forth by Pres-ton and Sibbes, said Erbery.[12] 'The spiritual man,' said Richard Sibbes, 'judgeth all things, yet he himself is judged of no man . . . All earthly things he commands . . . by the spirit of Christ in him he rules over all.'[13] 'If God be a father, and we are brethren, it is a level-ling word,' declared Sibbes; though the idea that justification was never lost was 'an error crept in among some of the meaner, ignorant sort of people'.[14] John Preston taught that the elect know *by their own experience* that the Bible is true and what God is: 'as he is described in the Scriptures such have they found him to be to them-selves.'[15] Bolton declared that 'the worldling is a wrongful usurper of the riches, honour and preferments of this life; . . . the saint, whilst he continues in this world, is a rightful owner and possessor of the earth.'[16] Tobias Crisp held that 'sin is finished'. 'If you be freemen of Christ, you may esteem all the curses of the law as no more concerning you than the laws of England concern Spain.' A believer cannot commit an unpardonable sin: his conscience is Christ. 'To be called a libertine is the most glorious title under heaven.'[17]

Allegorical writing of this sort was harmless enough in time of social peace, though the ecclesiastical authorities were never happy about it. It became dangerous in the revolutionary atmosphere of the 1640s when some of the lower classes began to take it literally. The doctrines were again harmless when taught by Thomas Traherne or quietist post-restoration Quakers. But in between, as the Revolution seemed to open up infinite possibilities, the glowing embers flashed flame.

In December 1643 Robert Baillie observed that the Independent party was growing, 'but the Anabaptists more, and the Antinomians most.' He noted that they were especially strong in the Army.[18] In Brownist congregations, he reported with horror, 'to the meanest servant they give power to admonish, reprove, rebuke and to separate from the whole church.' If the majority in a congregation should excommunicate their pastor, no synod or other external authority could do anything about it. Giving such a power of excommunication to every uncontrolled congregation, he observed ominously, 'driveth to universal grace'.[19] From this time onwards we get plentiful evidence of the emergence of a whole number of opinions which were later to be associated with the Ranters.

Thomas Edwards reported many sectaries who said Christ died for all, and a bricklayer of Hackney who said that Christ was not God, or alternatively that he himself was as much God as Christ was. A Rochester man who associated with Baptists said that Jesus Christ was a bastard; so did Jane Stratton of Southwark. Edwards's error number eight was 'right reason is the rule of faith ... We are to believe the Scriptures and the doctrines of the Trinity, incarnation, resurrection, so far as we see them agreeable to reason, and no further.' 'God loves his children as well sinning as praying.' Some sectaries hold they cannot sin, but if they sin, Christ sins in them.[20] In

1647 John Trapp reported a 'female Antinomian, who when her mistress charged her for stealing her linens' replied, 'It was not I, but sin that dwelleth in me.'[21] 'Every creature in the first estate of creation was God' (it is Edwards reporting again), 'and every creature is God, every creature that hath life and breath being an efflux from God, and shall return into God again, be swallowed up in him as a drop is in the ocean.' Further errors twenty-five and twenty-six in 1646 were 'that God is in our flesh as much as in Christ's flesh', and 'that all shall be saved at last'. Mrs Attaway and William Jenny held themselves as free from sin as Christ was when he was in the flesh, though Edwards regarded them as living in adultery. They believed in the mortality of the soul, and that there was no hell but what was in the conscience. A London lady declared that murder, adultery, theft, were no sins.[22] Sectaries believe that if a man were strongly moved to sin, after praying repeatedly, then he should do it, said a pamphlet of 1648 disapprovingly.[23]

So there was a breakdown of confidence in established forms of religion, pretty widespread, but conspicuously prevalent in London and the Army, especially among the young. Historians have discovered that among members of the Long Parliament and of the royal civil service the average age of those who adhered to the King in the civil war was lower than that of those who adhered to Parliament.[24] For this there were special reasons. In the 1630s, when Parliament never met, up-and-coming young gentlemen had to look to the court for a career. It was among those whose opinions and attitudes had been formed by the 1620s that steady adherents of Parliament were found. But it was very different among the population at large, at least in London and the Home Counties. The radicals, not unexpectedly, came from the younger generation of those who had no aspirations to an official career.

Thomas Edwards again and again emphasizes that it was 'many young youths and wenches' who 'all of them preach universal redemption'.[25] Baxter said that 'the remnant of the old separatists and Anabaptists in London' was small and inconsiderable in the years 1640–42; but 'they were enough to stir up the younger and unexperienced sort of religious people' and apprentices. William Dell in 1646 found that the young, 'as being most free from the forms of the former age, and from the doctrines and traditions of men', were most open to conviction.[26] John Crook as a London apprentice met with a company of young men to pray and talk about the things of God, much as John Lilburne had done earlier.[27] Anthony Pearson tells us that apprentices and young people joined the Ranters; Baxter that Quakers emptied the churches of Anabaptists and separatists, of 'the young, unsettled'.[28] We think of refusal of 'hat honour' and the use of 'thou' by Quakers as gestures of social protest, and so they were. But they also marked a refusal of deference from the young to the old, from sons to fathers. No one who has read Thomas Ellwood's vivid account of his struggle with his father[29] can doubt that the fiercest and most anguished battles were those waged within the home, between the generations. This aspect of the rise of Quakerism in gentry families perhaps deserves further consideration.

The soldiers who made the demonstration in Walton-on-Thames parish church quoted above were presumably young men. They abolished (i) the Sabbath as unnecessary, Jewish and merely ceremonial; (ii) tithes as Jewish and ceremonial, a great burden to the saints of God and a discouragement of industry and tillage; (iii) ministers as antichristian and of no longer use now Christ himself descends into the hearts of his saints; (iv) magistrates as useless now that Christ himself is in purity of spirit come amongst us and hath erected the kingdom of saints upon the earth; (v) the Bible, as beggarly rudiments, milk for babes; for now Christ is in glory amongst us and imparts a fuller measure of his spirit to his saints than the Bible can afford.[30] Robert Abbot in 1651 struck a modern note when he denounced 'many monstrous young men and women, so disorderly in their courses and so disguised in their attires that all ages . . . cannot give the like precedents. How do young women rejoice in baring their nakedness!'[31] (Nakedness is a relative concept: one critic of the Baptists expressed pious horror when, at a baptism, 'the nakedness of one of the women . . . was seen above her knees'. 'For this,' he added with relish, 'there were many witnesses.'[32])

The preachers of free grace – Saltmarsh, Erbery, Dell and others – aimed to liberate men and women from the formalism, the legal calculations of covenant theologians, and from the despair to which predestinarian theology reduced many who doubted their salvation. In the hands of men and women simpler and less theologically sophisticated, especially in this time of revolutionary crisis, their teachings were easily pushed over into Antinomianism, a sense of liberation from all bonds and restraints of law and morality. When Thomas Collier told the Army at the end of September 1647 that 'God as truly manifests himself in the flesh of all his [saints] as he did in Christ',[33] he must have known that many of the rank and file listening to him would believe themselves to be saints.

Given then this breakdown of confidence on the one hand, and the prevalent millenarian enthusiasm on the other, it is hardly surprising that men and women, faced with an unprecedented freedom of choice, passed rapidly from sect to sect, trying all things, finding all of them wanting. Again and again in spiritual autobiographies of the time we read of men who passed through Presbyterianism, Independency and Anabaptistry before ending as Seekers (Webster and Clement Writer[34]), as Ranters (Salmon, Coppin, Coppe, Clarkson and Francis Freeman[35]) or as Quakers (Deusbury, Howgill and Thomas Taylor[36]). Controversies over church government or over baptism – infant, adult, self-, by dipping or not at all – split congregations, produced endless conscientious scruples, endless bickerings. All the leading protagonists seemed equally certain, all appeared to have backing from Biblical texts or from the authority of the spirit within. Many concluded by questioning the value of all ordinances, of all outward forms, of all churches even.[37] Since the end of the world was probably near anyway, a resigned withdrawal from sectarian controversy was one solution, a rejection of all sects, of all organized worship. Such men were called Seekers – Walwyn, though he rejected the label,[38] Roger Williams,[39] John Saltmarsh, John Milton, possibly Oliver Cromwell himself. Edwards called Lawrence Clarkson a Seeker.[40] Many of these men had connections with the radicals, and were bitterly disappointed with the failure of the Army to bring about a democratic society in and after 1647. Whatever their disillusionment, the generation of the 1640s was carried along by millenarian enthusiasm. But what of their successors, in the flat and unexciting world of the 1650s? 'When people saw diversity of sects in any place,' wrote Richard Baxter, 'it greatly hindered their conversion.' Many 'would be of no religion at all'.[41]

II   WILLIAM ERBERY

William Erbery was described in 1646 as 'the champion of the Seekers'.[42] He had been ejected from his living in Cardiff in 1638 for refusing to read the Book of Sports. He was a convinced supporter of Parliament during the civil war, a chaplain in the New Model Army. Charles I, Erbery thought, had preferred 'none but the rich, his friends and favourites, a company of fools and flatterers, though the oppressed peeled nation was ready to perish'.[43] As an Army chaplain Erbery led other ranks in criticism of Presbyterian ministers, tithes and persecution. He quoted Boehme with approval.[44] Erbery preached universal redemption, Edwards tells us, and denied the divinity of Christ, as well as declaring that any layman may preach.[45] He proclaimed that 'the fullness of the Godhead shall be manifested in the flesh of the saints', as in Christ's flesh. Christ 'is still suffering till he shall rise in us'. Men therefore should 'sit still, in submission and silence, waiting for the Lord to come and reveal himself to them'. 'And at last, yea within a little, we shall be led forth out of this confusion and Babylon, where we yet are, not clearly knowing truth nor error, day nor night: but in the evening there shall be light.' His Presbyterian enemies accused him of claiming that 'the saints have a more glorious power than Christ . . . and do greater works than ever Christ did'. Erbery more modestly saw himself 'bewildernessed as a wayfaring man, seeing no way of man on earth, nor beaten path to lead him. Let him look upward and within at once, and a highway, the way is found in Christ in us, God in our flesh'. The saints shall judge the world:[46] God appearing in them shall punish kings of the earth upon the earth. And these saints were of the lower classes. 'God comes reigning and riding on an ass, that is revealing himself in majesty and glory in the basest of men.' Kings, lords and dukes 'all proceeded from a carnal pedigree'.[47]

'It was, as we conceived, high time to call Mr Erbery to an account,' reported the Presbyterian ministers sent down to Oxford to investigate the Army. Erbery, they said, was a Socinian, preaching damnable doctrine and blasphemous errors. He stirred up 'the multitude of soldiers' against the Presbyterian ministers. 'All well-grounded policy for the affairs of this life is grounded upon religion', and 'the Christian religion cannot be upheld without a Christian ministry'.[48]

In January 1648 Erbery called on the Army to destroy the power of the King and rectify popular grievances. He objected to the officers' version of the Agreement of the People because it established a state church and did not extend toleration to Jews, though he approved of most of it.[49] The Army, Erbery thought, had a double right to act in politics. King and Parliament 'were the two powers who kept the people of the Lord and the people of the land from their expected and promised freedoms'.[50] The Army 'had the call of the kingdom, petitioning by several counties and the common cry of all the oppressed in the land'. It acted 'in the immediate power of God . . . for all saints, yea for all men also'. 'God in the saints shall appear as the saviour of all men.' 'No oppressor shall pass through them any more.' 'The day of God has begun, though the saints have been and are still in confusion.' 'For a few days we cannot bear with the want of kings and rulers, but after many days' men will no longer miss them. The saints drew back when they should have gone on. The Army was at its best when it acted. 'But as for all their public speakings, their Declarations, Protestations, Remonstrances, 'tis not worth a rush.'

Erbery still waited to see 'God in the army of saints, wasting all oppressing powers in the land . . . God will do it in his time, . . . not only destroy Antichrist within . . . but all worldly oppressors by the mouth of the sword.'[51] In July 1652 Erbery wrote urging Oliver Cromwell to relieve the poor, as well as attacking tithes and lawyers' fees.[52] He advocated steeper taxation of 'rich citizens, racking landlords . . . and mighty moneyed men', to form 'a treasury for the poor'. 'The great design that God hath to do this day is to undo . . . the mighty ones of the earth, . . . that the outward and inward man may have deliverance at last.'[53] 'How many men are made poor by making a few ministers rich?' 'O that the poor might have their arrears out of the unreasonable gain of the gospel priests', who 'take up the fifth or fourth part of men's lands and labours'. The burden of tithes now in England is worse than under popery or in popish countries. There were no true ministers any longer. 'God in the last days will first appear . . . not in ministers at all but in the magistrate, both civil and martial.'[54]

John Saltmarsh had spoken of 'the apostasy of the churches'.[55] In Erbery's thinking this apostasy had prevailed for 'many hundreds of years'. 'When kingdoms came to be Christian, then kingdoms began to be churches; yea, churches came to be kingdoms, and national churches began. Then also Antichrist came to be great.' Popery, prelacy, presbytery had been the three Beasts; but the state church of the Commonwealth was no better. It was the last Beast or church-state. In 'our land in these last days the mystery of iniquity hath been most manifest'. In the depth of his disillusion Erbery declared that 'the mystery of Antichrist . . . is manifested in every saint, in every particular church'. 'The greatest work that God hath to do with you this day, is to make you see you are dead.'[56] 'God is going out and departing from all the preaching of men, that men may give themselves wholly to public acts of love to one another, and to all mankind; therefore all religious forms shall fall, that the power of righteousness may rise and appear in all.'[57]

'To be solitary and walk alone,' Erbery concluded, 'is a wilderness condition, which with God is the most comfortable state . . . In that apostasy we now are, we cannot company with men, no not with saints, in spiritual worship but we shall commit spiritual whoredom with them.'[58] In England 'the wickedness of the people of God will first appear . . . to all the world'. For having been 'set in power', 'every man may see the shame' if they 'prove oppressors, as former powers have been'. In power the 'seeming saints' must inevitably be corrupted. In civil government they were far superior to their predecessors. 'But as for spiritual graces, how soon have they withered in the wisest? Good men in Parliament, when come to power how weak were they? When was the Self-Denying Ordinance kept?' 'Godly men in the old and new modelled Army . . . their tears are all dried up, as withered grass . . . The flower is a finer thing than common grass, but falls sooner.' 'God has a people to call in their room. The people of God turn wicked men, that wicked men may turn to be the people of God.' 'The lords and nobles of old could do better with it [power], because gentlemen born; but when so much money comes into the hands of poor saints, oh how they hold it and hug it and hunger after it, as dogs do after dry bones!' 'In saints by calling shall the apostasy and falling away be first revealed to the full.'[59]

But Erbery managed to avoid self-righteousness. 'How often did my desire to be rich make me in fear to be poor,' he admitted; until he finally gave up his public stipend from tithes.[60] 'The life of the people of God, and mine also, is so unlike Christ that I have often wished . . . to go away from myself and from my people.' But 'they are mine and I am theirs'. By 1654 he had decided that, as against the Fifth Monarchists, the people of God should not meddle at all with state matters. Christ's kingdom is not of this world. 'You say that the worst of men speak well of the present government; and is it not well? and a fair way for peace and love?'[61] 'The people of God are in present power (as 'twas never before).' God 'hath stained the pride of all glory, and the glory of all flesh, tumbling the earth upside down and tossing to and fro the government thereof, that nothing but confusion hath appeared. What certainty then can be expected in such changes? What order in confusion? Yea, what truth, when God is making man a lie?'[62]

This attitude of resignation after the failure of the Barebones Parliament in December 1653 made John Webster feel he had to defend Erbery against the charge of falling off and compliance. Erbery knew, Webster said, 'that it was the wisdom as well as the obedience of the saints to make their captivity as comfortable as they could; but to shake off the yoke before the season came was to rebel against the Lord'. Erbery seems in fact to have been prepared to accept Cromwell as king.[63] Erbery, said Webster, 'was rather a presser forward than an apostate',[64] but he seems to have abandoned hope of a political solution in his lifetime. 'It may be other generations may see the glory talked to be in the last times, but we are cut off for our parts;

our children may possess it, but for our parts we have no hopes to enjoy it, or in this life to be raised out of our graves.' The English churches 'do live in Babylon. And there not they only, but all the scattered saints this day do dwell, and I also with them waiting for deliverance.'[65]

Erbery died in 1654, almost his last published words being 'I have been ever entire to the interest of this commonwealth.'[66] His epitaph was not unfittingly written by one of his friends:

> Some are dead that seem alive,
> But Erbery's worth shall still survive.[67]

III   THE RANTER MILIEU

Erbery was often accused of being 'a loose person or a Ranter', of having a ranting spirit;[68] he was also alleged – like the Ranters – to be devious, covering himself by double meanings.[69] Erbery denied the accusation of Ranterism, but not always wholeheartedly. He spoke of 'the holiness and righteousness in truth flowing from the power of God in us, which by the world hath been nicknamed with Puritanism, and in some now Ranting', though he refused to justify 'those profane people called Ranters', who blasphemed, cursed, whored, openly rejoicing in their wickedness.[70] He admitted that he 'was commonly judged by good men as one of those owning this principle and practising their ways', that 'I cry up the profane as most holy, and the saints of God to be the only Ranters; that . . . I hold fellowship with divers prodigiously profane and scandalous, . . . blasphemously counterfeiting the sacraments of the Lord's supper.' He denied saying that the Ranters were the best saints: his point had been that the self-styled saints were worse than Ranters, lusting after the wisdom, power, glory and honour of this present world. At least Ranters were honest about it. 'These, it may be, lie with a woman once a month, but those men, having their eyes full of adultery, . . . do lie with twenty women between Paul's and Westminster.'[71] This perhaps throws some light on Erbery's odd remark, quoted above, that 'wicked men may turn to be the people of God'.[72]

> 'Tis true, uncasing formal righteousness
> Which decks itself in strictest letter-dress,
> Thou didst some ways prefer the open sinner,
> Opposing coarse offenders to the finer.

So John Webster, noting that by 'some weaker spirits' Erbery's doctrine concerning 'the restitution of all things, the liberty of the creation, ... the saints' oneness in Christ with God' was misunderstood or led to practices which Erbery regretted. We can I think read a good deal between these defensive lines. Even in print Erbery was often very rude and coarsely jocular about what others might regard as sacred subjects. He thought that holy communion should be a full meal, with lots of drink. 'Why do they not say their prayers before a pipe of tobacco? a good creature.'[73]

It is clear that Erbery was very much at home in the world of taverns and tobacco in which many of the sects used to meet. 'Religion is now become the common discourse and table-talk in every tavern and ale-house,' men were complaining as early as 1641.[74] 'Ale-houses generally are ... the meeting places of malignants and sectaries,' a preacher told the House of Commons in July 1646.[75] Levellers used to meet in taverns: Nicholas Culpeper strove 'to make himself famous in taverns and ale-houses'; Baptist messengers met in inns, and Baptist services were the occasion of pipe-smoking.[76] 'Eat of Christ, therefore, the tree of life, at supper, and drink his blood, and make you merry,' wrote John Eachard, a Suffolk parson who spoke up for the common soldiers in 1645.[77] Winstanley agreed that holy communion was not a sacrament but eating and drinking in any house, 'in love and sweet communion with one another'.[78] Thomas Edwards reported 'an antinomian preacher in London', who 'on a fast day said it was better for Christians to be drinking in an ale-house, or to be in a whore-house, than to be keeping fasts legally'. Another sectary argued that drunkenness was no sin, but 'a help to see Christ the better by'. He was a staunch Parliamentarian, a sequestrator in Somerset.[79]

The analogy of modern drug-taking should enable us to understand that – in addition to the element of communal love-feast in such gatherings – the use of tobacco and alcohol was intended to heighten spiritual vision. Some years later the millenarian John Mason was excessively addicted to smoking, and 'generally while he smoked he was in a kind of ecstasy'.[80] (Tobacco was still a novel and rather naughty stimulant, though by 1640 it had risen to first place among London's imports.[81]) In New England Captain Underhill told Governor Winthrop 'the Spirit had sent into him the witness of free grace, while he was in the moderate enjoyment of the creature called tobacco'.[82] Was it in a tavern, or at a religious meeting, that Captain Freeman declared that he saw God in the table-board and in the candlestick?[83] Or that the trooper with an interest in comparative religion asserted, 'If I should worship the sun or the moon, or that pewter pot on the table, nobody has anything to do with it'?[84] When some Ranters wanted to get their own back on the prophets Reeve and Muggleton, who had damned them to all eternity, the inducement they offered 'three of the most desperate, atheistical' of their number 'to curse them and the Lord Jesus Christ their God' was the promise of 'a good dinner of pork'.[85] William Dell in 1653 mocked a phrase used by Sidrach Sympson, 'arts and tongues are the cups in which God drinks to us' as 'savouring of the Ranters' religion; as if God was the familiar companion of the clergy, and sometimes drank to them in a cup of Hebrew, sometimes in a cup of Greek . . .'[86]

At one Ranter meeting of which we have a (hostile) report, the mixed company met at a tavern, sang blasphemous songs to the well-known tunes of metrical psalms and partook of a communal feast. One of them tore off a piece of beef, saying 'This is the flesh of Christ, take and eat.' Another threw a cup of ale into the chimney corner, saying 'There is the blood of Christ.'[87] Clarkson called a tavern the house of God; sack was divinity.[88] Even a Puritan enemy expresses what is almost a grudging admiration for the high spirits of the Ranters' dionysiac orgies: 'they are the merriest of all devils for extempore lascivious songs, . . . for healths, music, downright bawdry and dancing'.[89] One of the accusations against Captain Francis Freeman was that he sang bawdy songs.[90]

Bunyan said the ideas of the Quakers were not much better than those of Ranters, 'only the Ranters had made them threadbare at an ale-house'.[91] Ranters met at a victualling house kept by one of their number in the Minories, Muggleton tells us; they also met at the David and Harp in Moor Lane, in the parish of St Giles, Cripplegate, kept by the husband of Mary Middleton, one of Lawrence Clarkson's mistresses.[92] Ranters 'had some kind of meetings', Fox says, 'but they took tobacco and drank ale in their meetings, and were grown light and loose'. They 'sung and whistled and danced'.[93] Bunyan thought Ranters talked too much:[94] this is indeed one contemporary meaning of the verb 'to rant'. Bunyan's comment may have its bearing on Quaker silence. Yet Fox understood the Ranters' point. When 'a forward, bold lad' offered him a pipe, saying, 'Come, all is ours', Fox (who was no smoker) 'took his pipe and put it to my mouth, and gave it to him again to stop him, lest his rude tongue should say I had not unity with the creation.'[95] 'My spirit dwells with God,' said Abiezer Coppe, 'sups with him, in him, feeds on him, with him, in him. My humanity shall dwell with, sup with, eat with humanity; and why not (for a need) with publicans and harlots?'[96]

'Unity with the creation', tobacco 'a good creature', parodying holy communion: we should never fail to look for symbolism in what appear the extravagant gestures of seventeenth-century radicals. Ranter advocacy of blasphemy, it has been well said, was a symbolic expression of freedom from moral restraints.[97] Abiezer Coppe was alleged on one occasion to have sworn for an hour on end in the pulpit: 'a pox of God take all your prayers'.[98] An obsessive desire to swear had possessed him in early life, but he resisted it for twenty-seven years. Then he made up for lost time. He would rather, he declared, 'hear a mighty angel (in man) swearing a full-mouthed oath' than hear an orthodox minister preach. 'One hint more: there's swearing ignorantly, i'th dark, and there's swearing i'th light, gloriously.'[99] Even Joseph Salmon, from the mystical and quietist wing of the Ranters, was also in the habit of using 'many desperate oaths'.[100]

Great tensions must lie behind this attitude to swearing, whether in the indulgence of Coppe after 1646, or in his earlier repression of the desire to swear, which the Quakers followed. Bunyan reveals similar tensions in *Grace Abounding*. Swearing was an act of defiance, both of God and of middle-class society, of the Puritan ethic. 'Many think to swear is gentleman-like,' as Bunyan put it.[101] Courtiers and members of the upper class could get away with swearing: royalists in the civil war were known to their opponents as 'Dammees'.[102] For the lower classes swearing was expensive: we recall the 'debauched seaman' who after being fined at the rate of 6d. for an oath put 2s. 6d. on the table and had his money's worth.[103] Lower-class use of oaths was a proclamation of their equality with the greatest, just as Puritan opposition to vain swearing was a criticism of aristocratic and plebeian irreligion.[104] But lower-class and Ranter swearing was also a revolt against the imposition of Puritan middle-class standards, interfering with the simple pleasures of the poor for ideological reasons. Bibliolatry led to a phobia about swearing; rejection of the Bible made it possible again, and with it a release of the repressions which gave the Puritan middle class their moral energy.

IV   RANTERS

Mr A. L. Morton, who knows more about the Ranters than anyone else, suggests that migratory craftsmen, freed by the temporary breakdown of the settlement system during the Revolution, men who were 'unattached and prepared to break with tradition', may have furnished much support for the Ranters.[105] We should bear in mind the whole mobile itinerant population, evicted cottagers, whether peasants or craftsmen, slowly gravitating to the big cities and there finding themselves outsiders, sometimes forming themselves into religious groups which rapidly became more and more radical. It is very difficult to define what 'the Ranters' believed, as opposed to individuals who are called Ranters. The same is true to a lesser extent of Levellers or early Quakers; but the Levellers did issue programmatic statements, and the pamphlets of Fox and Nayler can be accepted as authoritative for the Quakers. There is no recognized leader or theoretician of the Ranters, and it is extremely doubtful whether there ever was a Ranter organization. As so often in the history of radical movements, the name came into existence as a term of abuse.

There are very wide discrepancies between the theology of men like Salmon and Bauthumley, on the one hand, and the licentious practices of which rank-and-file Ranters were accused, though the ideas of Lawrence Clarkson perhaps help to bridge the gap. The same is also true of the early Quakers, whom contemporaries long tended to lump together with Ranters. There are two possible explanations for this last fact, and it is difficult to know which should weigh more heavily with us. On the one hand there is the unreasoning hostility of conservative critics, who believed that Ranter and Quaker ideas must lead to licentiousness and therefore assumed that they did; on the other hand there is the likelihood that many early rank-and-file Quakers had in fact not entirely shaken themselves free from Ranter ideas and practices.

Nevertheless, for a brief period between 1649 and 1651 there was a group which contemporaries called Ranters, about which they felt able to make generalizations. (I exclude eccentric individuals like John Robins and Thomas Tany, who were sometimes called Ranters: it is very difficult to extract any coherent principles from their expressed views.[106]) We hear of Ranters, as of Fifth Monarchists, after the execution of Charles I and the defeat of the Levellers: both these events no doubt relate to the origin of the two groups. 'All the world now is in the Ranting humour,' it was said in 1651.[107] Let us look at some first-hand witnesses. Ranters boast much of freedom, said a divine preaching before the Society of Astrologers in 1650, and say that God is not only in things divine but also in things diabolical. He equated them with the Family of Love.[108] A Southwark physician in 1652 defended them against time-serving saints because of their favourable attitude towards the poor.[109] John Reeve ascribed to Ranters 'a pretended universal love to the whole creation'. For a time he was attracted by their 'imagination of the eternal salvation of all mankind, though they lived and died under the power of all manner of unrighteousness'.[110]

Bunyan in the early fifties found some Ranter books held 'highly in esteem by several old professors'. One of his intimate companions 'turned a most devilish Ranter, and gave himself up to all manner of filthiness'. He denied the existence of God or angels, and laughed at exhortations to sobriety. Other persons, formerly strict in religion, were swept away by Ranters: they would condemn Bunyan as legal and dark, 'pretending that they only had attained to perfection that could do what they would and not sin' – a doctrine which Bunyan found very seductive, 'I being but a young man'. He was especially tempted to believe there was no judgment or resurrection, and therefore that sin was no such grievous thing – the conclusion that 'atheists and Ranters do use to help themselves withal', turning the grace of God into wantonness. Bunyan's answer to Ranters became the orthodox one: they lacked a conviction of sin.[111] Ranters, said Samuel Fisher in his Baptist period, despise the ordinances of Christ and 'run beyond the bounds of modesty and all good manners'. 'The rabble of the ruder sort of Ranters . . . are willingly ignorant, because of the tediousness of that thought to them, that there is any more coming of Christ at all.' Some deny the existence of Christ: others claim to be Christ or God.[112] George Fox in 1649 met Ranters who said they were God.[113] There is no Creator God but everything comes by nature, they were said to believe.[114]

Ephraim Pagitt thought 'the Ranter is more open and less sour' than a Quaker.[115] Ranters set up the light of nature under the name of Christ in man, declared Richard Baxter. With the spiritual pride of ungrounded novices in religion, they believed that God regards not the actions of the outward man, but of the heart: that to the pure all things are pure – which they took as licensing hideous blasphemy and continuous whoredom. Fortunately the horrid villainies of this sect speedily extinguished it, and reflected discredit on all other sects.[116] John Holland, a hostile but not obviously unfair witness, says Ranters call God Reason (as Gerrard Winstanley had done). One of them said that if there was any God at all, he himself was one. God is in everyone and every living thing, said Jacob Bauthumley: 'man and beast, fish and fowl, and every green thing, from the highest cedar to the ivy on the wall'. 'He does not exist outside the creatures.'[117] God is in 'this dog, this tobacco pipe, he is me and I am him';[118] he is in 'dog, cat, chair, stool'.[119]

The only name the Ranters appeared to accept for themselves collectively was 'My one flesh'. This and their salutation of 'fellow creature' were intended to emphasize unity, with mankind and with the whole creation. ('Fellow creature' was a phrase of Winstanley's.[120]) Abiezer Coppe and Joseph Salmon, like Winstanley, had a vision of this unity of all created things.[121] Their materialistic pantheism is a denial of the dualism which separates God aloft in heaven from sinful men on earth; which offers pie in the sky only when you die. God is not a Great Taskmaster: he is a member of the community of my one flesh, one matter. The world is not a vale of tears to be endured, expecting our reward hereafter. Ranters insisted that matter is good, because we live here and now.

To Ranters as to Winstanley, Christ's coming meant 'his coming into men by his spirit'. When he has so come into men's hearts, they no longer need 'such lower helps from outward administrations' as preaching, communion, study of the Bible, etc.[122] (That was written by Samuel Fisher in his Baptist period: one wonders how far he would have disagreed when he became a Quaker.) For Ranters Christ in us is far more important than the historical Christ who died at Jerusalem, and 'all the commandments of God, both in the Old and New Testaments, are the fruits of the curse'. Since all men are now freed of the curse, they are also free from the commandments; our will is God's will.[123] There are many stories of Ranters lighting a candle to look for their sins in broad daylight; 'but there were none,' said the Ranter in one such story, 'and that which they thought so great, unto him was so small that he could not see it.'[124]

The existence of evil was a subject to which Ranters paid a good deal of attention: simple believers found their arguments difficult to answer.[125] If God is omnipotent, some Ranters asked, why does he permit evil? Others denied that there was any such thing as sin; if there was, it must be part of God's plan.[126] The day of judgment is either 'an invented thing', 'a bugbear to keep men in awe', or it had begun already. There was no life after death: 'even as a stream from the ocean was distinct in itself while it was a stream, but when returned to the ocean was therein swallowed and became one with the ocean: so the spirit of man whilst in the body was distinct from

God, but when death came it returned to God, and so became one with God, yea God itself.' That was Lawrence Clarkson, who added that he would 'know nothing after this my being was dissolved'.[127] God has become a synonym for the natural world. To see God in the book of the creatures was a 'familistical ranting tenet' which Anna Trapnel was glad she had avoided in her despair in 1652–3.[128]

An extreme form of this doctrine attributed to Ranters was that 'those are most perfect . . . which do commit the greatest sins with least remorse'.[129] Clarkson came very near this, writing, 'till I acted that so-called sin I could not predominate over sin'. But now 'whatsoever I act is . . . in relation to . . . that Eternity in me . . . So long as the act was in God . . . it was as holy as God'. This, he insisted, covers 'those acts by thee called swearing, drunkenness, adultery and theft, etc.'.[130]

The Blasphemy Act of 9 August 1650 was aimed especially against the Ranters' denial of 'the necessity of civil and moral righteousness among men', which tended 'to the dissolution of all human society'. It denounced anyone who maintained him- or herself to be God, or equal with God; or that acts of adultery, drunkenness, swearing, theft, etc. were not in themselves shameful, wicked and sinful, or that there is no such thing as sin 'but as a man or woman judgeth thereof'. The penalty was six months' imprisonment for the first offence, banishment for the second, the death of a felon if the offender refused to depart or returned. Judges operating this Act seem to have stretched it very much in order to apply it only to those who genuinely taught that there was no difference between right and wrong. They refused to allow J.P.s, clergy and juries to extend it to the sincere if unorthodox religious opinions of a Ranter (or near-Ranter) like Richard Coppin[131] or a Quaker like William Deusbury.[132]

'Blasphemers' were less well treated in the Army.[133] Joseph Salmon and Lawrence Clarkson both left the Army in 1649, Jacob Bauthumley in March 1650.[134] Worst treatment of all seems to have been meted out by the English authorities in Scotland, where Oliver Cromwell told a woman Ranter, wife of a lieutenant, that 'she was so vile a creature as he thought her unworthy to live'.[135] A year earlier Lieutenant William Jackson was accused, among other things, of believing God to be the author of sin, and that he (Jackson) was as perfect then as he ever should be.[136] In 1656, in Dumfriesshire, 'Alexander Agnew, commonly called "Jock of Broad Scotland", was condemned to be hanged for denying that Christ was God, that the Holy Ghost existed, that a man has a soul or there is a heaven or a hell, or that the Scriptures are the word of God. He did not believe that he was a sinner or that prayer had any efficacy. He had nothing to do with God, Jock said; God was very greedy. 'He never received anything from God but from nature.' He was accused of broadcasting these views 'to the entangling, deluding and seducing of the common people'.[137] He seems to have been an early martyr of popular rationalism.

But the Ranters were not by nature martyrs. Like Lollards and Familists before them, they usually recanted when called upon to do so, though sometimes, like Coppe, very deviously.[138] Indeed, if there is no immortality, the satisfactions of martyrdom are less obvious: resistance to the death would call for a deeper and more consistently worked out ideology than most Ranters had. The revolutionary movement, moreover, was in decline before the Ranters appeared on the scene. Marian martyrs chose death where their Lollard predecessors would have recanted, because (among other things) the advances of Edward VI's reign had given a tremendous boost to their morale. But from the 1650s, apart from a courageous and already committed man like John Bidle the Socinian,[139] only those who passionately believed that Christ's kingdom was not of this world had the courage to resist unto death. One of the most important reasons for the survival of the Quakers was their stoutness under persecution on which even their enemies commented.[140]

V ABIEZER COPPE

Coppe was an Oxford undergraduate from Warwick. After acting as preacher to an Army garrison, he became leader of the drinking, smoking, swearing Ranters in 1649, at the age of thirty. In that year he published *Some Sweet Sips of some Spirituall Wine*, followed by his two *Fiery Flying Rolls*, a powerful piece of writing, in a prose style unlike anything else in the seventeenth century.

Coppe's message was delivered from 'my most excellent majesty and eternal glory (in me) ... who am universal love, and whose service is perfect freedom and pure libertinism'. It was that sin and transgression is finished and ended. God, 'that mighty Leveller', would 'overturn, overturn, overturn'. After bishops, kings and lords, it was the turn of the 'surviving great ones' to succumb to the Levellers. 'Honour, nobility, gentility, property, superfluity, etc.' had been 'the father of hellish, horrid pride, ... yea the cause of all the blood that hath ever been shed, from the blood of the righteous Abel to the blood of the last Levellers that were shot to death'. The Levellers died martyrs for their God and their country: their blood cries for vengeance. Now 'the neck of horrid pride' must be chopped off at one blow, that 'parity, equality, community' might establish 'universal love, universal peace, and perfect freedom'. 'The very shadow of levelling, sword levelling, man levelling, frighted you (and who ... can blame you, because it shook your kingdom?) but now the substantiality of levelling is coming.'

Coppe disavowed both 'sword-levelling' and 'digging-levelling'.[141] The betrayal of the Levellers had produced a great disillusion in him. But his pacifism was different from that which Quakers were later to profess. 'Not by sword; we (holily) scorn to fight for anything; we had as lief be dead drunk every day of the week, and lie with whores i'th market place; and account them as good actions as taking the poor abused enslaved ploughman's money from him ... for killing of men.' The doleful cries of poor prisoners, ' "Bread, bread, bread for the Lord's sake" pierce mine ears and heart, I can no longer forbear.' The rulers must 'bow before these poor, nasty, lousy, ragged wretches' and set them free. 'Hide not thyself from thine own flesh, from a cripple, a rogue, a beggar, ... a whoremonger, a thief, etc., he's thine own flesh.'[142]

It is worth quoting at some length, to give an idea of Coppe's highly personal style:

Thou hast many bags of money, and behold I (the Lord) come as a thief in the night, with my sword drawn in my hand, and like a thief as I am – I say deliver your purse, deliver sirrah! deliver or I'll cut thy throat.

I say (once more) deliver, deliver my money . . . to rogues, thieves, whores and cutpurses, who are flesh of thy flesh, and every whit as good as thyself in mine eye, who are ready to starve in plaguy gaols and nasty dungeons . . .

The plague of God is in your purses, barns, houses, horses, murrain will take your hogs (O ye fat swine of the earth) who shall shortly go to the knife and be hung up in the roof, except - - - -

Did you not see my hand, this last year, stretched out?

You did not see.

My hand is stretched out still - - - -

Your gold and silver, though you can't see it, is cankered . . .

The rust of your silver, I say, shall eat your flesh as it were fire . . .

Have ALL THINGS common, or else the plague of God will rot and consume all that you have.[143]

Coppe described how in the open streets he demonstrated against coaches and hundreds of men and women of greater rank, 'gnashing with my teeth at some of them, . . . falling down flat upon the ground before rogues, beggars, cripples'. 'Howl, howl, ye nobles, howl honourable, howl ye rich men for the miseries that are coming upon you . . . We'll eat our bread together in singleness of heart, we'll break bread from house to house.' 'The true communion amongst men is to have all things common and to call nothing one hath one's own.'[144]

In 1650 the *Fiery Flying Rolls* were condemned by Parliament to be publicly burnt, as containing 'many horrid blasphemies'. 'The two Acts of 10 May and 9 August 1650,' Coppe tells us, 'were put out because of me.' Coppe himself was examined by Parliament's Committee of Examinations, and committed to Newgate. In January he issued a partial recantation, and in May a fuller one. Even this is pretty qualified. Coppe complained that many errors have been wrongly attributed to him. He asserted the existence of sin, but took care to emphasize that there were 'little thieves and great thieves . . . little murderers and great murderers. All are sinners. Sinners all. What then? Are we better than they? No, in no wise.'[145] He affirmed the existence of God, and denied that man was God. But man is a partaker of the divine nature, and God can command anything, and so can free men from his own commandments. 'God forbids killing, but tells Abraham to slay his son; adultery, but tells Hosea to take a wife of whoredoms.' He tautologically denounced 'the community which is sinful', but added that 'if flesh of my flesh be ready to perish, . . . if I have bread it shall or should be his'.[146] Coppe agreed that adultery, fornication and uncleanness were sins, but emphasized that those that cry out against adultery or uncleanness in others were greatly guilty of heart-adultery. The sins he chose to stress were pride, covetousness, hypocrisy, oppression, tyranny, unmercifulness, despising the poor.

> The laying of nets, traps and snares for the feet of our neighbours is a sin, whether men imagine it to be so or no; and so is the not undoing of heavy burdens, the not letting the oppressed go free, the not healing every yoke, and the not dealing of bread to the hungry [etc., etc.], . . . whether men imagine it to be so or no.[147]

No wonder not all his contemporaries were impressed by his penitence.[148] Coppe and 'a great company of Ranters' came to see George Fox in prison in 1655: a good deal of drink and tobacco was consumed, to Fox's annoyance, and some familiar Ranter tenets were vented.[149] After the restoration Coppe changed his name and practised physic. He sometimes preached, but when he died in 1672 he was buried in the parish church of Barnes in Surrey. In *A Character of a true Christian*, published posthumously, Coppe still asserted that 'evil and good the Lord doth bless'. But of himself he said:

> Wholly he's resigned
> Unto the unconfined . . .
> When self is swept away and gone
> He says and lives, God's will be done.[150]

VI   LAWRENCE CLARKSON

In 1650 the Ranters were known as Coppinites or Claxtonians.[151] There is the less need to write at length on Lawrence Clarkson (or Claxton) since Mr A. L. Morton's admirable study.[152] Born at Preston, brought up among Lancashire Puritans, he served in the New Model Army.[153] Then he turned itinerant preacher, held a living at Pulham for a short time till he was turned out for preaching universal salvation. He was then successively a Baptist and (under the influence of Erbery) a Seeker, 'preaching for monies' in each faith. In 1647 he published a near-Leveller pamphlet of some power, *A Generall Charge or Impeachment of High Treason, in the name of Justice, Equity, against the Communality of England*. This seems to imitate Overton's controversial style, though it was not so well done. It was 'published for the redemption . . . of the long-lost freedom of the freeborn subjects of England'. 'We dare not contradict,' Clarkson's Commonalty naïvely said of Parliament, because 'they are our lords, our patrons and impropriators'. If we do, 'they will oppose us, imprison us, beggar us'.

> Who are the oppressors but the nobility and gentry [asks Experienced Reason], and who are oppressed, if not the yeoman, the farmer, the tradesman and the like? . . . Have you not chosen oppressors to redeem you from oppression? . . . It is naturally inbred in the major part of the nobility and gentry . . . to judge the poor but fools, and themselves wise, and therefore when you the commonalty calleth a Parliament they are confident such must be chosen that are the noblest and richest . . . Your slavery is their liberty, your poverty is their prosperity . . . Peace is their ruin, . . . by war they are enriched . . . Peace is their war, peace is their poverty.

Taxes rob the poor to pay the rich, and men that have no more religion than a horse act as censors of other men's writings. As so often with the radicals, Clarkson was fiercely hostile to the clerical profession which he had so recently quitted. 'Thousands better than your parish priests have saluted the gallows. It is more commendable to

take a purse by the highway than compel any of the parish to maintain such that seek their ruin, whose doctrine is poisonable to their
consciences.'[154]

In his Ranter period Clarkson held that God was in all living
things and in all matter. There was no external heaven or hell, no
resurrection of the body: 'that place called heaven would become a
hell to the body.' 'I really believed no Moses, Prophets, Christ or
Apostles.' All power and all acts, he thought, are from God, and
therefore there is no act whatsoever that is sinful before God, including the crucifixion of Christ.[155] Clarkson really did teach that

> there is no such act as drunkenness, adultery and theft in God . . .
> Sin hath its conception only in the imagination . . . What act soever
> is done by thee in light and love, is light and lovely, though it be that
> act called adultery . . . No matter what Scripture, saints or churches
> say, if that within thee do not condemn thee, thou shalt not be
> condemned.[156]

This sounds very shocking, but it is worth reminding ourselves that
Luther had preached 'Whatsoever thou shalt observe upon liberty
and of love, is godly; but if thou observe anything of necessity, it is
ungodly.' 'If an adultery could be committed in the faith, it would no
longer be a sin.'[157] And Calvin had said that 'all external things [are]
subject to our liberty, provided the nature of that liberty approves
itself to our minds as before God'. 'The consciences of believers may
rise above the Law, and may forget the whole righteousness of the
Law.'[158] Calvin hedged such phrases about with safeguards; but we
can see how easily his doctrine toppled over into Antinomianism. Sir
Thomas Overbury was consciously caricaturing when he described
his Precisian as one who 'will not stick to commit fornication or
adultery so it be done in the fear of God'.[159] But it was very near the
knuckle. All that was needed was assurance of election, of Christ
within you.

'Suppose a believer commit adultery and murder,' mused Tobias
Crisp; still he 'cannot commit those sins that can give occasion to
him to suspect that if he come presently to Christ, he would cast him
off'. Crisp inserted many qualifications, but he recognized himself

that 'the enemies of the gospel will make an evil construction' of his doctrine.[160] Another intermediary between Luther and the radicals of the Revolution was Robert Towne, curate of various places in the West Riding of Yorkshire and in Lancashire, who in July 1640 had to disclaim being a Grindletonian. If men 'believe sin, death and the curse to be abolished,' he wrote, 'they are abolished. They that believe on Christ are no sinners.' This passage is sandwiched between two quotations from Luther, and Towne goes on to ask 'Are we for this Familists?' Then Luther is a Familist. 'To faith there is no sin, nor any unclean heart.'[161]

Clarkson developed this considerably further. 'None can be free from sin till in purity it be acted as no sin, for I judged that pure to me which to a dark understanding was impure: for to the pure all things, yea all acts were pure.' 'So that see what I can, act what I will, all is but one most sweet and lovely ... Without act, no life; without life, no perfection.' Clarkson was already practising what he preached, escaping from one 'maid of pretty knowledge, who with my doctrine was affected', giving his body to other women whilst being 'careful for moneys for my wife', travelling the country with Mrs Star, and resisting the opportunity when 'Dr Paget's maid stripped herself naked and skipped' at a Ranters' meeting.[162]

In 1650 Clarkson was arrested and examined. As on a previous occasion he stood on his rights as 'a freeborn subject' and refused to answer incriminating questions. He was sentenced to banishment, but the sentence was not carried out, and he was released a month later. This lenient treatment presumably means that he recanted more easily than Coppe: henceforth we hear no more of Clarkson as 'the Captain of the Rant'. He remained a close associate of Major William Rainborough, brother of the more famous Colonel Thomas Rainborough. William became a Ranter.[163] After a period as an astrologer, and magician, Clarkson was converted by John Reeve, another ex-Ranter, to what was later called Muggletonianism. In 1659 Clarkson rebuked 'ranting devils' who continued to say that God was the author of evil and that 'for them sin is no sin'.[164]

VII   JOSEPH SALMON

Joseph Salmon appears to have been an officer in the Army. His first pamphlet, *Anti-Christ in Man*, was published in 1647. In this, like Erbery, he declared that 'the spirit of Antichrist . . . is in all of us'. 'Thou needest not go to Rome, Canterbury or Westminster, but thou mayst find that Antichrist in thee, denying Jesus Christ to be come in thy flesh.' 'Thy heart is that temple of God where this great Whore sitteth.' The Whore appeared in prayer, in fasting, in all outward ordinances and forms of worship.[165] At a time when Antichrist was variously identified with the Pope or the royalists, but was normally a real person or group of persons, this must have seemed a very strange and subversive doctrine. For Salmon the Biblical narratives were to be taken as allegories of what went on within the believer.[166] 'Thou art therefore to expect Jesus to come to judgment in thee, and the end of the world to be in thee' and in this life. 'This last day, this spiritual appearance of Christ in men and women, is the very origin of all these commotions that are amongst us . . . because the last day dawns, and the star of glory is risen more in one than in another.' 'The kingdom of God is come.'[167]

In 1649 he published *A rout, a rout*. This was 'intended especially to my fellow soldiers, those of the inferior rank and quality'. He had very little from the Lord to declare to the generals as yet. They were, he thought, 'the rod of God . . . In this day of the Lord's wrath you strike through king, gentry and nobility; they all fall before you.' But the motives of the Army leaders were not disinterested: they were really aiming only at self-preservation. The Lord 'will ere long cast his rod into the fire of burning and destruction. It will be a sweet destruction,' said Salmon with some relish: 'wait for it.'[168] The sword solved nothing: those who fear to lay down their swords lest they should lose their liberties 'are shut up in a darkness; . . . you fear the world, and they are afraid of you'. But soon 'the whole edifice of this swordly power shall be annihilated. The Lord will die with it, in it (or rather out of it and from it), and in this death he will destroy more than you have done all your lives' time.' Apart from Richard Coppin, this is the only reference I have come across during this period to the death of God.[169]

Salmon too was arrested in the round-up of Ranters in 1650, preaching to crowds in the street from his prison in Coventry. He was accused of decrying all forms whatsoever, by allegorizing the Scriptures.[170] For all his mystical quietism, it appears that he too swore many desperate oaths.[171] He was released in 1650 on promise of writing a recantation. This was *Heights in Depths and Depths in Heights*, published in the following year. Salmon now shared the general disillusion.

> The world travails perpetually, every one is swollen full, big with particularity of interest, . . . labouring to bring forth some one thing, some another, and all bring forth nothing but wind and confusion . . . There is a set time for every purpose under heaven; vanity hath its time also . . . It may be I am now casting stones against the wind (that is but vanity) . . . I have lived to see an end to all perfections.[172]

He had a Hobbist vision of 'the whole world consuming in the fire of envy one against another', from which quietism was the only escape. 'I am now at rest in the silent deeps of eternity, sunk into the abyss of silence, and (having shot this perilous gulf) am safely arrived into the bosom of love, the land of rest . . . My great desire (and that wherein I most delight) is to see and say nothing.'[173] He emigrated to Barbados, where in 1682 he (or someone else of the same name, described as a shoemaker) was in trouble for trying to organize an Anabaptist congregation.[174]

VIII   JACOB BAUTHUMLEY

Jacob Bauthumley was a Leicestershire shoemaker, and was still serving in the Army when he published *The Light and Dark Sides of God* in November 1650. This book was condemned as blasphemous, and Bauthumley was bored through the tongue. He advanced the pantheistic view already familiar among Ranters. 'Not the least flower or herb in the field but there is the divine being by which it is that which it is; and as that departs out of it, so it comes to nothing, and so it is today clothed by God, and tomorrow cast into the oven.' 'All the creatures in the world . . . are but one entire being.' 'Nothing that partakes of the divine nature, or is of God, but is God.' God cannot love one man more than another: all are alike to him. God 'as really and substantially dwells in the flesh of other men and creatures as well as in the man Christ'. Where God dwells is 'all the heaven I look ever to enjoy'.[175] 'Sin is properly the dark side of God, which is a mere privation of light.' 'God is no more provoked by sin to wrath than he is allured to blessing by my holiness.' God is 'glorified in sin'. 'The reason why we call some men wicked and some godly is not anything in the man, but as the divine being appears more gloriously in them . . . According to the counsel of his will, they did no more that crucified Christ, than they that did embrace him.'[176]

Hell and the devil are within us: otherwise we must imagine a hell in God. There is no hell hereafter. The devil is not a person, the resurrection is spiritual and inward, not of the flesh hereafter. The Bible speaks to us in language we can understand: the stories of Cain and Abel, Isaac and Ishmael, Jacob and Esau are allegories, not literal truths. We should not be guided by the Bible but by the mind of God within us. It is indeed sinful to perform an action authorized by the Bible if we are persuaded in our own spirit that we should not do it. Many of these positions were shared by Milton.[177] Bauthumley's was a quietist form of Ranterism, though he too shocked George Fox by participating in scenes of singing, whistling and dancing; but Bauthumley ended as a respectable citizen of his native Leicester, library-keeper and serjeant-at-mace.[178]

IX   RICHARD COPPIN

Richard Coppin denied being a Ranter, but his *Divine Teachings*, published in September 1649, was influential among Ranters; and it is difficult to think of any label which would describe him better. He was called a successor to Joseph Salmon. *Divine Teachings* was commended by the Leveller newspaper *The Moderate* as 'an excellent book'.[179] Coppin was a clergyman of the established church until 1648, after which date he became an itinerant preacher of universal salvation.

'God is all in one, and so is in everyone,' he wrote in *Divine Teachings*. 'The same all which is in me, is in thee; the same God which dwells in one dwells in another, even in all; and in the same fullness as he is in one, he is in everyone.' God's elect are no longer an oligarchy: protestant doctrine is carried to the most extreme democratic conclusions. 'We and the Scripture,' wrote Coppin, 'are graves in which this glorious God lies dead and buried'; through his resurrection in us we come to a right knowledge of him, ourselves and them. God is both teacher and learner.[180] God is in all believers; there is no heaven and hell except in man's own conscience. God is in hell as well as in heaven. Believers today have a fuller revelation than prophets and apostles. God now reveals himself in the poor and ignorant:

> not only poor as touching the world, but poor and ignorant in the things of God . . . The flesh of man . . . needs to have no greater torment to devour it, than the light of God's majesty appearing and dwelling in the heart of the creature . . . God dwells in us, as in a cloud of darkness . . . If this seed, which is God himself, . . . is not apprehended by us to be risen in us, then darkness prevails over our wills and . . . breaks the unity of all things, and breeds . . . nothing but trouble, distrust and confusion. Thus you may see that our trouble arises from our not seeing God to be risen in us . . . This is a marvellous thing indeed to all that know it not; but experience goes beyond all things.

God cannot be angry with the person of any man created by him. His judgments are cast 'not upon us, but upon sin in us, to its destruction and our salvation'. 'The new man sinneth not.'[181]

Coppin treated the stories of the Fall and the Day of Judgment as allegories. 'When a man is converted, that is the last day.'[182] There was no resurrection of 'this earthly body'. In a phrase which anticipates Milton's 'A Paradise within thee, happier far', Coppin wrote that man could return to 'a more excellent state' than the Paradise he had lost, 'through the birth of Christ'.[183] Those who could not admit 'all sin and transgression to be finished' strive to retain a kingdom for the devil and themselves.[184] Coppin claimed that 'whatsoever I did speak or write, it was ... my own experience in the Lord'. He had no use for the established church. 'What is the church but the townhouse, in which the priest, the town servant, is to do the town's work, for which he receives the town's wages?' Fortunately 'the anti-christian law of compelling men to church' was no longer in force, since the act of 1650 abolished compulsory Sunday church attendance. The clergy however still 'live by telling people of their sins'. 'But in the kingdom of Christ, which is a free kingdom, there is no ... sin unpardoned.' The torments of hell, Coppin said in somewhat papistical fashion, were not external; their effect was purgatory.[185]

In 1655 Coppin was arrested by Major-General Kelsey after a series of sermons in Rochester cathedral in which the preacher made clear the democratic consequences of his doctrine: 'No man can be assured of his salvation, except he see the same salvation in the same Saviour for all men as well as for himself, which is to love his neighbour as himself.'[186] By such arguments Coppin wound himself 'into the bosoms of (a many-headed monster) the rude multitude'. He was accused of relying on 'a party of soldiers and others that would have tumulted and mutinied for him'. He and his supporters were 'church and state Levellers'. He got six months in jail and Major-General Kelsey recommended that the troops should be removed from contact with the tainted townsmen.[187] Coppin remained impenitent: 'I will delight myself with the worst of men as well as with the best.' The manifestation of Christ within him, he felt, increased *pari passu* with men's persecution of him.[188]

X   GEORGE FOSTER

George Foster does not fit neatly into the category of either Leveller or Ranter. He represents what was probably a large group of men and women who moved from the one to the other, never wholly mastering the philosophy of either. ('The Levellers were a branch that sprouted forth of the Ranters,' Muggleton said;[189] though this can hardly be true chronologically unless we think of a pre-existing body of opinion from which Levellers and Ranters emerged.) The Warboys Baptists thought of Foster as a prophet of the Levellers, who announced 'that the time was then that God would love all men, and rich men should cast their gold and silver about the streets'.[190] This was a very degenerate version of the teaching of either constitutional Levellers or True Levellers, though it may come closer to popular sentiment than the more sophisticated theories which impress posterity.

Foster had a vision in which he saw a man on a white horse 'cutting down all men and women that he met with that were higher than the middle sort, and raised up those that were lower than the middle sort, and made them all equal; and cried out, "Equality, equality, equality" ... I, the Lord of Hosts have done this ... I will ... make the low and poor equal with the rich'. The Leveller martyrs Lockier and Thompson would now be avenged, though the instrument of God's vengeance, in Foster's view, seems rather unexpectedly to have been General Fairfax. God 'will make those that have riches give them to them that have none'. And 'there shall be no power and no law besides God'.[191]

God, 'that mighty Leveller', will root up all powers, whether kings or parliaments, and will make all common. The whole earth shall be a treasure for all and not for some. 'And if any say, "Why do they take away my goods?"' the answer will be ' "We have need of them, and we, in the name of our Creator, take them for to make use of them" ... And what will you say to this, O you great men that have abundance? ... The saints, even poor despised sectaries, shall see and know that all things are theirs.' 'Self-love shall cease ... and there will be no complaining in our streets, as there is now, crying out for "Bread, bread, for the Lord's sake." ' 'I pass this sentence on you, O rich men, that I will utterly destroy you', and the meaner sort will be restored from the slavery and bondage in which the rich have kept them. An international revolution would follow, leading to the gathering of the Jews in Italy in 1651, the destruction of Pope and

Great Turk by 1656, and the establishment everywhere of a classless society.[192]

Foster anticipated the verdict that has probably already formed itself in the reader's mind. 'Let not the notion of madness possess your spirits,' he wrote, 'as for you to think that I am mad; but rather that it is the pleasure of the Father to turn the world upside down, and so to make use of me as he did of his son Jesus Christ', who 'did do things contrary to the custom of the world in those days.' And Foster signed himself with the Ranter formula, 'one of your fellow-creatures'.[193]

XI   JOHN PORDAGE AND THOMAS TANY

It would be nice to know more about John Pordage in the period in which he tells us that 'notions of Ranterism . . . were everywhere frequently discoursed of'.[194] Pordage was the son of a London merchant, curate at Reading in the early 1640s, rector of Bradfield not later than 1647 – one of the richest livings in the county. He was later known as a disciple of Jacob Boehme and a Philadelphian. When he was in trouble in Berkshire in 1655 he was accused of some traditional Ranter views – of denying the historical Christ and believing that God was in every man; of saying 'it was a weakness to be troubled for sins'; and that marriage was a very wicked thing; of being a Familist.[195] But he was also accused of saying that there would soon be no Parliament, magistrate or government in England; that the saints would take over the estates of the wicked for themselves, and the wicked should be their slaves, that he cared no more for the higher powers than for the dust beneath his feet.[196] He was also involved in guilt by association. He knew Erbery. He kept open house at Bradfield, and a very remarkable collection of men seem to have taken advantage of this to stay with him for long periods. Among these were William Everard the Digger (or Robert Everard the Agitator),[197] Abiezer Coppe and Thomas Tany (Theaureaujohn). 'The chief person of his family communion,' Richard Baxter tells us of Pordage, was 'a gentleman and student of All Souls in Oxford', who was 'much against property, and against relations of magistrates, subjects, husbands, wives, masters, servants, etc.'[198] Pordage defended Abiezer Coppe, and expressed approval of Coppin's writings. In Pordage himself 'that inward spiritual eye, which hath been locked up and shut by the Fall' was 'opened in an extraordinary way'. It revealed to him that 'there were two invisible principles . . . two spiritual worlds extending and penetrating throughout this whole visible creation'.[199]

Pordage was alleged to be a follower of Thomas Tany, who 'hath been questioned for holding dangerous and unsound opinions, as that there is no hell, and the like'.[200] Tany, who adopted the name of Theaureaujohn at divine command on 23 November 1649, was probably, as he ingenuously confessed, mad;[201] but his madness took some very radical forms. He believed that God was in everything, and that man could not lose his salvation. He thought nevertheless that all religion was 'a lie, a cheat, a deceit, for there is but one truth, and that is love'.[202] In 1651 he had been indicted of blasphemous words, together with Captain Robert Norwood.[203] In December 1654 Tany burnt the Bible in St George's Fields 'because the people say it is the Word of God, and it is not'.[204] Tany thought that 'our lands being freed from the Norman subjection', in consequence of Parliament's victory in the civil war, 'we may lawfully claim our lands and inheritance in the commonwealth'; common lands should return to the common people.[205] Tany had some association with John Robins and with the Muggletonians, by whom he was denounced.[206]

XII   THOMAS WEBBE

Thomas Webbe, of an old Wiltshire clothing family, was rector of Langley Burhill. He was alleged to have obtained the living on promising not to accept tithes from his parishioners; and to have expressed from the pulpit a hope that he would live long enough to see 'no such thing as a parsonage or minister in England'. He made some very disparaging remarks about preaching in general, and his own in particular. A group around him was alleged to have formed a 'Babel of profaneness and community' in the early fifties. Webbe spoke up for Lilburne and against Parliament during the trial of the Leveller leader in 1649; he praised Coppe, and in 1650 exchanged friendly letters with Joseph Salmon. The latter used a phrase worthy of Blake: 'the Lord grant we may know the worth of hell, that we may for ever scorn heaven' – a phrase which Ephraim Pagitt thought worth quoting.[207] In 1650 Webbe was put on trial for adultery, then liable to the death sentence, but was acquitted, to the fury of local respectabilities. He was alleged to have said 'there's no heaven but women, nor no hell save marriage'. Another witness asserted that Webbe claimed to 'live above ordinances, and that it was lawful for him to lie with any woman'. He enjoyed music and mixed dancing, wore long shaggy hair and thought Moses was a conjuror. His enemies, who were counted among the enemies of the Levellers, got him ejected by the Committee for Plundered Ministers in September. 'O Sirrah, you know the law, do you?' he was told. 'You are one of Lilburne's faction, you shall be banished.'[208]

XIII THE END OF THE RANTERS

The geography of Ranterism has not yet been finally settled. Mr Morton places them mainly in towns, in the North Midlands (Coventry, Leicestershire, Derbyshire – especially the Peak District, Nottinghamshire); in Cleveland, the West Riding, Holderness, Lancashire, Cumberland, Westmorland, Cornwall.[209] We may add Huntingdonshire, Gloucestershire, Wiltshire, Poole and Wells, 'the seat of the old Ranters, Garment and Robins'.[210] In Wellingborough, centre of support for first Diggers and later Quakers, there were clearly Ranter influences too.[211]

Since the Ranters were, so far as we know, never organized, it is difficult to ascertain what became of their rank and file after the leaders had been picked off in 1650 and 1651. There are slight indications. In Lacock, Wiltshire, in 1656, William Bond said there was

no God or power ruling above the planets, no Christ but the sun that shines upon us; . . . if the Scriptures were a-making again then

Tom Lampire of Melksham would make as good Scriptures as the Bible. There was neither heaven nor hell except in a man's conscience, for if he had a good fortune and did live well, that was heaven; and if he lived poor and miserable, that was hell, for then he would die like a cow or a horse.

Thomas Hibbord of the same village said 'God was in all things; whatever sins he did commit, God was the author of them all, and acted them in him. He would sell all religions for a jug of beer.'[212] This group of Ranters may well have been connected with that around Thomas Webbe. Some Quakers associated the Muggletonians with Ranters, no doubt because of Reeve and Clarkson.[213]

Records have also been preserved of discussions in the 1650s between officers of the Baptist church at Fenstanton near Ely – a village which the Digger emissaries visited in 1650[214] – and members who picked up Ranter views, though sometimes they shade off into Quakerism. Rank-and-file members of the church were excommunicated for claiming 'some manifestations of the Spirit above the Scriptures' (1651), for saying 'the Scripture was but a dead letter', and that God was the cause of evil actions. John and Elizabeth Offley 'were grown to perfection', regarding the Apostles as 'imperfect creatures'. There was no sin, they added. Edward Mayle and his wife 'did not desire to be in such bondage' as to observe 'outward, ceremonial and carnal ordinances' (1652).[215] In 1653 Mrs Robert Kent 'spake many things which savoured of Rantism', claiming that she did the will of God in all things. Mrs Paul Wayt seemed to doubt whether there were ever such persons as the Virgin Mary or Jesus Christ. 'She knew it was truth according to the history, but not according to the mystery.' Fordam, a tanner, thought it was no sin if a man should steal his horse, 'believing that he had right unto him equal with him'. Mrs William Austin 'looked upon the Scriptures as nothing, she trampled them under her feet'. She had 'as lief be with the devil as with God' – or with her Baptist interlocutor, she added. 'He that died upon the cross at Jerusalem? He is nothing to me; I do not care for him.' John Harvey 'was in that condition that he could not sin'. He and others refused to argue with the Baptist emissaries who lacked their experiences, but 'we would not believe his fancy which he called experience'.[216] Edmund Hickhorngill, who lapsed from the Hexham church to become a Quaker, soon attained to 'a better and higher dispensation'. 'He propounds no other rule to himself but his reason, which if a man sin not against, he shall be happy enough.'[217] So we see radical religion passing into rationalism.

Gerrard Winstanley appears to have had some trouble in his Digger colony with Ranters who joined the community and 'caused scandal'.[218] They attached too much importance to 'meat, drink, pleasure and women'; lack of work 'inflames their hearts to quarrelling, killing, burning houses or corn'. Sexual promiscuity broke the peace in families and led to idleness, to a Hippy-like existence for which others had to pay by labour. It also led to venereal disease, the incidence of which in England had presumably increased in the wake of armies and camp followers. And the high-flown Ranter generalizations confused the simpler members of the community. Winstanley felt he had to vindicate the Diggers, who were themselves slandered as Ranters: he disclaimed 'excessive community of women'. But he was careful to add, even while denouncing Ranter ideas, 'Let none go about to suppress that ranting power by their punishing hand . . . If thou wilt needs be punishing, then see thou be without sin thyself.'[219] It may have been this experience with Ranters which convinced Winstanley of the need to have laws and rules in his ideal community, and punishments to deal with the idle and the ignorant, the unruly and the 'self-ended spirits'.[220]

10
Ranters and Quakers

> These things gave them [the Quakers] a rough and dis-
> agreeable appearance with the generality, who thought
> them turners of the world upside down, as indeed in some
> sense they were, but in no other than that wherein Paul
> was so charged, viz. to bring things back to their primitive
> and right order again.
>
> W. PENN, Preface to George Fox's *Journal*, I, p. xxxiv.

I FROM RANTERS TO QUAKERS

The object of this chapter is not to write a history of the early Quaker movement. Much work has been done on this since Braithwaite's admirable *The First Period of Quakerism*. Inevitably any historian writing about the Quaker movement is dazzled by the personality of George Fox, whose great *Journal* must be a principal source. By 1694 the Quaker movement was clearly Fox's movement. But in the 1650s this was not clear. Yet Fox's *Journal* is naturally written with a good deal of hindsight, and events and personalities of the 1650s have certainly been modified, whether by Fox himself or by his editors, in the light of later experience. This is not to suggest anything like deliberate distortion: simply that the story looks different when you know, or think you know, how it ended: when your object in writing is not merely to produce a correct record but to edify and confirm in their faith people living at the end of the story, for whom the beginning meant little, was already legendary.

Thus in Fox's *Journal* James Nayler plays a part only slightly greater than that of Trotsky in official Soviet histories of the Russian Revolution. Yet in the 1650s many regarded Nayler as the 'chief leader', the 'head Quaker in England'.[1] 'He writes all their books,' Colonel Cooper told the House of Commons in December 1656. 'Cut off this fellow and you will destroy the sect,' Mr Bond agreed.[2] Such opinions were perhaps incorrect even when they were uttered: but that they were expressed shows that Fox was by no means clearly the sole leader of the Quakers in the 1650s. I do not want to elevate Nayler against Fox, or to suggest that Nayler led a Ranter wing of the Quakers – though rivalries of personality as well as of principle are suggested by the famous occasion when Fox refused to let Nayler kiss his face or hand, and offered his foot instead.[3] I want rather to suggest that the whole early Quaker movement was far closer to the Ranters in spirit than its leaders later liked to recall, after they had spent many weary hours differentiating themselves from Ranters and ex-Ranters. It is perhaps a help for us to look at early Quakers in connection with that world of the Ranters in which Quakerism grew up, rather than through the spectacles of the respectable Quakers of the later seventeenth century.[4]

Reading Fox's *Journal* one at once becomes aware of a gap between the events described and the apparent reasons for them. *Why* did such vast crowds gather to hear Fox? Why and how were so many convinced? Why were priests, some magistrates, and some of the 'rabble' so enraged? Answers to these questions do not emerge from the story as Fox tells it. His preaching seems to consist mainly of pious exhortations hardly likely to be unacceptable to any Puritans. We have to go back to the pamphlet literature of the 1650s to discover what all the fuss was about.

Not indeed that there is any great theological novelty or interest in Fox's works of the 1650s, any more than in the *Journal*. He interrupts church services; he denounces. He proclaims the doctrine of the spirit within, which was already widespread. Fox in 1648 'found none that could bear to be told that they should come to ... that righteousness and the holiness that Adam was in before he fell'. We can well believe that this was a great revelation to him and to some of his hearers: but neither this doctrine, his claim to be the Son of God, nor his belief that Christ died for all men, were new, as we have seen. One may conjecture that Fox's 'great openings concerning the things written in the Revelations' meant more to him and to his audience when he declared them than when he wrote up his *Journal*.[5] The rage caused by early Quakers was, one suspects, more due to their refusal of hat honour, their 'thouing' and their attacks on steeplehouses and hireling priests than to any original ideas of Fox's. Many of his early pamphlets are trivial – e.g. *The Vials of the Wrath of God upon the seat of the Man of Sin* are mostly directed against football and wrestling.[6] Fox is at his best in *The Lambs Officer* of 1659, an extremely powerful Joycean monologue of denunciation, repetitive, almost liturgical, circling around one or two recurrent phrases – 'Come to the bar of judgment' – and insistent questions – 'Did not the Whore of Rome give you the name of vicars . . . and parsons and curates? . . . set up your schools and colleges . . . whereby you are made ministers?' 'Guilty or not guilty?'[7] It would make a magnificent broadcast if recited by a good actor. It may be significant that it was published in a year of political crisis, the last year of hope for the radicals.

The only explanation of popular hostility to the Quakers in the early 1650s that we get in the *Journal* is political: Quakers are called 'Roundheaded rogues'.[8] (Gerrard Winstanley in May 1648 makes it clear that the word 'Roundhead' was used especially against the political radicals.[9] Edward Burrough was mocked at as a Roundhead even in his pre-Quaker days.[10]) But there is little evidence in the *Journal* of any hostility from the common people on other than political grounds unless they were incited by a local parson. It was different of course with the gentry, who can hardly have appreciated Fox's apostrophe in 1653: 'O ye great men and rich men of the earth! Weep and howl for your misery that is coming . . . The fire is kindled, the day of the Lord is appearing, a day of howling . . . All the loftiness of men must be laid low.'[11] Most of the gentry in the North of England may anyway be deemed to have had royalist sympathies. The North was under military occupation in 1651–3. There had been areas of support for Parliament, in the West Riding and in east Lancashire; but the region as a whole was still smarting under defeat. The Committee for the Propagation of the Gospel in the North parts, set up in 1650, was an attempt at political re-education under military supervision. In Wales the Committee for the Propagation of the Gospel became 'the real government of Wales'.[12] We have less information about the Committee in the North, but undoubtedly it too had the strong support of the military authorities in those conquered counties.

Quakers then entered the area as a wing of the government party in the years 1651–3, enjoying the protection of the military authorities,[13] and of the occasional local gentleman of radical inclinations.[14] They had sometimes the more enthusiastic support of Army rank and file. Just as the bishops before 1633 had allowed Puritan preachers in the North who would not have been tolerated in the South, so those who administered the North (or Wales) could not afford to alienate Quaker missionaries, many of whom were ex-New Model Army soldiers, still supporters of Parliament against the King. Fox had been in prison for nearly a year at Derby in 1650, but in the North, as we can see from his *Journal* itself, he enjoyed a good deal of protection in the years 1651–2. Even hostile J.P.s (of whom there were many) had to proceed cautiously against him. Persecution began, spasmodically, from the end of 1652, when the dissolution of the Rump appeared imminent, and again after April 1653, when the gentry may have felt they were given a free hand, Fox was imprisoned at Carlisle. But then the relatively radical Barebones Parliament met: a letter from it got Fox released and his jailor put in his place in the dungeon.[15] In Wales too J.P.s protected Quakers as a lesser evil than papists or pagans.[16]

It was the Quakers themselves who alienated the clergy, some of whom in the North seem initially to have been sympathetic. Indiscriminate attacks on hirelings, tithes and the sanctity of ecclesiastical buildings made it impossible for any priest to support them and continue to hold his living. In the long run, it may be, the hostility of the intruded Puritan ministers did the Quakers no harm in public opinion in the North or in Wales; but in the short run the clergy seem easily to have been able to raise mobs against them – as Roundheads.

In 1654 Fox was arrested on suspicion of plotting against the government, but he was well received by Oliver Cromwell. Those who wished ill to Quakers were those who resented Army rule; their views were strongly represented in the Parliament of 1656, as we see from the debates about James Nayler. Dark hints were dropped that the spread of the Quakers had been due to official encouragement, indeed that Quakers were to be found in the government itself.[17] But by that time the Quaker campaign to conquer the South and East of England had been under way for two years, and their rapid expansion did indeed give men of property cause for alarm, make them apprehensive of 'some Levelling design' underlying the by then well organized Quaker movement.[18] The fact that Quakers were said to have reclaimed 'such as neither magistrate nor minister ever speak to'[19] might seem reassuring after Quaker pacifism was firmly established and known to be accepted by all members of the sect. But that was far from being the case in the mid-1650s. The remark does however give us an idea of the class to which Quakers appealed.

From the mid-1650s Quakers increasingly defined their beliefs, defensively, by negatives. They do not deny the existence of God or a historical Christ, of heaven or hell. They do not believe that all can attain perfection on earth. They are not against the authority of magistrates or parents. There is little enough in their published works (or in Fox's *Journal*) to tell us why such defences were necessary. But they tell us something important about the ambience from which the Quakers came, or, perhaps more accurately, about the ambience in the South and East which the Northern Quakers found when they invaded it after 1652. A diarist in Cheshire, for instance, tells us in 1655 that the Quakers 'denied the Trinity; ... denied the Scriptures to be the Word of God; they said that they had no sin'.[20] From this point of view Judge Hotham and Dr Robert Gell were right in their famous assertions 'had not the Quakers come, the Ranters had over-run the nation'.[21] This of course implies a difference between Quakers and Ranters, and a greater acceptability of the former to the ruling class, which I shall discuss later: but the Quakers could hardly have prevented Ranters from over-running the country unless their doctrines had initially been near enough to Ranterism to absorb many Ranters.

Thomas Collier in 1657 asserted that 'any that know the principles of the Ranters' may easily recognize that Quaker doctrines are identical. Both would have 'no Christ but within; no Scripture to be a rule; no ordinances, no law but their lusts, no heaven nor glory but here, no sin but what men fancied to be so, no condemnation for sin but in the consciences of ignorant ones'. Only Quakers 'smooth it over with an outward austere carriage before men, but within are full of filthiness' – and he gave Nayler as an example.[22] This passage was echoed almost word for word by both Bunyan and Baxter, though Bunyan improves the last phrase to 'only the Ranters had made them [these doctrines] threadbare at an ale-house, and the Quakers have set a new gloss upon them by an outward legal holiness'.[23] Bunyan lists Quaker beliefs in the early fifties: (1) The Bible is not the Word of God; (2) every man in the world has the spirit of Christ; (3) the Jesus Christ who was crucified 1600 years ago did not satisfy divine justice for the sins of the people; (4) Christ's flesh and blood is within the saints; (5) there will be no resurrection of the body; (6) the resurrection has already taken place within good men; (7) the crucified Jesus did not ascend above the starry heavens, (8) and shall not come again at the last day as man to judge all nations. On another occasion Bunyan lumped Ranters and Quakers together in condemnation because both permitted women ministers.[24] Clarkson, looking back from 1660, had no doubt that the early Quakers shared his beliefs about God, the devil and the resurrection: 'only they had a righteousness of the law which I had not'.[25]

Fox himself in 1654 witnessed that Ranters 'had a pure convincement', but they had 'fled the cross' and turned the grace of God into wantonness. He emphasized especially drunkenness, swearing, and 'sporting yourselves in the day-time'.[26] Fox had a short way with Ranters, who in his view bowed and scraped too much, were too 'complimental'. 'Repent, thou swine and beast,' was his reply to a civil greeting from one of them, followed by a reference to 'the old Ranters in Sodom'.[27] One wonders how far the Quaker denial of hat honour may have been fortified by opposition to Ranter practice. Anthony Pearson said in the same year 1654 that 'some that are joined to the Ranters are pretty people', but they contain 'so many rude savage apprentices and young people ... that nothing but the power of the Lord can chain them'.[28] The Quaker James Parnell in 1655 admitted that Quakers were accused to be one with Ranters. 'Some of them have tasted of the love of God, and grace of God, and have had appearance of God'; but they have turned the grace of God into wantonness, and 'have deceived many with their alluring speeches'. Their lascivious ways bring discredit on the truth of God.[29] Nayler, without naming the Ranters, said disapprovingly that 'the greatest profession now set up by many is to make the redemption of Christ a cover for all licentiousness and fleshly liberty, and say they are to that end redeemed'.[30]

Edward Burrough, who seems himself to have had Ranter leanings at one time, in 1656 admitted that Ranters 'have scorned self-righteousness'; their house had once been the house of prayer, though now it has become 'the den of robbers', cultivating false peace, false liberty and love and fleshly joy.[31] Fox himself tells us of many Ranter groups which ultimately became Quakers – in Cleveland, Nottinghamshire, Leicestershire, Sussex, Reading.[32]

In part, no doubt, enemies of the Quakers were anxious to associate them with Ranters in order to discredit them: 'Quakerism is become the common sink of them all' – Anabaptists, Antinomians, Socinians, Familists, Libertines, etc.[33] But there could be genuine confusion. In Poole, Dorset, and in Wiltshire, former Levellers were alleged to have become Ranters.[34] The Grand Jury of Gloucestershire in August 1655 petitioned against 'Ranters, Levellers and atheists, under the name of Quakers'.[35] Christopher Atkinson was accepted as a Quaker until in 1655 he fell 'into too much familiarity and conversation with some women-kind, especially such as (it seemed) were somewhat inclined to a spirit of Ranterism. He grew loose and ... committed lewdness with a servant-maid.'[36] Mary Todd, a London lady who at a meeting 'pulled up all her clothes above her middle, exposing her nakedness to all in the room', was disowned by Quakers, who said she was a Ranter: but the act of disavowal suggests that they felt some responsibility for her.[37] Thomas Laucock, who clapped his hands upon his heart and said heaven is 'within me, within me!' – was he a Ranter or a Quaker? His question, What is Christ – 'three or four storey high above sky?' – sounds Ranterish, but his interlocutor claimed to have got similar if less dramatic replies from George Fox and James Parnell.[38] We may also perhaps assume that Thomas Peacock was wrongly accused of being a Quaker. He said he could not sin, denied the existence of the devil, and asked 'Dost thou believe on that thief that was hanged at Jerusalem?'[39] But what group could such men belong to by the late 1650s? They were excommunicated by the Baptists.[40] An account in 1659 of 'the devil's changing his device from ranting to quaking' may correctly describe the course of many individuals. As late as 1668 Fox was insisting that some people called Quakers were really Ranters.[41]

Similarly the Quakers must have absorbed many ex-Levellers, including John Lilburne. Lilburne's acceptance of Quakerism in 1655, incidentally, was a very different act for the ex-revolutionary than if he had been convinced after 1660. A hostile pamphlet of 1653 said that the Northern Quakers 'teach the doctrine of levelling privately to their disciples'. The leaders were 'downright Levellers', only concealing their views from fear of suppression.[42] That need not be taken too seriously, but there are many such comments. Fuller made several identifications when he spoke of a man who was 'too rich and knowing to be a Leveller, an Anabaptist or a Quaker'.[43] In December 1656 an M.P. described Quakers as 'all Levellers, against magistracy and property'.[44] Fox said of the Levellers in 1654: 'You had a flash in your mind, a simplicity', but their minds 'run into the earth and smothered it, and so get up into presumption'. They would have had unity and fellowship 'before life was raised up in you': so their aspirations withered and were condemned in the light of true unity and true fellowship.[45]

The spread of Quakerism, emptying the churches of Anabaptists and separatists, witnessed *both* to the defeat of the political Levellers *and* to the continued existence and indeed extension of radical ideas. The multitude still 'much incline' to 'a popular parity, a levelling anarchy' in 1650.[46] As late as 1662 Samuel Fisher was having to defend Quakerism against accusations of 'this rude and levelling humour'.[47] It was well after the event that Thomas Comber suggested that the Quakers derived from Gerrard Winstanley.[48]

II   QUAKERS AND POLITICS

The first official declaration of absolute pacifism in all circumstances was made by the Quakers in January 1661, after a number of Friends had been arrested in the aftermath of Venner's unsuccessful Fifth Monarchist revolt. It was intended especially to protect Quakers against charges of sedition, but it also marks the beginning of an absolute refusal to accept civil or military office.[49] Many Quaker leaders were ex-soldiers – James Nayler, William Deusbury, Richard Hubberthorne, John Whitehead, Edward Billing, John Crook, Thomas Symonds, George Fox the Younger and others.[50] Some Quakers had been dismissed from the Army in the 1650s for disciplinary reasons,[51] but others seem not to have found military service incompatible with their principles.[52] Quakers also continued to serve in the Navy.[53]

Fox himself was offered a commission in 1651. In the *Journal* he tells us that he refused it on pacifist grounds, but in 1657 he urged 'the inferior officers and soldiers' of the Army on to conquer Rome.[54] After 1658 he was more cautious,[55] but as late as January 1660 a leading south Welsh Quaker asked Fox whether Quakers were free to serve in the Army.[56] It is at least possible that his refusal in 1651 sprang from political objections to the government of the Commonwealth rather than from pacifist principle. Burrough and Howgill were not pacifists in 1655, and the former and Hubberthorne advocated the use of force in 1659. Burrough thought the Army did much good until it turned to self-seeking.[57] In 1659, when the political situation was more to their liking, some Quakers re-enlisted in the Army.[58] Indeed, as late as 1685 a few Quakers are said to have turned out for Monmouth's rebellion.[59]

Nor did Quakers in the 1650s abstain from political activity. Their earliest pronouncement included a demand for annual Parliaments.[60] Quakers were suggested as J.P.s, and some may actually have served.[61] In 1659 they resumed political activity, organizing petitions, etc.[62] The Westminster Quaker, Edward Billing, published a tract containing thirty-one proposals for political action, most of them drawn from Leveller programmes. He had hoped to get his pamphlet endorsed by the Society of Friends before publication. They did not agree, but at least he had thought it possible. Such questions were still open.[63]

The published opinions of Quakers gave plenty of grounds for regarding them as political radicals in the 1650s. Edward Burrough, whom Professor Cole regards as the political spokesman of the Quakers in the 1650s rather than Fox, took it for granted that Friends had supported Parliament in the civil war.[64] Nayler, Howgill and Fox made similar assumptions.[65] On the eve of the restoration Nayler and Fox spoke out against monarchy almost as courageously as Milton. 'What a dirty, nasty thing it would have been,' Fox told the Council of Officers in 1659, 'to have heard talk of a House of Lords among them!'[66] All Quakers were pretty severe in their references to priests of the established church. 'Your downfall is near at hand,' they were told in 1653.[67] 'Their religion', Edward Burghall noted of Quakers in his Diary in 1655, 'consists chiefly in censuring others and railing upon them, especially ministers.'[68] Burrough called priests 'the fountains of all wickedness abounding in the nations'. Their tithes robbed the poor, being paid not only out of the land 'but out of men's labours therefor'. No tradesman had their trick of compelling people to buy their wares; without tithes 'they must either beg or work or worse for a livelihood'.[69] Anthony Pearson advocated helping the poor by abolishing tithes, as the rich had been helped by the abolition of the Court of Wards. The burden of tithes, he argued, made the cost of improving the waste too great for ordinary people to be able to afford, to the detriment of the national economy.[70]

'The earth is the Lord's and the fullness thereof,' wrote Nicholson in 1653. 'He hath given it to the sons of men in general, and not to a few lofty ones which lord it over their brethren.'[71] Burrough in 1659 denounced all 'earthly lordship and tyranny and oppression, . . . by which creatures have been exalted and set up one above another, trampling under foot and despising the poor'.[72] 'God is against you,' Nayler told 'covetous cruel oppressors who grind the faces of the poor and needy'. Howgill prophesied woe to 'you lofty ones of the earth, who have gotten much of the creation into your hands . . . and

are become lords of your brethren'.[73] Fox proposed that 'all the great
houses, abbeys, steeple-houses and Whitehall' should be turned into alms-houses, that monastic and glebe lands should be used to
support the poor, and that manorial fines should be turned over to
them.[74] He too prophesied woe to the rich in the day of the Lord now
appearing.[75] 'The mighty day of the Lord is now appearing,' John
Audland repeated to Bristol in 1658.[76] A Quaker in Furness had foretold the day of judgment for 1 December 1652 – though Fox warily
rebuked him for his rash precision. Samuel Fisher retained something of this apocalyptic sense of the nearness of God's coming even
after the restoration.[77]

Contemporaries could at least be forgiven for associating such
threats with radical political action. 'The time will come,' declared
another Quaker pamphlet of 1654, 'that as with the servant, so with
the master; and as with the mistress, so with the maid.'[78] It was easy to
suspect Quakers (like morris dancers from the North) of 'some levelling design'.[79] When Quakers assembled on moors in their thousands,
oblivious of any prohibition by magistrates, it was not altogether surprising that M.P.s thought they would 'overrun all, both ministers and
magistrates'.[80] 'We are a people accused to raise up a new war,' admitted Fox in 1654, though he denied both this charge and the accusation
that Quakers owned no magistracy.[81] Friends never plot or murmur
against magistrates, Nayler said; nevertheless, magistrates are not to
be obeyed when they command that which God forbids; and 'he that
is a self-lover, or proud, or covetous, or respects gifts or rewards' or
persons, 'cannot rule for God'.[82] If this was intended to be reassuring
it probably failed of its purpose.

Burrough admitted that the Quaker preacher is considered 'a sower
of sedition, or a subverter of the laws, a turner of the world upside
down, a pestilent fellow'.[83] He himself used very alarming military
metaphors about the coming of Christ. We may understand that for
Quakers Christ's coming was internal, not the physical descent which
Fifth Monarchists were predicting at precisely this time: but again this
was not so obvious to contemporaries when Burrough addressed himself *To the Camp of the Lord in England*.[84] The camp of Christ and
the camp of Antichrist had been used by Puritan ministers to describe

the two sides in the English civil war.[85] It is hardly surprising that some took Burrough literally when in 1654 he announced that 'the fire is to be kindled, . . . and the proud and all that do wickedly shall be as stubble . . . The sword of the Lord is . . . put into the hands of them which is hated and despised by the rulers and officers, which is scornfully called Quakers, but they shall conquer by the sword of the Lord.'[86] Theaureaujohn, who drew his sword in the lobby of the House of Commons in December 1654, and who symbolically burnt the Bible because it deceived the people, was believed to be a Quaker. This was no doubt a mistake, but it was shared by Bulstrode Whitelocke, later not unsympathetic to Quakers himself. Andrew Smith of Forfar, who stabbed Quartermaster Farley during divine service on the Sabbath, may not have been a Quaker either, but his principle of action – 'Jesus Christ commanded him so to do' – was similar to that which led Nayler in his entry to Bristol. Henry Cromwell in 1655 thought 'our most considerable enemy now' was the Quakers, whose principles seemed to him incompatible either with civil government or with the discipline of an army. Two years later Colonel Daniel equated the 'principles of quaking' with 'the Levellers' strain', and also regarded them as subversive of military discipline.[87]

Even what seems to us the innocent eccentricity of refusing to remove the hat in the presence of social superiors, or to use the second person plural to them, confirmed conservative contemporaries in their suspicions. The former was a long-standing gesture of popular social protest, practised not only by Marian martyrs but also by the seditious Hacket, Coppinger and Arthington in 1591,[88] by John Lilburne on many famous occasions, by Winstanley and Everard in the presence of Fairfax in 1649. We have only to read Thomas Ellwood's autobiography to grasp the fury it could cause in a normal gentleman when his son claimed to share the head of the household's exclusive privilege of wearing his hat when others went uncovered.[89] The gentle Fuller wrote in 1655:

> We maintain that Thou from superiors to inferiors is proper, as a
> sign of command; from equals to equals is passable, as a note of
> familiarity; but from inferiors to superiors, if proceeding from

ignorance, hath a smack of clownishness; if from affection, a tang of contempt ... Such who now quarrel at the honour will hereafter question the wealth of others. Such as now accuse them for ambition for being higher, will hereafter condemn them for covetousness, for being broader than others; yea, and produce Scripture too, proper and pregnant enough for their purpose as abused by their interpretation.

Unless they are repressed, 'such as now introduce Thou and Thee will (if they can) expel Mine and Thine, dissolving all property into confusion'.[90] (The 'clownish' Thou seems to have been normal usage among northern countrymen).[91] 'Bowing to superiors ... justified from Scripture' ran an item in the index of an anti-Quaker tract published in 1656.[92]

This gesture of social protest recurred in the French Revolution. 'Le chapeau est le signe de l'affranchissement,' declared Barrière in May 1789, arguing that the Third Estate should remain covered in the royal presence. Democrats should never doff their hats or bow to social superiors, declared Sanial in *Annales Patriotiques* three years later. 'By saying "Thou" to one another, we complete the collapse of the old system of insolence and tyranny,' Chalier told the Convention in 1793.[93]

III   JAMES NAYLER AND GEORGE FOX

The spokesman of political radicalism, in addition to Edward Burrough, was James Nayler, who has been described as the culmination of the Ranter tendency in Quakerism.[94] God 'made all men of one mould and one blood to dwell on the face of the earth,' Nayler wrote in 1654 in a denunciation of the rich.[95] 'Who could have believed,' he asked in the same year, 'that England would have brought forth no better fruits than these, now after such deliverance as no nation else can witness?'[96] Nayler made no secret of his continuing support for the Parliamentary cause, which he had served in the field for eight or nine years, 'counting nothing too dear to bring the government into your [Oliver Cromwell's] hands (for the liberty of freeborn men).' In

1659 Nayler was still calling on the Long Parliament to 'set free the oppressed people'. 'The simple-hearted' supporters of Parliament, who had been drawn in by 'fair pretences' were beginning 'to leave you and return home, as men disappointed of their expectation'.[97]

Ellwood, who was convinced by hearing Edward Burrough and James Nayler defending 'the universal free grace of God to all mankind', tells us that 'what dropped from J.N. had the greater force upon me, because he looked but like a plain simple countryman, having the appearance of a husbandman or a shepherd (whereas E.B. looked like a scholar, which made his argument the less remarkable).'[98] Nayler, in a phrase which Fox often used later, spoke in 1654 of ministers 'who plead for sin'.[99] 'No man,' he asserted, 'can be a minister of Christ, nor preach him truly, but who preacheth perfection, and that is the end of his ministry.' None can come to Christ but he who comes to perfection.[100] In 1656 Nayler taunted the Presbyterian clergy with still hankering after power. 'Was not this it you talked on, twenty, thirty, forty or fifty years since? Yet now further off from it than ever.' 'And thus he [the devil] makes you most afraid of freedom.'[101]

The events following Nayler's symbolic entry into Bristol in 1656, riding on a donkey and with women (including Erbery's widow – or daughter) strewing palms before him, are well known. Why was so much fuss made? There had been earlier Messiahs – William Franklin,[102] Arise Evans, who told the Deputy Recorder of London that he was the Lord his God,[103] Theaureaujohn, King of the Jews; Mary Gadbury was the Spouse of Christ, Joan Robins and Mary Adams believed they were about to give birth to Jesus Christ. They were comparatively leniently dealt with by local magistrates: a short prison sentence, perhaps a whipping for the women. But M.P.s spent six weeks denouncing Nayler with hysterical frenzy; many demanded sentence of death and Nayler was ultimately flogged and branded with a brutality from which he never recovered. The explanation must be that none of the others seemed so dangerous. Most were holy imbeciles, William Franklin a fraud. But Nayler was a leader of an organized movement which, from its base in the North, had swept with frightening rapidity over the southern counties. It was a movement whose aims were obscure, but which certainly took over many of the aims of the Levellers, and was recruiting former Levellers and Ranters. Bristol was the second city of the kingdom, where the Quakers had many followers. Above all, M.P.s were anxious to finish once and for all with the policy of religious toleration which, in their view, had been the bane of England for a decade. The government of the Protectorate, satisfactorily conservative in many ways, was still in their view woefully unsound in this respect. The fact that its relative tolerance resulted from its dependence on the Army only heightened the offence.

So conservatives in Parliament seized the occasion to put the whole Quaker movement in the dock, and the government's religious policy too. The hysteria of M.P.s' contributions to the debate shows how frightened they had been, how delighted they were to seize the opportunity for counter-attack. And the conservatives won their showdown with the government. Nayler was tortured, to discourage the others. Cromwell queried the authority for Parliament's action against Nayler,[104] but ultimately he made political use of the Nayler case to manoeuvre the Army into accepting Parliament's Petition and Advice, a constitution which established something like the traditional monarchy and state church, and drastically limited the area of religious toleration.

It was a parting of the ways for the Quaker movement as well as for the English Revolution as a whole. As early as 1653 the story that Nayler had been with the Levellers at Burford was being denied.[105] It was more difficult to deny a symbolic connection: 'part of the Army that fell at Burford was your figure', one of Nayler's followers was told by her husband. The Nayler case was a tragedy for the Quaker movement, already suffering divisions caused by the 'Proud Quakers' from 1654 onwards and the surviving strength of Ranters in the North Midlands.[106] Nayler's case strengthened the arguments for more discipline, more law and order in the Quaker movement, arguments which George Fox no doubt found temperamentally congenial. In 1657 Burrough was warning Quakers to beware of the Ranter spirit. Samuel Fisher spoke of Nayler's offence as revealing 'that old spirit of the Ranters, which makes head against the light of Christ condemning filthiness in every conscience'.[107]

Nayler himself in the depth of his humiliation rejected the support of 'many wild spirits, Ranters and such like', who refused to accept the hostile verdict of Friends. You have belied the Lord, Nayler told these Ranters in 1659, and said that 'sin and righteousness is all one to God', whom many Ranters openly deny. Their 'light answers' and 'mockings' 'have made heavy the burden of the meek and lowly, against whom you have sported'.[108] Nayler's experience, and still more his repentance, helped to restore a sense of sin to the Quaker movement. Nayler had believed that it was possible for a man to achieve Christ's perfection and perform Christ's works: his entry into Bristol was made in that spirit. But after his terrible punishment he was convinced that he had been in error, that 'the motions of sin did still work from the old ground and root'.[109] So he rebuked his Ranter defenders:

> do not say, All things are lawful, all things are pure, etc.; and so sit down and say you are redeemed and have right to all; but first pass through all things, one after another, as the light learneth you; and with a true measure see if you be from under the power of any. When you have proved this throughout all things, and found your freedom, then you may say, All things are lawful, and know what is expedient, and what edifies yourselves and others and the rest to reign over, without bondage thereto.[110]

Nayler had the right to say that, arrived at through his great suffering and shame. ('I found it alone, being forsaken. I have fellowship there with them who lived in dens and desolate places in the earth.')[111] But those phrases, 'what is expedient', 'what edifies', closed the door on much that had been courageous and life-giving in the early Quaker movement. Heresy and schism were endemic among Quakers for the rest of the century. The enormous problem of disciplining this amorphous movement fell principally to George Fox. For all protestant churches the appeal to conscience, to the inner voice, conflicted with the necessity of organization and discipline if the church was to survive. Luther's rejection of his own principles when quoted against him was only the first of many examples. If I am right in supposing that Quakers drew their rank and file largely from Ranter and Seeker groupings, then their problem was to impose discipline on the most individualist of all nonconformists. It cost Fox much heart-searching and enmity before he convinced the movement.

'The saints of God may be perfectly freed from sin in this life so as no more to commit it,' Burrough had said; and I quoted Fox himself earlier on the preachers who 'plead for sin'.[112] But gradually the need to draw lines between themselves and Ranters, and to eliminate Ranters within their own ill-defined ranks, led Quakers to place more emphasis on human sinfulness, even among Friends. The absolute individualism of the appeal to Christ within every man had to be curbed. Quakers ceased to perform miracles, and the book of miracles which George Fox had carefully collected as evidence of the truth of Quaker doctrine was suppressed.[113] As Messianic hopes faded, so attitudes towards society and the state had to be defined. It seems to have been the approach of the restoration that decided Fox in favour of pacifism and non-participation in politics.[114] His turn witnesses to acceptance of the fact that the Kingdom of God is not coming in the near future. So long as that had appeared to be on the agenda, political attitudes had necessarily to remain fluid. But now the problem is one of the relationship of the Society of Friends, a sect (for all its unique features) like any other sect, to the world in which it has to continue to exist. For this Ranterism was not enough.

William Penn wrote of the Ranter wing among Quakers:

> They would have had every man independent, that as he had the principle in himself, he should only stand and fall to that, and nobody else; and though the measure of light and grace might differ, yet the nature of it was the same; and being so, they struck at the spiritual unity which a people guided by the same principle are naturally led into ... Some weakly mistook good order in the government of church affairs for discipline in worship, and that it was so pressed or recommended by him [Fox] and other brethren. And they were ready to reflect the same things that Dissenters had very reasonably objected upon the national churches, that have coercively pressed conformity to their respective creeds and worships.

Penn said that it was a Ranter error to suppose that Christ's fulfilling of the law for us discharged us of all obligation and duty required by the law, as it was a Ranter error to suppose that all things a man did were good if he was persuaded they were good.[115]

The later Quaker problem was to win agreement on objective standards of good and bad, lawful and sinful. And this, Penn argued in almost Hobbist vein, necessitated church 'power' of some kind. Otherwise 'farewell to all christian church order and discipline', which would be 'an inlet to Ranterism and so to atheism'.[116] That seems pretty fairly to state the dilemma of a highly individualistic religion which grew up in a millenary atmosphere and was at first organizationally influenced mainly by a desire to hinder hindrances to spiritual freedom. But now it had to face the problem of continuing to exist in an uncongenial world that was here to stay. That necessitated discipline and organization, a more regular preaching ministry. No longer, in William Penn's words, could men afford 'to wait for a motion of the spirit for everything'.[117] Penn was a man with a large private income, the son of an admiral, a friend of James II. The man who above all made the 'adjustment to the state', who theologized the Quakers' return to sin,[118] was Robert Barclay, son of an old Scottish landed family related to the Stuarts, who was also to be seen at James II's court. In addition to his famous *Apology* (English translation 1678) Barclay published an attack on *The Anarchy of the Ranters and other Libertines* in 1676.

A whole series of splits within the Quaker movement occurred. In the 1650s there were the Proud Quakers, who showed clear ranting tendencies. They used profane language, were lax in conduct; some of them were football players and wrestlers. Their leader, Rice Jones of Nottingham, set up an ale-house.[119] After the restoration John Perrot had a direct command from God that hats should be worn during prayer. And indeed if Christ in man could not doff his hat to his earthly father, why should he to his Father in heaven? Ranters had kept their hats on during prayer: so did Nayler in the Bristol period. But Perrot went on to deny all human arrangements for worship, even meeting at stated times and places. Fox said that Perrot preached 'the rotten principles of the old Ranters', and associated him with Nayler, many of whose former partisans supported Perrot. Edward Burrough also straddled the gap between Ranters and Quakers. He may originally have had Ranter sympathies; at one time he worked closely with Perrot, and he retained confidence in him longer than any other Quaker leader.[120]

Fox's reply was to tighten the organization of government in the Society of Friends, and this in its turn led to the Story–Wilkinson separation in the 1670s. The dissidents opposed subordination of the *individual* light within to the sense of the meeting, and objected to the hierarchical structure – a national church! – of women's meetings, monthly and quarterly meetings. They spoke of courts, sessions, synods, Popes, bishops, edicts and canons, and rejected on principle the condemnation of individual Quakers by any church meeting. The Story–Wilkinson separation was joined, we are told, by 'a great many of the looser sort', 'some libertine spirits', who, in Penn's words, 'tread down your hedge under the specious pretence of being left to the light within'. The separatists felt that the new organization was 'an infringement upon individual liberty', that it denied the continuing presence of Christ within *all* believers.[121] In such trivia, if they are trivia, did the Ranter element in Quakerism perish. A royalist poet commented:

> The Quaker who before
> Did rant and did roar
> Great thrift now will tell ye on.

But the royalist was unimpressed by the change, or at the mercy of his rhyme, for he concluded 'But it tends to rebellion'.[122]

Ranterism was better at destruction than construction. In 1650 it was by listening to the errors of 'Diggers, Levellers and Ranters', that Baptist churches in Huntingdonshire and elsewhere were 'shaken' and 'broken up'.[123] In Cleveland in 1651 it was meetings that had been 'shattered' under Ranter influence that turned to the Quakers.[124] The communal sense of the Quaker meeting was later fitted into the discipline of something very like a national church. It was not a compulsive discipline, as Fox, Penn and Barclay repeatedly emphasized; but the difference had to be explained again and again to those who did not like it. It meant an end to the absolute individualism in which the spirit of God led each Friend independently.[125]

Fox's position is logical, once the world and sin are accepted. Since part of the strength of the inner light, of conscience, is its ability to change with a changing intellectual climate, it is not surprising that in the England of Charles II the Quaker consensus came down on the side of discipline, organization, common sense. The eccentricities of Quakerism were quietly dropped. Some were so hallowed by time and George Fox's own personality – like hat honour, 'thou' and grey homespun – that they were preserved as intriguing museum pieces, a party badge or test of loyalty, long after they had lost their first significance. But going naked for a sign, miracles and the other individualist exuberances of early Quakers and Ranters disappeared as the inner light adapted itself to the standards of this commercial world where yea and nay helped one to prosper.[126] It is as pointless to condemn this as a sell-out as to praise its realism: it was simply the consequence of the organized survival of a group which had failed to turn the world upside down.

So Fox in the *Journal* was not suppressing the past, not deliberately rewriting history. His inner voice was telling him different things in the 1680s from what it had told him and James Nayler thirty years earlier. And since the voice of Christ is one, to all men and at all times, it must have said the same then as it said in the 1680s.[127] James Nayler became a black shadow lying across memory. The relation of Quakers to Ranters is complex, and we may do Fox an injustice by using the *Journal* against him at too early a date. But it would be nice to know what element of after-wisdom is contained in Fox's description, his gratified description, of how at one and the same meeting in Yorkshire in 1654 he stopped the mouths of Ranters and converted the Lady Montague.[128]

Seen in this light, the famous remark of Hotham to Fox in 1652 may look rather different from the interpretation usually put on it. Quakers prevented the nation being overrun by Ranters, said the Justice; without Quakers 'all the justices in the nation could not have stopped it with all their laws, because (said he) they would have said as we said and done as we commanded, and yet have kept their own principle still. But this principle of truth, said he, overthrows their principle, and the root and ground thereof.'[129] Assuming it is correctly reported (perhaps quite a large assumption), this is not a simple statement like 'Methodism saved England from a French Revolution.' J.P.s could never have destroyed Ranterism because Ranters would compromise, recant, and yet remain of the same opinion still; but the Quakers' principle led them to bear witness in public, and so to be far less dangerous. For if they were to survive, their public witness forced on them the organization which destroyed the Ranter element in their faith.[130] One of the many Ranter characteristics of the followers of Story and Wilkinson was readiness to flee from persecution.

And yet, even after Fox had died, his wife Margaret, in her moving testimony concerning him, recalled that on the second day of her acquaintance with him Fox declared 'You will say that Christ saith this, and the apostles say this; but what canst thou say?' 'It cut me to the heart,' Margaret Fox recalled; 'I saw clearly we were all wrong. So I sat down in my pew again and cried bitterly.' He 'opened us a book that we had never read in, nor indeed had never heard it was our duty to read in it, to wit the light of Christ in our consciences'.[131] We can perhaps visualize the 28-year-old shepherd in the church, his hair provocatively long,[132] asking the simple question that put his congregation above Christ and the apostles. Or consider his other this-worldly questions, asked in 1659. Will any 'believe that you are Christians that will mar the workmanship of God? . . . Did not Christ come to . . . save men's lives and not destroy them?'[133] Quaker perfectionism may in the century after 1660 have degenerated into 'a shallow humanism' under Fox's influence.[134] But there were worse creeds in the seventeenth century than humanism.

Samuel Fisher and the Bible

The believer is the only book in which God now writes his
New Testament.

> WILLIAM DELL, *The Trial of Spirits* (1653), quoted
> by R. M. Jones, *Mysticism and Democracy*, p. 104.

I   SAMUEL FISHER

Samuel Fisher, son of a hatter at Northampton, was educated at
Trinity College and the Puritan New Inn Hall, Oxford. Although a
lecturer in Kent in the 1630s, he underwent Presbyterian ordination
in 1643, but resigned his living when he became a Baptist. As pastor
to a congregation in Ashford he maintained himself by farming. In
1654 he became a Quaker. He died of the plague in 1665.

In his Baptist period Fisher published a lengthy defence of dipping
as against sprinkling. He called sprinklers Rantizers ($\dot{\rho}\alpha\nu\tau\dot{\iota}\zeta\omega$, I
sprinkle), which no doubt seemed quite a good joke then: it enabled
him to depict Baptists as occupying a middle position between 'the
Rantizer and the Ranter, the one hereticizing in the excess by adding
a new thing, the other in defect by owning nothing'.[1] He rebuked 'the
rabble of the ruder sort of Ranters and ungodly scoffers', some of
whom deny 'that there was any Christ'. 'What little reason the
Ranter had,' he complained, 'to redeem himself from that bondage
which he deems to be in the observation' of ordinances 'before the
time appointed, much more to run beyond the bounds of modesty
and all good manners also, as not all but many if not the most of

these do, first or last, who despise any of the ordinances of the Lord Jesus.'[2] 'The Rakesham Ranter . . . regards neither God nor devil, and reckons on all Christ's commandments as not worth a rush . . . Some Ranters are not ashamed to say that they are Christ and God, and there is no other God than they and what's in them.'[3] Fisher clearly took pains with his style, which has something of Rabelais and something of Martin Marprelate in it – buffooning and alliterative. He uses abbreviations, e.g. PPP for Pope, Prelates, Presbyters (or sometimes Priests), and called on the latter to 'depart from that papistical posture of parish churches and pastoral relation to such as are not sheep'.[4]

He employed the same alliterative popular style from time to time after his conversion to Quakerism, referring to 'the teachers and textmen tangled in their own talkings about their text'.[5] 'We do not affirm Christ himself to be in all men; . . . nevertheless all . . . have some measure or other of his light.'[6] Heaven is neither only above nor only below the firmament: it is 'in every humble, broken and contrite spirit'. The saints may attain to a state of perfection and freedom from sin in this life.[7] God will save all that are truly willing in his way to be saved from their sins by him. Christ came intentionally to save all men; if all men are not saved it is through their own default. The light of nature equals grace, 'God's law or light in the conscience of all men'.[8] 'Are ye not ashamed,' he asked defenders of the Eternal Decrees, 'thus to engross the grace of God . . . among yourselves and a few like your sinning selves? . . . For the elect are very few with you.' 'Are ye not ashamed to make God not only tyrannical but hypocritical and as dissembling as yourselves?' If a king offers pardon to 1000 men on terms which 999 of them could not perform, it is not mercy in him to pardon the thousandth. This makes God 'a merciless tyrant and arrant hypocrite' – as though he offered meat to a man locked in the stocks, saying ' "Why wilt thou starve, thou self-murdering man? Come to me, and here is meat for thee . . . But if thou wilt not come I will knock thy brains out." ' Or like one who says 'he truly desires to make me his heir, . . . conditionally I will take a journey to the man in the moon first, to get it confirmed there; . . . but if I refuse to go thither he will kill me'.[9] Most of this is traditional Quaker doctrine, though expressed with Fisher's peculiar homely humour. More interesting is Fisher's application of the doctrine to Biblical criticism.

II   THE BIBLE

Among many possible approaches to the Bible, two stand out among the radicals. One was to use its stories as myths, to which each could give his own sense, a sense that need not consider the original meaning of the text – rather as Bacon used classical myths in *The Wisdom of the Ancients*. Winstanley employed this method, as did some Ranters and some Quakers. Thomas Edwards's twenty-ninth Error was 'We did look for great matters from one crucified at Jerusalem 1600 years ago, but that does us no good; it must be a Christ formed in us.'[10] Winstanley among others contrasted the historical Christ with the Christ within: the distinction between 'the history' and 'the mystery' was made by John Everard and by Ranters like Salmon and Coppe, as well as by Arise Evans and Ranter-influenced Baptists.[11] 'A chief one of the Army,' Erbery tells us, 'would once usually say that the flesh of Christ and the letter of Scripture were the two great idols of Antichrist.'[12]

Another approach denied the infallibility of the Bible, or submitted it to close textual criticism. Winstanley shared this approach too. He severely criticized those who based their belief merely on the letter of the Bible. 'There are good rules in the Scripture,' he wrote condescendingly, 'if they were obeyed and practised.'[13] But he would not make the Bible his main source for a code of conduct. One of Winstanley's chief complaints against the clergy was that they claimed a monopoly of interpreting the Bible, and suppressed the free spirit in the uneducated. 'You say you have the just copies of their writings; you do not know but as your fathers have told you, which may be as well false as true if you have no better ground than tradition.' Which translation is the truest? There are many. Different sects, different truths. 'And thus you lead the people like horses by the noses, and ride upon them at your pleasure ... How can these Scriptures be called the everlasting gospel, seeing it is torn in pieces daily amongst yourselves, by various translations, inferences and conclusions.' The spirit in men today is above the gospel, he concluded. 'The Scriptures were not appointed for a rule to the world to walk by without the spirit . . . For this is to walk by the eyes of other men.' Instead Winstanley praised those who 'become like unto wise-hearted Thomas', that 'believe nothing but what they see reason for'.[14]

Ranters were said to hold that the Bible 'hath been the cause of all our misery and divisions, . . . of all the blood that hath been shed in the world' – a view that Bunyan's Mr Badman repeated.[15] There will never be peace, some Ranters said, till all Bibles are burned – as soldiers did in Winstanley's parish church in 1649, as Thomas Tany and some followers of Perrot did. The Bible, Ranters declared, was not directed at England or any church or man in England – which suggests a more rational historic approach to Biblical studies than was common in the seventeenth century.[16] This approach might be bolstered by Biblical scholarship. Thus Walwyn was alleged to have said that 'the Scripture is so plainly and directly contradictory to itself' that he did not believe it to be the Word of God.[17] Lawrence Clarkson found 'so much contradiction' in the Bible that 'I had no faith in it at all, no more than a history'. There were men before Adam, and the world would continue to exist eternally.[18] To Andrew Wyke, a mechanic of Colchester and his lady friend, who went to visit Coppe in prison in Coventry, 'the Scriptures . . . were no more than a ballad'.[19] 'The Bible was the plague of England,' a Bristol grocer said. 'A pack of lies,' declared John Wilkinson of Leicester.[20] Bauthumley, who allegorized the Bible, concluded that it is no better than any books by good men.[21] Henry Oldenburg quotes many examples of fundamental criticisms of the Biblical narrative current in England in 1656: 'the whole story of the creation seems to have been composed in order to introduce the Sabbath . . . from motives of merely political prudence . . . Moses concocted the whole story.'[22]

Half-way between mythologizing the Bible and rejecting it as a guiding document was selective interpretation. Each sect and congregation practised this to a greater or lesser extent. As Dr Capp points out,[23] Fifth Monarchists ignored some inconvenient texts in the Bible, by mutual agreement. One of many objections to academic scholars, to university-trained priests (though not one that was often expressed), was their ability to remind men of texts it was not convenient to remember, which were difficult to fit into the agreed synthesis. Accurate scholarship, knowledge of the total Bible, could be constricting. Mechanick students of the Bible were more creative, more boldly innovating, *because* they were selective in their approach, more responsive to problems of their own world which demanded new solutions.

Milton and Henry Parker both raised this to a theory, the theory that the Bible must be subordinated to human convenience. It 'ought to be so in proportion as may be wielded and managed by the life of man without penning him up from the duties of human society'. Or as Parker put it, 'we ought to be very tender how we seek to reconcile that to God's law which we cannot reconcile to man's equity, or how we make God the author of that constitution which man reaps inconvenience from'.[24] 'No ordinance,' said Milton, 'human or from heaven, can bind against the good of man.' 'The general end of every ordinance . . . is the good of man; yea, his temporal good not excluded.'[25]

There is a grandeur about this arrogance which reminds us of Perrot refusing to doff his hat to the Almighty.[26] It was based, as so often with Milton, on sound scholarship. For the text of the Bible is so distorted and corrupted that we cannot rely on it as a guide: we can trust nothing but our own reason in deriving judgments. Our reason possesses an illumination superior to Scripture.[27] Milton was glad to find that ideas at which he arrived by searching his own conscience could be found in the Bible; but they had greater authority for him because they were in his conscience than because they were in the Bible. Similarly Jacob Bauthumley did not 'expect to be taught by Bibles or books, but by God'. 'The Bible without is but a shadow of that Bible which is within', though he thought either can deceive us.[28] John Everard said that 'letter learning' or 'university knowledge' was inferior to the religious experience of those who 'know Jesus Christ and the Scriptures experimentally rather than grammatically, literally or academically'.[29]

The Scriptures, Winstanley argued, should be used to illustrate truths of which one is already convinced. A man subject to Reason 'needs not that any man should teach him'.[30] 'What the Lord opened in me,' Fox put it, 'I afterwards found was agreeable' to the Bible. 'That which may be known of God is manifest within people,' he declared in 1658; 'thou needest no man to teach thee.' The Bible is not the most perfect rule of faith and life to the saints, Edward Burrough agreed.[31] At a less scholarly level we see the same process at work in the *Records of the Churches of Christ gathered at Fenstanton, Warboys and Hexham*. There we hear men and women rejecting the Bible, or parts of it which they do not like, in the name of a spirit within them. They are in effect applying Milton's test of the convenience of men in society, but they could always be out-quoted (though not convinced) by the greater knowledge shown by the Baptist organizers.[32]

In 1657 the Worcester clothier Clement Writer attempted to sum up this approach in his *Fides Divina*. He argued that the Bible could not be infallible because of its many errors of transcription and translation, and because there was no agreement about which books were inspired and which not. 'No testimony that is fallible and liable to error can possibly be a divine testimony.' 'The Scripture reports the miracles; can the miracles reported by the Scripture confirm that report?'[33] Writer repeatedly claimed to be 'destitute of school-learning and human arts and sciences'. 'I shall not say that human learning is a special limb of that Beast, but I will say that Antichrist shall never attain to that his advancement but by the special assistance and means of human learning.' He wrote neither for the learned nor for 'the careless vulgar', but for 'the middle sort and plain-hearted people'. He believed that 'if any divine right remains now in England, it is in the people of England'. But his outlook by the mid-1650s was as pessimistic as Erbery's. We can no more 'call back the light of the glorious gospel when it is withdrawn by God, as now apparently it is' since the apostasy. 'This Babylonish darkness . . . is like to continue.' Our duty is therefore to tolerate one another, to pray and to wait.[34] Baxter regarded Writer as an infidel.[35]

The scholarly underpinning of this position was done more effectively by Samuel Fisher in his *The Rustics Alarm to the Rabbies* of

1660. Holding that the spirit is far more important than the letter of the Bible, Fisher asks how reliable is the existing text? It is silly to call it the Word of God. There is no evidence of divine authority for the present canon of the New Testament. The Apocrypha is at least as reliable in text, and as likely to be divinely inspired, as many of the books of the Bible: many books of both Testaments have been lost. Would God allow this to happen to divinely inspired texts?[36] Nor will it do to say that the universal reception of the present canon guarantees divine inspiration: what about the Koran, 'the public possession of many generations and in actual authority among men as a standard throughout the whole world of Mahometanism?'[37]

Even John Owen admits that transcribers have made a number of small mistakes: what guarantee have we that they did not occasionally corrupt the text in more than trifles?[38] What with problems of Hebrew points, the numerous different transcriptions and translations and now printers' errors in addition, the Bible is a 'huge heap of uncertainties'. Fisher quotes Owen to the effect that 'when the foundation of faith is utter uncertainty, then the faith can be . . . no more than mere fancy and uncertainty'. But so is faith based on the assumption that the Bible as we now have it is the Word of God. It is rather, Fisher said in words which anticipate Spinoza, 'a bulk of heterogeneous writings, compiled together by men taking what they could find of the several sorts of writings that are therein, and . . . crowding them into a canon, or standard for the trial of all spirits, doctrines, truths; and by them alone'.[39]

Hence controversies over the text of the Bible between protestants and catholics, and horrible wars of religion. Protestants thought 'all would be unity itself among them' once they turned from traditions of the church to the text of the Bible: but among the reformed clergy the Bible increases rather than diminishes strife. 'Dark minds diving into the Scripture divine lies enough out of it to set whole countries on fire.' The letter in fact 'is too weak an engine to set to rights what's out of order'. 'Till men turn to the light and Word within' there will be no peace.[40]

Fisher's is a remarkable work of popular Biblical criticism, based on real scholarship. Its effect is to demote the Bible from its central position in the protestant scheme of things, to make it a book like any other. After a century during which men had died to bring the Word of God in the vernacular to the common people, during which the main stimulus to popular education in protestant countries had been the desire to equip ordinary laymen to read the Scriptures, here is Fisher coolly saying that there are enough Bibles for anyone who can read and has money to buy them. The Bible is read too much and heard too often.[41] The martyrs would have been shocked to see protestantism come to that: their persecutors would smile ironically. For Fisher's book marks the end of an epoch, the epoch of protestant Bibliolatry. Diversity of sects, each with its own interpretation of the Bible, had dissolved protestant unity: Fisher virtually abandoned any hope of unity of interpretation, and so of any external unity. It is the end of the authority of the Book; but by no means a return to the authority of tradition. It is simply the end of authority.

Fisher, whilst admitting that there is no agreement on interpretation even among those who have the light, bravely counters by asserting that the fact that men disagree about measurements does not mean that there is no such thing as a yard. His yard is in fact no more and no less than renaissance scholarly standards of textual criticism applied to the Bible. What is important is that Fisher wrote in the vernacular, in a racy, popular style; and that no one could accuse him of being an infidel. His work remained a Quaker textbook for more than a century. It is difficult to over-estimate its significance in this period. In the white heat of controversy in the 1640s and 50s the inner light could replace the Bible without shattering the foundations. But afterwards, all passion spent, God's kingdom having failed to come, Fisher's approach to the Bible, recollected in tranquillity, in apathy, inevitably led to scepticism. The appeal to the 'light within', a light which some even of the heathen philosophers had,[42] then became very difficult to differentiate in practice from simple human reason. When Vanbrugh's Lady Brute countered the New Testament command to return good for evil by saying 'that may be a mistake in the translation',[43] who knows how much she owed to Clement Writer and Samuel Fisher? After the revolutionary decades, after Winstanley, Hobbes, Writer and Fisher, the

Bible would never be the same again. But to university divines, Fisher, like William Dell, must have seemed to be committing treason to the clerical caste, by using the apparatus of scholarship to expose the scholarly mysteries to public obloquy: the rabbis particularly disliked being alarmed by rustics. Fisher deserves greater recognition as a precursor of the English enlightenment than he has yet received.

12
John Warr and the Law

Law . . . is but the declarative will of conquerors, how they will have their subjects to be ruled.

WINSTANLEY, Fire in the Bush (1650),
in Sabine, p. 464.

I   THE LAW

It was clearer to Winstanley than to most radicals that the state and its legal institutions existed in order to hold the lower classes in place. I have quoted elsewhere evidence to support his view.[1] In Chancery no less than at common law rank counted: the word of a gentleman of good standing would be accepted against that of a maidservant even if supported by another witness.[2] 'When a felony or murder is committed,' observed Francis Osborne, 'the next poor houses are ordinarily searched.'[3] Many of the New Model Army thought reform of the law was one of the things they had fought the civil war for.[4] They wanted the mysteries of the mumbo-jumbo men made available in the vernacular, they wanted legal proceedings and writings in English, not Latin or law French; they wanted local courts and trials by laymen, elected J.P.s, a codified law, no lawyers and no fees.[5] 'The laws of kings,' Winstanley wrote, 'have been always made against such actions as the common people were most inclinable to, on purpose to ensnare them into their sessions and courts; that the lawyers and clergy, who were the king's supporters, might get money thereby and live in fullness by other men's labours.'

'The law is the fox, poor men are the geese; he pulls off their feathers and feeds upon them.'[6] 'Clergymen and common lawyers are the chiefest oppressors' in the land, Erbery agreed; prisoners and the poor 'are the chief among the oppressed'.[7] The Quaker Francis Howgill thought the only use of 'the law as it now is' was 'for the envious man who hath much money to revenge himself upon his poor neighbours'.[8] Burrough wrote against 'the great and heavy oppressions of the law', the enrichment of lawyers at the expense of the poor, for whom 'the remedy is worse than the disease'. He and Fox, like Winstanley, denounced the death penalty for theft.[9]

George Fox the Younger subsumed this into a general attitude towards the state:

the rich covetous oppressing men, who oppresseth the poor, they have the only power to choose law makers, and they will choose to be sure such as will uphold them in their oppression; and the poor man that is oppressed, though he had no power allowed him to choose, yet he must be subject to the laws which they make who are his oppressors, or else he is accounted a rebel.[10]

Even Oliver Cromwell, as late as 1650, said 'the law as it is now constituted serves only to maintain the lawyers and to encourage the rich to oppress the poor'.[11]

We could quote endlessly. But in the upside-down world, where there is no property, there will be 'no need of judges'. 'Take a cobbler from his seat, or a butcher from his shop, or any other tradesman that is an honest and just man, and let him hear the case and determine the same, and then betake himself to his work again.'[12] 'There is no need of them [lawyers], for there is to be no buying and selling; neither any need to expound laws, for the bare letter of the law shall be both judge and lawyer.'[13] John Rogers, John Spittlehouse and Peter Chamberlen called for judges to be elected.[14]

The nearest the radicals could hope to get to this ideal in the old world was by elevating the jury above the judges. 'Mechanics, bred up illiterately to handicrafts', could judge as well as lawyers trained in the handicraft of writing,[15] just as they could preach as well as university-educated divines. Lawyers are the Norman army of Antichrist's laity, declared John Rogers, as priests are Antichrist's clergy.[16] Henry Marten, commanding an irregular regiment of plebeians under the banner *For the People*, told a jury in the summer of 1648 to keep on their hats in the presence of the judge, in order to show that they were chief judges in the court.[17] 'A damnable blasphemous heresy,' Judge Jermyn significantly called it when Lilburne aired the same doctrine.[18] Levellers, Diggers and Quakers refused to pay lawyers' fees, insisting on defending themselves, often with very good effect. George Fox, who like Lilburne knew a good deal of law, like Lilburne addressed himself to the jury, not the judge. He repeated the Leveller and Fifth Monarchist demand that all the law should be 'drawn up in a little short volume, and all the rest burnt'.[19] The Quakers William Penn and William Mead were defendants in Bushell's Case in 1670, which made history by establishing the right of the jury to return a verdict with which the judge disagreed.

Despite the strength of the case for legal reform, despite the efforts both of the Rump's committee for reform of the law and of the Barebones Parliament, the reformers failed. 'Property is little if liberty be encroached on,' said Charles Cocke, opposing law reform in 1656; 'and liberty little if property be taken away.'[20] The words would have appealed to Ireton and to Baxter: the sentiment commended itself to the men of property. 'And so, as the sword pulls down kingly power with one hand, the king's old law builds up monarchy again with the other,' said Winstanley. 'The old laws cannot look with any other face than they did: though they be washed with Commonwealth's water, their countenance is still withered.'[21] Lawyers supported first the offer of the crown to Cromwell, then the restoration of Charles II. The law remained unreformed till the nineteenth century.

II   JOHN WARR

But the radicals certainly had the best of the argument. Most interesting of them all is John Warr. He is known to historians as a legal writer who advocated fundamental reforms of the law. 'When the poor and oppressed want right, they meet with law ... Many times the very law is the badge of our oppression, its proper intention being to enslave the people.' Without fundamental reform of the law the people cannot be free: 'an equal and speedy distribution of right ought to be the abstract and epitome of all laws'. When the law was in a known language, as before the Norman Conquest, a man might be his own advocate.[22]

But this reforming tract was based on a deeper and less well-known philosophy, of which hints peep through even here. 'At the foundation of governments justice was in men before it came to be in laws.' But now 'lust by the adoption of greatness is enacted law ... Laws upon laws do bridle the people ... An usurper reigns, and freedom is proscribed like an exile, living only in the understandings of some few men.' The oppressed man stands in no more need of this 'mere web, a frothy and contentious way of law, ... than the tender-hearted Christian' stands in need of Thomas Aquinas 'to resolve him in his doubts'. 'The notion of fundamental law is no such idol as men make it' (e.g. the Levellers). 'For what, I pray you, is fundamental law but such customs as are of the eldest date and longest continuance? ... The more fundamental a law is, the more difficult, not the less necessary, to be reformed.' 'But yet the minds of men are the great wheels of things; thence come changes and alterations in the world; teeming freedom exerts and puts forth itself.' The law can be 'reduced to its original state, which is the protection of the poor against the mighty'.[23]

A sketch of Warr's underlying philosophy had been published the preceding year in *Administrations Civil and Spiritual*. This is a remarkable application to legal thinking of the radical protestant emphasis on the religion of the heart: it is legal theory based on the inner light. Warr sees history as a dialectical interaction between two forces, Equity (Reason) and Form (Use and Custom), the religion of principles and the religion of ceremonies. (Equity is of course not used in the legal sense: Warr thought the Court of Chancery was first erected 'merely to elude the letter of the law, which though defective yet had some certainty; and, under a pretence of conscience, to devolve all causes upon mere will, swayed by corrupt interest'.[24]) Warr shared the general prejudices of the radicals in religious matters, though he expressed them in his own way. 'The distinction of the clergy and laity came up under the protection of Form ... Clerical and fleshly interests may be maintained in a Presbyteral as well as a Papal way', and indeed in an Independent way. Law reform is part of a general spiritual revolution. As Equity gradually prevails over Form, worldly interests fall. 'The time of restitution or redemption of principles from that thick darkness wherein they have lain is that which the saints long after and count it their honour to be employed in, ... the redemption of the world from its civil darkness.' This darkness, however, exists *within* men: it consists of ignorance of Equity and acceptance of an ideology of Form. Outward yokes are but badges of our inward darkness.[25]

In this cosmic battle of the principles, for Warr, God is on Reason's side, though Form tries to creep under the protection of Reason. What Warr wants to do is

> only to free the clear understanding from the bondage of the Form and to raise it up to Equity, which is the substance itself. For though the dark understanding may be restrained or guided, yet the principled man hath his freedom within himself, and walking in the light of Equity and Reason (truly so called) knows no bounds but his own, even Equity.[26]

In England the law is a means by which the rich oppress the poor: in so far as Reason accepts this, it is guilty of disobedience and rebellion. (Some disobedience is more lawful than subjection, as in the Revolt of the Netherlands against Spain, or of Parliament against Charles I: but this is not the case here.) 'The destruction of the world, or the present state of things, will be a great loss to some, but a mighty advantage to the world in general, when Equity shall be advanced in its perfect height (the clear image of God in the world).' This will be a sufficient compensation for all our sufferings, losses, bloodshed. 'You'll say, this principle overthrows all order, magistracy, government, and lets loose the reins to all licentiousness, and makes the world an heap?' All such prejudices must be removed. The Forms of the world have only 'a counterfeit order, ... which brings fleshly ease'; but God delights to overthrow this order and to set up his own 'confusion', which indeed is the best order. The death of Form 'may well be called a resurrection of the dead'.[27]

The distinction between Form and Reason, Precedent and Equity, Law and Grace, runs through seventeenth-century radical thought, though Warr makes exceptionally clear sense of it. *The Army Declaration* of 14 June 1647 distinguished between the letter and 'the equitable sense' of laws. The officer is but the Form or letter of the Army, said Richard Overton in *The Hunting of the Foxes*: the equitable or essential part is the soldiery.[28] 'It matters not what the forms be, so we attain the ends of government,' wrote *Mercurius Politicus* on the eve of the expulsion of the Long Parliament by Oliver Cromwell, who himself was not 'wedded and glued to forms of government'.[29] John Cook objected to 'this over-doting upon old forms'.[30] What is especially interesting is Warr's fusion of his religious ideas with his driest and most technical legal analysis. Warr's philosophy, with its mythological use of the Bible, its lack of enthusiasm for fundamental law, appears to be closer to that of Winstanley than to that of the Levellers. But analogies spring to mind from all sides. Abiezer Coppe in 1649 made use of similar pairs of opposites – Form/Power, Type/Truth.[31] Thomas Sprat in 1667 pointed out that in war as in philosophy 'greater things are produced by the *free* way than the formal'.[32]

In *The Priviledges of the People* (1649) Warr applied his analysis more directly to politics. The divisions of the civil war resulted from men's minds being 'prejudiced with corrupt interests of one sort or other . . . But is Truth divided? Is there not one common principle of freedom which (if discovered) would reconcile all?' Prerogative and privilege (even privilege of Parliament) are altogether inconsistent with true freedom. To claim 'to serve for the county' as M.P. may be as hypocritical as the Pope claiming to be the servant of the church. There are some sparks of freedom in the mind of most, and these are God's image in the mind. 'God favours all weak things.' The whole body of the people is above their rulers, whether one or more. 'True majesty is in the spirit, and consists in the divine image of God in the mind.' The princes of the world, falling short of this, have replaced it with outward badges of fleshly honour, empty shows, void of substance. Weak though these are, they have dazzled our eyes, owing to the darkness which is in us. When we ourselves shall be raised up to an inward glory, then shall we be able to judge of that majesty and glory which rests upon another. ''Tis not possible for a people to be too free,' wrote Warr, but with Milton he recognized that liberty in its full appearance would darken the eye newly recovered from blindness: so gradualism was in order.[33]

There would be plenty of would-be legal reformers in England during the revolutionary decades: but I know none with such a systematic philosophy. Indeed, I know of no one, except perhaps Winstanley, who so comprehensively (and yet so concisely and elegantly) attempts to link the inner light to political democracy and legal revolution. It would be nice to think we need not equate our author with the John Warr who was an extensive purchaser of crown lands, mainly in south-western England and Wales: but no doubt he too, like Wildman, had a legal living to earn.[34]

13

The Island of Great Bedlam

> If madness be in the heart of every man, Eccles. 9.3, then this is the island of Great Bedlam ... Come, let's all be mad together.
>
> W. ERBERY, *The Mad Mans Plea* (1653), p. 8.

I   RADICAL MADNESS

A characteristic of a primitive society is an interest in, and awe and tolerance of, madness. In seventeenth-century England it was fashionable to go to Bedlam to gape at poor lunatics; masques of madmen dancing appear frequently in Elizabethan and especially Jacobean drama. Court fools, and fools in aristocratic houses, are a special case of this: one suspects they were not often as witty as Shakespeare's, though no doubt some wise men played the fool to get a living. A few intelligent rulers, by listening to their fools, may have broken through the cloud of flattering courtiers who stood between them and public opinion.[1] It was a step forward when a radical separatist like Henry Barrow objected on principle to bishops keeping fools to entertain them.[2] The Stuarts were the last English kings to employ a court fool; the last fool known to have been kept by an English landed family died in Durham in 1746, the year when the last attempt to restore the Stuart line was defeated.[3] 'Gone are the halcyon days of the jesters,' John Owen asserted in 1655.[4] Aubrey illustrates another way in which sensitivity was increasing. 'Till the breaking out of the civil wars,' he wrote, Tom O'Bedlams ('poor distracted men that had been put into

Bedlam') 'did travel about the country', being licensed to go begging on 'recovering to some soberness'. But 'since the wars I do not remember to have seen any of them'.[5]

Awe and tolerance of the mad are illustrated by the relative immunity which a man like Arise Evans, or a lady like Eleanor Davies, enjoyed until they overstepped the bounds of the politically endurable. Arise Evans could hang about Charles I's court for days on end, and deliver a message from God to the King announcing that he and his kingdom were to be destroyed. Meanwhile bishops ran away at the sight of him, and the royal Secretary of State asked for the prayers of 'God's secretary'. In the 1640s Evans got only a brief spell in Bridewell for telling the City's Deputy Recorder that Arise Evans was the Lord his God. Later he called on Oliver Cromwell and stayed to midnight; he pestered the Council of State to restore the son of the King whom they had executed; and republican officers defended him in long arguments at Whitehall.[6] The Commonwealth did not even imprison him as Charles and the Deputy Recorder had done. Lady Eleanor Davies *printed* verses predicting the violent overthrow of Charles I, and was sent to Bedlam. The accuracy of her prophecies gave her 'the reputation of a cunning woman amongst the ignorant people'.[7] Nevertheless, so long as the holy imbecile had no disciples, he or she – unlike James Nayler in 1656 – had a great deal of latitude.[8] Prophets could be used to further others' political purposes, as Arise Evans may have been; Professor Underdown suggests Cromwell and Ireton made use of the prophetess Elizabeth Poole in the anxious weeks before the execution of Charles I.[9]

In the freer circumstances of the 1640s and 50s most 'madmen' appear to be political radicals. For this there could be many explanations. One is popular in our day – that mental breakdown is a form of social protest, or at least a reaction to intolerable social conditions: those who break down may be the truly sane. One wonders how conscious Shakespeare was of what he was doing when he put significant social criticism into the mouths of fools and those, like Lear, under extreme mental stress. This is certainly an explanation to bear in mind when considering those radicals often dismissed as 'the lunatic fringe'. The effort to grasp new truths, truths which would turn the world upside down, may have been too much for men like Thomas Tany and George Foster.[10] A partial lapse from 'sanity' may have been the price to be paid for certain insights.

Abiezer Coppe describes himself as

> charging so many coaches, so many hundreds of men and women of the greater rank, in the open streets, with my hand stretched out, my hat cocked up, staring on them as if I would look through them, gnashing with my teeth at some of them, and day and night with a loud voice proclaiming the day of the Lord throughout London and Southwark. [This was, he admitted], strange carriage . . .
>
> I am about my act, my strange act, my work, my strange work, that whosoever hears of it, both his ears shall tingle.
>
> I am confounding, plaguing, tormenting nice, demure, barren Micah with David's unseemly carriage, by skipping, leaping, dancing like one of the fools, vile, base fellows, shamelessly, basely, and uncovered too, before handmaids . . .
>
> It's a joy to Nehemiah to come in like a madman and pluck folk's hair off their heads, and curse like a devil - - - and make them swear by God - - - (Nehem. 13).[11]

Quakers going naked for a sign, George Fox crying out 'Woe to the bloody city of Lichfield', were symbolical gestures. Fox felt it necessary, long after the event, to rationalize his behaviour in Lichfield, singularly unconvincingly.[12] Such actions were also deliberate forms of advertisement, whether self-advertisement or advertisement for the cause, in so far as these could be distinguished. Mr Thomas suggests that prophecy was an easy way for a member of the lower classes to win attention, especially perhaps a lower-class radical.[13] We note the sexual overtones in Coppe, his desire to shock; though the connection between sexual innuendo and class hostility is in itself interesting. Many radicals recognized, with Coppe, that their views were so extreme that they must appear mad to normal members of the ruling class.

Lilburne in 1640 suggested that God 'doth not choose many rich, nor many wise, . . . but the fools, idiots, base and contemptible poor men and women in the esteem of the world'.[14] Here the note is social, as in Coppe's 'vile, base fellows': the ideas are mad because they reflect the outlook of a lower class. Similarly Winstanley in 1649 said that 'the declaration of righteous law shall spring up from the poor, the base and despised ones and fools of the world'. 'The law of love in my heart,' he wrote on another occasion, 'does so constrain me, by reason whereof I am called fool, madman.'[15] 'In the eye of the world,' Winstanley wrote later, 'a man is a fool before he be made wise.'[16] God prefers his own 'confusion' to man's 'order', Warr agreed.[17]

There was good Biblical authority for becoming 'a fool for Christ'. Even the aristocratic Milton claimed to be foolish with 'such a folly as wisest men going about to commit have only confessed and so committed', though his folly was greater.[18] *Divinity and Philosophy Dissected* (Amsterdam, 1644), attributed to Giles Randall, was 'set forth by a mad man'. 'That which is foolishness with God is wisdom with man,' Clarkson had observed in 1646.[19] Joseph Salmon in 1649, threatening the leaders of the Army, wrote: 'I was once wise as well as you, but now I am a fool, I care not who knows it, . . . and it is for your sakes that I am so.'[20] The younger Isaac Penington in 1650 began 'to prefer folly at my very heart above wisdom . . . There is a more sweet, quiet and full enjoyment of oneself in a state of folly than in a state of wisdom . . . In this state of folly I find a new state of things springing up in me.'[21] This did not stop him writing about *The Fundamental Right, Safety and Liberties of the People* (1651). William Covell in 1660 told the restored Charles II that men who 'are counted as mad as Paul was oftentimes speak forth the words of truth and sobriety'; and he went on to recommend very radical reforms.[22] John Crook abandoned his position as a Justice of the Peace 'to be a fool for Christ' when he was converted to Quakerism by William Deusbury.[23]

William Erbery in *The Mad Mans Plea* combined rough buffoonery at the expense of the Baptist Edmund Chillenden and his military congregation with serious polemical purpose. Addressing 'the Lord's fools and mad folks', Erbery asserted that with God 'fools are the wisest men, and madmen the most sober-minded (as babes are the highest men).' 'The prophet then is a fool, and the spiritual man is mad.' Erbery casts some light on the Baptist and Quaker practice of interrupting services and insulting ministers when he wrote that since the church is now become a harlot,

> men therefore must now be sober to God, but stark mad with the church, in plaguing, vexing and destroying all her delicacies ... If God had not made me a fool, surely I should never have made the ministers mad ... Babylon's last fall will be in the fall of these last churches, who shall be thrown down ... by the mighty approach of God in his people (Rev. 18). Neither is it by controversy (as before) nor by disputes (as now), but by derision and scorn.

Ridicule and derision, mocking and playing the fool, Erbery thus regarded as the best polemical instruments. He was writing at the time of the Barebones Parliament, when he (wrongly) believed that 'the present powers are resolved that their ministers shall tell no more lies to the nation', and still hoped that 'this land (though the house of bondage) shall one day break forth into singing, and smile at those empty forms of religion'.[24]

There is another possibility: that men were simply covering up, allowing themselves to express dangerous thoughts under cover of insanity or delusions, from which one could retreat afterwards. This may have been the case when Theaureaujohn proclaimed 'Know that I am a madman' in 1651.[25] He was probably right; but he expressed very seditious views in his madness. Coppe was generally believed to have simulated madness when he was examined by a Parliamentary committee in 1650, 'flinging apples and pears about the room' (nutshells, according to another account).[26] One wonders how the fruit came to be there so usefully, and whether perhaps some symbolical gesture was intended: by their fruits ye shall know them, empty kernels. Salmon in his work of recantation, *Heights in Depths*, said that in his Ranter days he 'walked in unknown paths, and became a madman, a fool among men'. He 'stumbled and fell into the snare of open error and profaneness, led and hurried (by what power let the wise judge) in a principle of mad zeal'.[27] There can be no doubt that the Ranter Thomas Webbe was being prudent when he called himself Mad Tom in a pamphlet foretelling the downfall of Charles II in 1660.[28]

But not many of the radicals were prudent, certainly not Tany.

George Foster reminded those of his readers who were inclined to dismiss him as insane that Jesus Christ too had behaved eccentrically by the standards of his time. Foster himself might also be an agent of God to turn the world upside down.[29] Isaac Penington had similar views. 'He who made all things, and hath often preferred folly to bring wisdom down, may be about the same work again in a way as uncouth, unexpected, yea impossible to the present wise men as those ways he formerly picked out still were to the wisest in those generations.'[30] In the early 1650s the sword of the New Model Army had succeeded in uniting the island of Great Britain under a single government for the first time in its history; but neither Foster nor Tany nor even Penington were the men to unite the island of Great Bedlam.

So what are we to conclude? Self-advertisement by the lower orders? Delivering dangerous opinions in a way which would enable them to be disowned? Mental breakdown? The strain of novelty? An element of provocation, a desire to shock, was certainly there. But the radicals, especially Ranters and early Quakers, seem also to have accepted the irrational element in human experience, and irrational behaviour, more than most of their contemporaries. There is something surrealist about Coppe.[31] God within man could after all speak from the irrational as well as from the rational consciousness: God is by definition beyond human reason. He could be a synonym for mere self-expression, self-assertion, regardless of the content of what was expressed. This perhaps was what Winstanley wished to guard against when he insisted that God and Reason were one. Rational moderate enjoyment of the world gave the whole body quiet rest and peace; 'that immoderate ranting practice of the senses is not the true life of peace'.[32]

II   EVERARD

We may take another example of a man with a respectable political record, who yet on occasion appears to be a madman or a charlatan or both. This is Everard, a member of John Pordage's 'family communion'. This Everard was 'first a separatist, then a scoffer at ordinances, ... then a blasphemer'. He was also a conjuror, who during a stay with Pordage at harvest time in 1649 raised wonderful apparitions – 'a giant with a great sword in his hand' and 'a great dragon ... with great teeth and open jaws, whence he often ejected fire against me' (Pordage). Some of these apparitions were accompanied by noisome poisonous smells and loathsome hellish tastes of sulphur. But there were also visions of good angels, with correspondingly agreeable smells and tastes. All these continued for the three to four weeks of Everard's stay, and made Dr Pordage take to the virgin life, to avoid the kingdom of the Dragon. Everard was also 'seen at London in a frantic posture' about the same time; he became 'mad and frantic' and was 'committed by authority to Bridewell'.[33]

It is not clear whether this Everard is the Digger William Everard, whom Fairfax in April 1649 thought 'no better than a madman', when he called himself a prophet 'of the race of the Jews' and retailed stories of his visions.[34] Winstanley, in a mysterious phrase never satisfactorily explained, spoke of him as 'Chamberlen the Reading man, called after the flesh William Everard'.[35] A William Everard, who first appears from Reading in February 1643, acted as a regular spy for Sir Samuel Luke, Scoutmaster-General to the Earl of Essex's army, in the early months of that year.[36] Four years later a William Everard, who may well have been the same man, was an Agitator and promoter of the Agreement of the People in the New Model Army. He was arrested for participation in the mutiny at Ware in November 1647, and was alleged to have been involved in a conspiracy to kill the King, together with Captain Bray and William Thompson. In December he was released from imprisonment, but cashiered. This would fit the Digger Everard, who we know had been dismissed from the Army. In the early stages of the Digger movement Everard rather than Winstanley seems to have been its spokesman. Contemporary news-sheets suggest that Everard left the Digger colony at St George's Hill at the end of April 1649 in order to join the mutiny which Fairfax and Cromwell suppressed at Burford. If this is correct it would help to connect the two William Everards, since after Ware the Agitator William Everard had been a fellow-prisoner with Thompson, who led some of the troops which revolted in May

1649.[37] It would also supply a reason, otherwise lacking, for his disappearance from the Digger story and for his appearance at Bradfield at harvest-time, since if he had indeed been in arms after leaving St George's Hill he would be seeking an inconspicuous refuge. Pordage's living at Bradfield was near Reading, where he had earlier been a curate, and so may well have been known to 'the Reading man'. But the suggestion that William Everard was at Burford may be due to contemporary confusion with Robert Everard, who certainly was.

Robert Everard had also been an Agitator, who took part in the Putney Debates. He may or may not be the same as the Captain Robert Everard who left the Army after the Battle of Worcester in 1651, and in 1652 was alleged to be disseminating Arian and Socinian heresies in Newcastle upon Tyne.[38] This Robert Everard published several pamphlets between 1649 and 1652, defending adult baptism and denying original sin. Whichever was Pordage's Everard, there seems to have been some method in his madness.[39]

14
Mechanic Preachers and
The Mechanical Philosophy

> One sort of children shall not be trained up only to book
> learning and no other employment, called scholars, as
> they are in the government of monarchy; for then through
> idleness and exercised wit therein they spend their time
> to find out policies to advance themselves to be lords and
> masters above their labouring brethren.
>
> WINSTANLEY, *The Law of Freedom* (1652)
> in Sabine, p. 577.

I   MAGIC AND SCIENCE

I discussed above the hopes of establishing a science of Biblical
prophecy, and the effects this had on popular millenarianism.[1] Side
by side with this, and even more plausible at the time, were the vast
prospects raised by the sixteenth- and early seventeenth-century
magi/scientists, that new methods of controlling the world of nature
and of man might be found. Hermeticists hoped to revive the *prisca
theologia*, the timeless magical wisdom of the Ancients; Paracelsans
expected by drawing on the experience of craftsmen to found a
new science of alchemy/chemistry; astrologers, Mr Thomas has suggested, were groping towards a social science, a science of man in
society.[2]

All these dreams still seemed realizable. We know now that no
science of prophecy, whether Biblical or astrological, emerged: no science of natural magic nor of alchemy. But until the later seventeenth

century this was not clear: great scientists like Dee, Kepler, Tycho Brahe, Napier, Boyle, were all interested in those subjects. William Perkins was addicted to magic as an undergraduate; John Preston when a young don studied astrology.[3] So cool and level-headed a sceptic as John Selden was at once a supporter of the new heliocentric astronomy and a great admirer of Robert Fludd.[4] Francis Bacon himself had been inspired by the Hermetic religio-social ideal of controlling nature. Although he rejected the superstitious claims of magic and astrology, which attempted to dominate nature from outside, he thought they contained a core of knowledge about the physical universe which could be used. He looked to the example of craftsmen as a model of scientific experiment: nature cannot 'be commanded except by being obeyed'.[5]

Bacon's influence was spread wide in England after 1640, thanks especially to the exertions of Samuel Hartlib, and to the invitation to Comenius to come to England. The Comenian fusion of Baconianism and Hermetic natural philosophy laid great emphasis on the social and democratic possibilities of the new science. Hartlib for two decades popularized in England a programme of social, economic, religious and educational reform which influenced men of the calibre of Boyle and Petty. In the euphoria of the early 1640s this programme, which appeared to have the blessing of the Parliamentary leaders, joined with millenarian enthusiasm in creating visions of a Utopia in England soon. (Cf. Hugh Peter's recommendation to Parliament in 1646 that the state should further 'the new experimental philosophy'.[6]) The Comenians[7] appealed especially to craftsmen, who formed the bulk of the religious sects, by their call for a wide extension of educational opportunity, for new teaching methods (using the vernacular, not Latin; emphasizing things, not words; experience, not books); for pooling and making widely available all existing scientific information (notably via Hartlib's Office of Addresses) and for directing science to the relief of man's estate – just as much as by their desire for peace and tolerance among protestants, and for union against the dark forces of papal reaction. 'We are all fellow-citizens of the world, all of one blood, all of us human beings,' wrote Comenius in words which Winstanley and Webster echoed.[8] This was what attracted Boyle in 1646–7. The members of Hartlib's 'Invisible College' practised 'so extensive a charity that it reaches unto everything called man', taking 'the whole body of mankind for their care'.[9]

Mr Thomas has shown how widespread was interest in alchemy and astrology in the 1640s and 50s, not least among religious and political radicals. It was not accidental that Ralpho, Hudibras's squire, was at once a sectary, a Hermetic philosopher and a Behmenist.[10] The victory of Army and Independents over the Presbyterians William Lilly interpreted as a victory for the friends of astrology. Mr Thomas gives evidence to show that Richard Overton sought political advice from the astrologer Lilly at a crucial stage in April 1648; other serious rational politicians who consulted professional astrologers include Cornet Joyce, Mrs John Lilburne, Hugh Peter, several Agitators, Anabaptists, Ranters and Quakers. Lawrence Clarkson took up astrology in 1650; John Pordage practised it. So did the members of Hartlib's Invisible College; Gerrard Winstanley and John Webster recommended that it should be taught. George Fox in 1649 was no less worried by the influence of astrologers than of priests. Astrology was 'a study much in the esteem of illiterate Ranters', said a pamphlet of 1652.[11] As late as 1663 a Quaker said to be under Ranter influence thought the 'conjunction of the stars was hopeful for the nation'.[12] Those – Presbyterians especially – who opposed astrology raised the question of whether 'human curiosity should be allowed to play freely upon the works of creation': though such opposition seems to have done the astrologers more good than harm.[13]

Alchemy/chemistry, and especially chemical medicine, had radical associations. For Familists and Behmenists, so influential on Ranters and Quakers, alchemy was an outward symbol of internal regeneration.[14] John Webster, Erbery's heir, had been a pupil of the Transylvanian chemist Hans Hunneades, who worked at Gresham College. Webster also pressed the study of alchemy and natural magic on the universities, and was attacked as a proponent of the 'Familistical-Levelling-Magical temper'.[15] One alchemist, of whom Sir Isaac Newton thought very highly, hoped in 1645 that 'within a few years', thanks to alchemy, 'money will be like dross', and so 'that prop of the antichristian Beast will be dashed in pieces ... These things will accompany our so long expected and so suddenly approaching redemption', when 'the new Jerusalem shall abound with gold in the streets'.[16] That was nearly as subversive as Winstanley.

Chemistry became almost equated with radical theology. Webster himself hailed Erbery as 'chemist of truth and gospel'. Francis Osborne in 1656 said that the Socinians were 'looked upon as the most chemical and rational part of our many divisions'.[17] Samuel Fisher in 1662 praised 'that chemical divinity, that God is declaring forth the mysteries of his kingdom by', in reply to Bishop Gauden's sneer at 'canting or chemical divinity, which bubbles forth many specious notions in fine fancies and short-lived conceptions'.[18] Richard Overton in 1643 had proposed a scientific experiment to test the immortality of the soul; George Fox and Edward Burrough in 1658 similarly proposed experiments to test the miracle of the mass.[19] Henry Pinnell translated Paracelsus in 1657, with an Apology in which the translator praised the Hermetic philosophy and insisted that, so far from making 'void the Word of the Lord by his works', he wanted to 'establish the one by the other'. 'Every part of the creation doth its part to publish the great mysteries of man's salvation.'[20] One of the Fellows of the short-lived Durham College was Israel Tonge, an alchemist; another, William Sprigge, agitated for the teaching of chemistry in the universities.[21]

So astrology, alchemy and natural magic contributed, together with Biblical prophecy, to the radical outlook. In 1646 Benjamin Bourne declared that 'the Familists are very confident that by knowledge of astrology and strength of reason they shall be able to conquer over the whole world'.[22] As Mr Thomas points out, in the astrologers' 'assumption that the principles underlying the development of human society were capable of human explanation we can detect the germ of modern sociology'. 'Astrology, though beginning as a system of explanation, ... ended as one which held out the prospect of control.' That is why conservative theologians were so hostile to it.[23] It also explains its attractions for the radicals: rather like sociology in mid-twentieth century English universities.

Reliance on dreams and visions – Descartes and Lord Herbert of

Cherbury no less than Fox or Winstanley – was also not entirely irrational. The sudden insight, summing up mental processes that have been continuing for some time, is something we are all familiar with. It could seem like a revelation, especially when it came in the hours of darkness. But if you believed the insight was divinely inspired, this gave it authority both for you and for your audience. So new and unconventional insights could be propounded and accepted. A group which Fox met in 1647, who 'relied much on dreams', ultimately became Quakers.[24] Many Anabaptists, Ranters and Quakers practised faith healing, a layman's medicine, or rather the medicine of lay believers.[25] But the miraculous cures claimed by the early Quakers were suppressed by their successors: Penn and Ellwood do not refer to them.[26]

The supporters of alchemy, astrology and magic were unfortunate in backing the right horse at the wrong time. Alchemy was to develop into the science of chemistry, though it had to wait for the next great upheaval of the French Revolution for this to be completed.[27] Social sciences have emerged more slowly in the nineteenth and twentieth centuries, and they are not conscious of any debt to astrology. But the cosmic hopes which the Hermetic philosophy seemed to open up were not wholly unreasonable in the mid-seventeenth century when magic and science were still advancing side by side. Isaac Newton first turned to the study of mathematics in order to investigate the scientific claims of judicial astrology.[28] He remained interested in alchemy throughout the creative period of his life. 'The last of the magicians,' Lord Keynes called him.[29] From our twentieth-century vantage point we see the path of science advancing inexorably through the mechanical philosophy and the gradual elimination of magic from all spheres[30] – except, unfortunately, the core of Newton's law of gravity, the unexplained 'force' which acts by apparently non-material, non-mechanical means across vast distances. Ignoring this, we assume that the triumph of mechanism was inevitable from the start. But Winstanley, for whom God and matter were one, said 'God is still in motion', and urged us to pursue 'the motional knowledge of a thing as it is'. For 'truth is hid in every body'.[31] Great though the achievements of the mechanical philosophy were, a dialectical element in scientific thinking, a recognition of the 'irrational' (in the sense of the mechanically inexplicable) was lost when it triumphed, and is having to be painfully recovered in our own century. We smile when we read Samuel Hering asking for special university courses on Jacob Boehme; but at least one modern historian of science has suggested that it was exactly Boehme's sort of leaven that was missing in English scientific thinking during the later seventeenth and eighteenth centuries.[32] The radicals were wrong; but they are beginning to look less stupidly wrong than they did once.

A generation ago even so sensitive a commentator as Sabine was a little embarrassed by Winstanley's suggestion that nature itself had been corrupted by the Fall of Man. He dismissed as 'naive' and 'simple-minded' the idea that natural disasters like 'the risings up of waters and the breakings forth of fire to waste and destroy are but that curse, or the works of man's own hands that rise up and run together to destroy their maker, and torment him that brought the curse forth'.[33] Winstanley, however, as so often, is putting startlingly new content into traditional forms of language. If we bear in mind that for him the Fall was caused by covetousness and set up kingly power, we may rather think today that this is one of the profoundest of Winstanley's insights. As we contemplate our landscape made hideous by neon signs, advertisements, pylons, wreckage of automobiles; our seas poisoned by atomic waste, their shores littered with plastic and oil; our atmosphere polluted with carbon dioxide and nuclear fall-out, our peace shattered by supersonic planes; as we think of nuclear bombs which can 'waste and destroy' to an extent that Winstanley never dreamed of – we can recognize that man's greed, competition between men and between states, are really in danger of upsetting the balance of nature, of poisoning and destroying the fabric of the globe. We are better placed to appreciate Winstanley's insight that in a competitive society the state is just a part of the competitive system. Perhaps it was over-simplified to believe that harmony and beauty will be restored to nature, as well as society, as soon as community of property is established. But what are the chances of priority being given to 'the beauty of the commonwealth' before there has been a change in social relations?

For Winstanley social revolution is the same thing as men learning to 'live in community with the globe and . . . the spirit of the globe', in accordance with the laws of nature: letting Reason rule in man as it does in the cosmos.

Rejection of non-mechanistic explanations was in part – and only in part – ideologically motivated. Stable laws of nature went with a stable society. Now that God was located within every human heart, it was inconvenient to have him intervening in the day-to-day running of the universe. Both popular magic and catholic magic upset the ordered cosmos. After 1660 everything connected with the political radicals had to be rejected, including 'enthusiasm', prophecy, astrology as a rival system of explanation to Christianity, alchemy and chemical medicine. Proponents of the latter were dismissed as 'fanatics in physic', 'a sort of men not of academical but mechanic education', supporters of 'the late rebellion', who wanted to open medicine to 'hatters, cobblers and tinkers'.[34] Naturally enough, as the iatrochemists and alchemists failed to win acceptance, as they found themselves spurned by official scientific bodies, so they became increasingly wild and irrational.[35] Thus society's verdicts are self-confirming.

It was 'plebeians and mechanics' whom Bishop Parker denounced in 1681 for having 'philosophized themselves into principles of impiety'. They 'read their lectures of atheism in the streets and highways'. I was guilty of undue foreshortening when in my *Intellectual Origins of the English Revolution* I described the mechanical philosophy as the philosophy of rude mechanicals.[36] I should have differentiated more sharply between 'mechanic atheism' and the mechanical philosophy proper. One part of the reason for the acceptance of the latter was that it seemed to offer an academic alternative to the mechanic atheism to which some of the radical congregations under mechanic preachers were tending.

The triumph of the mechanical philosophy ultimately created further problems for Christianity, as some parsons had foreseen it would. Witches, malignant spirits and the devil had been useful explanations for the existence of evil and suffering, useful scapegoats. Who was to blame if they were not? 'Deny spirits and you are an atheist,' divines said.[37] Since God could not be dispensed with, the feelings of sin and guilt previously purged by punishing heretics and witches were increasingly turned inwards: the Puritan sense of guilt was part of the price paid for the gap between ideology and technology.[38]

II DIVINITY, LAW, MEDICINE

Academic scientists were as anxious in restoration England to dissociate themselves from atheism as from enthusiasm, to show that science proved the existence of God and a law-abiding universe. Charles II was wise to become patron of the Royal Society as well as head of the Church of England: the one was as useful against mechanic atheism as the other was in curbing mechanic preachers. But many babies went out with the bath water as the Royal Society trumpeted its respectability and concentrated on utilitarian experiments. The wide vision, especially the social vision, of the radical Baconians was totally lost; some glimpses only survived in the Dissenting Academies. For the nonconformist sects, as they abandoned hope of turning the world upside down, as they re-admitted sin, accepted existing society and the state, withdrew from politics to an exclusively other-worldly religion – so they lost their sympathy for and understanding of the earthly aspirations of Hermetic philosophy, of magic.[39]

The radicals of the English Revolution made a last attempt to see the universe as a whole, science and society as one. Copernican astronomy had ended the distinction between heavenly and sublunary: the radicals aimed at completing this by ending the distinction between specialists and laymen. They wanted to drive scholastic theologians out of the universities, to end the dominance of Latin, Greek and Hebrew; but they did not want science to be handed over to a new set of mumbo-jumbo men. Dee, Bruno, Fludd and many others had aspired to understand the whole universe in all its aspects. Comenius was perhaps the last serious thinker to attempt an all-embracing synthesis and apply it to human life. Winstanley wanted science, philosophy and politics to be taught in every parish by an elected non-specialist, drawing on the pool of scientific and other information which something like Hartlib's Office of Addresses would have furnished.[40] He and the radical scientists wanted science to be applied to the problems of human life: this was the practical significance of their emphasis on astrology, alchemy and natural magic. Their defeat, however scientifically necessary and desirable, also meant the end of dreams of an all-embracing *Weltanschauung* accessible to ordinary people. Newton was as incomprehensible to the average mechanic as Thomas Aquinas. Knowledge was no longer shut up in the Latin Bible, which priestly scholars had to interpret; it was increasingly shut up in the technical vocabulary of the sciences which the new specialists had to interpret. 'And pray you what is the difference?' the radicals might have asked.

I do not wish to suggest that many of the plebeian radicals were aware of this philosophical and cosmological dispute in the background, though I suspect some of them had a greater understanding of it than historians have had until very recently. But their specific grievances fall into place against this backcloth. What rank and file radicals wanted was democratization – of religion by mechanic preachers and abolition of tithes, democratization of law by decentralization of courts, abolition of feed lawyers, democratization of medicine by abolition of the College of Physicians' monopoly and the provision of free or cheap medical remedies for all. In all three spheres the enemy was monopoly.

Industrial monopolies had collapsed in 1641, but as Lilburne pointed out in 1645, book-printing was still engrossed by the Stationers' Company, preaching by the black-coated ministers, administration of justice by lawyers and judges, 'thieves *cum privilegio*'.[41] The liberty of the commonwealth, Nicholas Culpeper declared in 1649, is infringed by the three monopolies of priests, physicians and lawyers.[42] The lower orders, Goodall said much later, wanted medicine thrown open to tinkers, 'tailors to invade the bar and jugglers the pulpit'.[43] We are told of rank-and-file soldiers, patients in St Bartholomew's Hospital in 1647, who petitioned for the appointment of a young surgeon of whom they approved; others tried to get rid of a politically undesirable sister.[44] Winstanley in 1652, Samuel Hering in 1653, demanded a free national health service; the latter wanted lawyers, like parsons, schoolmasters and physicians, to be paid by the state and charge no fees.[45] Petty wanted state-sponsored teaching hospitals.[46] John Cook the regicide proposed free medical treatment for the poor.[47] William Dell, the main burden of whose attack is directed against the clergy, thought physic and law should be taught in universities only when thoroughly reformed from their corruptions 'both for practice and fees'.[48] John Webster, who pressed science and natural magic on the universities, was as anxious as Dell and Winstanley that they should no longer train ministers.[49]

The mechanic preachers proposed to democratize religion. Any man or woman who had the spirit of God might preach, better than a university-trained divine who lacked the spirit. The scientific radicals adopted a similar attitude to medicine. The revolutionary decades, wrote John Heydon in 1664, 'admitted stocking-weavers, shoemakers, millers, masons, carpenters, bricklayers, gunsmiths, porters, butlers etc. to write and teach astrology and physic'.[50] Nicholas Culpeper, apothecary and avowed republican, denounced as a Seeker and atheist, conducted a campaign against the monopoly of the College of Physicians parallel to that which Winstanley, Webster and Dell carried on against the universities. Culpeper translated into English the sacred text of the College, the *Pharmacoepia Londinensis*, so that medical prescriptions would be available to the poorest. He hoped it would make every man his own physician, as the translation of the Bible made every man his own theologian (and as Lilburne hoped every man would become his own lawyer).[51]

Clarkson for a time practised astrology; Coppe and Walwyn after 1660 took up medicine as a profession. Winstanley was certainly acquainted with the Paracelsan tradition, from which he no doubt took the antithesis of light/darkness which pervades his thought as it does that of Clarkson, Bauthumley and the Quakers, the Children of Light.[52] Winstanley may also have learnt from this source that 'to know the secrets of nature is to know the works of God', 'the secrets of nature' being a familiar phrase in this tradition.[53] Winstanley also appears to have known something of anatomy, correctly locating the pericardium.[54] George Fox always retained an interest in medicine.

The Revolution which started by a wave of popular anger at the cruel sentences passed on the Rev. Henry Burton, lawyer Prynne and

Dr Baswick, ended by pillorying the three professions of divinity, law, medicine, which, Fox said, had abandoned the wisdom, faith and equity of God. Parsons of the state church early became the principal enemy of the radicals. Lawyers, physicians, surgeons, apothecaries, schoolmasters, 'the new professional groups', thriving with expanding demand among the middle classes, 'came to form one of the dominant elements, sometimes the predominant one, in the parliamentarian county committees'.[55] The extruded traditional gentry hated them because they were consolidating the Revolution; disappointed radicals hated them because they were frustrating its further extension. The radicals ended by advocating not only mechanic preachers but also mechanic doctors, mechanic lawyers and judges. Winstanley carried the principle further still, calling for a non-professional citizen army, ready to act as a check on any who attempted to upset the freedom of the commonwealth.[56]

III UNIVERSITIES

The radicals' vision included a reformed educational system, which would realize something like Comenius's ideal: universal education in the vernacular for boys and girls up to the age of eighteen, followed by six years at the university for the best pupils. 'They are eagerly debating on the reformation of schools in the whole kingdom,' wrote Comenius in 1641, 'that all young people should be instructed, none neglected'.[57] During the Revolution a new university was started at Durham, and others were proposed for London, York, Bristol, Exeter, Norwich, Manchester, Shrewsbury, Ludlow, Cornwall, Wales, the Isle of Man: there were also proposals for an increase in the number of schools.[58] In Wales a great number of new schools were actually started. Professor Stone believes that there was a 'substantial increase in lower-class literacy throughout the revolutionary decades'.[59] William Petty in 1648 advocated 'colleges of tradesmen', where able mechanicians should be subsidized to perform experiments, as well as 'literary workhouses' for poor children.[60] William Dell called for schools in all towns and villages, with grammar schools in cities and larger towns, and universities in every great city. Undergraduates should work their way through the university, earning their living in some useful calling part of the day or every other day.[61] Winstanley too wanted universal education, regardless of class or sex, to be combined with manual work so as to ensure that no privileged class of idle scholars should arise 'which occasions all the trouble in the world'.[62]

Dell also criticized the social role of universities, suggesting that 'all divinity is wrapped up in human learning to deter the common people from the study and inquiry after it, and to cause them still to expect all divinity from the clergy, who by their education have attained to that human learning which the plain people are destitute of'. From this swaddling of divinity in human learning 'must it sadly follow, that all who want human learning must needs also want divinity; and then how shall poor plain people, who live in lawful callings, and have not the leisure to attain human learning, how shall they do to be saved?'[63] 'The subtle clergy,' Winstanley agreed, 'do know that if they can but charm the people by this their divining doctrine, to look after riches, heaven and glory after they are dead, that then they shall easily be the inheritors of the earth, and have the deceived people to be their servants.'[64]

Universities were thus crucial to seventeenth-century society. They trained the opinion-formers, the persuaders. To the radicals they seemed to embody and justify fundamental assumptions of propertied society – that all Englishmen were members of the national church, like it or not; that only gentlemen educated in the classics might preach. They seemed to deny by implication the fundamental protestant doctrine of the priesthood of all believers, to restrict its application to educated clerics. For this reason Elizabethan Brownists and Barrowists had thought universities were 'the very guard of Antichrist's throne'.[65] What was new in the revolutionary decades was that such views were discussed openly, both by intellectual radicals and by mechanick preachers, one of whom was reported as saying in 1647 'that universities is of the devil and human learning is of the flesh'.[66] Roger Williams, Erbery, Coppin, Robert Norwood, Fox, Nayler, Farnsworth, Samuel Fisher, John Webster, all agreed with Winstanley and Dell that universities should not be used for the training of ministers.[67] Hugh Peter occupied a half-way position when he advocated gathering up 'godly youths out of shops' and sending them for improvement – perhaps to an Oxford College set aside for the purpose. The training was clearly not to be primarily in 'arts and tongues'.[68]

'The universities,' wrote Thomas Hobbes, 'are the fountains of the civil and moral doctrine from whence the preachers and the gentry ... sprinkle the same upon the people.' Consequently 'the instruction of the people dependeth wholly on the right teaching of youth in the universities'. This succinct analysis of the social role of universities in mid-seventeenth-century England helps us to understand the hostility of radicals to them, especially as Hobbes added 'a university is an excellent servant to the clergy'.[69] Those who wished to abolish a state church, tithes and parochial livings naturally wished to change the universities, whose principal function was training ministers to occupy these livings. For those who thought that 'if Christ call him and pour forth his spirit on him, that and that only makes him a true minister',[70] knowledge of Latin, Greek and Hebrew was irrelevant to his training, and the whole function and purpose of Oxford and Cambridge seemed distorted. Cobbler How, Lord Brooke, Roger Williams, Henry Denne, Richard Overton, William Walwyn, Edmund Chillenden, Gerrard Winstanley, William Dell, John Milton, Roger Crab, Richard Coppin, John Canne, Henry Stubbe, George Fox, Richard Farnsworth and Samuel Fisher might all be quoted to this effect.[71]

'It is one of the grossest errors that ever reigned under Antichrist,' Dell told his Cambridge congregation in 1651, 'to affirm that the universities are the fountain of the ministers of the gospel', or that the clergy should be a separate caste.[72] But if universities ceased to train a privileged caste of clergy, and devoted themselves to serving the secular interests of the commonwealth, then a religious reformer like Dell could agree with secular reformers like John Hall and Noah Biggs in urging the study of anatomy and 'mechanic chemistry, the handmaid of nature, that hath outstripped the other sects of philosophy', together with a review of old experiments and traditions.[73] John Webster

wanted astronomy, natural magic, chemistry, astrology, medicine all
to be studied at the universities. He knew he would be regarded as
'an absolute Leveller' for his pains, though he denounced the many-
headed monster.[74] He was quite right: John Wilkins, Seth Ward and
Thomas Hall all attacked him as a Leveller.[75] Winstanley, who felt
that 'the secrets of the creation have been locked up under the traditional, parrot-like speaking from the universities and colleges for
scholars',[76] had every hope of a rapid advance for such studies in his
ideal commonwealth. There the functions of parson, doctor and lawyer would all be taken over by a single elected member of the parish,
presumably without special training, who once a week should lead
discussion classes in philosophy, medicine, history, civic studies.[77]

It is sadly ironical that the time when Winstanley was thus visual-
izing a democratization and widespread dissemination of all
knowledge was almost precisely the time at which significant spe-
cialization began to set in. The last of the polymaths were dying out
just as Winstanley hoped to establish a minor polymath in every
parish. His scheme was not utterly utopian, since it was linked with
Comenian plans for collecting and disseminating information,
including scientific information and information about inventions.
We can hardly say that Winstanley's vision was impossible; we can
only say that it was never tried.

The restoration enabled the universities to survive, almost
untouched by the scientific ideas which had invaded them during the
Revolution. But continuing unchanged in a revolutionized society
meant that their social role was transformed. They retained an
intimate association with the Anglican church even though the latter
had now lost its exclusive monopoly position. They also retained a
classical emphasis when Latin had ceased to be either the main
source of scientific information, or the language of international
scholarship, or even the effective language of the élite professions,
divinity, law, medicine.[78] So Oxford and Cambridge became isolated
from the main stream of national and international intellectual life,
a backwater, just as nonconformists, excluded from the universities,
evolved in dissenting academies a culture which was as one-sided on
the other side – utilitarian, provincial, sectarian. The split which

Winstanley had hoped to bridge, between useless specialized scholars and ill-educated practical men, remained. In Winstanley's society the two cultures would have been one.

Not only did England enter the epoch of the Industrial Revolution with a ruling élite ignorant of science; the scientists of the Royal Society themselves abandoned the radicals' 'enthusiastic' schemes for equal educational opportunity. So the reservoir of scientific talent in the lower classes which these schemes had envisaged remained untapped, and 'England advanced towards the technological age with a population ill-equipped to take the fullest advantage of its resources'.[79]

15
Base Impudent Kisses

It is a curious fact that with every great revolutionary movement the question of 'free love' comes into the foreground. With one set of people as a revolutionary progress, as a shaking off of old traditional fetters, no longer necessary; with others as a welcome doctrine, comfortably covering all sorts of free and easy practices between man and woman.

FREDERICK ENGELS, 'The Book of
Revelation', in *Progress*, Vol. II, 1883.

I THE PURITAN SEXUAL REVOLUTION

In one of many stories of Ranters searching for sin in broad daylight with the aid of a lighted candle, the lady found it, to her satisfaction, in a gentleman's codpiece.[1] Then as now, 'sin' usually meant sex for Puritans. The sexual revolution which was an important part of the introduction of the protestant ethic meant replacing property marriage (with love outside marriage) by a monogamous partnership, ostensibly based on mutual love, and a business partnership in the affairs of the family. The wife was subordinate to her husband, but no slave. The abolition of monasteries and nunneries symbolized the replacement of the celibate ideal ('stinking chastity' as Bale called it[2]) by the concept of chastity in marriage. The dual standard of sexual conduct was replaced, at least as an ideal, by a single standard applied to both sexes.

This revolution has been described, with some exaggeration, as more important than the Great Rebellion.[3] It took a long time to complete, if indeed it has yet been completed. But the revolutionary decades saw a significant acceleration of the process, as well as attempts to transcend it. Historians of literature have made us familiar with controversies on the Jacobean stage over marriage and the position of women. By and large the popular theatre for which Shakespeare wrote was in favour of monogamous wedded love; the aristocratic coterie theatre was more cynical and contemptuous in its attitude towards women.[4] This may in the main be attributed to a rise in economic importance of those middling-sized households, in town and country, in which the wife was a junior partner in the business.

Landowners, down to Samuel Richardson's Harlowes in the eighteenth century, naturally regarded marriage as too serious a property transaction to be left to children: this is a theme in many of those books of *Advice to a Son* so popular among the gentry at this time, presumably because standards were changing, and parents thought that advice was needed. Nor were children always romantic. The terms of Edmund Verney's proposal in 1661 chill the heart: 'We are the most convenient matches in England, one to the other,' he assured the lady of his choice, 'because the best part of our estates join.'[5] In the medieval tradition with which C. S. Lewis has made us familiar,[6] sexual satisfaction still seemed to the Inns of Court poets something to be sought outside marriage.

> Let haberdashers marry, and those poor
> Shop traffickers that spend their precious hours
> In narrow lanes

said a character in one of Davenant's plays, probably acted in 1639.[7] So long as the Court of Wards existed, the marriage of a tenant-in-chief (and that meant most great landowners) could hardly be anything but a property transaction. Abolition of the Court in 1646 must have increased the chance of an heir or heiress choosing for himself. As Harrington pointed out, 'the lower sort' were far freer in this respect than the nobility and gentry.[8] Some of the less attractive aspects of the Puritan view of marriage should therefore be seen in relation to what preachers (and popular dramatists) were up against. Intolerance of marital infidelity, the desire to impose severe penalties for adultery, were part of the battle against property marriage, for love in marriage.

In many ways the legal position of women was inferior to that of men. They were still burnt for husband-murder: murdering one's wife was only a hanging matter. A wife so indecent as to sit in the same pew with her husband at church was liable to penalties in the ecclesiastical courts.[9] But women's position was improving, most of all in London, naturally enough. There it was actionable to call a woman 'whore', and wife-beating was also an offence.[10] (Dutch merchants were still horrified by the Englishman's habit of beating his wife, though this was frowned on in Yorkshire.)[11] But the position of women was much better in fact than it was in theory, law still not having caught up with economic change. 'A wife in England,' wrote the bachelor John Chamberlain, 'is *de jure* but the best of servants, having nothing in a more proper sense than a child hath.' But 'their condition *de facto* is the best in the world, such is the good nature of Englishmen towards their wives.' Italians said England was the paradise of women as well as the purgatory of servants and the hell of horses.[12] 'English wives,' the old-fashioned John Smyth grumbled, 'challenge more liberty and incline more to sovereignty than those of other nations.'[13] A Russian visitor to London in 1645–6 confirmed that women rule their houses and their husbands; he added that they were also more honest.[14] For a woman to be truly independent meant putting herself outside society and rejecting her sex. The heroine of Middleton's *The Roaring Girl* wore men's clothes and defended herself with her sword.

The new ethic was reflected in Puritan doctrines of the helpmeet, insistence on the wife's rights (in subordination) in the family partnership, on marriage for love and on freedom of choice for children (though not disregarding the parents' views).[15] The qualifications have to be put in, and Puritanism was not a monolithic creed. Some old ideas died hard: the equation of adultery with theft, because the wife is the husband's property, can be found in many theologians popular with Puritans, from Bullinger onwards.[16] Yet William Gouge in his influential *Of Domesticall Duties* argued very clearly that the husband's adultery was as bad as the wife's: there was no dual standard for him, nor for William Perkins or Daniel Rogers. Gouge urged young men to marry for love. Daniel Rogers almost incited children to resist if parents refused consent to the marriage of their choice.[17] Eve, Thomas Goodwin pointed out, was taken from Adam's side – not from his foot.[18] Sibbes had some reason on his side when he asked 'would you have a milder government than that of a husband, which though it be not a parity, yet it comes as near as can be?'[19] This was doctrine to appeal to moderate constitutionalists, as patriarchialism seemed to go with the Divine Right of Kings.

Milton was very surprised, and so are we, to discover how many early protestant theologians sanctioned divorce,[20] some of them insisting on equal rights for women in this respect, e.g. Bishop Hooper and *The Reformation of the Ecclesiastical Laws*.[21] Divorce was easier in Puritan New England than in Old.[22] Hugh Peter in 1651 was thus not startlingly original when he advocated divorce as well as civil marriage; for the latter there had been agitation in Parliament as early as 1576.[23] A family structure appropriate to industrialism was established in England well before the Industrial Revolution, which it may have facilitated. This seems a parallel phenomenon to that noted by Mr K. V. Thomas – that 'magic lost its appeal before the appropriate technical solutions had been devised to take its place.'[24]

Women had played a prominent role in the heretical sects of the Middle Ages, and this tradition came to the surface again in revolutionary England. Sects allowed women to participate in church government, sometimes even to preach.[25] Women voted in Hugh Peter's church at Rotterdam in the 1630s.[26] Female preachers abound in the horrified pages of Thomas Edwards. 'If a toleration were granted,' he wailed, 'they should never have peace in their families more, or ever after have command of wives, children, servants' – a note that recurs.[27] A respectable divine like Samuel Torshell sold the pass when he wrote in 1645 that there was no difference between men and women in the state of grace. 'The soul knows no difference of sex.'[28] Theologically impeccable, it was socially imprudent to emphasize that in the 1640s. Fox was carrying the idea only a little further when he asked 'May not the spirit of Christ speak in the female as well as in the male?'[29] But women sectaries did more than preach, bad though that was. They threatened to subvert the marriage bond. Unequal marriages were antichristian yokes, they said: a wife might forsake an antichristian husband, a husband an antichristian wife. Mrs Attaway did just that, in the company of William Jenny.[30]

Elizabethan Familists divorced, as they married, by simple declaration before the congregation. Before 1640 such customs had been concealed by sects existing precariously underground or in exile. But during the Revolution they were practised and defended in public: the social impact was profound. Mr Thomas points out some consequences of open and widespread advocacy of religious equality for women. If the religious sanction for the father's headship of his family, or the king's fatherhood of his people, is taken away, the whole of society and all its institutions are open to review from the point of view of the inner light, reason, natural right, popular consent, common interest. Mr Thomas quotes attacks made during the Revolution, sometimes by women themselves, on their limited educational opportunities, their confinement to domestic duties, their subjection to their husbands and the injustices of a commercial marriage market.[31]

Mrs Chidley in 1641 argued that a husband had no more right to control his wife's conscience than the magistrate had to control his.[32] The Fifth Monarchist John Rogers forbade men to despise women 'or wrong them of their liberty of voting and speaking in common affairs. To women I say, I wish you be not too forward' (as, by all accounts, his own wife was); 'and yet not too backward, but hold fast your liberty . . . Ye ought not by your silence to betray your liberty.'[33] Quakers – following the example of Familists and some Baptists – practised marriage by declaration before the congregation, with no other civil or religious ceremony. Winstanley advocated a similar proceeding.[34] Quakers also abandoned the wife's promise to obey her husband, since man and wife were as equal in the new life as they had been before the Fall. George Fox on marrying Margaret Fell engaged not to meddle with her estate, to the amazement of the lawyers.[35] Gerrard Winstanley summarized the best of the radical protestant tendency for his ideal community: 'every man and woman shall have the free liberty to marry whom they love, if they can obtain the love and liking of that party whom they would marry. And neither birth nor portion shall hinder the match, for we are all of one family, mankind.' The communal storehouse, he added with a realistic touch, would provide marriage portions.[36]

We should add the liberating effect of the breakdown of church courts and therefore of supervision over the sexual lives of ordinary people, 'upon a groundless suspicion of unchastity . . . to drain the people's purses'.[37] The suspicions may not all have been groundless. We are told that at least one out of every three brides in seventeenth-century England was pregnant when she was married; and that bastardy was commoner in England than in France.[38] The most recent historian of law reform during the interregnum sees the revolutionary decades as a period of greater freedom from moral supervision than any before or immediately after. The 1650 Act against adultery, Mr Veall thinks, was not enforced.[39] Henceforth 'sin' was not a crime. Soon, in the eyes of Ranters, sexual intercourse outside marriage ceased to be sinful. 'Vice, these late years,' wrote Fuller in 1647, 'hath kept open house in England . . . No penance for the adulterer, stocks for the drunkard, whip for the petty larcener.'[40] 'In Captain Chillington's [sic] church,' Erbery mocked, 'there's neither penance nor stool of repentance for men who lie with their maids.'[41]

Another way in which Edmund Hall alleged that church courts had extorted money was by fines for marrying without a licence. The issuing of marriage licences, Dr Marchant tells us, had been 'a growth industry' in the years before 1640. They were not cheap. Of 509 licences issued in Norwich diocese in the years 1636–7, all but 13 cost 3s. 6d. or more. At York in the 1630s the average price was about 10s. Such licences were, Dr Marchant suggests, a status symbol which only the upper and middle classes could afford: they must have predisposed the poor to despise church marriage.[42]

The revolutionary decades saw an astonishing outburst of uninhibited speculation, which included the relation of the sexes among many other themes. Several besides Milton advocated freedom of divorce (Hugh Peter, Mrs Attaway). Francis Osborne discussed

polygamy and marriage by annual contract, renewable;[43] the Har-
ringtonian and republican Henry Nevile, accused of atheism and
blasphemy in the Rump Parliament in 1659, in *The Isle of Pines*
(1668) depicted a cheerfully happy polygamous utopia.[44] Petty and
others discussed 'Californian marriage', interesting sexual combinations of 1 + 4 and 5 + 1 + 1.[45] John Hall argued the case for female
nudism, not (as the Adamites were alleged to do) as a symbol of
regained innocence, but because nakedness would be less provocative than the clothes which women wore – a view which owed
something to reports from the New World, popularized by Mont-
aigne and in England by Robert Burton. John Bunyan agreed with
the point.[46] George Fox in 1647 came across a group which held that
women had no souls, 'adding in a light manner, no more than a
goose'.[47] The Muggletonians thought that in heaven we shall be

> All males, not made to generate,
> But live in divine happy state.[48]

It was Robert Herrick, bachelor, royalist and anti-Puritan, who
prayed for an 'unlearned wife'.[49]

II BEYOND THE PURITAN SEXUAL
REVOLUTION

When we get to the Ranters we see some consequences. John Robins
gave his disciples authority to change wives and husbands – and
changed his own 'for an example'.[50] Lawrence Clarkson raised this
to a theory of complete sexual freedom, and Abiezer Coppe carried
the attack even further, into the monogamous family itself. 'Give
over thy stinking family duties,' he wrote. It is never quite clear when
Coppe is speaking in his own person and when on behalf of God (if
indeed he differentiated clearly). But the following passage seems to
belong to God: 'Give over, or if nothing else will do it, I'll at a time
when thou least of all thinkest of it, make thine own child ... lie
with a whore - - - before thine eyes.' We must become like little
children again: 'and to such a little child, undressing is as good as

dressing; . . . he knows no evil.' Coppe seems to have transferred to his own person here, warning us that he is only hinting his meaning when he writes:

> Kisses are numbered among transgressors – base things – well! by base hellish swearing and cursing (as I have accounted it in my time of fleshly holiness) and by base impudent kisses (as I then accounted them) my plaguey holiness hath been confounded . . . And again, by wanton kisses, kissing hath been confounded; and external kisses have been made the fiery chariot to mount me into the bosom of . . . the King of Glory . . . I can . . . kiss and hug ladies, and love my neighbour's wife as myself, without sin.[51]

Coppe had to disavow, among other errors, 'that adultery, fornication and uncleanness is no sin', and 'that community of wives is lawful'.[52]

For Clarkson the act of adultery was not distinct from prayer: it all depended on one's inner approach. 'To the pure all things, yea all things, are pure,' he emphasized, adultery included.[53] That was written in 1650: looking back ten years later Clarkson thus described his Ranter principles: 'No man could be freed from sin, till he had acted that so-called sin as no sin . . . Till you can lie with all women as one woman, and not judge it sin, you can do nothing but sin . . . No man could attain to perfection but this way.' Clarkson in 1659 denounced 'ranting devils' who make God 'a cloak for all their lascivious lust'; they say that 'for them all women are as one woman', and continue to practise what he had formerly preached. But in the early 1650s he had no qualms. 'Most of the principal women came to my lodgings for knowledge,' he tells us, 'but at last it became a trade so common that all the froth and scum broke forth into the height of this wickedness.'[54] (Clarkson is writing after his conversion to Muggletonianism: his tone would no doubt have been different earlier. But there is no reason to disbelieve him.) His itinerant life gave him opportunities, and enabled him to escape from embarrassing relationships. Historians have perhaps not yet reflected sufficiently on the importance of social and physical mobility in expanding the possibilities of freedom, including sexual freedom, especially for women.[55]

It seems indeed to have been perfectly simple for any couple to team up together and wander round the country, preaching and presumably depending on the hospitality of their coreligionists or those whom they could convince. William Franklin and Mary Gadbury did this, the only remarkable thing about them (and the only reason why we know their story) being that Mary Gadbury (who could not sign her name) believed that Franklin was her Lord and Christ, and called herself the Spouse of Christ. This rather naturally attracted attention. Sin, Mary assured an inquiring clergyman, is taken away when men and women come to be in Christ. When they were tried at Winchester in January 1650, Mary Gadbury assured the court that 'she companied not with him in an uncivil way, but as a fellow-feeler of her misery; at which last word, the whole court laughed exceedingly ... A fellow feeler indeed.' Franklin, a rope-maker whose 'language was wholly according to the Familists' dialect', rather tamely abandoned his claim to be Christ; Mary Gadbury, indignant at this betrayal, suffered the additional humiliation of being whipped.[56] Bunyan tells us that he himself heard a man 'in Oliver's days' advise a girl whom he was tempting 'to commit uncleanness with him' to say, 'when you come before the judge, that you are with child by the Holy Ghost'.[57]

Hostile accounts naturally made the most of such stories, and there are many graphic descriptions of Ranter orgies by pamphleteers who had mastered the modem journalist's ability to titillate whilst reprehending.[58] Clarkson in his Baptist days was accused by a county committee of lying in the water with a 'sister' whom he was dipping at night. Clarkson's presence of mind rarely failed him, and he replied 'Surely your experience teaches you the contrary, that nature hath small desire of copulation in water' – 'at which they laughed'.[59] Similar accusations were made against many other radicals: there was a popular song about a Quaker who practised bestiality. A committee solemnly reported to Parliament in 1656 that Nayler's principles permitted him to lie 'with any woman that is of his own judgment'.[60] Coppe, according to an even less reliable source, 'commonly lay in bed with two women at a time'.[61]

We need not take any of these stories seriously, though Coppe certainly liked to shock. And we should allow a good deal for symbolic gestures. If men and women believe that they have 'attained to that perfection in Christ already which they lost in Adam', it was logical, if chilly, to assume that 'they may go naked as he did, and live above sin and shame'.[62] We recall too the many occasions on which very respectable Quakers 'went naked for a sign', with only a loin-cloth about their middles for decency's sake. But the core of truth which does emerge is that Ranters systematically proclaimed the right of natural man to behave naturally. In word and deed some of them deliberately flouted the inhibitions which the Puritan ethic was imposing. Clarkson had something like a philosophy of free love,[63] and there is reasonable documentation for John Holland's remark: 'They say that for one man to be tied to one woman, or one woman to one man, is a fruit of the curse; but, they say, we are freed from the curse, therefore it is our liberty to make use of whom we please.'[64] Lieutenant Jackson in Scotland in May 1650 was reported as saying that if we were not free to enjoy another man's wife the creature was kept in bondage; the creatures can do nothing otherwise than as moved and acted by God.[65]

It would have been difficult at the time, and is impossible now, to assess the relative importance of repressed exhibitionism and serious symbolic propaganda. In 1652 a lady stripped naked during a church service, crying 'Welcome the resurrection!' The incident was remarkable principally because it took place in the chapel at Whitehall; such occurrences were less rare at Ranter and Quaker meetings.[66]

Ranterism easily passed over into its apparent opposite extreme, asceticism. Fox fasted for ten days, Miles Halhead for a fortnight, Nayler for a day or two longer. James Parnell died after a ten days' fast. Anna Trapnel fasted for twelve days, Sarah Wight, allegedly, for fifty-three.[67] John Pordage was reported as saying that marriage was a very wicked thing, and to have denied the lawfulness of having children by one's husband. He was also, logically enough, accused of having had an illegitimate daughter, and of defending polygamy, though he admitted preferring virginity to matrimony.[68] Quaker asceticism led to reports that 'the Quakers would have no children'. George Fox 'never thought of such things' as 'the procreation of children': 'I judged such things as below me.'[69] Winstanley, no ascetic, made one valid point against this 'excessive community of women called Ranting'.

> The mother and child begotten in this manner is like to have the worst of it, for the man will be gone and leave them, and regard them no more than other women . . . after he hath had his pleasure. Therefore you women beware, for this ranting practice is not the restoring but the destroying power of the creation . . . By seeking their own freedom they embondage others.[70]

Sexual freedom, in fact, tended to be freedom for men only, so long as there was no effective birth control. This was the practical moral basis to the Puritan emphasis on monogamy. The fact that it has since lost this basis tends to make us forget how important it was in its time. Unless the seducer was a Don Juan rich enough to maintain a bastard and its mother (as Charles II and the court wits of the restoration could) sexual liberty was a hit-and-run affair. Many putative fathers must have taken to the road, leaving the mother and the parish authorities to carry the baby. We can see here perhaps yet another attraction of the itinerant life for a Ranter like Lawrence Clarkson. The prudent and stay-at-home, like Samuel Pepys, preferred to philander with other men's wives: to lay their eggs, cuckoo-like, in others' nests. This is why cuckoldry is such an unfailing – and to us boring – joke on the coterie stage. Many were the complaints in the early seventeenth century that City wives were becoming too independent to appreciate the compliment which an aristocratic suitor paid them.

Ranters, I am suggesting, gave ideological form and coherent expression to practices which had long been common among vagabonds, squatter-cottagers, and the in-between category of migratory craftsmen.[71] Over such itinerants church courts and J.P.s had little control: *de facto* marriage and divorce must have been common. 'Vagabonds,' it was said in 1654, 'be generally given to horrible uncleanness, they have not particular wives, neither do they range themselves into families, but consort together as beasts.'[72] The Gubbings of Devon are no doubt an extreme case. They were outside the law, 'exempt from bishop, archdeacon and all authority either ecclesiastical or civil'. They lived like swine and 'multiplied without marriage'.[73] But Norden the surveyor also spoke of people bred amongst the woods, 'dwelling far from any church or chapel', who were 'as ignorant of God or of any civil course of life as the very savages amongst the infidels'.[74] Contemporaries explained the whoredoms of the Welsh by the mountain air: the modern historian more wisely sees them as the natural product of a society which refused to accept English protestant marriage laws.[75] (John Knox had experienced similar difficulties in tightening up the marriage bond in Scotland.)[76] We can only guess how much infanticide accompanied these informal marriages, or more casual liaisons; but presumably infant mortality would in any case be especially high among such social groups.

Rejection of church marriage by Clarkson, Winstanley, Ranters, Quakers, was in one sense a traditional lower-class attitude, looking back to Lollard and Familist practice.[77] But the Ranters, by rejecting sin, proclaiming free love and raising the matter as one for public rational discussion, went further than their predecessors could, and pushed through to a concept of the relation of the sexes which was more libertine than anything publicly defended hitherto. Clarkson at least hoped that his ethic would free men and women from tormenting themselves for imaginary sins. 'Happy is the man that condemns not himself in those things he alloweth of.'[78] Unfortunately Ranter theology leapt ahead of the technical possibilities of their society: equal sexual freedom for both sexes had to wait for cheap and effective methods of birth control. Middleton's Roaring Girl could retain her independence only by remaining chaste. It would be interesting to know how much truth there was in the propagandist assertion of *The Routing of the Ranters* that among Ranters 'the woman doth commonly make choice of the man she will dwell with'.[79] But early Quakers seem to have anticipated theories of painless child-birth, even though their reasoning – that they had been brought into the condition in which Adam and Eve were before the Fall – would not commend itself to a modern gynaecologist.[80]

The Revolution helped many women both to establish their own independence and to visualize a total escape for the poorer classes.

Mary Cary in 1647 got as far as saying that 'We all condemn that antichristian principle in Popery [and elsewhere, *mutatis mutandis*, though she did not emphasize this] to enjoin all to believe as the Pope believes.'[81] Next year she described herself as a 'minister', and justified Parliament's war against the King from Revelation. She dated the resurrection of the two witnesses prophesied in Revelation XI to 5 April 1645, the day the New Model Army marched forth, and referred to the 'great victory' which had occurred in the summer of 1647.[82] In 1651 Miss Cary drafted *A New and more exact Mappe or Description of New Jerusalems Glory*, starting from the assumption that in 1645 Jesus Christ had begun to take his kingdom. 'The time is coming,' she assured her readers, when 'not only men but women shall prophesy; not only aged men but young men, not only superiors but inferiors; not only those who have university learning but those who have it not, even servants and handmaids.' 'Before twenty or ten or five years pass we shall undoubtedly see much more of this spiritual glory upon the saints than now there is'; and she described the material utopia which awaited the saints on earth. 'They shall have abundance of gold and silver.'[83] Mary Cary subsequently became Mrs Rande, under which name in 1653 she urged the Barebones Parliament to abolish tithes and lawyers, relieve the poor and reform the universities.[84] It may be a coincidence that in 1669 the Grand Duke of Tuscany said the Ranters were 'so called from Alexander Ranta, a tailor', for he was not at all well informed in such matters of detail.[85]

There were, finally, tendencies among the radicals which survived to counteract the gloomy 'Puritanism' which set in after 1660 and the defeat of the real Puritans. The Quaker doctrine of perfectibility continued to testify against hatred of the body, even if Fox did think begetting children beneath him. For he also said 'the outward body is not the body of death and sin; the saints' bodies are the members of Christ and the temples of the living God.'[86] Quakers thought lacemaking an unsuitable occupation for members of their Society, but they had no objection to brewing or keeping an ale-house. ('Why not?' Samuel Fisher asked of the latter occupation; 'the calling being . . . honest . . . though often much abused'.)[87] Among Milton's many unorthodoxies, he made romantic love of man for woman a principal cause of the Fall, and endowed the angels with sex, as well as with the capacity to appreciate food – the basis of both ideas being that matter is good and rightly to be enjoyed.[88] What happened to the ideas which radicals for a brief period publicized, and which then returned to obscurity, we do not know. But Mr A. L. Morton has established that Blake at least inherited ideas similar to those of the Ranters, as well as knowing his Milton intimately.[89]

16
Life Against Death

Sir Thomas Bitefig:— First then,
I charge thee, lend no money; next, serve God;
If ever thou hast children, teach them thrift:
They'll learn religion fast enough themselves.

CARTWRIGHT, *The Ordinary*, Act V, scene i.
(Published 1651, but the author died in 1643)

I THE PROTESTANT ETHIC

I shall assume without argument that there is such a thing as the
protestant ethic: an emphasis on the religious duty of working hard
in one's calling, of avoiding the sins of idleness, waste of time, over-
indulgence in the pleasures of the flesh. This ethic was most easily
absorbed by the industrious middle classes in town and country –
yeomen, craftsmen, merchants, some gentlemen. It gave a moral
energy, a conviction of righteousness, that enabled them to carry out
heroic feats of political revolution, and to endure that more hum-
drum day-to-day struggle to save and accumulate the capital which
was indispensable to business success. It also convinced many of
them that it was a religious duty to impose regular, disciplined
labour on the lower classes (and occasionally, more daringly, on the
idle upper classes): at least to create social conditions which discouraged idleness. This meant opposing observance of saints' days, and
the traditional village festivals and sports, as well as sexual
irresponsibility.

I want to emphasize the extent of the revolution in man's thinking and feeling which imposition of the protestant ethic involved. Protestant preachers in the late sixteenth and early seventeenth century undertook a cultural revolution, an exercise in indoctrination, in brainwashing, on a hitherto unprecedented scale. We only fail to recognize this because we live in a brainwashed society: our own indoctrination takes place so early, and from so many directions at once, that we are unaware of the process. Brainwashing is something which other peoples do. Only in our own day, with the beginnings of the widespread rejection of the protestant ethic in our society, and with examples of alternative indoctrinations in other societies, can we grasp the vastness of the achievement of those who initially imposed it – even though it took several generations.

The preachers knew what they were doing. Their language is revealing. They were up against 'natural man'. The mode of thought and feeling and repression which they wished to impose was totally unnatural. 'Every man is by nature a rebel against heaven,' declared Richard Baxter, 'so that ordinarily to plead for a democracy is to plead that the sovereignty may be put into the hands of rebels.'[1] Only the strongest religious convictions could steel men to face the sacrifices, the repressions, the loss involved: and it took generations for those attitudes to be internalized. 'It is the violent only that are successful,' wrote the gentle Richard Sibbes: 'they take it [salvation] by force.' Professor and Mrs George have collected much evidence of the hostility which men in the central Puritan tradition, Perkins, Sibbes, Bolton, Adams, felt towards idleness, 'the very rust and canker of the soul', 'itself against the law of Scripture'.[2] There is a terrifying crescendo in the words of Mrs Joceline's *The Mothers Legacie* (1622): 'Be ashamed of idleness, as thou art a man, but tremble at it, as thou art a Christian ... God hates the slothful ... What more wretched estate can there be in the world? First to be hated of God as an idle drone, not fit for his service, then through extreme poverty to be contemned of all the world.'[3] 'One grain of time's inestimable sand,' wrote Roger Williams, 'is worth a golden mountain: let us not lose it.'[4]

There were plenty of idle, lazy natural men, of course. The preachers agreed that the theology of popery was 'set up by the wit of man to maintain stately idleness'.[5] What really horrified them was to find a similar tendency in certain brands of radical protestantism. Under Elizabeth the view was attributed to the Libertines that 'a man ought not to weary his body in travail and labour; for they said the Holy Ghost would not tarry in a body that was weary and irksome.'[6] This was a striking counter-argument to the doctrine of the dignity of labour which was such an important component of the protestant ethic. It is the assimilation by a lower social class of the values of the leisured aristocracy. There were interesting possibilities here, which Ranters developed. The idea fitted in with the economic ethic of cottagers who would work only when the price of corn was high: when bread was cheap, labour was dear, if indeed it could be obtained at all. This refusal to accept the principle of supply and demand infuriated economists, from Petty onwards.[7] Most of the tenets of the Familists, Thomas Weld declared in 1644, 'tended to slothfulness, and quench all endeavour in the creature'.[8] 'In the ordinary constant course of his [God's] dispensation,' the New England Synod of 1637 told Mrs Hutchinson, 'the more we endeavour, the more assistance and help we find from him.'[9]

Familism, from which the thought of so many of the radicals derives, was thought to encourage moral sloth and therefore idleness in callings. Samuel Rutherford thus caricatured the effects of Dell's teaching: 'All husbandmen sit idle, all tradesmen buy and sell and labour with your hands no more, be at rest and quiet, take Mr Dell's word, God's undertaking takes away all reforming in men, all undertaking in second causes.'[10] According to an anti-Ranter pamphlet, 'that idleness is the mother of all mischief was never so evidently proved as by the ... Ranters, a people so dronish that the whole course of their lives is but one continued scene of sottishness.'[11] If the lower orders are idle they may even be able to enjoy themselves! It was idleness which brought Nayler to 'these high notions', Luke Robinson told the House of Commons in December 1656; hard labour would restore him to his senses.[12] (Without wishing to labour it, we may quote Mrs Thirsk's point that in sixteenth- and seventeenth-century England pastoralists were regarded as lazy by contrast with husbandmen.[13] John Everard allegorized this to make the true shepherd 'depend more upon God and his providence' than husband-men, who rely upon their own labour and toil, 'and think thereby to cozen God, expecting he will reward them'.[14] Aristocratic sentimen-talization of the pastoral existence was possible because shepherds were, or were thought to be, non-manual workers, who had plenty of time for sporting with Amaryllis in the shade.)

In my *Society and Puritanism* I illustrated the Puritan horror of waste of time, the inculcation of habits of punctuality and orderli-ness of life.[15] The English reformed church in Amsterdam in the 1630s enforced punctuality and *voluntary* performance of duties on its members by fines. The standards which were imposed by the Con-sistory Courts of the Dutch reformed church, unlike those of the English church courts, were those of capitalist business life.[16] By the end of the century this discipline, this sense that time is money, this *voluntary* commitment to duty, had been internalized by the bulk of the English middle class, labouring 'as ever in my great task-master's eye'. It had become a custom, a habit taken for granted. But not by the lower classes, as Milton's metaphor suggests.

Men so different as Richard Bancroft, Henry Barrow and Thomas Hobbes all pointed out that the Puritan preachers turned a relatively blind eye to the sins of rich business men.[17] Calvinism, which helped so many yeomen, merchants and craftsmen to live, labour and some-times prosper, turned a less friendly face on those whose efforts did not meet with the good fortune which was also necessary if a man was to get on in that uncertain world, and on those unable or unwill-ing to keep up unremitting self-discipline. Calvinism called up the terrors of hell and damnation for those whom an arbitrary God did not choose to favour: despair and thoughts of suicide, as we have seen contemporaries witnessing,[18] might be by-products of Calvin-ism. For the ungodly lower orders it offered – or Presbyterians thought it should – a harsh and bracing discipline.

Presbyterian discipline was an attempt to dragoon them into acceptance. The New Model Army frustrated this attempt, and Pres-byterians were not able to take the place of the Army in 1660. After the restoration the sectarian communities took over more gentle indoctrination of their members, something of an élite: the mass of the lower classes remained resistant until coerced by the brutal economic pressures of the eighteenth-century Industrial Revolution.[19] This led to assumptions of a dual standard of rationality. The men of property, employers, were deemed (by themselves and their ideologues) to be capable of reasoned calculation in a way that their employees were not.[20] Only a few theorists resisted the whole attempt at regimentation for labour: or at least only in the 1640s and 1650s could their views get into print.

The author of *Tyranipocrit Discovered* was one of these. He referred in 1649 to 'this hypocritical doctrine, to be rich and godly'.[21] He did not exaggerate. William Ames explained that riches lawfully gotten, though not good in themselves, were the gifts of God: not to be forsaken unless the special will of God required it. Evangelical poverty is spiritual, and may consist with great riches: the more usual sort of poverty may be regarded as a punishment or affliction. Prosperity is approved by God: parsimony and frugality are virtues.[22] This gets the best of every world: riches can be despised and enjoyed at the same time, and the special will of God was not always easy to identify. Influential City preachers like Sibbes, Gouge and Thomas Taylor all taught their congregations that riches could be sanctified: the Scriptures teach us how to use them lest we be tempted to prefer a state of poverty.[23]

It was only a very short step to Sir William Temple, who thought the man that shall not provide for his family 'worse than an infidel'.[24] Hugh Peter in 1651 said 'a well-monied man that is prudent by God's blessing gets up above his neighbours', and a sermon of 1655 dedicated to the Lord Mayor of London asserted that

> industry and diligence in a lawful and warrantable vocation and calling, in order to gain a competent provision of earthly things for our children and relations, is not condemned in sacred Writ, but commended . . . Grace in a poor man is grace and 'tis beautiful; but grace in a rich man is more conspicuous, more useful.[25]

It is laudable and a duty to provide for our families, declared the Rev. Joseph Lee in 1656;[26] to choose the less gainful way, when God showed a lawful way to make money, was refusing to be God's steward, Richard Baxter thought.[27] I shall quote below Abiezer Coppe's furious retort to this very prevalent line of argument. George Fox in his *Journal* noted, with positive gratification, that Quaker uprightness led to worldly prosperity.[28] The doctrine of predestination, said the author of *Tyranipocrit Discovered*, encouraged rich presumptuous sinners to sin through security.[29] Dr Macfarlane and Mr K. V. Thomas suggest that the guilty conscience of individualists, breaking the traditional decencies of the code of village society, took refuge in witchcraft accusations which singled out their victims as enemies of God.[30]

One consequence of the protestant ethic was an emphasis on the importance of property rights. During the Revolution, and especially in the economic crisis of the years 1647–50, men asked what moral justification there could be for the exclusive property rights of the rich when the poor were starving. Here is Baxter's reply:

> Whensoever the preservation of life is not in open probability like to be more serviceable to the common good than the violation of property will be hurtful, the taking of another man's goods is sinful, though it be to save the taker's life … Therefore ordinarily it is a duty rather to die than to take another man's goods against his will.

Property, said Baxter, anticipating Locke, 'is in order of nature antecedent to human government'. One of Oliver Cromwell's criticisms of Fifth Monarchists was that they did not recognize property as one of the badges of the kingdom of Christ.[31]

The testing time for Calvinism came in the 1640s, when the preachers had aroused hopes of a better society which remained unfulfilled, and when an atmosphere of freedom prevailed in which voices of protest against the harshness of the Calvinist discipline could not be silenced. On all sides both the Presbyterian system and the Eternal Decrees came under attack, and now not merely from sceptical scholars like William Chillingworth, John Hales and John Selden, but from crude materialistic Ranters, some of whom disliked Calvinism because it stifled the human spirit, others, it may be suspected, because they did not like work.

II   BEYOND THE PROTESTANT ETHIC

Professor C. H. George quotes Falstaff's defence of his activities as a highwayman: 'Why, Hal, 'tis my vocation, Hal. 'Tis no sin for a man to labour in his vocation.'[32] There was plenty for enemies of the protestant ethic to be ironical about. Some Puritan preachers had sailed dangerously near the wind when they denounced idle gentlemen who 'live in no calling'.[33] *More Light Shining in Buckinghamshire* argued that gentlemen were the real vagabonds, who do not labour in a calling: by their own and by God's law they should be punished. 'So first go hang yourselves for your great thefts of enclosures and oppressions, and then afterwards you can go hang your poor brethren for petty thefts.'[34] Winstanley extended the Puritan emphasis on the dignity of work to something like a labour theory of value:

> No man can be rich but ... either by his own labours, or by the labours of other men helping him. If a man have no help from his neighbours, he shall never gather an estate of hundreds and thousands a year. If other men help him to work, then are those riches his neighbours' as well as his ... Rich men receive all they have from the labourer's hand, and what they give, they give away other men's labours, not their own.

All landlords are thieves. Winstanley's conclusion, so different from that of the preachers, was that both landlordism and wage labour should be abolished, 'for this brings in kingly bondage'.[35]

Sin itself looked different to the proponents of an upside-down world? Winstanley asked, who were the greatest sinners in the world? He replied that 'the greatest sin against universal love' was 'for a man to lock up the treasuries of the earth in chests and houses, and suffer it to rust or moulder, while others starve for want to whom it belongs – and it belongs to all.' Winstanley answered Ireton's phrase at Putney, 'Liberty cannot be provided for in a general sense if property be preserved' with a phrase no less trenchant: 'There cannot be a universal liberty till this universal community be established.' His second deadly sin might be a reply to Baxter on the sanctity of private property: it was

> for any man or men, first to take the earth by the power of the murdering sword from others; and then by the laws of their own making [to] hang or put to death any who takes the fruits of the earth to supply his necessaries, from places or persons where there is more than can be made use of by that particular family where it is hoarded up.[36]

Lionel Lockier argued that 'formal saints' were more guilty than Ranters of spending extravagantly when their fellows stood in need: servants are made to labour on the Sabbath and the poor starve in the church porch:

> And all that hold community
> By them as Ranters counted be.[37]

Mr Covetousness, in Bunyan's *Holy War*, 'covers himself with the name of Good-Husbandry'.[38]

Ranters gave fullest expression to moral indignation against the humbug to which the protestant ethic could give rise – 'thy stinking family duties and thy Gospel ordinances as thou callest them ... under them all lies snapping, snarling, biting, besides covetousness, horrid hypocrisy.'[39] 'Hypocritical darkness hath ... overspread ... almost all family worship,' Winstanley agreed.[40] This 'Pharisee in man is the mother of harlots,' Coppe continued, 'and being the worst whore cries Whore first; and the grand blasphemer cries out Blasphemy, blasphemy, which she is brim full of.'[41] But Coppe's case can only be made at length:

> Follow me, who last Lord's Day, September 30, met him in open field, a most strange deformed man, clad with patched clouts: who looking wishly on me, mine eye pitied him; and my heart, or the day of the Lord, which burned as an oven in me, set my tongue on flame to speak to him, as followeth:
> How now, friend, art thou poor?
> He answered, Yea, master, very poor.

Whereupon my bowels trembled within me and quivering fell upon the worm-eaten chest (my corpse, I mean) that I could not hold a joint still.

And my great love within me (who is the great God within that chest, or corpse) was burning hot towards him; and made the lock-hole of the chest, to wit, the mouth of the corpse, again to open. Thus:

Art poor?

Yea, very poor, said he.

Whereupon the strange woman who flattereth with her lips and is subtle of heart, said within me:

It's a poor wretch, give him two-pence.

But my EXCELLENCY and MAJESTY (in me) scorned her words, confounded her language, and kicked her out of his presence.

But immediately the WELL-FAVOURED HARLOT (whom I carried not upon my horse behind me, but who rose up in me), said:

It's a poor wretch, give him 6d., and that's enough for a squire or knight to give to one poor body.

Besides (saith the holy Scripturian Whore) he's worse than an infidel that provides not for his own family.

True love begins at home, etc.

Thou and thy family are fed, as the young ravens, strangely. Though thou hast been a constant preacher, yet thou hast abhorred both tithes and hire; and thou knowest not aforehand who will give thee the worth of a penny.

Have a care of the main chance,

And thus she flattereth with her lips, and her words being smoother than oil, and her lips dropping as the honeycomb, I was fired to hasten my hand into my pocket; and pulling out a shilling, said to the poor wretch, give me sixpence, here's a shilling for thee.

He answered, I cannot, I have never a penny.

Whereupon I said, I would fain have given thee something if thou couldst have changed my money.

Then said he, God bless you.

Whereupon, with much reluctancy, with much love, and with amazement (of the right stamp) I turned my horse's head from him, riding away . . .

And behold the plague of God fell into my pocket, and the rust of my silver rose up in judgment against me, and consumed my flesh as with fire ... and the 5 of James[42] thundered such an alarm in mine ears that I was fain to cast all I had into the hands of him, whose visage was more marred than any man's that ever I saw.

This is a true story, most true in the history.

It's true also in the mystery.

And there are deep ones couched under it, for it's a shadow of various glorious (though strange) good things to come.

Well! To return - - - After I had thrown my rusty cankered money into the poor wretch's hands, I rode away from him, being filled with trembling, joy and amazement, feeling the sparkles of a great glory arising up from under these ashes.

After this, I was made (by that divine power which dwelleth in this Ark, or chest) to turn my horse's head - - - whereupon I beheld this poor deformed wretch looking earnestly after me: and upon that was made to put off my hat and bow to him seven times, and ... I rode back to the poor wretch, saying, Because I am a King I have done this, but you need not tell any one.[43]

After the white-hot anger and pity of that strange passage, almost anything else sounds tame. But Nayler has analogous words, which ironically pick up many of the traditional Puritan phrases in a way that could hardly be to the liking of the later Fox:

> Saith God, Thou shalt not covet ... Saith Antichrist, Thou must live by the wits that God hath given thee, and this is not covetousness but a provident care; and he that will not provide for his family is worse than an infidel, and if thou stand to wait upon God and do not help thyself by thy wits, both thou and thine may be poor enough.[44]

Of Presbyterian sabbatarianism Nayler said 'you have ... a day to abstain from the world, and days to conform to the world': and he mocked their fear of freedom.[45]

The author of *Tyranipocrit Discovered* made some gentler points against the selfishness and hypocrisy to which Puritanism could give rise:

I would not dispraise faith, but I would praise love, and prefer love above and before all . . . Man may profit man, but no man can profit God; and therefore, if we will do good, we must do it to mankind, and not to God without [i.e. outside] man . . . Faith no doubt is a comfortable thing for him that hath it, but another's faith cannot help me.

It would be less hypocritical to prefer hate to love than to put all emphasis on a faith which does not issue in charitable works.[46] 'Talking of love is no love,' Winstanley added; 'it is acting of love in righteousness.'[47] Roger Crab in 1657 argued that it was impossible to love your neighbour as yourself whilst accumulating property: 'all our properties are but the fruit of God's curse.'[48]

Antinomianism is a democratization of the Calvinist doctrine of election, a logical extension of protestant individualism. All protestants had emphasized that religion must be based on inner conviction; but radical Puritans most of all. 'God in this Gospel reformation aims at nothing but the heart,' declared William Dell.[49] The middle class of Geneva, Amsterdam, London, East Anglia, had found the protestant ethic, the dignity of labour and hatred of idleness, written on their hearts: the environment in which they lived and worked had put it there. Not so cottagers, casual labourers. Labour is one thing for small masters whose wealth is directly related to their labour: if they do not work neither shall they eat. But the wage labourer works, in part at least, that another may eat. So long as he gets his wages, he is not interested in what he produces, or how much. The inner voice speaks differently to communities drawn from the lowest classes. Idleness is not a sin; adultery is no sin to the pure in heart. Love is more important than faith.

One final blasphemy: some radicals denied the civilizing mission of white Anglo-Saxon protestants. Already in 1646 Thomas Edwards reported seditious spirits who were questioning Englishmen's rights in Ireland. Walwyn suggested they had no business to be there at all: 'the cause of the Irish natives in seeking their just freedoms . . . was the very same with our cause here in endeavouring our own rescue and freedom from the power of oppressors.' Why should not the Irish enjoy the liberty of their consciences, Walwyn asked. They are a better-natured people than we. Thus he 'puzzled the judgments and consciences of those that otherwise would promote the happy work' which terminated at Drogheda.[50] Samuel Rutherford observed that it was 'sundry Antinomians' who thought Irish papists should be allowed 'to enjoy their religion'.[51]

The author of *Tyranipocrit Discovered* in 1649 lumped together French and Spanish brutality towards Waldensians, Moors and Dutch, and 'how the English hunted the poor Irish'. He extended this to a denunciation of commercial empire in general:

> Our merchants, they travel by sea and land to make Christian pros-
> elytes, chiefly our Indian merchants; but consider their practices,
> and the profit that we have by their double dealing, first in robbing
> of the poor Indians of that which God hath given them, and then in
> bringing of it home to us, that we thereby may the better set forth
> and show the pride of our hearts in decking our proud carcasses, and
> feeding our greedy guts with superfluous unnecessary curiosities.

Yet 'although their dealing concerning the Indians' goods be bad, yet they deal worser with their persons: for they either kill them, which is bad, or make them slaves, which is worse. I know not what to say concerning such impious proceedings with them poor innocent people.'[52] The Diggers spoke on behalf of 'all the poor oppressed people of England and the whole world', and hoped that the law of freedom would go from their country to all the nations of the world. Burrough echoed Winstanley when he asked 'Hath not God made of one mould and one blood all nations to dwell upon the face of the earth?'[53] Yet in the 1650s Oliver Cromwell was trying to use an aggressive imperialist foreign policy as a means of reconciling royalists to his rule, not unsuccessfully. This harnessing of the military tastes of a section of the gentry to colonial expansion survived for more than two centuries, until 'the poor oppressed people of England' again made themselves heard in politics.

Puritans had expended so much energy denouncing papist good works, done for what they believed to be the wrong reasons, that their faith sometimes produced no good works at all. Levellers and Quakers, like the author of *Tyranipocrit*, insisted that faith must issue in works.[54] The true light, said Margaret Fell, could be distinguished from a hypocritical pretence only if words were tested by deeds, and deeds by their effect on the community – meetings, families, neighbours.[55] Thanks to the inner light, wrote Penn, 'where once nothing was examined, nothing went unexamined. Every thought must come to judgment, and the rise and *tendency* of it be well approved before they allow it any room in their minds.'[56]

Most radicals preferred doers to talkers, rejected a fugitive and cloistered virtue.[57] The supreme exponent of the philosophy of action as opposed to contemplation was Winstanley. 'Thoughts run in me,' he said, 'that words and writings were all nothing and must die, for action is the life of all, and if thou dost not act thou dost nothing.' It is 'action whereby the creation shines in glory'. University ministers under 'a covetous proud black gown … would always be speaking words, but falls off when people begins to act their words'. But 'God is an active power, not an imaginary fancy'. 'So that this is the great battle of God Almighty; light fights against darkness, universal love fights against selfish power; life against death; true knowledge against imaginary thoughts.'[58]

III A COUNTER-CULTURE?

The Ranter ethic, as preached by Coppe and Clarkson, involved a real subversion of existing society and its values. The world exists for man, and all men are equal. There is no after-life: all that matters is here and now. 'In the grave there is no remembrance of either joy or sorrow after,' said Clarkson.[59] Nothing is evil that does not harm our fellow men – as many of the existing institutions of society do, and as the repressive humbug and hypocrisy of the self-styled godly certainly do. 'Swearing i'th light, gloriously', and 'wanton kisses',[60] may help to liberate us from the repressive ethic which our masters are trying to impose on us – a régime in which property is more important than life, marriage than love, faith in a wicked God than the charity which the Christ in us teaches.

It was a heroic effort to proclaim Dionysus in a world from which he was being driven, to reassert the freedom of the human body and of sexual relations against the mind-forged manacles which were being imposed.[61] 'Without act, no life,' Clarkson echoed Winstanley, 'without life, no perfection; and without perfection, no eternal peace and freedom indeed, in power, which is the everlasting Majesty, ruling, conquering and damning all into itself, without end, for ever.' We might very nearly be reading Blake. Clarkson looks forward to Blake again when he concludes that to the truly pure 'Devil is God, hell is heaven, sin holiness, damnation salvation: this and only this is the first resurrection.'[62] The world is turned upside down. Men must no longer, wrote Coppe in 1649, 'hunger or hanker after the flesh-pots of the land of Egypt (which is the house of bondage), where they durst not minish ought from the bricks of their daily task'; they should look for and hasten to 'spiritual Canaan (the living Lord), which is a land of large liberty, the house of happiness, where, like the Lord's lily, they toil not but grow in the land flowing with sweet wine, milk and honey ... without money'.[63] This is the Land of Cokayne, of tipsy topsy-turvydom. It was a revised version of the dream of the medieval peasant, as was the heaven on earth which George Foster and Mary Cary had foreseen.[64]

The Ranters' emphasis on love is perhaps mainly a negative reaction to nascent capitalism, a cry for human brotherhood, freedom and unity against the divisive forces of a harsh ethic, enforced by the harsh discipline of the market, as hitherto masterless men are drawn into the meshes of the harsh competitive society. The negativeness of the Ranter reaction allowed links to be formed, as we have seen, with the royalist aristocracy, whose oaths and whose compliments the Ranters aped.[65] Much of Ranterism was less a new ethic than an expression of traditional attitudes, some of which derived from the leisured ruling class – dislike of labour, sexual promiscuity, swearing, an emphasis on works rather than faith. All these linked the upper and lower classes in opposition to the intermediate proponents of the protestant ethic. The greatest of the royalist journalists, Sir John Berkenhead, used to look back nostalgically to happier times when there had been no need for newsbooks.[66] But now the many-headed monster had to be courted, and how better appeal to Dionysian elements among the opposition to Puritanism than by the bold baw-dry of royalist newspapers?[67] Thomas Morton of Merrymount in New England in the 1620s encouraged servants to revolt against their masters, danced round a maypole and 'maintained (as it were) a school of atheism'. Morton was naturally a royalist during the civil war.[68] Maypoles and the Merrie Monarch had the same sort of appeal after the restoration.[69]

Royalists in the 1650s made more directly political overtures to the Levellers, some of whom entered into negotiations with them, unlike the more consistently republican Diggers.[70] In Winstanley's pamphlet of 1650 calling on men to support the Commonwealth in the hope of further advance in a radical direction, he attacked Rant-ers whose sexual libertinism was disrupting the Diggers' attempt at disciplined communal cultivation of the waste. Their sexual prac-tice, he suggested, merely stood traditional values on their head; it was not the transvaluation of values which, in their different ways, both the protestant ethic and Digger communism achieved.[71] Win-stanley wanted to transcend the forces of his society, to build up through love a more positive unity based on rational acceptance of a self-imposed labour discipline within the cooperative community. He was as fiercely opposed as Ranters to the 'clergy power', which restrains 'the liberty of the inward man, not suffering him to act in the liberty of himself; for he makes a man a sinner for a word, and so he sweeps the stars of heaven down with his tail, he darkens heaven and earth and defiles body and mind'.[72]

There had been moments when it seemed as though from the fer-ment of radical ideas a culture might emerge which would be different both from the traditional aristocratic culture and from the bourgeois culture of the protestant ethic which replaced it. We can discern shadows of what this counter-culture might have been like. Reject-ing private property for communism, religion for a rationalistic and materialistic pantheism, the mechanical philosophy for dialectical science, asceticism for unashamed enjoyment of the good things of the flesh, it might have achieved unity through a federation of com-munities, each based on the fullest respect for the individual. Its ideal would have been economic self-sufficiency, not world trade or world domination. The economically significant consequence of Puritan emphasis on sin was the compulsion to labour, to save, to accumulate, which contributed so much to making possible the Industrial Revolution in England. Ranters simply rejected this: Quakers ultimately came to accept it. Only Winstanley put forward an alternative. Exploitation, not labour, was the curse of fallen (i.e. covetous) man. Abolish exploitation with the wage relationship, and labour in itself, to contribute to the beauty of the commonwealth, would become a pleasure.[73] Coolly regarded, we must agree that this was never more than a dream: the counter-acting forces in society were too strong. It came nearest to realization in the Digger communities, which might have given the counter-culture an economic base. Their easy dispersal, and the transition from unorganized Ranter individualism to the organized Society of Friends, registers the fading of the dream into the half-light of common day.

One of the fascinating problems in the intellectual history of seventeenth-century England is the collapse of Calvinism. It was as though it had performed its historic task with the establishment of a society in which the protestant ethic prevailed. Before 1640 Calvinism had been attacked from the right by sacramentalist Laudian Arminians; during the Revolution it was attacked by rationalist Arminians of the left – John Goodwin, Milton, Quakers. Presbyterian discipline was unpopular both with the ungodly lower classes and with upper-class anti-clericals. More serious, Calvinism had proved unable to maintain its defences against Antinomianism. So long as the elect were respectable bourgeois Puritans, their sense of freedom through cooperation with God brought no fundamental danger to the social order. But it was impossible, once discipline broke down, to decide who the elect were. The radicals rejected as hypocrites those Puritans whose faith did not result in works of love. Artisan Fifth Monarchists proclaimed that they were the saints who should rule. Mechanick preachers and lower-class Quakers were convinced that the holy spirit was within them. Some Ranters preached a dionysiac Antinomianism that would have subverted all the moral standards of a propertied society.

Failure to agree on who the elect were drove the men of property back to works – by their fruits ye shall know them. Standards and norms of conduct could be established and enforced by lay J.P.s, with no danger of a clerical Presbyterian discipline. This was a very different theology of works from that of Catholics or Laudians; it was non-sacramental, in no way dependent on a mediating priesthood. It avoided both types of clericalism. And the sects themselves, once they had accepted the world and the sinfulness of man, cooperated in enforcing a morality of works on their members. We are all so much Arminians now that it requires a great imaginative effort to think oneself back into the pre-revolutionary society which Calvinism dominated.

Something analogous occurred during the French Revolution. Middle-class revolutionaries proclaimed the Rights of Man, and seem to have been genuinely taken aback when the Fourth Estate claimed that they too were men. The distinction between active and passive citizens fulfils the same function as that between godly and ungodly: the latter is more convenient because less precisely definable. But both justification by faith and the Rights of Man suffer from the same inescapable contradiction: in order to give the not-yet-privileged confidence to fight against the old type of inequality it is necessary to appeal to that in them which unites them against the privileged: their common humanity, the equality before God of those who believe themselves to be his elect. The 'bourgeois' doctrine of equality always has the suppressed premise that some are more equal than others. The Puritans, to do them justice, did not suppress their premise. Haller perceptively wrote:

> Orthodox Calvinism levelled all men under the law, made all equal in their title to grace, and then denied to most all prospect of realizing their hopes. It made individual experience of God all-important, and then denied freedom to the individual will. It evoked energy and tried to direct it within preordained channels.[74]

17
The World Restored

Peace never comes amongst those sad disasters
Into that land where servants beat their masters.

> THOMAS JORDAN, Lord Mayor's Pageant,
> 18 December 1659, in F. W. Fairholt, *Lord Mayors'*
> *Pageants* (Percy Soc. – Early English Poetry, Ballads
> and Popular Literature, X, 1847) ii, p. 211.

I   1649–1660

Many complained in and after 1649 that the Revolution had not realized the glorious hopes of the preceding years. 'The new tyrants which have driven out the old,' said the author of *Tyranipocrit Discovered*, 'are in all things so bad [as] or worse than the old tyrants were, only they have, or pretend to have, a better faith and a new form of tyranny.'[1] It was not so much the person of Charles I that can hurt me, said Major White in the same year, 'as the power that is made up in the kingly office by the corrupt constitution'.[2] 'Truly tyranny is tyranny in one as well as in another,' Winstanley wrote, 'in a poor man lifted up by his valour as in a rich man lifted up by his lands'[3] – in the Grandees of the Army as in the gentry of the House of Commons, in fact. As the change of institutions failed to bring about the hoped-for transformation, Winstanley, Dell, Erbery, Vavasor Powell and others warned the Army leaders against avarice, ambition, luxury. They were in danger of rearing a more stubborn and intractable despot at home than ever they encountered in the field, Milton told them. Unless they changed their ways, they would become royalists themselves.[4]

After the 'glorious rich providence of God to England' – the 'quashing of the Levellers' at Burford in May 1649[5] – once it had been decided that there was to be no further social revolution, it was inevitable that those who had done well out of the civil war should seek to consolidate their position. This, they came to recognize, could best be achieved by compromise with their defeated enemies, even at the price of retaining or restoring much of the old order. The alternative of continuous revolution, or a further extension of democracy, was too frightening to contemplate. As early as 1650 the Independent John Price, Walwyn's old adversary, asked 'Were it not better we should have' a government 'of the Great Turk than of the rabble rout?'[6] He expected any reasonable and educated man to agree with him. After 1653, if not earlier, almost all trends of opinion among the propertied class combined to denounce Levellers and levelling – the Protector Oliver Cromwell, the republican James Harrington, heads of Oxford and Cambridge colleges, town oligarchies, agricultural reformers, the author of *The Whole Duty of Man*, Presbyterian divines and their sectarian critics.[7] Once the Nayler case had broken the radical-political back of Quakerism, the men of property seemed secure from the perils which had environed them since 1647. But the security was illusory. After Oliver Cromwell's death in 1658, his son Richard fell out with the generals, and a period of desperate confusion ensued, in which radical groupings and opinions revived.

Alarming ideas were abroad again. A series of pamphlets by William Covell, who carefully described himself as a gentleman and disavowed being 'a Leveller who would destroy property', nevertheless proposed to settle all waste lands and commons on the poor for ever, to establish cooperative communities with no buying and selling among their members, to tax the rich in order to pay for the maintenance of the aged, and to abolish the state church. He wrote from Enfield, where there had earlier been a Digger colony, and where in 1659 there were anti-enclosure riots.[8] 'Peter Cornelius' (Plockhoy) thought private property was one of the main causes of want, abuse and corruption. He put forward schemes for cooperative cultivation and communal living, with free social services. Like Winstanley, he appealed to the law of nature which entitled all mankind to some means of subsistence. Like Winstanley, he was passionately anti-clerical and wanted to abolish tithes.[9] William Sprigge also proposed to abolish tithes, and attacked hereditary nobility. He and many other followers of James Harrington campaigned for an agrarian law to limit the accumulation of landed capital.[10] Another pamphleteer revived the assertion that the Army embodies 'the ordinary and common bulk of the people, which are the greatness and strength of the nation'. He added, more ominously, that it was 'a time of breaking and pulling down all worldly constitutions . . . We are upon our march from Egypt to Canaan, from a land of bondage and darkness to a land of liberty and rest.'[11] Even Milton, not usually very conscious of economic problems, closed his *Proposals . . . for the Preventing of a Civil War* (?1659) with a plea for 'the just division of waste commons'.[12]

What made such pronouncements especially frightening to the propertied class was the reappearance of Agitators in the Army.[13] It looked like a return to 1647, complicated by fears of Quakers and 'bloody Anabaptists', now better organized than any radical groups had been twelve years earlier.[14] The Army leaders were accused of arming Anabaptists and Quakers, with the result that 'a mean and schismatical party must depress the nobility and understanding commons'. The words were used by an old Parliamentarian as he rose in revolt in order to bring about a restoration of monarchy.[15] The Fifth Monarchist Christopher Feake was accused of wanting to destroy aristocracy and gentry,[16] and in 1661 the manifesto of Fifth Monarchists in arms did in fact denounce 'the old, bloody, popish, wicked gentry of the nation'.[17] 'We lay at the mercy and impulse of a giddy, hot-headed, bloody multitude,' declared the Rev. Henry Newcome after it was all over.[18] 'Were not this multitude restrained they would presently have the blood of the godly,' Richard Baxter agreed.[19] The crucial question was asked by a pamphleteer in 1660: 'Can you at once suppress the sectaries and keep out the King?'[20] Most middle-of-the-road Puritans and supporters of Parliament had by that time decided that they could not.

In 1641 Sir Thomas Aston had defined 'true liberty' as knowing 'by a certain law that our wives, our children, our servants, our goods are our own'.[21] The word liberty had received many different definitions since then, but by 1660 a majority of the men of property had come to see a lot in Sir Thomas's point of view. Wives, property, employees: it would be a relief to know that they were all safely under control. In 1657 General Monck, who more than any other single individual was to make the restoration, told Richard Cromwell that though 'the greatest part of the people are not the best part', nevertheless 'the most considerable . . . of those that are the best . . . have a great regard to discipline in the Church of God'.[22] Two years later a pamphleteer noticed 'the old spirit of the gentry brought in play again', opposing an 'earthly, lordly rule' to 'the growing light of the people of God'.[23] It was this 'growing light' that made 'the most considerable' forget their objections to bishops.

II   AFTER 1660

It was significant for the future history of England that the Convention Parliament of 1660 was not summoned by the King: it summoned him. Bishops and Lords were brought back too. Radicals were purged from the government of corporations, by the simple process of offering them the oaths of supremacy and allegiance, since refusal to swear was one of the hall-marks of sincere sectaries. Just to make sure, however, the Corporation Act of 1661 also gave local commissions (composed of the neighbouring gentry, who would know their men) power to displace any oath-takers if the commissioners 'shall deem it expedient for the public safety'. The Act against tumultuous petitioning hit at one of the main forms of popular political activity. Henceforth it was illegal to collect more than twenty signatures to any petition 'for alteration of matters established by law in church or state', unless the petition had first been approved by three or more J.P.s or by the majority of the Grand Jury of the county – men of property again. Since the abolition of church courts J.P.s had taken over many of their functions,[24] and they maintained wide supervisory powers even after ecclesiastical courts had nominally been restored.

The Act of Settlement of 1662 put an end to the mobility which had been an essential part of popular liberty in the revolutionary decades. Its preamble made clear that it was aimed against those 'poor people' who 'do endeavour to settle themselves in those parishes where there is the best stock, the largest commons or wastes to build cottages, and the most woods for them to burn and destroy; and when they have consumed it, then to another parish, and at last become rogues and vagabonds'. That is an exact description of the lowest classes whom the Diggers had tried to mobilize to help themselves.[25] But now the gentry were securely in the saddle again. J.P.s were enabled to allow migration of labour where it was economically necessary, but to check it where it seemed to them to serve no useful purpose. Similarly J.P.s could displace squatters on the waste – and many of them were expelled from their cottages – but could also license them where their labour was needed. Landowners could once again enclose and remove timber, unchecked. Copyholders had no security of tenure, no protection against being 'devoured by fees'.[26]

The game laws were made even more ferocious against all but the well-to-do: after 1671 *gamekeepers* had the right to search houses and confiscate weapons. The concentration of power in the hands of the landed class could hardly have been better illustrated. Enclosure and the game laws deprived cottagers of many of their traditional sources of food. No wonder forest and pasture areas continued to be centres of radical dissent, whilst parson and squire were consolidating their control over the agricultural villages, and the gentry in the House of Commons (thanks to the disbandment of the Army) were free to persecute dissenters in the towns. J.P.s took vigorous action against vagrants.[27] Not less effective, as Winstanley had learnt in 1649 and the Fenstanton Baptists in 1653, and as Bunyan confirmed in 1658, were the threats of raising rents or eviction by which 'rich ungodly landlords' could persuade tenants not to go out 'to hear the Word'.[28]

'The rich will rule the world,' sighed the well-to-do Richard Baxter philosophically; 'and few rich men will be saints ... We shall have what we would, but not in this world.'[29] Not in this world: the words were often heard now. In 1649 'many Christian people' in Norfolk had faced the question: 'Christ saith, My kingdom is not of this world. How then can it now be expected?' They replied: 'But he doth not say, It shall not be upon the earth nor while the earth remains (see the contrary, Rev. 5.10).'[30] But those confident days were over. Erbery was saying as early as 1654 that the people of God should not meddle with state matters.[31] But not even Quakers pursued that line consistently before 1660.[32] After the restoration, however, Edward Burrough told Friends 'our kingdom and victory is not of this world, nor earthly', and backed up this new position with a historical argument. The Lord had suffered the restoration to take place 'as a rod of God in his hand, to correct and smite many people' – in particular the Parliamentarians who, forgetful of the Lord and his mercies, had failed to carry out their reforming promises. God had suffered it for reasons known to himself only. In these circumstances there is nothing to do but accept. But he hinted delicately that 'force and cruelty will never make the King happy, ... for the people are wise and understanding, and will not long bear any degree of the yoke of slavery'.[33] It was, as it were, a minimum pacifist position.

Sin came back, first as the means by which radicals explained to themselves their failure to achieve victory for God's cause on earth: not only Quakers, who rejected Christ in Nayler, but also Milton, the theme of whose great philosophical poem was 'man's first disobedience', and its consequences, and how Paradise *within* could be regained on earth. But sin also protected property and an unequal society. Isaac Barrow wrote in 1671:

All things at first were promiscuously exposed to the use and enjoyment of all, every one from the common stock assuming as his own what he needed. Inequality and private interest in things ... were the by-blows of our Fall; sin introduced these degrees and distances, it devised the names of rich and poor; it begot these ingrossings and enclosures of things; it forged those two pestilent words, *meum* and *tuum*, which have engendered so much strife among

men ... We mistake if we think that natural equality and community are in effect quite taken away.

But the good doctor's message was not that his congregation should
therefore reject private property: it was that sin, like the poor, was
always with us, and that there was nothing that we – still less the
poor – could do about it; but bounty to the humble poor would earn
its reward.[34]

For the poor the message was slightly different, but drawn from
the same premises. *The Whole Duty of Man* urged:

> Be often thinking of the joys laid up for thee in heaven and then, as
> a traveller expects not the same conveniences at an inn as he hath at
> home, so thou hast reason to be content with whatever entertain-
> ment thou findest here, knowing thou art upon thy journey to a
> place of infinite happiness which will make an abundant amends for
> all the uneasiness and hardship thou canst suffer in the way.[35]

That was exactly the message that Levellers, Diggers and Ranters
had challenged.

But the experience of the revolutionary decades could not so easily
be wished away. Consequently many, bishops included, deliberately
preached a dual standard, a noble lie, so as to persuade the more
intelligent of the men of property not to attack the socially necessary
myths which they did not themselves accept. Marvell quotes Samuel
Parker as saying:

> Put the case, the clergy were cheats and jugglers, yet it must be allowed
> they are necessary instruments of state to awe the common people into
> fear and obedience, because nothing else can so effectively enslave
> them ('tis this it seems our author would be at) as the fear of invisible
> power and the dismal apprehensions of the world to come.[36]

Rakehelly courtiers might blaspheme and fornicate so long as they did
not justify such practices openly. Rake Rochester indeed was convinced on his death-bed by Gilbert Burnet, far from being the most
illiberal of Anglicans, of the *social* necessity of Christianity.[37] The
Hon. and Rev. Dr John North, his brother tells us, was an Arminian

by conviction. But he thought Calvinism, 'with respect to ignorant men, to be more politic and thereby, in some respects, fitter to maintain religion in them, because more suited to their capacity. But that is referred to art, and not to truth, and ought to be ranked with the *piae fraudes* or holy cheats'.[38] To such ends had the revolutionary creed of Calvinism come, after shaking Europe for a century and a half. It was in a work entitled *The Reasonableness of Christianity* that John Locke wrote: 'day-labourers and tradesmen, the spinsters and dairy-maids' must be told what to believe. 'The greatest part cannot know and therefore they must believe.'[39] But at least Locke did not intend that priests should do the telling: that was for God himself.

There were no Lord Mayor's shows in London between 1640 and 1655. When they were revived in the latter year the preacher told the Lord Mayor (who no doubt knew already) that 'for anniversary shows and harmless and merry recreations, without a moderate permission of them, very little to content the multitude'.[40] The greatest show of all was monarchy. The extraordinary popularity of *Eikon Basilike* from the 1650s, despite Milton's furious attack on it, had put conservatives wise to the social significance and uses of divine kingship. Rude plebeian soldiers had referred to their royal prisoner as 'Stroker', 'in relation to that gift which God had given him' of being able to cure the King's evil. Leveller journalists had mocked a story that Charles I's spittle had cured a sick child.[41] But now plebeian soldiers and Levellers were silenced. The tremendous ceremonial of the coronation was accompanied by a revival of 'touching' on a grand scale. Charles II is alleged to have 'touched' over ninety-two thousand persons during his reign, though I do not know who counted. On one occasion half a dozen of those hoping for a cure were trampled to death in the press.[42] We are in the world of synthetic monarchy, of government by manipulation. The bought cheers at the restoration look forward to the bought anti-popery of the years 1679–81.

There is plenty of evidence for different sentiments among the populace. 'A pox on all kings. I do not give a turd for never a King in England,' said a London lady. A Wapping man 'would gladly spend five shillings to celebrate the execution of the King', and would not mind being the executioner himself. 'We lived as well when there was no King,' said a Yorkshire yeoman; he hoped to do so again. A Londoner in 1662 hoped that 'all the gentry in the land would kill one another, that so the commonalty might live the better'. A constable who had helped to hand some regicides over for execution in 1660 found that in consequence he had 'quite lost his trade among the factious people of Southwark'. It was a Surrey man who 'hoped ere long to trample in the King's and bishops' blood'.[43] For the church hierarchy was no more popular. In 1669 Edward Chamberlayne recorded that 'the clergy . . . are accounted by many as the dross and refuse of the nation . . . It hath been observed, even by strangers, . . . that of all the Christian clergy of Europe . . . none are so little respected, beloved, obeyed or rewarded as the present . . . clergy of England.' The Grand Duke of Tuscany, who visited England that year, was one such stranger.[44] Pepys and Samuel Butler both use the word 'hatred' to describe the popular attitude towards the clergy.[45] But Isaac Barrow claimed that the Church of England enjoys 'the favour of the almost whole nobility and gentry'.[46] No doubt he was right too.

For some at least the revolutionary decades had been a period of intense strain: for such the fear of freedom was removed by the return to the old familiar forms. A last outburst of despairing prophecies of the end of the world, 'produced by fanatics to rouse the vulgar',[47] rebounded as the fatal year 1666 came and went. London was burned, but England and its King, bishops and social system survived. There was a considerable literature denouncing 'vulgar prophecies'[48] among other suspect forms of enthusiasm. Thomas Sprat claimed it as the job of science and the Royal Society 'to shake off the shadows and to scatter the mists which fill the minds of men with a vain consternation'. Prodigies and prophecies could be self-validating by breaking men's courage and preparing them for disasters 'which they fondly imagined were inevitably threatened them from heaven'. This had been 'one of the most considerable causes of those spiritual distractions of which our country has long been the theatre'.[49] The ending of belief in day-to-day divine intervention in politics helped to produce an atmosphere in which science could develop freely; elevation of the mechanical philosophy above the dialectical science of radical 'enthusiasts' reciprocally helped to undermine such beliefs.

'Fanaticism' and 'enthusiasm' were the bugbears of polite and scholarly restoration society. The carefully cultivated classicism of the age of Dryden and Pope was (among other things) the literary form of this social reaction. For the radicals Latin and Greek had been the languages of Antichrist,[50] as they were the languages of the universities, law, medicine, the three intellectual élites.[51] Dr P. W. Thomas has shown us how the classical principles of regularity and propriety had appealed to isolated royalist intellectuals during the decades of defeat. They saw themselves as preservers of literary culture in a time of barbarism. They deplored excess, emphasized decorum and obedience to the rules, in all walks of life.[52] The classical revival may thus have played its part against the dionysian freedom favoured by the Ranters.[53] Blake – as so often the inheritor of this tradition – wrote 'The classics! It is the classics, and not Goths nor monks, that desolate Europe with wars.'[54]

Among scientists and most ex-Parliamentarians, latitudinarianism prevailed after 1660, a limited toleration, a desire to comprehend moderate dissenters within the state church. The latitude men agreed with respectable dissenters in insisting on the maintenance of 'a face of godliness'. Strict Sabbath observance, Baxter argued, 'will make men to be in some sort religious whether they will or not: though they cannot be truly religious against their will, it will make them visibly religious'.[55] Such 'visible religion' was exactly what the radicals had denounced as Antichrist sitting in the Church of England.

'The scum of the people', 'the rascality and rout', had always been against Parliament and Puritans, partly no doubt through ignorance and clerical influence, but partly too through hatred of a Presbyterian discipline, of the forcible inculcation of the protestant ethic, of Puritan hostility to traditional popular festivals and sports.[56] So long as a Presbyterian disciplinary system seemed a possibility, it was rational to prefer bishops if they were the only alternative. By 1660 Richard Baxter had become reconciled to episcopacy as the only chance of getting any discipline at all;[57] others may have accepted bishops rather than risk having too much discipline. In fact church courts and their excommunications were less effective even against the lower classes after 1660 than they had been before 1640. From 1687 they faded out altogether. Such discipline as was imposed was done voluntarily by the sects for their own members.[58] This was a great if unsung victory for popular liberty, at all events in the towns: men and women were left alone more than they had ever been before 1640, certainly far more than the Presbyterians had hoped in the forties.

Moral disciplining of the lower classes passed to J.P.s,[59] and was more effective in agricultural districts than in towns or pastoral/industrial areas. It is doubtful even whether attempts were still made to compel the poorer classes to come to church on Sundays. It had been difficult enough before the breakdown of church courts, before the Act of 1650 which ended compulsory attendance.[60] In many London parishes the church could not have held all the parishioners if they had attended, and the growing habit of renting pews helped to exclude the poor.[61] In some rural parishes a squire like Addison's Sir Roger de Coverley attended church 'in order to count the congregation' and 'see if any of his tenants are missing'.[62] The churchwardens of a Hertfordshire village of 1677 thought it worth reporting that 'several of the inhabitants come constantly to church'.[63] The various royal indulgences, and then the Toleration Act of 1689, finally deprived the Church of England of its monopoly position. So 'the rabble', saved from Ranters, was left to its own devices. There was thus social sense in the alliance of the highest and lowest classes, the hardest swearing classes, against the smug hypocrites in between.

In 1646 the friends of Overton's Mr Persecution wanted the jury which tried him to include Rude-multitude as well as Satan, Antichrist and Sir John Presbyter.[64] This alliance produced not only church and king mobs but also a deliberate sentimental cultivation of the traditional aspects of agricultural Merrie England, maypoles, cakes and ale, as against the triumphant bourgeois ethic. It has its expression too in the literary glorification of the highwayman, often a ruined ex-Cavalier who robs the rich but spares the poor, and who also had no use for an ethic of hard work.[65] Restoration comedy does not merely pick up the old Inns of Court naughtiness: it has also learnt something from the Ranters, whom Samuel Sheppard depicted as *The Joviall Crew*.[66] The lowest classes, whom the sects had neglected (except for Ranters, perhaps to some extent early Quakers), got their revenge by rabbling dissenters for the next century and more.

As a military and political operation the restoration was a great success. Most of the Army was disbanded, but selected regiments, carefully purged, were retained as garrisons for key towns. At Plymouth a citadel was built as a check on the inhabitants who had 'showed themselves on a former occasion to be open to sedition'.[67] The Corporation Act ejected radicals from the government of towns: the act against tumultuous petitioning, the restoration of the censorship and the end of religious toleration deprived them of the possibility of political action. 'The honest inhabitants of the now woeful town of Mansoul', in Bunyan's inimitable summary, cowered at home whilst 'red-coats and black-coats walked the town by clusters, blaspheming God and protecting the Diabolians'.[68] The tendency among the sects towards pacifism and withdrawal from politics was encouraged by this mixture of pulpit cajolery and military repression. Those least amenable would emigrate – or would be transported. Yet, notwithstanding these draconian measures, even as late as the end of 1687 Gilbert Burnet believed that 'a rebellion of which he [William of Orange] should not retain the command would certainly establish a commonwealth'.[69] Prudently, the men of property invited William in time, and he brought a large professional army with him: so the unreliable James II could be hustled off the throne without danger of popular revolt.

In one way or another law and order were thus preserved long enough for the agricultural improvers to be proved right. Destruction of timber by squatters and miners, together with marling the soil, extended the area of arable or mixed husbandry at the expense of forests and pasture. Disafforestation, fen drainage, enclosure of commons and capital investment in agriculture – all these in the long run *did* make England a richer country, did create new demands for a permanent class of landless wage labourers, however much this new status was felt as unfreedom. By the 1690s restrictions on mobility could safely be modified.[70] Economic expansion, ironically, came especially in the North and West, where clover enabled marginal land to be brought under cultivation when enclosed, where cheap labour attracted industry and the expansion of colonial trade and shipping under the stimulus of the Navigation Act benefited the outports. The growing respectability and quiet dedication to industry of so many Quakers shows how their mood adapted to the new economic possibilities.

John Evelyn in 1664 attributed the 'furious devastation of so many goodly woods and forests' to the punitive taxation of the revolutionary decades and to the activities of Parliamentary sequestration committees as well as to 'the multiplication of glass-works, iron-furnaces and the like'. But now he had hopes, via enclosure, of reafforestation.[71] The agricultural writer John Houghton counted enclosure of commons and disparking of parks among the beneficial consequences of 'his Majesty's most happy restoration'.[72] In 1690 Sir William Petty remarked that over the past forty years the power and wealth of England had increased, thanks especially to fen-drainage, watering dry grounds, improving forests and commons, cultivating heath and barren grounds with clover and sainfoin.[73] Dr Kerridge suggests that by 1700 three-quarters of English enclosures had already taken place.[74] Even a radical like Moses Wall in 1659 had seen 'an improving of our native commodities, as our manufactures, our fishing, our fens, forests and commons, and our trade at sea, etc.' as the way forward not only to 'a comfortable subsistence' for the nation but also to 'progressency ... in liberty and spiritual truths'.[75] The Revolution began with Oliver Cromwell leading fen-men in revolt against court drainage schemes; its crucial turning point was the defeat of the Leveller regiments at Burford, which was immediately followed by an act for draining the fens; it ended with the rout of the commoners and craftsmen of the south-western counties in the bogs of Sedgmoor.

18
Conclusion

Revolutions of ages do not oft recover the loss of a rejected
truth, for the want of which whole nations fare the worse.

J. MILTON, *Areopagitica* (1644) in *Complete Prose
Works*, II, p. 493.

I   TEEMING FREEDOM

The philosopher Thomas Hobbes in his analysis of sense experience
stressed the importance of change in stimulating mental activity – 'it
being almost all one for a man to be always sensible of the same
thing and not to be sensible of anything'.[1] One achievement of this
period is its insights into the historical process itself, an 'awareness
of great forces at work in society', whether in Hobbes's *Behemoth*,
Marvell's *Horatian Ode*, Harrington's *Oceana*, or Winstanley's
writings.[2] These insights were lost at the restoration, and this aspect
of historical writing advanced little in the next century. I have tried
to stress in this book the most unusual stimuli which during the
revolutionary decades produced a fantastic outburst of energy, both
physical and intellectual. The civil war itself, the intellectual forcing
house of the New Model Army and its Army Council, regicide, the
conquest of Ireland and Scotland, the Dutch and Spanish wars, physical and social mobility, the continuous flow of pamphlets on every
subject under the sun – one could list a great many more ways in
which this energy manifested itself.

For a short time, ordinary people were freer from the authority of church and social superiors than they had ever been before, or were for a long time to be again. By great good fortune we have a pretty full record of what they discussed. They speculated about the end of the world and the coming of the millennium; about the justice of God in condemning the mass of mankind to eternal torment for a sin which (if anyone) Adam committed; some of them became sceptical of the existence of hell. They contemplated the possibility that God might intend to save everybody, that something of God might be within each of us. They founded new sects to express these new ideas. Some considered the possibility that there might be no Creator God, only nature. They attacked the monopolization of knowledge within the privileged professions, divinity, law, medicine. They criticized the existing educational structure, especially the universities, and proposed a vast expansion of educational opportunity. They discussed the relation of the sexes, and questioned parts of the protestant ethic.

The eloquence, the power, of the simple artisans who took part in these discussions is staggering. Some of it comes across in print – Fox the shepherd, Bunyan the tinker, Nayler the yeoman. We tend to take them for granted. But far more must have been lost, even of those men and women who left writings. And what of those who did not? The 'men of acute wit and voluble tongues', as an enemy described them, who visited Coppe in jail at Coventry in 1650?[3] How overwhelmingly right Milton's pride had been in the 'noble and puissant nation, rousing herself like a strong man after sleep and shaking her invincible locks, . . . a nation not slow and dull, but of a quick, ingenious and piercing spirit, acute to invent, subtle and sinewy to discourse, not beneath the reach of any point the highest human capacity can soar to'.

How right too was Milton's confidence that God's Englishmen had significant and eloquent things to say, which only the 'tyrannical duncery' of bishops had prevented them from saying; and that any future attempt to censor them would be 'an undervaluing and vilifying of the whole nation', a reproach to the common people.[4] One wonders how often in the 1650s and 60s, for all his growing disillusionment with the political gullibility of ordinary people, he nevertheless reflected on what they had created. Henry Power, a

Halifax man, summed up between ten and twenty years after *Areopagitica*, when Milton's hopes were failing him:

> This is an age wherein all men's souls are in a kind of fermentation, and the spirit of wisdom and learning begins to mount and free itself from those drossy and terrene impediments wherewith it has been so long clogged ... Methinks I see how all the old rubbish must be thrown away, and the rotten buildings be overthrown and carried away with so powerful an inundation. These are the days that must lay a new foundation of a more magnificent philosophy never to be overthrown.[5]

What do we conclude? We do not need persuading, today, that liberty of printing ought to be given a trial. That hard-fought battle has been won. We take the victory for granted, and are sometimes sceptical of the results now that printing has become big capitalist business. But to appreciate what it meant, to recover the intoxicating excitement – not only of being able to print what one thought, but of being able to *say* what one thought – we have to return to those marvellous decades when it seemed as though the world might be turned upside down.

There is still a freshness about their writings which comes across. Historians may trace sources in Italian Neo-Platonists and German Anabaptists, but what gives life and vigour to these ideas is the relevance which men felt that they had to the affairs of England in the revolutionary decades. The ideas may (or may not) be second-hand; the passion behind them is not. Many radicals claimed to have received their truths not from books or from men but from God, from the spirit within. No doubt they deceived themselves: they gave form and shape to vague ideas that were in the air. But the form and shape were their own, drawn from the experience of their daily life in England during the years when John Warr's 'teeming freedom' exerted itself.

We must not sentimentalize: I have picked out the most favourable examples. Magic and superstition still played a big part in popular thought, as was shown in the brief outburst of witch persecution in Suffolk in 1645. A lot of nonsense was talked and written. Nevertheless, if we compare the two great set debates on religious toleration which survive from this period, the Whitehall debates of

December 1648 and January 1649 and the Nayler debates of December 1656, a clear distinction emerges. In the former the representatives of the New Model Army, London Levellers and radical divines, all show a degree of tolerance astonishing for the age. Wildman speculated that the sun or the moon might reasonably be thought to be God: he and others wished to deprive the magistrate of any power in religious matters at all. The generals were less certain, and Ireton uneasily asked whether toleration was to 'debar any kind of restraint on anything that any will call religion?'[6]

In the second Parliament of the Protectorate the gentry, the principal lawyers of the country, and a few big merchants, sat in judgment on the Yorkshire yeoman who had entered Bristol on a donkey. The hysterical savagery which they showed is in striking contrast to the civilized decency of the Whitehall debates. A few courageous Army officers defended Nayler, together with one or two members of the government whose policy of toleration was under attack. Nayler's aims, Colonel Sydenham declared, border 'near a glorious truth'. But the consciences of many M.P.s, especially those who were just about to offer the crown to Oliver Cromwell, could not be reconciled to allowing Nayler to live. It was doubtful whether Parliament had any right to punish Nayler at all, and after nearly a month of debate this consideration among others helped to produce a more merciful sentence. And what was it? To be flogged through the streets of London, his tongue to be bored with a hot iron, his forehead branded; then to be sent to Bristol for a second flogging: and to be kept in prison until Parliament decided otherwise.[7] Flogging followed by exposure in the pillory was designed to break a man's spirit. It rarely failed except when – as with Lilburne in 1638 – the victim was sustained by the solidarity of the watching crowd, which might itself restrain the executioner's hand. But a pitiless punishment approved by a hostile crowd was society's most brutally effective way of reasserting its standards against a movement which was divided and in retreat. Nayler underwent his ordeal with fortitude, but physically he never recovered from it; he died three years later at the age of 43.

The M.P.s in 1656 were frightened – frightened of what they believed to be the Quaker threat to magistracy and ministry, to a state church and the stability of the social order. One of the fiercest was Francis Drake, lord of the manor of Cobham, the Diggers' persecutor.[8] But fear will not in itself explain the difference between the atmosphere of the two debates. For the participants in the Whitehall debates in the winter of 1648–9 were approaching the greatest crisis of the Revolution, the trial and execution of Charles I. Some of those who took part in the discussions suffered the terrible death of a traitor after the restoration: the bodies of Cromwell and Ireton were dug up and hanged. Many of the others led a hunted existence, underground or in exile. They knew at the time of the debates what risks they were running. If anyone had cause for nervous panic, it was they, not the M.P.s of 1656. The former had a confidence in reason, in the goodness of man, which in retrospect appears naive and touching. The latter were savage because they had no assurance that what they wanted to defend could be preserved by any other means than savagery.

Their attitude had been expressed by Clement Walker in 1649: the Army radicals had encouraged social insubordination by stimulating discussion. But 'there can be no form of government without its proper mysteries, which are no longer mysteries than while they are concealed. Ignorance, and admiration arising from ignorance, are the parents of civil devotion and obedience.'[9] 'The more liberty, the greater mischief,' Major-General Skippon succinctly told Parliament in December 1656. 'I would not have a people know their own strength,' Luke Robinson agreed.[10]

Part of the ebullience I have been discussing springs from the youth of the actors. Young men of ability have far more chance of coming to the top in a revolution. I have already quoted accounts of the appeal of religious radicalism to the young.[11] Brailsford pointed out how very young were the Agitators of 1647.[12] It was true of higher ranks in the Army too. Fairfax was Commander-in-Chief of the New Model Army at the age of 33, Ludlow military ruler of Ireland at the same age. Henry Ireton was only 40 when he died in 1651. John Lambert was perhaps the second most powerful person in the kingdom at the age of 35; his political career was finished when he was 41, though he languished for another 23 years in gaol. The New Model offered one career to the talents; but leaders of democratic sects also had to establish their ascendancy in open competition, and most of them were very young when they entered on these careers. Bidle was born in 1616, Nayler in 1617 or 1618, Coppe in 1619, Fox in 1623, John Rogers in 1627, Richard Hubberthorne in 1628, Edward Burrough in 1634. All were under thirty when the civil war ended. James Parnell was still not 20 when he died in 1656. It was a young man's world while it lasted.

II EXPERIENCE

In the radicals' mode of thought two strands are twisted. One is belief in the evolution of truth, continuous revelation. John Robinson preached the doctrine in his farewell sermon to the Pilgrim Fathers in 1620,[13] so it is fitting that the belief is often related to the discovery of the New World. Thus John Goodwin in 1642 argued that 'if so great and considerable a part of the world as America is . . . was yet unknown to all the world besides for so many generations together: well may it be conceived, not only that some but many truths, yea and those of main concernment and importance, may yet be unknown.'[14] Thomas Goodwin announced that 'a new Indies of heavenly treasure . . . hath been found out! . . . Yet more . . . may be.'[15] Lord Brooke and the five Dissenting Brethren of the Westminster Assembly looked forward to a state of permanent reformation.[16] John Saltmarsh, Walter Cradock and many others saw their own age as one of an outpouring of the spirit: they hoped that a thousand flowers would bloom.[17] This was a great argument for religious toleration, in *Areopagitica* and in the anonymous *The Ancient Bounds* (1645), which insisted that truth 'cannot be so easily brought forth' without liberty of conscience; 'better many errors of some kind suffered than one useful truth be obstructed or destroyed'.[18] 'The daily progress of the light of truth,' said Milton, 'is productive far less of disturbance to the church, than of illumination and edification.'[19] Through revelation of new truths to believers, traditional Christianity could be adapted to the needs of a new age; the everlasting gospel within responded more easily and swiftly to the pressures of the environment than did traditions of the church or the literal text. History is a gradual progress towards total revelation of truth.[20]

What then is the test of the new truth? It is plain blunt common sense. The Baconian emphasis on things rather than words, the scientists' emphasis on the test of practice, on experiment, both point that way. Hobbes argued against the arid rationalism of the Schoolmen who 'speak without conception of the things, and by rote, one receiving what he saith from another by tradition'. Ordinary men know just as well as the learned what is meant by an empty vessel, 'namely that there is nothing in it that can be seen; and whether it be truly empty the ploughman and the Schoolman know alike'.[21] Appeal to the collective common sense of ordinary men and women was what the sectaries meant when they appealed to experience, experiment: the experience must have been felt by the recipient very powerfully, but he must also be able to communicate it to his peers, and they must find it acceptable.

Here we come to the second principle of the radicals – reliance on the holy spirit within one, on one's own experienced truth as against traditional truths handed down by others. How else can revelation be continuous? This emphasis was common to Milton, Dell, Winstanley, Bunyan, Ranters and Quakers. Clearly it could have very radical consequences indeed: everything that is traditional is suspect just because it is traditional. In time of revolution men think aggressive thoughts, and these can be recognized by others as valid, as divinely inspired. Experience could be used alike against history and against the Bible. Thomas Collier, preaching to the Army at Putney in 1647, offered to confirm one of his points from Scripture, 'although I trust I shall declare nothing unto you but experimental truth'.[22] 'Experience goes beyond all things,' Coppin declared.[23] The Antinomian Henry Pinnell contrasted the way 'a man knows a thing by reading of it' with 'experimental certainty of it in himself'.[24]

One consequence of the stress on continuous revelation and on experienced truths was that the idea of novelty, of originality, ceased to be shocking and became in a sense desirable. 'All that I have writ concerning the matter of digging,' Winstanley wrote in December 1649, 'I never read it in any book, nor received it from any mouth . . .

before I saw the light of it rise up within myself.'[25] He emphasized that the *Law of Righteousness* about which he wrote was *New*. Originality was a test of sincerity and genuineness. 'Men must speak their own experienced words, and must not speak thoughts.' 'This question,' he told the clergy, 'is not to be answered by any text of Scripture . . . but the answer is to be given in the light of itself, which is the law of righteousness . . . which dwells in man's heart.'[26] Winstanley agreed with John Wilkins that it was the devil who persuaded men that novel ideas, drawn from experience, were a sign of error.[27]

To this emphasis on experience, on things rather than words, several streams contribute. There is the radical protestant insistence on relying on your own feelings, not on the words of others – 'as a man rehearseth a tale of another man's mouth', said Tyndale, 'and wotteth not whether it be so or no as he saith, nor hath any experience of the thing itself'.[28] 'True experience of Christ,' the Puritan Thomas Taylor wrote a century later, 'is experimental.' It is not acquired 'out of books or relations . . . but by experience of himself'.[29] 'I aim not at words but things' were the opening words of Lord Brooke's *A Discourse . . . of . . . Episcopacie* (1641). A parallel development took place among scientists. William Gilbert praised true philosophers who looked for knowledge 'not only in books but in things themselves'.[30] John Wilkins was summing up the Baconian tradition when he said 'it would be much better for the commonwealth of learning if we would ground our principles rather upon the frequent experience of our own than the bare authority of others.'[31] John Hall was Comenian as well as Baconian when he advanced the educational principle that it was 'better to grave things in the minds of children than words'.[32] Henry Stubbe indeed said it was Bacon who inspired Englishmen with 'such a desire of novelty as rose to a contempt' of the established order in church and state, and was responsible for the civil war.[33]

The religious doctrine of the evolution of truth or of the Everlasting Gospel achieved the same effect. 'If thou wilt needs condemn whatever savours of novelty,' William Dell expostulated, 'how shall the truths we yet know not be brought in, or the errors that yet remain with us be purged out?' We must 'wholly . . . forsake the doctrines of men', and 'lay by all those opinions that we have sucked in from our very cradles'. Thus purged we can hear what Jesus Christ will say to our spirits, and stick to it, 'though never so differing from the opinions and doctrines of this present age, as well as of the former'.[34] With Winstanley as we have seen God and Reason became one; the Christ within our hearts preached secularism.

But treachery lurked in the inner light. In time of defeat, when the wave of revolution was ebbing, the inner voice became quietest, pacifist. This voice only was recognized by others as God's. God was no longer served by the extravagant gesture, whether Nayler's entry into Bristol or the blasphemy of the Ranters. Once the group decided this way, all the pressures were in the direction of accepting modes of expression not too shocking to the society in which men had to live and earn their living.[35] The radicals were so effectively silenced that we do not know whether many held out in isolation with Milton. We do not even know about Winstanley. But what had looked in the Ranter heyday as though it might become a counter-culture became a corner of the bourgeois culture whose occupants asked only to be left alone.[36] The inner light which formerly spoke of the perfectibility of the saints now came to re-emphasize sin. We should not attribute this to the skill, inspiration or wickedness of George Fox or of anyone else. Fox was only the agent: Nayler or Burrough in his place would no doubt have had to act similarly. The openness of the religion of the heart, of the inner voice, to changes in mass moods, to social pressures, to waves of feeling, had made it the vehicle of revolutionary transformations of thought: now it had the opposite effect. The 'sense of the meeting' accepted the 'common sense' of the dominant classes in society. 'Inspiration,' said Davenant, was 'a dangerous word which many have of late successfully used.'[37] It was to cease to be an ideal to be aimed at for a century or more, till the romantic revival.

III   THE BOND OF UNITY

The inner light, then, was not for the sectaries mere absolute individualism, any more than the appeal to private interpretation of the Bible was. The appeal to texts and traditions was not merely antiquarian: the past was called into existence to redress the balance of the present. Printing and the protestant emphasis on education had made available translations not only of the Scriptures but also of other hitherto arcane documents. Nicholas Culpeper translated the *Pharmacoepia Londinensis* out of Latin into English so that poor men and women could cure themselves. Just as the Levellers elevated the jury over the judge, so the radical sectaries no longer looked up to the specialized, educated priest as the arbiter of precedent.[38] For them the verdict lay with the congregation of believers, each member of which respected the spirit within all his fellow priests. The ideal was a society of all-round non-specialists helping each other to arrive at truth through the community.

Acceptance of interpretations of the Bible by a congregation guarantees their relevance for the given group, is a check against mere anarchic individualism. Today, in our atomized society, the appeal to the individual conscience, to the integrity of the isolated artist, is ultimately anarchistic, the extreme of illusory withdrawal from society. But in the seventeenth century the inner light was a bond of unity because God *did* in fact say similar things to the mechanics who formed his congregations. 'The light which shineth in every one of us,' said Burrough, brings us to perfect knowledge 'as to it our minds become turned and our hearts inclined.'[39] Silent meetings needed no priest to guide them in their search for unanimity: Winstanley, Erbery and Fox hoped to bring people 'to the end of all outward preaching'.[40] Winstanley waited 'the Lord's leisure with a calm silence'; Joseph Salmon's 'great desire' was 'to see and say nothing'.[41]

There had been a unity in opposition to the old régime in church and state which extended over a broader spectrum of society, but even after this disintegrated, the classes to whom the sects appealed had much in common. Winstanley visualized national divisions being swallowed up in brotherly unity – though particular churches must first 'be torn to pieces'.[42] For him the inner light or Reason is what tells a man that he must do unto others as he would they should do unto him: that he must cooperate. So he, and he alone, really transcended the dichotomy of individualism/collectivism through his vision of a society based on communal cultivation and mutual support. But Ranters too had a yearning towards unity.[43] The Quakers were ultimately to give organizational form of a sort to this unity through 'the sense of the meeting'.

The tragedy of the radicals was that they were never able to arrive at political unity during the Revolution: their principles were too absolutely held to be anything but divisive. It was small consolation for Samuel Fisher to be able to jibe at John Owen in 1660: formerly you called us fanatics, now you are called one yourself.[44] The printer Giles Calvert's shop perhaps came nearest to uniting the radicals in spite of themselves – 'that forge of the devil from whence so many blasphemous, lying scandalous pamphlets for many years past have spread over the land'.[45] Mr Morton stresses the importance of Calvert as a unifying force. He printed translations of Henry Niclaes and Jacob Boehme, the works of Saltmarsh, Dell, some Levellers, most of Winstanley, the Wellingborough broadsheet, many Ranters and very many Quakers, as well as the last speeches of the regicides in 1660. Two years later he was still inciting the publication of seditious literature, and after his death in 1663 his widow continued his policy. When Clarkson in 1649 wished to get in touch with Ranters he was referred to Giles Calvert.[46]

IV   SECTS AND SECTARIANISM

Fox's achievement was to form a disciplined sect, with a preaching ministry, out of a rabble of ex-Ranters and others new to the idea of thinking for themselves about religion. The task was immense: but success brought its disadvantages. We can approach this by asking, Who supported the itinerant preachers – Baptists, Ranters, Quakers? They had to live; and there were so many of them, in cut-throat competition. *Some* organization was essential. This was the great failure of the Ranters – their inability (or unwillingness) to organize. A man with Lawrence Clarkson's charisma seems to have made money enough, but he ended up a Muggletonian, responsive to the crack of the leader's whip.[47] Fox and other Quaker missionaries could on occasion sleep in a ditch or under a haystack, but his ministry was more effective when he found a Hotham, a Fell, to put him up at the manor house. I quoted above Coppe's rueful reflections on the insecurity and financial temptations of the itinerant preacher's life.[48] There was inevitable pressure on all sects to seek some support from some men of property: and this in time exacted its price. The insidious pressures of the world bore down on the children of light even as they organized to turn the world upside down.

In the last resort, perhaps, Quakers did not want to overturn the world, any more than constitutional Levellers wanted to overthrow the sanctity of private property.[49] Quakers wanted life to be lived better, more honestly; they wanted to end the haggling and swindling of the market, by insisting that their yea was yea and their nay nay. This introduction of modern business standards of behaviour (to which Bunyan's *Mr Badman* also contributed) was a great achievement, a greater revolution than we often recognize, just because it was so complete and final. One has to live in a pre-capitalist society to appreciate the difference. Every credit to the Quakers: they deserved the prosperity they were already beginning to win, despite persecution, before Fox's death. But this was not overturning the world as Diggers, and even Ranters, had hoped.

We can see sectarian organization hardening in those marvellous dialogues recorded in *Records of the Churches of Christ gathered at Fenstanton, Warboys and Hexham*. There we hear the common man and woman struggling for self-expression against the dead weight of the culture of centuries. Inevitably the organizers of the sects used the Bible against what they called the 'fancies' of those whom the spirit was still moving in ways that were becoming unpopular; inevitably the rebels had to reject the Bible, even though they could not produce scholarly reasons for doing so that could compete with the learning of Henry Denne, the Levellers' 'Judas Denne'.[50] Modern Biblical scholarship has caught up with and justified them: conviction of sin has to take more sophisticated forms today than 'the Bible says so'.

But the organizers of the sects faced a dual problem. In the Fenstanton discussions, in addition to conformist pressure, and the pressure of landlords, driving men to go to their parish churches, we see that men also have a sense that so long as they would conform outwardly to the state church they had a chance of being left to their own devices. The Baptists did not let them alone. They made too high demands for normal frail humanity. So long as the end of the world seemed imminent, psychological tension could be maintained, and intense moral pressure was tolerable. But not for the everyday world. And when in the restoration period fierce persecution came, this produced a different sort of tension, which drove all but the most dedicated believers back to the state church. So the sects became restricted to a self-selected élite, the elect: they could not be for the average sensual man. The English Communist Party in the 1930s used to be described as having the largest ex-membership of any party. All the seventeenth-century sects, as they established themselves, must have acquired a very large ex-membership. This explains what we have already noted, some genuine popular welcome back for the old church, cakes and church ales, even if not for bishops.

Yet the sects did play an important role as centres of social services, giving some protection for their members in the tough world of early capitalism.[51] The Fenstanton Baptists distributed poor relief, and used it as an instrument of social control. A woman who went to the parish church – 'forced so to do for the maintenance of herself and children', as she claimed – got seven shillings to satisfy her necessities as soon as she had repented.[52] As the world closed in on the sects, their organization tightened and was more and more used to impose social attitudes. In 1655 the church resolved that no 'member of the congregation whatsoever shall travel from place to place without the advice and consent of the congregation to whom he belongeth', such consent to be in writing. No more free-lance itinerant ministers, going where and with whom the spirit suggested! Two years later they resolved that it was unlawful for a family 'to keep a daughter at home, maintaining her in idleness', when she was capable of earning her living. The parents were 'sharply reproved for their sin', and exhorted to put their daughter to service.[53] In the 1670s Bunyan's church showed great severity against those of its members who did not pay their debts, and Bunyan himself advised deacons to use poor relief to encourage industry and discourage idleness.[54] Here is another reason why in the later seventeenth century the nonconformist sects ceased to proselytize among the urban poor: they had enough to do to survive and look after their own. It was yet another argument against doing anything to frighten off members who began to prosper.

So, paradoxically, the sects' acceptance of responsibility for their own poor compelled them to impose labour discipline on their members; and they would do this far more effectively than an external Presbyterian disciplinary system could have done. As the economy slowly progressed, the greatest extremes of starvation disappeared anyway: Professor Jordan's men of charity could invest all their surplus in production now, confident that between them the sects and the state would look after the poor. However laudable the provision of social insurance by the sects, it involved a total acceptance of the unequal world. It is far from the Leveller demand for the restitution to the poor of embezzled charities, from the Digger demand for the occupation of common lands, from the Digger and Ranter wish to see community of goods. The radicals no longer hoped to turn the world upside down: they competed desperately as they adapted themselves to it. The sects became sectarian.

Hotham was quite right, we may conclude, to think that for his society Quakers were preferable to Ranters. The Society of Friends formed a responsible, disciplined body out of a shapeless, nameless mass. They were anxious for their reputation, more and more came to preserve the bourgeois decencies. At an alleged 'Ranters' Parliament' of 1650 'many queries were propounded in behalf of the poor of their fraternity; desiring to know how they should be maintained notwithstanding the falling off of many hundreds of the great ones. To which answer was made, that they should borrow money and never pay it again.'[55] The story may be apocryphal, but the dilemma it records was real. How could the allegiance of the poor be retained without forfeiting the support of 'great ones'? And if a sect attracted too much support from great ones, could it preserve its original principles? The Ranters never formed a sect at all in this sense, never achieved the discipline necessary to maintain their own poor and so preserve a cohesive unity. If they had done so, they might have lost all that was distinctly Ranter anyway.

Winstanley and Erbery believed that too much discussion led only to division.[56] As sects crystallized out, such unity as the radicals had ever had was finally destroyed. After 1649 all trends of opinion disavowed the Levellers, often meaning by them the True Levellers. Even Coppe disclaimed 'sword-levelling' and 'digging-levelling'. Coppin, John Spittlehouse, John Webster, Nayler and the Quakers all had to counter accusations of being Levellers.[57] Ranters disrupted the Digger community; Winstanley denounced Ranting, though carefully saying that Ranters must not be persecuted. Baptists excommunicated Ranters and Quakers; Quakers attacked Baptists and Ranters as antichristians. To judge by the surviving church books, excommunication was one of the principal activities of the early sects. The maintenance of internal purity disrupted unity: without internal purity survival as a sect was impossible. Here too there was no obvious solution. There was still broad agreement on political aims – opposition to tithes, to the state church and its ministry, to the law, to the existing franchise; but on theological issues, on the Second Coming, they split. In 1659 this disunity prevented the concerted action which alone might have saved the Good Old Cause; in 1660 its consequences were revealed in all their political ugliness. All sects were anxious to disavow those to the left of themselves, to show how moderate and respectable they were really.[58]

And yet, viewed internally, the discipline and internal unity were necessary for each sect's survival in an increasingly unsympathetic environment. Quaker expansion no doubt suffered from the defection of Proud Quakers, Ranters, supporters of Perrot and of Story and Wilkinson. Yet would the Society of Friends have survived at all without these purges? Would they have attracted and retained the support of men like William Penn and Robert Barclay? Could they have afforded, in hard financial terms, not to have such support?[59]

V   DEFEAT AND SURVIVAL

The great period of freedom of movement and freedom of thought was over. For 20 years men had trudged backwards and forwards across Great Britain, in the Army, in search of work, in the service of God. The mixing, the cross-fertilization, must have been immense. After the restoration officers of the New Model returned to their crafts.[60] Preaching tinkers returned to their villages, or like Bunyan went to gaol. Levellers, Diggers, Ranters and Fifth Monarchists disappeared, leaving hardly a trace. Coppe changed his name and became a physician. Salmon, Perrot and many others emigrated. Nayler and Burrough died, Fox disciplined the Quakers: they succumbed to the protestant ethic. Property triumphed. Bishops returned to a state church, the universities and tithes survived. Women were put back into their place. The island of Great Bedlam became the island of Great Britain, God's confusion yielding place to man's order. Great Britain was the largest free-trade area in Europe, but one in which the commerce of ideas was again restricted. Milton's nation of prophets became a nation of shopkeepers.

As the completeness of the radicals' defeat became evident, Erbery and Salmon deliberately sought refuge in silence,[61] Coppe recanted, Lilburne turned Quaker, Clarkson Muggletonian. The conclusion of Winstanley's last pamphlet acknowledges defeat:

> Truth appears in light, falsehood rules in power;
> To see these things to be is cause of grief each hour.
> Knowledge, why didst thou come, to wound and not to cure? . . .
> O power, where art thou, that must mend things amiss?
> Come, change the heart of man, and make him truth to kiss.

His last words were a call to death to reunite him with the material creation:

> O death, where art thou? Wilt thou not tidings send?
> I fear thee not, thou art my loving friend.
> Come take this body, and scatter it in the Four,
> That I may dwell in One, and rest in peace once more.[62]

Yet nothing ever wholly dies. Great Britain no doubt fared the worse in some respects for rejecting the truths of the radicals in the seventeenth century, but they were not utterly lost. Just as a surviving Lollard tradition contributed to the English Reformation over a

century after the defeat of Lollardy, just as a surviving radical protestant tradition contributed to the English Revolution, and both
have still to be rediscovered by historical research, so the radicals of
the English Revolution perhaps gave more to posterity than is immediately obvious. The broadside ballad of 1646, *The World is Turned
Upside Down*,[63] may well have been the old song of that name which
was popular in the eighteenth century. It is said to have been played,
appropriately enough, when Cornwallis surrendered to the American revolutionaries at Yorktown in 1781. Thomas Spence, who
rejected monarchy, aristocracy and private property in land, and
wanted democratic village communities to become sole owners of
the land, published in 1805 a broadside called *The World Turned
Upside Down*.[64] The phrase was used by the Shakers, a Lancashire
group who were 'commissioned of the Almighty God to preach the
everlasting gospel to America' in 1774. Their membership was drawn
from artisans, labourers and servants; they believed that they had
actually risen with Christ and could live without sin; they danced,
sang and smoked at their meetings.[65] We can find other hints. William Pleasants, a lay clerk of Norwich cathedral around 1700, was
alleged to think 'there is no heaven but a quiet mind and no hell but
the grave'.[66] John Wesley in 1746, talking to Antinomians in Birmingham, reports one whose views were virtually indistinguishable
from those of the Ranters. He lived by faith and so was not under the
law. Wesley asked him 'May you then take anything you will anywhere? Suppose out of a shop, without the consent or knowledge of
the owner?' 'I may if I want it; for it is mine: only I will not give
offence.' Wesley's next question was predictable: – 'Have you also a
right to all the women in the world?' The answer showed that the
man in question was not just trying to annoy, but was describing a
thought-out position: it was 'Yes, if they consent.'[67]

We need not bother too much about being able to trace a continuous pedigree for these ideas. They are the ideas of the underground,
surviving, if at all, verbally: they leave little trace. It is unlikely that
the ideas of the seventeenth-century radicals had no influence on the
Wilkesite movement, the American Revolution, Thomas Paine or the
plebeian radicalism which revived in England in the 1790s. Unlikely:

but such influence is difficult to prove. Among so much that was unrecorded we can perhaps trace a surviving influence for Samuel Fisher's Bible criticism;[68] but even that seems ultimately to have been forgotten. A ballad attributed to James II's reign is a satire on 'Lubberland', and may hint at ideas similar to those of the radicals; but there is no specific reference. In Lubberland there will be

> No law nor lawyers' fees . . .
> For everyone does what he please
> Without a judge or jury . . .
> They have no landlords' rent to pay,
> Each man is a freeholder.[69]

We may perhaps wonder where Defoe got some of his ideas from:

> The very lands we all along enjoyed
> They ravished from the people they destroyed . . .
> All the long pretences of descent
> Are shams of right to prop up government.
> 'Tis all invasion, usurpation all . . .
> 'Tis all by fraud and force that we possess
> And length of time can make no crime the less . . .
> Religion's always on the strongest side.[70]

Harrington was no doubt the main influence on Defoe's thought about property, and there is no evidence that he had read Winstanley. But the passage is considerably more radical in its implications than anything Harrington ever wrote – and Defoe did rise with Monmouth in 1685.

There were other poets too. Oliver Goldsmith knew about the Levellers, and Blake owed much to the radicals of the seventeenth century.[71] Dionysus proved difficult to naturalize in Britain, where his name tended to be translated as John Barleycorn. But Burns perhaps records something of the tradition. The words 'rant' and 'ranting' (never used pejoratively) are favourites of his, and he more than once signed himself 'Rab the Ranter'. There is no reason to postulate any reference to the seventeenth-century Ranters in this. More significant is that Burns repeats many of the themes of the seventeenth-century radicals – fierce anti-clericalism, respect for honest poverty (or even the honest immoralism of itinerant beggars – 'a fig for those by law protected') as against kings, aristocrats and the judges who 'are their engines', hatred of the smug hypocrisy of Holy Willie and his like, scepticism about the existence of hell (except as a social deterrent –

> The fear of hell's a hangman's whip
> To haud the wretch in order),

ribaldry about the Bible, a love of freedom (associated on occasion with love of liquor), a belief 'that Man is good by nature' and that international brotherhood is coming: his sexual practice disregarded the conventional ties of marriage.[72]

More work could probably discover more connections, or possible connections. The Brontës' Haworth was in the Grindletonian area, where down to the early nineteenth century 'Oliver's days' were remembered as a golden age.[73] The 'faith in the potentialities of activism . . . displayed by the radical groups of the Interregnum', Mr K. V. Thomas tells us, was 'dashed by the restoration; but the notion that political remedies could be found for social and economic discontent was less easily checked'.[74] The radicals' postulate of economic solutions to society's problems must have helped to bridge that gap between the waning of magical beliefs and the rise of modern technology to which Mr Thomas has drawn attention.[75] Even more important, perhaps, for our generation, were their glimpses of a possible society which would transcend the property system, of a counter-culture which would reject the protestant ethic altogether. Some of these insights survived to do their subversive work on readers of Milton and Bunyan, regarded in the eighteenth century as the most respectable pillars of religious orthodoxy.[76]

Again and again in this book we have noticed the seventeenth-century radicals shooting ahead of the technical possibilities of their age. Later Biblical scholarship and anthropology make better sense than they could of the mythological approach to the Bible; cheap and easily available contraceptive devices make better sense of free love. Modern physics and chemistry are catching up with the dialectical element in their thought; modern anthropology is a science of society

which does not rely on the stars, modern theories of painless child-
birth make no theological assumptions about the Fall of Man. The
concept of evolution makes it possible to conceive of a universe with
no external first cause.[77] The technological possibilities may now
exist even for a community in which the creation of unemployment
need not be regarded as a principal task of government, and in which
'the beauty of the commonwealth' could take precedence over private profit, national power or even the G.N.P. My object is not to
patronize the radicals by patting them on the head as 'in advance of
their time' – that tired cliché of the lazy historian. In some ways they
are in advance of ours. But their insights, their poetic insights, are
what seem to me to make them worth studying today.

VI   THEN AND NOW

There are two ways of looking at a revolution. We can observe the
gestures which symbolize and focus whole ages of struggle – Sir John
Hotham shutting the gates of Hull in the white face of Charles I; the
women bringing up the ammunition at Lyme Regis; an axe flashing
in the January sun outside Whitehall; Nayler riding into Bristol on
his ass, with women strewing palms in his path. But there are also
the longer, slower, profounder changes in men's ways of thinking,
without which the heroic gestures would be meaningless. These
elude us if we get too immersed in detail; we can appreciate the
extent of the changes only if we stand back to look at the beginning
and the end of the Revolution, if we can use such inaccurate terms
about something which is always beginning and never ends. From
the longer range we can appreciate the colossal transformations
which ushered England into the modern world. And we can, perhaps, extend a little gratitude to all those nameless radicals who
foresaw and worked for – not our modern world, but something far
nobler, something yet to be achieved – the upside-down world.

After the defeat of the radicals in 1660, and the final elimination
of the old régime in 1688, the rulers of England organized a highly
successful commercial empire and a system of class rule which

proved to have unusual staying power. The protestant ethic dominated at least those thoughts and feelings which could be expressed in
print. The society produced great scientists, great poets: it invented
the novel. Newton and Locke dictated laws to the intellectual world.
It was a powerful civilization, a great improvement for most people
on what had gone before. But how absolutely certain can we be that
this world was the right way up – the world in which poets went
mad, in which Locke was afraid of music and poetry, and Newton
had secret, irrational thoughts which he dared not publish?[78]

Blake may have been right to see Locke and Newton as symbols of
repression. Sir Isaac's twisted, buttoned-up personality may help us to
grasp what was wrong with the society which deified him. So may
Dean Swift, the fiercest critic of the new world in which money ruled,
whose 'excremental vision' extended backwards to a golden age when
gold and repression were alike unknown.[79] This society, which on the
surface appeared so rational, so relaxed, might perhaps have been
healthier if it had not been so tidy, if it had not pushed all its contradictions underground: out of sight, out of conscious mind.[80] The
protestant ethic so dominated the moral attitudes of the middle
classes, the mechanical philosophy so dominated scientific thinking,
that the Licensing Act could be allowed to lapse in 1695 – not on the
radicals' libertarian principles, but because censorship was no longer
necessary. Like Newton, the opinion-formers of this society censored
themselves. Nothing got into print which frightened the men of property. What went on underground we can only guess. A few poets had
romantic ideas out of tune with their world; but no one needed to
take them too seriously. Self-censored meant self-verifying.

Upside down is after all a relative concept. The assumption that it
means the wrong way up is itself an expression of the view from the
top. Marx spoke of finding Hegel standing on his head and turning
him the right way up: but that was not Hegel's impression of his own
position. Marx thought the Prussia of his time was an upside-down
world.[81] The idea that the bottom might come to the top, that the
first might be last and the last first, that 'community . . . called Christ
or universal love' might cast out 'property, called the devil or covetousness', and that 'the inward bondages of the mind' (covetousness,

pride, hypocrisy, fears, despair and mental breakdown) might be 'all occasioned by the outward bondages that one sort of people lay upon another'[82] – such ideas are not necessarily opposed to order: they merely envisage a different order. We may be too conditioned by the way up the world has been for the last three hundred years to be fair to those in the seventeenth century who saw other possibilities. But we should try.

'If you should destroy these vessels,' Edward Burrough told the all-powerful restoration government, 'yet our principles you can never extinguish, but they will live for ever, and enter into other bodies to live and speak and act'.[83] The radicals assumed that acting was more important than speaking. Talking and writing books, Winstanley insisted, is 'all nothing and must die; for action is the life of all, and if thou dost not act, thou dost nothing.' It is a thought worth pondering by those who read books about the seventeenth-century radicals, no less than by those who write them. Were you doers or talkers only? Bunyan asked his generation.[84] What canst *thou* say?

APPENDIX I
Hobbes and Winstanley:
Reason and Politics

> This same power in man that causes divisions and war is
> called by some men the state of nature, which every man
> brings into the world with him . . .
>   Here is disorder, therefore this subtle spirit of darkness . . .
> tells the people, You must make one man king over you all and
> let him make laws, and let everyone be obedient thereunto.
>   WINSTANLEY, *Fire in the Bush* (1650), and *The Law*
>   *of Freedom* (1652) in Sabine, pp. 493, 531.

Thomas Hobbes has properly no place in this book, in so far as it is
a study of the left wing of radical Puritanism. Hobbes was no Puritan: he was a dependant of the great aristocratic and royalist family
of the Cavendishes. He fled from England in 1640, remaining abroad
throughout the civil war. For a time he was tutor to Prince Charles
in exile. Hobbes returned to England only at the end of 1651, after
the Commonwealth had suppressed the radicals. Yet Hobbes had a
grudging admiration for the achievements of the Revolution he
thought should never have been allowed to happen. 'If in time as in
place,' he once said, 'there were degrees of high and low, I verily
believe the highest of time would be that which passed betwixt 1640
and 1660.'[1] The royalist Earl of Clarendon thought Hobbes no better
than a Leveller in his belief in human equality and a career open to
the talents, denouncing Hobbes's 'extreme malignity to the nobility,
by whose bread he hath been always sustained'.[2] Hobbes was often
intellectually of the radicals' party.

We can see Hobbes and Winstanley at two opposite poles. Hobbes's philosophy is a secularized version of the protestant ethic: Hobbes's man in the state of nature is Calvin's natural man – selfish, dominated by evil passions, a lonely individual. Protestantism relied on the sense of guilt, of sin, to internalize an ethic of effort, thrift, industry. Hobbes hoped to achieve the same ends by an appeal to rational science, calculation of profit and loss, expediency, utility: not fear of hell but fear of social disorder. Hobbes has rightly been seen as the high priest of competitive individualism. He stripped bare the essence of capitalist society, and attempted to create a science of politics which would be convincing, if unpalatable, to all rational men. Winstanley attempted something similar on the basis of collectivist assumptions. He is less ruthlessly systematic than Hobbes, but he too aimed at producing a rational political system, the advantages of which would be self-evident to all men in so far as they were ruled by Reason.[3] But Winstanley started by rejecting both the 'sin' of the theologians and the competitive individualism of Hobbes.

Yet both Winstanley and Hobbes were determined to penetrate to the bedrock of politics, to disregard the inessential; both were acute observers of the brutally competitive society in which they lived. So they have curiously much in common. Both reject the Bible as a source of political guidance, and indulge in some daring Biblical criticism.[4] Both are sceptical about hell. Hobbes was probably a deist, but it is doubtful if he was a Christian: he was prepared to accept Christianity as the religion authorized by the sovereign authority under which he lived. Each was prepared to use Biblical texts to add conviction to a conclusion at which he had arrived by rational argument. Hobbes lacks even Winstanley's mythological interest in the Bible as a means of conveying poetic truth, though Hobbes treats the state of nature as a myth. Both were fiercely anticlerical, for the clergy were the main threat to the authority both of Hobbes's sovereign and of Winstanley's Christ in man. Both disapproved of persecution, but Hobbes disliked claims to revelation or inspiration no less. Neither of them expected salvation from an other-worldly saviour; Hobbes looked to Leviathan, the mortal God, Winstanley to Reason, Christ in men and women. Both believed in the equality of man. Both held that 'property, ... depending on sovereign power, is the act of that power'. Both rejected scholastic divinity, Winstanley because it 'leaves the motional knowledge of a thing as it is'. 'God is still in motion,' he said, and motion is growth. Hobbes held that 'life itself is but motion'; 'the nature of motion' is 'the gate of philosophy universal'. Both thought that no commonwealth had yet been established on true principles, and hoped by their writings to remedy that defect.[5]

Hobbes saw that in a society composed of equal and competing individuals there would be an inevitable tendency towards anarchy unless there were a sovereign with, in the last resort, absolute authority. Few indeed of the radicals tackled this central problem of political theory – the problem of the state and its relation to systems of property. The Levellers never faced it squarely, and had no reply to Ireton's insistence at Putney that liberty and property were ultimately incompatible.[6] Winstanley was the only radical who both grasped Hobbes's problem and provided an alternative solution. Winstanley may even refer to Hobbes in the passages quoted as epigraph to this appendix. The first was written in 1650, a year before *Leviathan* was published, though Hobbes's views had been known since 1640. Whether Ireton or Winstanley had read Hobbes is an interesting question, but the answer to it does not matter very much for our purposes. The society itself gave birth to Hobbist ideas, in others as well as Hobbes.[7] It was the society, not merely a particular political thinker, that Winstanley was rejecting when he denied that all men are naturally competitive. But he might well have Hobbes's state of nature in mind when he wrote: 'Imagination fears where no fear is: he rises up to destroy others, for fear lest others destroy him: he will oppress others, lest others oppress him; and fears he shall be in want hereafter, therefore he takes by violence that which others have laboured for.' Imagination 'fills you with fears, doubts, troubles, evil surmisings and grudges, he it is that stirs up wars and divisions, he makes you lust after everything you see or hear of'. As long as imagination rules, a sovereign state is necessary – 'the government of highwaymen'; but that is an additional reason for getting rid of property and competition, for letting Reason rule.[8]

Winstanley's answer to Hobbes derived from his transmutation of the myth of the Everlasting Gospel.[9] In the third age, which Winstanley thought was beginning in his time, Christ was appearing in sons and daughters, guiding 'all men's reasoning in right order to a right end'. He would make all men righteous, i.e. all will voluntarily 'live in community with the globe and . . . the spirit of the globe', in accordance with the laws of nature, with Reason which guides the consciences of men and is the law of the universe.[10] Then the state will have no coercive functions except to preserve the community against any resurgence of individual selfishness.

Hobbes had attempted to found a science of politics through his laws of nature, which were 'precepts or general rules found out by reason'. If men understood these laws of nature, which also extended to society, then they would accept them and draw the necessary rational consequences for their own good. Any other course is as irrational as kicking against the pricks or trying to make water flow uphill. Hobbes included individualism and competition within his basic psychology of man, and drew the conclusion that absolute subjection to the sovereign was to the interest of each individual. His rigorous logic is so powerful that it is very difficult to break its chain: it has to be challenged in its assumptions, in its psychology. This Winstanley did, in a passage which follows immediately after the first passage quoted as epigraph to this appendix. Man, he argued, is naturally sociable. 'Look upon a child that is new-born, or till he grows up to some few years; he is innocent, harmless, humble, patient, gentle, easy to be entreated, not envious.' Man falls when, growing up in the competitive world, he surrenders to covetousness. But there is nothing inevitable or necessarily permanent in this. Reason is in each one of us, and Reason rejects the covetousness which underlies private property. Cooperation and mutual help are dictated by Reason for the preservation of the human race. 'Let Reason rule in man, and he dares not trespass against his fellow-creature, but will do as he would be done unto. For Reason tells him, is thy neighbour hungry and naked today, do thou feed him and clothe him, it may be thy case tomorrow, and then he will be ready to help thee.'[11] Consequently Winstanley sees the third age, the age of the

303

spirit, not as an age of inspired zealots but as a time when Christ rising in men and women will at last bring them to understand the laws of the universe, and to see that community, cooperation, is one of these laws. Then no one will want to kick against the pricks.

Hobbes thought all men were capable of understanding his laws of nature, though any man might reject or disregard them on a short-term calculation of his own advantage. But this could only have disastrous consequences for himself and society. Unbridled selfishness would lead to universal conflict, and so ultimately to a state of war. Therefore the sovereign, any sovereign, had to be elevated and obeyed. Hobbes believed, however, that he had established a science of politics which would convince enough men for enough of the time: the sovereign's job would then be to coerce the irrational, or any of us in our irrational moments. Before he wrote, he thought, there had been no science of politics, and consequently no state had been established on sound principles.

Winstanley's Reason sometimes sounds like an anticipation of Rousseau's General Will. Its light is in all men, but does not completely dominate the thinking of any single individual all the time: some calculate that it is to their advantage to compete and destroy one another. 'Many times men act contrary to Reason, though they think they act according to Reason.' Under kingly power this is the norm. But this will change as Reason itself 'knits every creature together into a oneness, making every creature to be an upholder of his fellow, and so everyone is an assistant to preserve the whole'. The less selfish men are, the more closely will they approximate to this Reason, which 'guides all men's reasoning in right order and to a right end'. For all humanity is one. Winstanley believed that Christ rising in men and women would convince all, even the rich who in the short run appeared to lose, that cooperation and mutual help are the merest common sense, are *natural*, and that in the end rich men too would gain by the establishment of communism. This would however involve a more fundamental revolution in men's attitudes than acceptance of the Hobbist philosophy. 'This great change, or setting up this new law of righteousness, ruling in everyone, . . . will be a great day of judgment. The righteous judge will sit upon the throne in every man and woman.'[12] *True Magistracy Restored* was the subtitle of *The Law of Freedom*: the restoration must come from below.

Hobbes's intellectual radicalism was a strong influence on the wits at Charles II's court,[13] but his political philosophy ultimately proved unacceptable to the respectable men of property who dominated post-restoration England. It was unacceptable because it was so hopelessly rational. Hobbes stripped society and the state of all the flummery which the compromise of 1660 made it essential to restore – hereditary monarchy and aristocracy, bishops. Authority was what men of property yearned for in 1659–60. But as society settled down again into something that tried to resemble the comfortable old ways, Hobbes's astringent political philosophy yielded place to that of Locke. Locke's ideas – by Hobbes out of the protestant ethic – were less ruthlessly logical, less brilliantly clear-cut, less shocking to traditionalists. They fitted the world in which kings ruled by the grace of God but could be turned out if they did not rule as the men of property wished; in which the church showed men the way to heaven but bishops were appointed by politicians.

Hobbes had his moment, as he rightly saw, in 1651, when the sovereign body of men had none of the traditional attributes of divine right, hereditary right or ecclesiastical blessing. His was by far the most thoroughgoing of many attempts at that time to establish a theory of *de facto* authority.[14] The important question for such theories was not who the sovereign was but whether or not he did his job of holding competitive individualist society together. Winstanley challenged the *de facto* theory at its strongest: if competitive individualist property relations were abolished, then the problem of sovereignty would sink into insignificance. Just as sin did not cause property, but *vice versa*, so only the abolition of property could get rid of the coercive state and the preachers of sin, both of which had come into existence to protect property. The weakness of Winstanley's position, as Hobbes would have pointed out, lay in his assumption that Reason would say the same thing to all men and women. It was an assumption similar to that which Rousseau made about the General Will. But, said Hobbes, 'commonly they that call for right reason to decide any controversy do mean their own'.[15] At least Winstanley's way out of this dilemma, a day of judgment in the heart of every man, is more plausible than Rousseau's hope that the pluses and minuses will somehow cancel out. But Hobbes would feel that both of them underestimate the extent to which the complex of property relations, state power and ideology tends to be self-perpetuating because self-justifying.

Karl Marx in a perceptive passage said that with Hobbes the bloom is off Baconian materialism. Science has lost its joy, its excitement, its freshness: reason is reduced to calculation, to counting the cost. For Hobbes, reason 'is nothing but reckoning (that is adding and subtracting) of the consequences of general names agreed upon for the marking and signifying of our thoughts'.[16] But for Winstanley Reason is Love, is Christ rising in the sons and daughters of God: the bloom is restored to science, to the universe which is the clothing of God. Winstanley's mythological, poetic approach is at the opposite pole to Hobbes's abstractions, just as it is poles apart from Hobbes's Calvinist assumptions about the inherent selfishness and competitiveness of natural man. Hobbes thought that man's ruling passion was fear of death: Winstanley wanted all men to choose life, and to have it more abundantly. Davenant wrote from a very different point of view, but he expresses what Winstanley meant by love:

> In Love's free state all powers so levelled be
> That them affection governs more than awe.[17]

Milton and Bunyan:
Dialogue with the Radicals

Therefore we dare not despair, but will look for, wait for,
and hope for deliverance still.

BUNYAN, *The Holy War* (1682) in
Works, III, p. 353.

I MILTON

If we were not so over-awed by Milton the great poet we should long
ago have recognized his role as a precursor of the Ranters. In 1641
he went out of his way to compare 'such as are now called Familists'
with primitive Christians. This was an astonishing act, at a time
when even Lord Brooke denounced Familists, before even the Leveller Walwyn had spoken up for them. Already Milton shared the
millenarian hopes of the radicals.[1] He earned his place in *Gangraena* as a divorcer: Milton retaliated by linking 'shallow Edwards
and Scotch what d'ye call' (?Baillie) in common ignominy. Milton
accepted the soul-sleeping doctrines of Richard Overton's *Mans
Mortallitie*. In *Areopagitica* Milton attacked censorship before
publication because revelation is progressive, because new truths are
being revealed to believers in the 1640s: Clement Writer echoed
him.[2] In his *Treatise of Education* Milton hoped that learning would
undo the consequences of the Fall, 'repair the ruins of our first
parents': the hope realized (very differently) at the end of *Paradise
Lost*. All these views can be related to the Familist tradition. The
grounds on which Milton defended divorce are the obverse of a belief

that marriage must be based on love, and surprisingly reminiscent of Clarkson's views on sex: a man may put away his wife if he does it 'with the full suffrage and applause of his conscience . . . claiming by faith and fullness of persuasion the rights and promises of God's institution'. The elect need not be bound by the Mosaic Law. Milton came even closer to Clarkson's position when he wrote in *Areopagitica*:– 'To the pure all things are pure, not only meats and drinks but all kinds of knowledge, whether of good or evil.'[3]

The same emphasis on God within us which pervades the divorce pamphlets and *Areopagitica* underlies Milton's attitude towards the Bible and his rejection of sabbatarianism: 'If I observe the Sabbath in compliance with the decalogue, but contrary to the dictates of my own faith, conformity with the decalogue, however exact, becomes in my case sin and a violation of the law.'[4] This echoes the passage from Bauthumley which I quoted above.[5] Milton, like Winstanley, Coppe, the author of *Tyranipocrit Discovered* and James Nayler, rejected a 'fugitive and cloistered virtue', and praised only a faith which results in charitable works: 'that faith alone which acts is counted living'.[6] His hatred of priests, an established church, forms, ceremonies and tithes was as fierce as that of any of the radicals. He rejected the distinction of clergy and laity, and thought 'the meanest artificer' might exercise a gift of preaching.[7] He deplored, in true Ranter style, clerical attempts to impose 'imaginary and scarecrow sins'.[8] And though Milton spoke of Christ in *believers'* hearts, nevertheless in *Areopagitica* he denounced censorship as an insult to the common people, not merely to believers. In *Comus* he advocated a more equitable distribution of this world's goods; as late as 1659 he was arguing for 'a just division of wastes and commons'.[9] Milton's proud defence of regicide was on the radical ground that 'no man who knows aught can be so stupid to deny that all men naturally were born free'. Kings and magistrates are 'deputies and commissioners' of the people. To think otherwise 'were a kind of treason against the dignity of mankind'.[10] Milton never obeyed the Council of State's instruction to write against the Levellers, though he was not backward in using his pen against the Commonwealth's enemies from the other flank.[11] He shared the internationalist hope of seeing other nations of the earth recovering that liberty which they so long had lost.[12]

But it is not only in his prose pamphlets that we can see affinities between Milton and the radicals. It is the poetry that is truly subversive – often against Milton's intellectual convictions. He treats hell and the devil in the same mythological way as Winstanley, as a means of depicting inner psychological conflicts, or simply to make a good story. Classical and Biblical myths are mingled in a way which shows that neither is to be taken literally. Hell is internal. Heaven is an allegory for the earth. When at the crisis of *Paradise Lost* Adam realizes that Eve is lost because she has eaten the apple, he cries out

> How can I live without thee, how forgo
> Thy sweet converse and love so dearly joined
> To live again in these wild woods forlorn . . .
> Flesh of flesh,
> Bone of my bone thou art, and from thy state
> Mine never shall be parted, bliss or woe.

There is complete ambivalence in Milton's attitude here. Professor Waldock rightly calls it 'a fundamental clash: it is a clash between what the poem asserts, on the one hand, and what it compels us to feel, on the other'.[13] Philosophically, Milton accepts God's will, realizes that there must be order, discipline, obedience: yet at the crucial moment his heart warms to Adam, sacrificing all for love. The emotion underlying the poem is more subversive than the poem's argument.

Adam's fall was due not to pride or intellectual curiosity, as it well might have been if Milton had followed Genesis and the commentators. It was due to love, love for woman; and to a preference for society rather than a lonely rectitude in individual isolation. It is not quite what we should expect from the poet traditionally seen as the high priest of self-righteous protestant individualism. And the conclusion of *Paradise Lost* too – 'a Paradise within thee, happier far' – echoes (however unconsciously) Coppin, and is an elaboration of the radicals' view that man can attain to a pre-lapsarian state here on earth.[14] Milton's very unusual emphasis on the physical aspects of love between the angels, and on their enjoyment of food, becomes perhaps less eccentric if we relate it to the radicals' doctrine that matter is God, that physical existence here on earth is good and to be enjoyed for its own sake.[15] Milton goes out of his way to glorify the nakedness of Adam and Eve before the Fall, and to stress that their sexual love was consummated, 'Whatever hypocrites austerely talk.' Milton was as severe as Winstanley or Erbery on those 'that practised falsehood under saintly show'. Hypocrisy is 'the only evil that walks Invisible except to God alone'. Milton emphasizes that there was no private property before the Fall. Labour is not really a curse: Adam worked in Paradise before the Fall, and even after it 'idleness had been worse'.[16]

Milton so successfully concealed his Arianism in *Paradise Lost* and *Paradise Regained* that commentators were deceived until the publication in 1825 of the *De Doctrina Christiana*; but once we have the clue there are many hints. Men are, like Christ, 'the sons of God', as they had been for Winstanley. When Jesus brought back 'through the world's wilderness long wandered man Safe to eternal Paradise of rest', Paradise was regained 'by one man's firm obedience fully tried Through all temptation', not by the vicarious suffering of Christ on the cross. The 'one just man' can be Noah or Samson or Christ, or (one suspects) Milton. All this too is of a piece with the radical treatment of the Christian myth as an allegory of the conflicts in the heart of each believer, and with their increasing emphasis on works rather than faith; it assumes the interregnum discussion about the Fall.

The rejection in *Paradise Regained* of premature political solutions – 'his weakness shall o'ercome Satanic strength' – reminds us of Erbery and the Quakers. The insistence that Christ's kingdom is not of this world is also a continuation of the lifelong battle of Milton (and the radicals) against the union of church and state, coercion of consciences by the civil power. It was Satan who was convinced that Christ aimed at an earthly kingdom. The confidence that despite the political catastrophe of 1660 Christ's kingdom will still come – 'but what the means Is not for thee to know nor me to tell' – also recalls the Quaker analysis of the restoration.[17] But *Samson Agonistes* shows us that Milton still had confidence in ultimate political victory, even if he could not envisage the means by which it would be achieved. Milton had nailed his republican colours to the mast in *The Readie and Easie Way to establish a Free Commonwealth*, that very brave book. Although after the restoration he wrote under a strict censorship and was himself deeply suspect, Milton still managed to convey many radical opinions in the later poems – using e.g. 'the parsimonious emmet' as a 'pattern of just equality' in a future republic – covering himself by an ambiguous 'perhaps'. His last published work – an at first sight surprising panegyric of the papist King of Poland, John Sobieski – was in fact a masterpiece of double-talk. Sobieski was a king who carried out a forceful nationalist foreign policy, and so an obvious foil to Charles II. But the contrast was the more piquant in that in 1672 a statue of Charles II had been unveiled by the Tory Lord Mayor of London which was an adaptation of a statue of John Sobieski. Many were the witticisms at the expense of this statue, including poems by Marvell (probably) and Rochester.[18]

I am not suggesting that Milton was a crypto-Ranter, or even that he shared many of the views of the radicals. It could indeed be argued that *Paradise Regained* is in some respects an anti-Ranter poem. Whether or not Ellwood suggested the subject, it was written at a time when Milton was close to the Quakers, and the Quakers very occupied with Perrot and other ranting tendencies. When Satan offers Christ food and drink in the wilderness Christ rejects Clarkson's doctrine that to the pure all things are pure; but when good angels provide food Christ eats heartily. He is as moderate, as sensible, as middle-of-the-road as the Quakers were becoming by 1667. For him as for Quakers, the 'spirit of truth . . . in pious hearts' offered

> an inward oracle
> To all truth requisite for men to know.[19]

Milton was a leisure-class intellectual, who never knew what it was to labour under a small taskmaster's eye.[20] His contempt for the common people is explicit, at least from 1645 onwards. What I do suggest is that some of Milton's religious and political convictions, as revealed in the prose pamphlets, derive from the radical traditions of the Familist underworld and that it is very likely that some Ranters drew on them via Milton. *Pace* M. Saurat, this underground tradition seems to me a more plausible source than the *Zohar*, though Milton may have read that too. He could have learnt that sin is the privation of light from Bauthumley's *Light and Dark Sides of God*, and the light/darkness antithesis pervades the thought of many other radicals as well as of Milton.[21]

Milton, I am suggesting, combined radical intellectual convictions with patrician social prejudices, rather as Oliver Cromwell combined some genuinely radical religious beliefs with the normal social assumptions of a country gentleman. If we think of Milton as living in a state of permanent dialogue with radical views which he could not altogether accept, yet some of which he valued very highly indeed, it may throw light even on the great poetry. We may recall his friendship with Quakers after the restoration, although he (like Erbery) appears not to have associated himself with any religious sect.

Such an approach to Milton helps me, at any rate, to absorb the argument of William Empson's brilliantly provocative *Milton's God*. At first sight Empson's thesis, attractive though it is, raises doubts because it appears to suggest that Milton the poet knew truths which Milton the theologian denied – not emotional truths, like the power of love, but philosophical truths, like the nature of God. If he was not stupid or confused, he must have been writing in an elaborate code. But if Milton was carrying on a continuous dialogue with the radicals it becomes easier to think of him rejecting with his intellect truths of which he was well aware and which one half of his being accepted. If Milton had allowed himself consciously to accept the view of Winstanley, Erbery and some Ranters, that the God whom most Christians worshipped was a wicked God, his life would have lost its structure, would have fallen in ruins about his head like the temple of the Philistines. He had to justify the ways of God to men in order to justify his own life, the sacrifice of his eyes. No Ranter could have written *Paradise Lost*: the tension would have been lacking. God's ways were justifiable to all except the obscure few 'who think not God at all'. Those others

> who doubt his ways not just . . .
> Give the reins to wandering thought . . .
> Till by their own perplexities involved
> They ravel more, still less resolved,
> But never find self-satisfying solution.

History was meaningless, there was no hope for the future, unless one could believe that God, in his own good time, would bring about the changes which the revolutionaries had failed to achieve. In the last two books of *Paradise Lost*, Michael, at God's express command, encourages fallen Adam with a pre-view of future history. Those who lost their confidence in God's purposes,

> The conquered also, and enslaved by war,
> Shall with their freedom lost all virtue lose
> And fear of God, from whom their piety feigned
> In sharp contest of battle found no aid
> Against invaders; therefore cooled in zeal
> Thenceforth shall practice how to live secure,
> Worldly or dissolute, on what their lords
> Shall leave them to enjoy . . .
> So all shall turn degenerate, all depraved . . .
>   Tyranny must be,
> Though to the tyrant thereby no excuse.

> So virtue given for lost,
> Depressed and overthrown . . .
> Revives, reflourishes, then vigorous most
> When most unactive deemed.

Paradise Lost, *Paradise Regained*, and *Samson Agonistes* are all, in my view, wrestling with the problem of the failure of the Revolution, trying to apportion blame and look forward from defeat. Samson, like the New Model Army, was a public person:[22]

> I was no private, but a person raised
> With strength sufficient and command from heaven
> To free my country.

He accepted Dalila's charge that he had betrayed himself. We recall Milton's warning in 1654 to the ambitious generals, that they would themselves become royalists if they did not abandon avarice and ambition.[23] 'I formed them free,' God says of the rebel angels,

> And free they must remain
> Till they enthral themselves.

They fell 'self-tempted, self-betrayed'. Satan was in consequence 'not free, but to thyself enthralled'. The argument from necessity, which Oliver Cromwell and Satan used, was 'the tyrant's plea'.

Yet Empson is right to suggest that Milton was in some sense aware of the terrible collapse that was always possible. Milton was not of the devil's party without knowing it: part of him knew. The revolutionary Milton admires much in Satan – as in Adam at the moment of the Fall – that reflects the characteristics of unrestrained romantic individualism, which are present in Milton as they had been in Marlowe, as they were in the Ranters. But Milton had concluded that these qualities can be dangerous to society unless they are controlled. Satan represents the way in which the Good Old Cause had been perverted, whether by ambitious generals or undisciplined rank and file. It is significant that the view that Satan was the true hero of *Paradise Lost* flourished with the revival of revolutionary romanticism, with Blake and Shelley and Byron.[24] We are meant to admire Tennyson's Ulysses when he says:

> Though much is taken, much abides; and though
> We are not now that strength which in old days
> Moved earth and heaven; that which we are, we are;
> One equal temper of heroic hearts,
> Made weak by time and fate, but strong in will
> To strive, to seek, to find, and not to yield.

We are not meant to admire Milton's Satan when, in similar circumstances, he asked:

> What though the field be lost:
> All is not lost; the unconquerable will,

And study of revenge, immortal hate,
And courage never to submit or yield:
And what is else not to be overcome?

Satan's conception of liberty is for Milton a false conception:

The mind is its own place and in itself
Can make a heaven of hell, a hell of heaven . . .
Better to reign in hell than serve in heaven.

That seemed fine to the romantic anarchists of the late eighteenth and early nineteenth centuries. But Milton had seen where unrestrained individualism led to. The conclusion of *Paradise Lost*, though apparently expressing a similar sentiment, is vastly different. Adam leaves Paradise to find 'A Paradise within thee, happier far': the Fall is after all fortunate, whatever we think of those who brought it about. But Adam will find this Paradise only if he can add:

Deeds to thy knowledge answerable, add faith,
Add virtue, patience, temperance and love.

This is not romantic self-realization; it is adaptation to the world and its laws, the laws of God for man. The Quakers made a similar adaptation, but without the tension, the inner contradictions which produced Milton's poetry. It is Milton's glory that in the time of utter defeat, when Diggers, Ranters and Levellers were silenced and Quakers had abandoned politics, he kept something of the radical intellectual achievement alive for Blake and many others to quarry.

II BUNYAN

With Bunyan too I would stress the radical ambience, though in his case rather for its influence on him than (as with Milton) for his influence on it. Bunyan, like Winstanley, Fox and many others, shared the despairs, the temptations, the atheism of the early fifties. His theology developed in controversy with Ranters and Quakers.[25] If Milton had intellectual affinities with the radicals but was set apart from them by his patrician assumptions, Bunyan shared the social and political attitudes of the radicals but not their theology. In 1654 and many times later he denounced kingly oppressors.[26]

He cared about 'the old laws, which are the Magna Carta, the sole basis of the government of a kingdom'. They 'may not be cast away for the pet that is taken by every little gentleman against them'.[27] In *The Holy War* it made him 'laugh to see how old Mr Prejudice was kicked and tumbled about in the dirt'.[28] And his own comment on the behaviour of the propertied Puritans, slipped unobtrusively into *The Pilgrim's Progress*, is the best commentary I know on the restoration. 'Did you not know,' Faithful asks, 'about ten years ago, one Temporary in your parts, who was a forward man in religion then?'[29]

One object of the restoration had been to put tinkers back into their callings.[30] But Bunyan remembered a lot from the revolutionary decades. 'More servants than masters,' he wrote, 'more tenants than landlords, will inherit the kingdom of heaven.' God's own, he wrote in the same year 1658, 'are most commonly of the poorer sort'. Unlike gentlemen, 'they cannot, with Pontius Pilate, speak Hebrew, Greek and Latin'. Bunyan reflected on 'the sad condition of those that are for the most part rich men'.[31] Worldly Wiseman, Formalist, Hypocrisy, like Antichrist, were all gentlemen: Madam Bubble, 'the Mistress of the world', was a gentlewoman. Mrs Wanton was 'an admirably well-bred gentlewoman'. Mr By-ends was 'a gentleman of good quality', related to lords, parsons and the rich. The Pilgrims, on the other hand, were 'of base and low estate', and uneducated. Faithful was brought before Lord Hate-Good for slandering several of the nobility and 'most of the gentry of our town'. ('Sins are all lords and great ones', is Bunyan's marginal note.)[32] In *The Holy War* he gives us a long list of Diabolian lords and gentlemen (though vagabonds are also Diabolians). Mr Lustings is 'a man of high birth'. The devils are clearly very well bred: they bow and scrape to one another.[33] Mr Badman was 'a person of quality'; 'Cain's brood' were 'lords and rulers'.[34] Even Giant Pope is armigerous: 'his escutcheon was the stake, the flame and the good man in it'.[35]

Bunyan's parents had been cottagers, and his wife described him in 1661 as 'a tinker and a poor man, therefore he is despised and cannot have justice'.[36] 'In danger to be removed like a cottage'[37] was a proverbial phrase for Bunyan; his Dives described Lazarus as 'a scabbed creep-hedge'. We can see *The Pilgrim's Progress* as the greatest literary product of this social group, the epic of the itinerant. 'As I walked through the wilderness of this world', Bunyan laid himself down to sleep in a den which he 'lighted on', as George Fox and so many other itinerants did: *Pilgrim's Progress* was the dream he then dreamed.[38]

Royalty had ceased to be peripatetic, had ceased to go on progress except on rare occasions, just at the time when the lowest class of the population appears to have been most mobile. Was the title of Bunyan's epic, whose apt alliteration we take so entirely for granted, intended to suggest that his Pilgrim was a king? We recall Coppe's 'Because I am a king I have done this' to the beggar whom he befriended.[39] The burden on the back was the symbol of the lowest grade of masterless man; but Bunyan's Pilgrim also has the freedom of the masterless. He is not tied to the soil. He can leave home when he wishes, go where he wishes: his wife can follow him if she wants to. It is the widest democratization of potential salvation – not merely to the static humble poor, dependent on their superiors, but to men and women who can take their lives into their own hands, help themselves in the confidence that if they do God will help them.

We call Bunyan a Calvinist, but his is a Calvinism with a difference. He shares Winstanley's activism. 'Were you doers, or talkers only?' God will ask at the day of judgment.[40] Heaven has to be striven for. Contrast the high Calvinism of Samuel Hieron: 'the kingdom of heaven is as a reward of inheritance'. This 'breaketh the neck of all merit . . . If heaven were the hire of servants, or the booty of purchasers, it were something to the purpose; but being the reward of sons, . . . there is no colour of desert'.[41] Hieron's is a theology which makes sense to men who have inherited their wealth and social position: Bunyan's is the outlook of mobile small craftsmen, itinerants. Society has been loosened up; desert and works creep into all the theology of the later seventeenth century, even that which we call Calvinist. 'The soul of religion is the practical part,' said Christian.[42]

We can parallel Bunyan's attitude from earlier writers like Sibbes: it is in the Puritan tradition, hardly the heresy M. Talon thought it.[43] But it also relates to the demand of Winstanley, Coppe and the author of *Tyranipocrit Discovered*, that faith shall issue in works. The subversiveness of Bunyan is both in his flat, matter-of-fact, real-life narrative, and in his themes. The hero of *The Pilgrim's Progress* is one of the people: the law and its courts, he knows, will not give him justice. The spiritual autobiography itself becomes subversive when its hero is a lower-class itinerant whose major temptations occur when playing tip-cat. There could be no more banal villain than the petty-bourgeois Mr Badman, though like Satan in *Paradise Lost* he is often very much livelier than the virtuous characters. Episodes like his courtship and second marriage look forward to Defoe in theme as well as in style.[44]

Yet for all the realism of the narrative Bunyan's Pilgrim is travelling to his upside-down world, which is almost as concrete and materialistic as Mary Cary's had been twenty years earlier. Only now it is not to be found on earth – just as for centuries before the Revolution had been the case. The masterless man assumes he must bear his burden in this world. He too has adapted to a society which Mary Cary and others hoped was about to be overthrown. Just as George Fox came to accept sin, just as sin looms much larger in *Paradise Lost* than in *Areopagitica*, so the particular poignancy of *The Pilgrim's Progress* (as of *Paradise Lost*) springs from the tension between the vision and the reality, the upside-down world and the all too real world. Milton persuaded himself that it had been a fortunate Fall. I do not think Bunyan would have agreed. He knew more about the heaviness of the burden, more about the puzzling world of Mr Badman, the free market and petty commercial morality, than Milton ever did, living without labour on the income his father's usury had left him. But each of them, starting from fallen man, can show the divine in man slowly winning its way back, in Milton's case to 'a Paradise within thee, happier far'; in Bunyan's to a confidence that triumphed over the torments and early death which were the fate of the itinerant.

Bunyan's Christian got rid of his burden only after he had turned away from the world and its works through the strait gate, and had accepted the cross. Then the burden rolled off his back, no thanks to any effort of his. If natural man could cast off the burden by his own exertions, he would cast off God too: he would be back in the state of equality which existed before man created God, before priests and kings persuaded men that the root of evil is man's sin, not inequality. Salvation must be the arbitrary gift of God's grace from outside, because the essence of the Fall had been a breach of God's arbitrary, irrational prohibition – though the idea of sinfulness came to incorporate any kind of anti-social behaviour. Bunyan disliked arbitrary little gentlemen who cast away the old laws; but he accepted that they, like the poor, will be with us till the end of the world.

III   SOME OTHERS

If there is anything in the analysis I have essayed in this book, it might suggest fresh approaches to other aspects of later seventeenth-century literature. Both Milton and Bunyan create for their characters what I have called a 'Robinson Crusoe situation', the isolation of the hero or heroine from social ties, as in Hobbes's state of nature.[45] The Lady in *Comus* is lost in the wood, Adam and Eve took 'their solitary way' from Paradise to the world, Christ faces Satan alone in the desert, Samson was never more alone than when he stood surrounded by his enemies in Dagon's temple. Bunyan's Pilgrim deserted wife and children in quest of salvation; Robinson Crusoe is preceded by Henry Nevile's *The Isle of Pines*.[46] The authors' reason for creating this situation, whether conscious or not, was to free the individual from inherited traditions, customs and laws, leaving him to work out his salvation alone in the sight of God only. In the light of our present analysis we may perhaps link this tendency to set the individual free from social norms with the Ranter rejection of conventional morality as well as with Locke's *tabula rasa*.[47] We may indeed see it as the application to literature of the doctrine of the inner light, the quintessence of radical individualism.

The affinities which I suggested between Ranters and royalists in their opposition to the protestant ethic[48] no doubt worked both ways, and continued to apply after the restoration. The wits of Charles II's court, insecurely restored to the highest positions in a society increasingly alien to them because increasingly commercial, were in a sense themselves outsiders, social misfits. Hence their desire at all costs to *épater* the triumphant *bourgeoisie*. They were not above reproducing the ideas of the radicals, or the radical ideas of Hobbes, for this purpose. Only in court circles, indeed, were men free to air such dangerous thoughts once the censorship clamped down. Samuel Butler, for instance, asked why female honour consisted only in 'not being whores: as if that sex were capable of no other morality but a mere negative continence.' He said that clergymen expose the kingdom of heaven to sale, in order with the proceeds to purchase as much as they can of this world. 'These officers and commanders of the Church Militant are like soldiers of fortune that are free to serve on any side that gives the best pay.' He attacked the mumbo-jumbo of priests and lawyers alike. 'Courts of justice for the most part commit greater crimes than they punish.' He elevated reason above faith.[49]

The comments of Osborne, Stillingfleet, Burnet and others, quoted above,[50] suggest that there was complete continuity between pre- and post-restoration 'atheism' and hostility to priestcraft. They make nonsense of the idea that there was in reaction against Puritanism a 'restoration spirit' which was in part a French import. The 'restoration spirit' was at least as much a product of 'the Puritan Revolution' as a reaction against it: or in so far as it was a reaction, this reaction came originally from the radical left wing of the Puritans. Just as the prose in which restoration comedy is written draws at least in part on the norms established by radical (and royalist) pamphleteers during the Revolution, so the ideas of restoration drama also have their roots in the ideas of the radicals whom this book has studied. We think of the fierce libertarianism of Otway, of his lines

> Conscience! a trick of state, found out by those
> That wanted power to support their laws;
> A bugbear name, to startle fools; but we
> That know the weakness of the fallacy,
> Know better how to use what nature gave.
> That soul's no soul which to itself's a slave.

> Who anything for conscience' sake deny
> Do nothing else but give themselves the lie.[51]

We think of Mrs Aphra Behn, few of whose characters have a good word to say for matrimony if they could get into bed together without it. Her own private life would have fitted into the world of the Ranters. Her Widow Ranter, depicted as a sympathetic character, is a hard-drinking, hard-smoking lecher, who defends herself with her sword like the Roaring Girl.[52] ''Tis as natural for wives as for subjects to rebel' against despotism, said the hero of the Duke of Buckingham's *The Militant Couple*.[53] Vanbrugh's Lady Brute was no doubt not the only one to make use of Biblical criticism similar to that of Clement Writer and Samuel Fisher.[54] When the reaction against restoration comedy came, its spokesman was not a Puritan but the high Anglican Jeremy Collier. He carefully documented links between the anti-clericalism and irreligion of the dramatists and social levelling and 'downright porter's rhetoric'.[55]

Rochester, to take another example, rejected hell, the devil and personal immortality as

> senseless stories, idle tales,
> Dreams, whimsies and no more.
> Our sphere of action is life's happiness,
> And he who thinks beyond thinks like an ass.

He worried about the compatibility of evil with divine omnipotence. He was sceptical about miracles, rejected much of the moral code of the Old Testament, and could not believe the stories of the creation and the Fall 'unless they were parables'. Rochester paraphrased Winstanley's 'action is the life of all' –

> Thoughts are given for action's government;
> When action ceases, thought's impertinent.[56]

Burnet's fascinating discussions with Rochester have striking analogies to conversations which must have gone on between Ranters and Quakers. Rochester used the arguments of Writer and Fisher against the sacred character of the Bible (which is not to say that he derived his arguments from these authors). He thought that all came by nature, still questioned the existence of eternal punishment, rejected monogamy as an unreasonable imposition on the freedom of mankind. He complained to Burnet of 'the jugglings of priests'. 'Why,' he asked, 'must a man tell me that I cannot be saved unless I believe things against my reason, and then I must pay him for telling me of them?' Burnet in his turn thought Rochester's 'philosophy for reforming the world' was too speculative. Burnet (like Milton, like the Quakers) made little of predestination but a great deal of the moral teaching of Christianity. The escape which he offered Rochester from his materialist scepticism was by the experience of feeling 'a law within himself'. The argument of his which carried most weight with Rochester was that libertinism was anti-social. Rochester agreed not to attack Christianity even before he was convinced of its truth.[57]

Professor Pinto's analysis of Rochester's dilemma comes very near to our analysis of the radicals during the interregnum. Rochester, he suggests, was trying to escape from 'a world which had been suddenly transformed by the scientists into a vast machine governed by mathematical laws, where God has become a remote first cause and man an insignificant reas'ning Engine'; he was trying to escape from 'the Cartesian-Newtonian world picture, a civilized city of good taste, common sense and reason'. But Rochester was also, I think, trying to escape from the protestant ethic, which adds force to Professor Pinto's comparison with Blake. Professor Pinto lists Rochester's three alternative solutions as (i) 'the ideal of the purely aesthetic hero, . . . a purely selfish ideal'; (ii) 'the ethical hero, the disillusioned and penetrating observer'; (iii) 'the religious hero', rejecting the shams of the social world for 'virtue conceived as poor, homeless, rejected and outcast' – an itinerant or cottager, we might almost say.[58]

It is difficult to know how seriously to take Rochester's republicanism. It could hardly be expressed more vigorously:

> Monsters which knaves 'sacred' proclaim,
> And then like slaves fall down before 'em.
> What can there be in kings divine?
> The most are wolves, goats, sheep or swine.

> Then farewell sacred majesty,
> Let's put all brutish tyrants down;
> When men are born and still live free,
> Here every head doth wear a crown.
>
> I hate all monarchs and the thrones they sit on,
> From the Hector of France to the cully of Britain.[59]

We do not know, either, where Rochester got his ideas from. Coming up to such an exciting college as Wadham in such an exciting year as 1660, it seems unlikely that all he learnt at Oxford was how to drink. He certainly read Hobbes: we do not know whom else.

We may find many radical ideas, defused of their revolutionary content, in the writings of the blameless Anglican clergyman, Thomas Traherne. We noted him undergoing sceptical doubts during his undergraduate career at Oxford.[60] He later overcame these, but retained a sense of God immanent within the creation: science helps us to know God through knowing the real world.[61] Traherne carefully studied the Hermetic philosophy, sought out the 'secrets of nature' and saw infinity in a grain of sand.[62] He equated life with motion, and thought that 'practice and exercise is the life of all'. 'Philosophers are not those that speak but do great things.' Like Winstanley, Traherne believed that men were born innocent, and that they fell because of the covetousness prevalent in the society in which they grew up; but something of Christ remained in all men.[63] But Traherne's communism, unlike Winstanley's, was in the imagination only:

> Cursed and devised proprieties
> With envy, avarice
> And fraud, those fiends that spoil even Paradise,
> Fled from the splendour of mine eyes . . .
>
> Proprieties themselves were mine.[64]

'All was mine': Traherne does not seem to have shared the Digger hope that all mankind might have equal rights, nor even the Ranter claim that 'all is ours'. 'In the great historical revolutions', Marcuse wrote, 'the imagination was, for a short period, released and free to enter into the projects of a new social morality and of new institutions of freedom; then it was sacrificed to the requirements of effective reason.'[65] Our story ends by pointing towards the Age of Reason rather than the upside-down world. But the English Revolution's 'teeming freedom' did liberate the imagination as Christ rose, however briefly, in sons and daughters.

Notes

I INTRODUCTION

1. Sabine, p. 252.
2. See ch. 13 below.
3. E. Welsford, *The Fool* (1935), ch. IX.
4. I. Morley, *A Thousand Lives* (1954), p. 78.
5. See p. 288 below.

2 THE PARCHMENT AND THE FIRE

1. 'The Many-Headed Monster in late Tudor and Early Stuart Political Thinking', in *From the Renaissance to the Counter-Reformation: Essays in Honour of Garret Mattingly*, ed. C. H. Carter (1968), pp. 296–324.
2. John Barclay, *Icon Animorum* (1614), Englished by T.M[ay] (1631), pp. 104–8.
3. L. Boynton, *The Elizabethan Militia, 1588–1638* (1967), pp. 62, 108–11, 119, 220–21, 249–50; *The Earl of Hertford's Lieutenancy Papers, 1603–1612*, ed. W. P. D. Murphy (Wiltshire Record Soc., 1969), p. 72.
4. C. Russell, *The Crisis of Parliaments* (Oxford U.P., 1971), p. 244. I am grateful to Mr Russell for pointing out to me that the county concerned was Herefordshire, not Hertfordshire as misprinted in his book.
5. See pp. 24–5 below.
6. D. B. Quinn, *The Elizabethans and the Irish* (Cornell U.P., 1966), p. 157.
7. R. Hooker, *Of the Laws of Ecclesiastical Polity* (Everyman edn) II, pp. 5–6.

8. R. Welford, *History of Newcastle and Gateshead* (1884–7) III, pp. 315–16. See p. 53 below.

9. C. Oman, *Elizabeth of Bohemia* (1964), p. 294.

10. Quoted by M. Ashley, *Life in Stuart England* (1964), pp. 21–2.

11. In Joan Thirsk (ed.), *The Agrarian History of England and Wales, IV, (1500–1640)* (Cambridge U.P., 1967), pp. 620–21.

12. Robert Wharton, *A Declaration to Great Britain and Ireland, shewing the downfall of their Princes, and wherefore it is come upon them* (1649), p. 3.

13. *Lowndes MSS.* (H.M.C.), p. 549.

14. L. J. Ashford, *The History of the Borough of High Wycombe* (1960), pp. 133–4. I am grateful to Dr A. M. Johnson for pointing out to me that this election was for the Short, not the Long Parliament.

15. *C.S.P.D., 1639–40*, pp. 608–9; M. R. Freer, 'The Election of Great Marlow in 1640', *J.M.H.*, XIV, pp. 434–45.

16. William Lilly, *Several Observations on the Life and Death of King Charles* (1651) in *Select Tracts*, ed. F. Maseres (1815) I, pp. 169–70; M. James, *Social Problems and Policy during the Puritan Revolution* (1930), p. 375.

17. [Bruno Ryves] *Angliae Ruina* (1647), p. 176.

18. M. Prestwich, *Cranfield: Politics and Profits under the Early Stuarts* (Oxford U.P., 1966), pp. 569, 577.

19. D. Underdown, *Pride's Purge*, p. 60.

20. Quoted by P. Zagorin, *The Court and the Country* (1969), p. 323.

21. [Ryves] *Angliae Ruina*, p. 96. ('Gentlemen should be as rare as white bulls in Norfolk,' one of Ket's rebels had said nearly a century earlier.)

22. E. Warburton, *Prince Rupert and the Cavaliers* (1849) II, pp. 104–5; *Beaufort MSS.* (H.M.C.), p. 23, which gives an economic explanation of this social phenomenon; cf. Edward Hyde, Earl of Clarendon, *History of the Rebellion*, ed. W. D. Macray (Oxford U.P., 1888) II, p. 464.

23. S. R. Gardiner, *The Great Civil War* (1891–3) III, p. 209.

24. Prestwich, op. cit., p. 570.

25. Charles I's Answer to the Nineteen Propositions, 18 June 1642.

26. W. Drummond, *The Magical Mirror* (1639), quoted by D. Masson in *Drummond of Hawthornden* (1873), p. 306.

27. J. W. Willis-Bund, 'A Civil War Parliament Soldier: Tinker Fox', *Associated Architectural Societies' Reports and Papers*, XXV, pp. 373–403.

28. A. G. Dickens, *Lollards and Protestants in the Diocese of York, 1509–1559* (1959), p. 13.

29. ibid., pp. 9, 17. James Nayler, whom we shall frequently meet later, was born near Wakefield. See pp. 186–94 below.

30. J. A. F. Thomson, *The Later Lollards* (Oxford U.P., 1965), p. 247. The jibe was common: see Dickens, op. cit., p. 18.

31. Dickens, op. cit., pp. 12, 47–8.

32. K. V. Thomas, *Religion and the Decline of Magic* (1971), pp. 168–70.

33. See C. Burrage, *The Early English Dissenters* (Cambridge U.P., 1912), 2 vols, *passim*; H. F. M. Prescott, *Mary Tudor* (1952), p. 108.

34. D. B. Heriot, 'Anabaptism in England during the 16th and 17th centuries', *Transactions of the Congregational History Soc.*, XII, p. 271.

35. J. Knewstub, *A Confutation of Monstrous and Horrible Heresies taught by H. N.* (1579), quoted by R. M. Jones, *Studies in Mystical Religion* (1909), p. 443.

36. Strype, *Annals*, II, pt i, p. 563; cf. *C.S.P.D., 1648–9*, p. 425.

37. Perkins, *Works*, III, p. 392; cf. my *Antichrist in Seventeenth-Century England* (Oxford U.P., 1971), pp. 142–3, 145.

38. Strype, *Annals*, II, pt i, p. 487; pt ii, p. 289; ed. A. Peel, *The Seconde Parte of a Register* (1915) I, p. 230; J. Rogers, *The Displaying of an horrible secte*, sig. Kv; cf. J. O. W. Haweis, *Sketches of the Reformation and Elizabethan Age taken from the contemporary pulpit* (1844), p. 200; G. H. Williams, *The Radical Reformation* (Philadelphia, 1962), pp. 479–84, 788–90; G. K. Hyland, *A Century of Persecution* (1920), pp. 102–12, 332–3. See p. 29 below for Ely, 'that island of errors and sectaries'.

39. P. Collinson, *The Elizabethan Puritan Movement* (1967), pp. 92–7.

40. T. Cooper, *An Admonition to the People of England*, ed. E. Arber (1895), pp. 9, 175; cf. pp. 102–3, 118–19, 139, 144–5, 148, 159. My italics.

41. Quoted by L. Stone, *The Crisis of the Aristocracy, 1558–1641* (Oxford U.P., 1965), p. 406; Collinson, op. cit., p. 147.

42. F. W. X. Fincham, 'Notes from the Ecclesiastical Court Records at Somerset House', *T.R.H.S.*, 4th Series (1921), p. 136.

43. Hooker, *Of the Laws of Ecclesiastical Polity* (Everyman edn) I, p. 148; cf. I. Walton, *The Life of Mr Richard Hooker* (1655) in *Lives* (World's Classics edn), p. 185.

44. Brightman, *The Revelation of St John Illustrated* (4th edn, 1644), p. 139. First published, posthumously, in 1615; Brightman died in 1607.

45. Ed. R. F. Williams, *Court and Times of Charles I* (1848) II, p. 71.

46. Lambeth MS. 943, f. 721. Colnbrook will recur in our story. See p. 91 below.

47. *The Souldiers Catechisme* (1644), pp. 20–21.

48. Clarendon, *History of the Rebellion*, I, p. 449.

49. [Anon.] *A Letter from Mercurius Civicus to Mercurius Rusticus* (1643) in *Somers' Tracts* (1748–51) V, p. 415; cf. J. Nalson, *An Impartial Collection* (1682) II, p. 760.

50. [Ryves] *Angliae Ruina*, p. 26.

51. [W. Chestlin] *Persecutio Undecima* (1681), pp. 4, 6–7 (first published 1648); E. L. Warner, *The Life of John Warner, Bishop of Rochester* (1901), p. 33; P. Barwick, *Life of Dr John Barwick*, ed. G. F. Barwick (1903), p. 177.

52. T. Adams, *Works* (1629–30), p. 76.

53. E[dmund] H[all], *A Scriptural Discourse on the Apostasie and the Antichrist* (1653), sig. B 3v–B 4.

54. E. Calamy, *Englands Looking-glasse* (1642), p. 59.

55. E. How, *The Sufficiency of the Spirit's Teaching* (8th edn, 1792), p. 51 and *passim*. First published in the Netherlands in 1639.

56. Ed. C. H. Firth, *Ludlow's Memoirs* (Oxford U.P., 1894) I, p. 367.

57. T. Hobbes, *Philosophical Rudiments* (1651) in *English Works*, ed. Sir W. Molesworth (1839–45) II, p. 79.

58. Tyndale, *Doctrinal Treatises* (Parker Soc., 1848), p. 247.

59. Hooker, *Works* (Oxford U.P., 1836) III, p. 402; *The Laws of Ecclesiastical Polity* (Everyman edn.) I, p. 132.

60. G. Goodman, *The Court of King James I* (1839) I, p. 421.

61. Ed. W. Notestein, *Journal of Sir Simonds D'Ewes* (Yale U.P., 1923), p. 340.

62. Wolfe, pp. 118–19.

63. J. Selden, *Table Talk* (1847), pp. 196–7; F. Osborne, *Political Reflections upon the Government of the Turks*, in *Miscellaneous Works* (1722) II, p. 238.

64. See my *Antichrist in Seventeenth-Century England*, pp. 78–88.

65. For the respective shares of Foxe and Brightman in establishing this tradition, see the Oxford D.Phil. thesis of Mrs K. R. Firth, 'The Apocalyptic Tradition in Early Protestant Historiography in England and Scotland, 1530–1655' (1971).

66. See pp. 92–8 below.

67. [Thomas Goodwin] *A Glimpse of Sions Glory*, in Woodhouse, p. 234.

68. Woodhouse, loc. cit.

69. Sir E. Dering, *A Collection of Speeches* (1642), p. 166.

70. *Beaufort MSS.* (H.M.C.), pp. 23, 27–8.

71. [Chestlin] *Persecutio Undecima*, p. 8.

72. S. Marshall, *Reformation and Desolation* (1642), p. 45.

73. T. Scott, *Vox Populi* (1620), sig. B2–B3v; *The Second Part of Vox Populi* (1624), p. 16.

74. *Portland MSS.* (H.M.C.) III, p. 86; cf. Sir Thomas Aston, Bart, *A Survey of Presbitery* (1641), sig. I 4v.

75. T. Edwards, *Gangraena*, pt III (1646), pp. 147–8.

76. See my *Economic Problems of the Church* (Oxford U.P., 1965), *passim*, and Margaret James, 'The Political Importance of the Tithes Controversy in the English Revolution, 1640–1660', *History*, XXVI, pp. 1–18.

77. R. Blome, *The Fanatick History* (1660), p. 5.

78. W. Gouge, *Of Domesticall Duties* (1626), pp. 331–2.

79. [Walwyn] *The Power of Love* (1643) in Haller, *Tracts on Liberty in the Puritan Revolution, 1638–1647* (Columbia U.P., 1933) II, p. 273; for Milton see p. 395 below.

80. J. Aubrey, *Brief Lives* (Oxford U.P., 1898) I, p. 279. For Familism see pp. 26–8 above.

81. Ludlow, *Memoirs*, I, pp. 545–6.

82. J. Lilburne, *Londons Liberty in Chains* (1646), p. 42; [Anon.] *Light Shining in Buckinghamshire* (1648), p. 13, in Sabine, p. 622. For this pamphlet see also p. 117 below.

83. R. Overton, *A Remonstrance of Many Thousand Citizens* (1646), p. 12, in Haller, *Tracts on Liberty*, III, p. 362.

84. Dell, *Several Sermons and Discourses* (1709), p. 638.

85. [Ryves] *Angliae Ruina*, p. 27.

86. Wolfe, p. 188.

87. Woodhouse, pp. 55–7, 61, 69–71. See p. 67 below for the Putney Debates.

88. Sabine, pp. 337, 181–2.

89. ibid., pp. 473–4. See ch. 7 below.

3 MASTERLESS MEN

1. For the Authorized Version of Acts xvii, 1–6 see epigraph on p. xv above. There the Geneva Bible's 'vagabonds' have become 'lewd fellows of the baser sort'. The object of the Geneva comment is to turn the accusation of sedition, of subverting the state of the world, away

from religious radicals and to apply it to lower-class itinerants. The subverters studied in this book were often both religious radicals and itinerants.

2. T. Middleton, *The Mayor of Queensborough*, Act II, scene iii. First printed 1661, though Middleton died in 1627.

3. J. Strype, *Annals of the Reformation . . . during Queen Elizabeth's happy reign* (Oxford U.P., 1824) I, pt ii, p. 296; ed. W. Tite, *Diary of John Manningham* (Camden Soc., 1868), p. 73.

4. *P. and R.*, pp. 227–9; *S. and P.*, p. 457.

5. e.g. Peter Chamberlen, *The Poore Mans Advocate* (1649), p. 47.

6. Such populations existed on a smaller scale in other towns, but there they could more easily be controlled by ruling oligarchies with the support of the local gentry.

7. Perhaps we should differentiate between City mobs and the freer population of the suburbs. The inhabitants of Southwark called on the Army to intervene in London in August and September 1647, to overthrow Presbyterian control of the City based on some 'mob' support (B. Whitelocke, *Memorials of the English Affairs* [1682], pp. 263–5). See pp. 356–8 below.

8. See epigraph to this chapter.

9. The sects 'may well have functioned as a home-from-home for first generation immigrants,' says Mr K. V. Thomas, op. cit., p. 153; cf. *S. and P.*, pp. 286–7, and pp. 373–6 below.

10. J. Strype, *Life . . . of . . . Edmund Grindal* (Oxford U.P., 1821), p. 572.

11. Quoted by Stone, *The Crisis of the Aristocracy*, p. 265.

12. Marprelate, *The Epitome* (1589), sig. E IV.

13. Dell, op. cit., p. 18.

14. Sabine, p. 284.

15. *Fenstanton Records*, p. 82.

16. Isobel Ross, *Margaret Fell* (1949), p. 119.

17. Robert Powell, *A Treatise of . . . Courts Leet* (1642), pp. 52–3.

18. Thirsk, *Agrarian History*, IV, pp. 38, 95–9; P. A. J. Pettit, *The Royal Forests of Northamptonshire* (Northamptonshire Record Soc., 1968), pp. 142–7, 158, 162–3, 171.

19. R. H. Hilton, 'The Origins of Robin Hood', *P. and P.*, 14; M. H. Keen, 'Robin Hood – Peasant or Gentleman?', ibid., 19; D. M. Bergeron, *English Civic Pageantry* (1971), esp. pp. 56, 70–71, 82.

20. Hilton, *The Decline of Serfdom* (Economic History Soc., 1969), pp. 19–23; J. Birrell, 'Peasant Craftsmen in the Medieval Forest', *A.H.R.*, XVII, pp. 91–107.

21. P. Massinger, *Plays* (1897), pp. 469, 487; cf. *Englands Helicon, 1600* (1949), pp. 197–8.

22. C. H. Firth, *Essays Historical and Literary* (Oxford U.P., 1938), p. 25; cf. p. 358 below.

23. Ed. M. Sylvester, *Reliquiae Baxterianae* (1696) I, pp. 14, 89; Baxter, *Poor Husbandman's Advocate*, ed. F. J. Powicke (1926), pp. 26–7, written 1691; cf. V. H. T. Skipp, 'Economic and Social Change in the Forest of Arden, 1530–1649', *A.H.R.*, XVIII, Suppl., pp. 84–111.

24. cf. W. G. Hoskins, *The Midland Peasant* (1957), p. 204.

25. Everitt, in Thirsk, *Agrarian History*, pp. 463, 562–3, 573; Strype, *Annals*, II, pt i, p. 487.

26. D. M. Loades, *Two Tudor Conspiracies* (Cambridge U.P., 1965), pp. 206–7; ed. E. Arber, *An Introductory Sketch to the Marprelate Controversy* (1895), pp. 116, 131.

27. *C.S.P.D., 1595–7*, pp. 343–4; cf. my *Reformation to Industrial Revolution* (Penguin edn), pp. 93–100.

28. J. Nalson, *An Impartial Collection* (1682) I, p. 285; ed. A. Browning, *Memoirs of Sir John Reresby* (1936), p. 309n.

29. *Privy Council Registers, 1637–8* (facs., 1967), pp. 434, 457, 521, 523.

30. Hodges, op. cit., p. 55.

31. A. Everitt, *Change in the Provinces in the Seventeenth Century* (Leicester UP., 1969), p. 42.

32. Thirsk, *Agrarian History*, pp. 54, 111–12, 411–12, 435, 463 and *passim*; D. G. C. Allan, 'The Rising in the West', *Economic History Review*, Second Ser., V, pp. 76–85; G. R. Lewis, *The Stannaries* (Harvard U.P., 1924), pp. 174–5; cf. my *Reformation to Industrial Revolution*, pp. 62–3, 89.

33. Sabine, p. 359.

34. J. C. Holt, 'The Origins and Audience of the Ballads of Robin Hood', *P. and P.*, 18, p. 9.

35. Edward Fairfax, *Daemonologia* (1621) (ed. W. Grainge, 1882), pp. 34–5. Fairfax was uncle of the Parliamentary general. Cf. the enchanted forest in Milton's *Comus*.

36. Thirsk, *Agrarian History*, pp. 112, 251; Everitt, *Change in the Provinces in the Seventeenth Century*, pp. 22–3; *The Community of Kent and the Great Rebellion* (Leicester U.P., 1966), pp. 86, 225, 297; 'Nonconformity in Country Parishes', *A.H.R.*, XVIII, Suppl., pp. 178–99; Edwards, *Gangraena*, pt III, p. 98; Pettit, *Royal Forests of Northamptonshire*, p. 173.

37. E. Kerridge, 'The Revolts in Wiltshire against Charles I', *Wiltshire Archaeological and Natural History Magazine*, LVII (1958), pp. 66–71; *V.C.H., Wiltshire*, IV, pp. 406–7, 412–14, 417, 427, 431–2.

38. K. V. Thomas, op. cit., pp. 162, 165; A. L. Morton, *The World of the Ranters* (1970), p. 130; J. D. Hughes, 'The Drainage Disputes in the Isle of Axholme', *The Lincolnshire Historian*, II, pp. 13–34; cf. pp. 26–8 above, 122 below, and for Erbery see pp. 192–7 below.

39. Ed. J. T. Rutt, *The Parliamentary Diary of Thomas Burton* (1828) I, p. 170.

40. M. Walzer, *The Revolution of the Saints* (Harvard U.P., 1965), esp. pp. 308–16.

41. R. Brome, *The Dramatic Works* (1873) III, p. 376. Played 1641, first published 1652. There are some relevant comments on Brome in Ian Donaldson's *The World Upside-Down* (Oxford U.P., 1970), chapter 4. I am sorry I did not read this interesting book before writing my own.

42. Ed. P. Clark and P. Slack, *Crisis and Order in English Towns, 1500–1700* (1971), p. 154; cf. A. Macfarlane, *The Family Life of Ralph Josselin* (Cambridge U.P., 1970), pp. 89, 114, 205–6, who appears equally sceptical.

43. W. Cradock, *Glad Tidings* (1648), p. 50.

44. N. Cohn, *The Pursuit of the Millennium* (1957), pp. 330–3; pp. 316–17 below.

45. Ed. N. Penney, *Extracts from State Papers relating to Friends* (1913), p. 43; cf. E. Burrough, *The Memorable Works of a Son of Thunder and Consolation* (1672), p. 500; Burton, *Parliamentary Diary*, II, pp. 112–14.

46. Clarkson, *The Lost Sheep Found* (1660) in Cohn, op. cit., p. 346; ibid., p. 332. For Clarkson see pp. 160–62, 316 below.

47. Ed. J. Thirsk and J. P. Cooper, *Seventeenth-Century Economic Documents* (Oxford U.P., 1972), p. 107.

48. Thirsk, *Agrarian History*, pp. xxxv, 11.

49. Pettit, op. cit., p. 133.

50. C. E. Hart, *The Free Miners of the Forest of Dean* (Gloucester, 1953), pp. 174–5.

51. E. R. Foster, *Proceedings in Parliament, 1610* (Yale U.P., 1966) II, pp. 280–81; cf. *Commons Debates, 1621*, ed. W. Notestein, F. H. Relf, and H. Simpson (Yale U.P., 1935) II, p. 332, V, p. 113; W. Notestein, *The House of Commons, 1604–1610* (Yale U.P., 1971), p. 243.

52. Thomas Tenison to Henry Oldenburg, 7 November 1671, in *The Correspondence of Henry Oldenburg* (ed. A. R. and M. B. Hall, Wisconsin U.P.) VIII (1971), p. 345.

53. Quoted in T. G. Barnes, *Somerset, 1625–1640* (1961), p. 151.

54. S. Hartlib, *Londons Charitie Stilling the Poore Orphans Cry*, quoted by Sabine, p. 14.

55. S. Fortrey, *Englands Interest and Improvement* (1663), pp. 19–20; cf. Adam Moore, *Bread for the Poor* (1653), p. 6.

56. E. M. Trotter, *Seventeenth Century Life in the Country Parish* (1919), pp. 135–9.

57. A. Moore, *Bread for the Poor*, p. 39; cf. p. 6.

58. Pseudomismus, *Considerations concerning Common Fields and Enclosure* (1665); John Moore, *The Crying Sin of England of not caring for the poor* (1653), p. 11. Moore was quoting the alleged remark of an advocate of enclosure, but 'Pseudomismus' did not complain that he misrepresented (op. cit., p. 25); cf. also Blith, *The English Improver Improved* (1652), Preface and Appendix.

59. J. Norden, *The Surveyors Dialogue* (1618), pp. 8–11, 113–14; cf. *P. and R.*, p. 190; ed. R. D. Ratcliffe, *The Chorley Survey* (Lancashire and Cheshire Record Soc., vol. 33, 1896), p. 55 seq.

60. B. Osborne, *Justices of the Peace, 1361–1848* (Shaftesbury, 1960), pp. 120–24.

61. See p. 269 below.

62. *P. and R.*, pp. 179, 190–3; Sabine, pp. 363–4, 638; D. A. Johnson and D. G. Vaizey, *Staffordshire and the Great Rebellion* (Stoke-on-Trent, 1964), pp. 26–7, 66–7.

63. A. Moore, op. cit., p. 32; Sabine, p. 506.

64. J. Smith, *Englands Improvement Revived* (1670), p. 18.

65. A. Moore, op. cit., p. 27.

66. S. Hartlib, *Legacy of Husbandry* (1655), p. 43.

67. Ed. K. M. Burton, *A Dialogue Between Reginald Pole and Thomas Lupset* (1948), pp. 140–41.

68. D. Brailsford, *Sport and Society* (1969), p. 9; Boynton, *The Elizabethan Militia*, p. 68.

69. A. Moore, op. cit., p. 7; J. Thirsk, 'Seventeenth Century Agriculture and Social Change', *A.H.R.*, XVIII, Suppl., p. 169.

70. Penry Williams, 'The Activity of the Council in the Marches under the Early Stuarts', *Welsh History Review*, I, p. 141; W. Sheppard, *Englands Balme* (1656), pp. 201–2; Sabine, p. 612.

71. D. H. Pennington, 'Staffordshire in Civil War Politics', *North Staf-fordshire Journal of Field Studies*, V, p. 15. Cf. Sir W. Davenant's poem, 'The Countess of Anglesey lead Captive by the Rebels at the Disforresting of Pewsam', in *Shorter Poems* (ed. A. M. Gibbs, Oxford U.P., 1972), p. 125. This was in 1623–4.

72. Pettit, *Royal Forests*, pp. 47–9, 115, 119, 125.

73. *C.S.P.D., 1654*, pp. 71–2.

74. A. Moore, op. cit., esp. dedication to the Lords of Wastes and Commons; Pseudomismus, op. cit., pp. 37–8; Lee, op. cit., pp. 27–9. Cf. J. Thirsk, 'Seventeenth Century Agriculture and Social Change', pp. 167–9.

75. Sir F. Pollock and F. W. Maitland, *History of English Law* (Cambridge U.P., 1911) I, p. 627.

76. Winstanley, *A Watchword to the City of London and the Army* (1649) in Sabine, p. 322; R. Coster, *A Mite Cast into the Common Treasury* (1649), ibid., p. 656.

77. Chamberlen, *The Poore Mane's Advocate*, pp. 5–6.

78. T. Adams, *Works*, p. 54.

79. G. M. Hipkin, 'Social and Economic Conditions in Holland Division of Lincolnshire', *Reports and Papers of the Architectural Societies of Lincolnshire, Yorkshire, Northamptonshire and Leicestershire*, XL (1930–31), p. 236.

80. R. H. Tawney, *The Agrarian Problem in the Sixteenth Century* (1912), p. 141.

81. Sabine, p. 387.

82. Underdown, op. cit., p. 284. Pyne protected Quakers and other radicals (ibid., pp. 36, 317). Poole was a Ranter centre. But there were limits to Pyne's radicalism; he opposed Levellers and those who threw down the fences of a royalist encloser of the forest (ibid., p. 329).

83. Thirsk and Cooper, *Seventeenth-Century Economic Documents*, pp. 135–40.

84. Ed. E. H. Bates Harbin, *Somerset Quarter Sessions Records, 1646–1660* (Somerset Record Soc., 1912), p. 286.

85. A. H. Johnson, *The Disappearance of the Small Landowner* (Oxford U.P., 1907), p. 47.

86. See p. xv above. The Geneva version, more plausibly, had 'removed like a tent'.

4 AGITATORS AND OFFICERS

1. Thirsk, *Agrarian History*, pp. 435, 562–3, 573.

2. Ed. D. H. Pennington and I. A. Roots, *The Committee at Stafford, 1643–1645* (Manchester U.P., 1957), p. lxii.

3. E. Broxap, *The Great Civil War in Lancashire, 1642–1651* (1910), p. 60.

4. *Mercurius Aulicus*, 13–20 April 1645, p. 1546; A. Clark, *Raglan Castle and the Civil War in Monmouthshire* (Chepstow, 1953), pp. 26, 71.

5. William Sedgwick, *A Second View of the Army Remonstrance* (1649), pp. 5–7; [Anon.] *The Armies Vindication of This Last Change* (1659), pp. 2–6.

6. *Reliquiae Baxterianae*, I, p. 53.

7. See pp. 82–3 below.

8. G. Wither, *The Speech Without Doore* (1644), p. 5.

9. Webster's chaplaincy has been questioned, but he specifically described himself as 'late chaplain in the Army' as well as surgeon in Col. Shuttleworth's regiment (W. S. Weeks, *Clitheroe in the Seventeenth Century*, Clitheroe [n.d., ?1928], p. 176).

10. op. cit., p. 6.

11. Woodhouse, p. 184. See p. 46 below.

12. [F. Cheynell] *An Account Given to the Parliament by the Ministers sent by them to Oxford* (1646[–7]), pp. 13–18; cf. Edwards, *Gangraena*, III, p. 250. For Erbery see pp. 143–7 below.

13. H. Pinnell, *A Word of Prophecy concerning The Parliament, Generall and the Army* (1648), pp. 2–17.

14. Woodhouse, pp. 390–96.

15. T. Collier, *An Answer to a Book written by one Richard Sanders* (1652), p. 41; see p. 144 below.

16. [Anon.] *A Vindication of certaine Citizens* (1646), pp. 6–9. The version of the sermon printed by Dell does not contain the phrase quoted, but suggests that the power of the spirit was in all the saints; cf. my *Antichrist in Seventeenth-Century England*, pp. 97–8, 124.

17. W. Bridge, *The Wounded Conscience Cured* (1642), pp. 4–5, 41–4, 53.

18. E. Bowles, *Plaine English* (1643), pp. 25–6. I owe this reference to the kindness of Professor C. M. Williams.

19. Sabine, pp. 371, 305.

20. Baxter, *The Holy Commonwealth* (1659), p. 231.

21. *Mercurius Politicus*, 87, 29 January–5 February 1652, p. 1385; *The Case of the Commonwealth* (1649), pp. 71, 69, 79. I owe this reference to the kindness of Mr I. McCalman.

22. [Anon.] *Apologie of the Agitators of Eight Regiments of Horse* (28 April 1647); J. Rushworth, *Historical Collections* (1680) VI, p. 479; ed. C. H. Firth, *Clarke Papers* (Camden Soc.) I (1849), p. 7; ed. H. Cary, *Memorials of the Great Civil War* (1842) I, p. 234; *C.J.*, V, p. 345; Francis White, *The Copy of a Letter Sent to His Excellency Sir Thomas Fairfax* (1647), p. 8.

23. [Anon.] *An Apologie of the Soldiers to all their Commission Officers* (1647), quoted by Woodhouse, p. [21].

24. Rushworth, op. cit., VI, p. 485; [Anon.] *The Red-Ribbond – News from the Army* (27 May 1647), p. 5.

25. Lilburne, *Jonahs Cry from the Whales Belly* (1647), p. 14.

26. *The Vindication of the Officers*, in Rushworth, op. cit., VI, p. 469; cf. *Clarke Papers*, I, p. xix: 'Those resolutions to stand for freedom and justice began among the soldiers only'; Woodhouse, pp. 397, 437–8, 453; Wolfe, p. 360.

27. Rushworth, op. cit., VI, p. 498; H. N. Brailsford, *The Levellers and the English Revolution* (1961), p. 96.

28. Whitelocke, op. cit., p. 253.

29. Rushworth, op. cit., VI, p. 514.

30. *Clarke Papers*, I, p. 120; cf. *A True Impartial Narrative* (17 June 1647), p. 3; Lilburne, *An Impeachment of High Treason against Oliver Cromwell* (1649), p. 54; Cary, op. cit., I, p. 224; Gardiner, *Civil War*, III, p. 273; Whitelocke, op. cit., p. 253.

31. Woodhouse, p. 403.

32. Wolfe, pp. 243–6; cf. Fairfax, *Short Memorials*, in *An English Garner*, ed. E. Arber (1895–7) VIII, pp. 569, 572.

33. Brailsford, op. cit., pp. 181, 410–12. The whole of Brailsford's ch. X is relevant.

34. [Anon.] *Londons Lawles Liberty . . . presented to the Adjutators of the Army* (September 1647).

35. C. Walker, *History of Independency* (1661) I, p. 59. First published 1649.

36. G. Unwin, *The Gilds and Companies of London* (1925), pp. 338–9.

37. *Mercurius Anti-Britanicus*, 3 (August 1645); *Mercurius Britanicus*, 17, 42, 63, 130 (1645). I owe these references to the unpublished thesis of Mr Ian McCalman, 'A Study of the Writings of Marchamont Nedham, 1620–1678, Journalist and Medical Writer'.

38. W. Lilly, *The Starry Messenger* (1645), p. 23; cf. *An Astrologicall Prediction* (1648), p. 17.

39. [B.?] Nicholson, *The Lawyers Bane* (1647), p. 5.

40. See pp. 21–2 above.

41. *Walwins Wiles* (1649) in H. and D., pp. 300, 302. Walwyn said that the stories against him were collected in 1646 (*Walwyns Just Defence*, 1649, in ibid., p. 353).

42. Wolfe, p. 184.

43. *Two Letters writ by Lieut-Col. John Lilburne ... to Col. Henry Marten* (1647), p. 6.

44. John Naylier, late Quarter-Master to Captain Bray, *The Newmarket Colonel* (1649), pp. 4–11; *Papers from the Armie* (October 1647).

45. Ed. W. C. Abbott, *Writings and Speeches of Oliver Cromwell* (Yale U.P., 1937–1947) I, p. 507; Wolfe, p. 46.

46. H. and D., pp. 301, 384.

47. Gardiner, op. cit., III, pp. 363, 370; Woodhouse, p. 15. For Bray see pp. 44–6 below.

48. *The Grand Plea of Lieutenant-Colonel John Lilburne* (1647), p. 19.

49. White, *The Copy of a Letter*, pp. 7, 11–12; Gardiner, op. cit., IV, pp. 302–3; Woodhouse, p. 174.

50. Woodhouse, pp. 452–5; Brailsford, op. cit., pp. 288–9; *Papers from the Armie* (October 1647).

51. Gardiner, op. cit., IV, pp. 16–17.

52. Woodhouse, pp. 442, 454.

53. R. L., *The Justice of the Army Against Evil-Doers Vindicated* (1649), pp. 1–4.

54. Whitelocke, op. cit., p. 280. See pp. 45–6, 89, 216–18 below for Eyres, Everard and Thompson. William Thompson had been in trouble over a pub brawl in September 1647, but this may have been a pretext for cashiering him. The soldiers of his regiment stood by him till after Ware (R. L., op. cit., pp. 7–9).

55. Lilburne, *The Juglers Discovered* (1 October 1647).

56. [Wildman] *Putney Projects* (1647), p. 27; *Letter from the Agitators of the Five Regiments of Horse* (28 October 1647); *Letter from the Agitators of the Army* (11 November 1647); Woodhouse, p. 452.

57. Brailsford, op. cit., pp. 342–3; Underdown, op. cit., pp. 268, 298.

58. Underdown, op. cit., pp. 118–19; Abbott, op. cit., I, p. 698.

59. [Anon.] *A Modest Narrative of Intelligence* (5–12 May 1649). For 1659–60 see p. 267 below.

60. Woodhouse, p. 438.

61. Rushworth, op. cit., VII, pp. 944–5.

62. Firth, *Essays Historical and Literary*, p. 130.

63. T. Collier, *A Vindication of the Army Remonstrance* (n.d., ?1649), sig. A 2, p. 26; W. Erbery, *The Lord of Hosts: or, God guarding the Camp of the Saints* (1653) in *The Testimony of William Erbery* (1658), pp. 25–42.

64. Wolfe, pp. 237, 276.

65. Walker, *History of Independency*, I, p. 140.

5 THE NORTH AND WEST

1. See my 'Puritans and "the dark corners of the land" ', *T.R.H.S.*, 1963, pp. 77–102; 'Propagating the Gospel', in *Historical Essays, 1600–1750*, ed. H. E. Bell and R. L. Ollard (1963), pp. 35–59; *S. and P.*, pp. 186–9, 202.

2. Lord Brooke, *A Discourse opening the Nature of that Episcopacie which is exercised in England* (1641) in Haller, *Tracts on Liberty*, II, p. 151.

3. Baxter, *The Holy Commonwealth*, p. 90.

4. *The Testimony of William Erbery*, p. 126; cf. pp. 135–7, 140; T. Rees, *History of Protestant Nonconformity in Wales* (2nd edn, 1883), p. 67.

5. B. R. White, 'The Organization of the Particular Baptists, 1646–1660', *Journal of Ecclesiastical History*, XVII, pp. 210–12.

6. Burrough, *Works*, p. 11; cf. sig. e 3, and epigraph to this chapter; cf. G. Fox, *Mans Coming up from the North* (1653).

7. [Anon.] *A Brief Narrative of the Irreligion of the Northern Quakers* (1653); E. Pagitt, *Heresiography* (5th edn, 1654), p. 136.

8. P. Hobson, *Fourteen Queries* (1655), Preface; *Fenstanton Records*, p. 352.

9. *Mr Peters Last Report of the English Warres* (1646), p. 13; Rees, *Protestant Nonconformity in Wales*, pp. 90–93; cf. D. Mathew, 'Wales and England in the early 17th century', *Trans. Hon. Soc. of Cymmrodorion*, 1955, p. 38.

10. G. Fox, *The Short Journal* (Cambridge U.P., 1921), p. 42; M. Coate, *Cornwall in the Great Civil War* (Oxford U.P., 1933), pp. 347–8; Braithwaite, pp. 206–10, 232–40, 385; ed. E. B. Underhill, *The Records of the Church meeting in Broadmead, Bristol, 1640–1687* (Hanserd Knollys Soc., 1847), pp. 515–17.

11. R. Marchant, *The Church under the Law* (Cambridge U.P., 1969), ch. 2 and 4, pp. 195–203, 230.

12. [F. Cheynell] *An Account Given to the Parliament*, p. 34.

13. Edwards, *Gangraena* (1646) I, pp. 123, 125, 216; II, p. 122; III, pp. 41, 52–3; Underdown, op. cit., p. 14; cf. my 'Propagating the Gospel', p. 55, and p. 31 above.

14. H. Palmer, *The Duty and Honour of Church Restorers* (1646), pp. 42–7.

15. *Mercurius Politicus*, 23 (7–14 November 1650), pp. 331–2. I owe this reference to Mr McCalman; cf. R. Howell, *Newcastle upon Tyne and the Puritan Revolution* (Oxford U.P., 1967), pp. 218–22.

16. C. Walker, *History of Independency*, Part II, p. 156.

17. K. H. D. Haley, *The First Earl of Shaftesbury* (Oxford U.P., 1968), p. 97.

18. Stone, 'The Educational Revolution', *P. and P.*, 28, p. 47.

19. W. Notestein, *English Folk* (1938), p. 275.

20. Dickens, *Lollards and Protestants in the Diocese of York, passim*; Thomson, *The Later Lollards, passim*; H. Barbour, *The Quakers in Puritan England* (Yale U.P., 1964), p. 86. See pp. 11–12, 28–9 above.

21. See pp. 55–8 below.

22. J. F. Chanter, *The Life and Times of Martin Blake* (1910), p. 52.

23. Clarendon, *History of the Rebellion*, II, pp. 461, 464, 470–72; III, pp. 80, 129–30; V, p. 472.

24. *P. and R.*, pp. 21–3, 207–8; ed. C. Hill and E. Dell, *The Good Old Cause* (1949), pp. 239, 249–54, 278–9.

25. I. Tullie, *A Narrative of the Siege of Carlisle*, in *Carlisle Tracts*, ed. S. Jefferson (1840), pp. 1–3.

26. Dell, *Several Sermons*, p. 79.

27. R. C. Richardson, *Puritanism in North-Western England: A Regional Study of the Diocese of Chester to 1642* (1972), *passim*.

28. Professor Underdown comments on the disproportionate incidence of political radicalism among members of the Long Parliament from Yorkshire, Durham and Northumberland (op. cit., pp. 228–9).

29. Thirsk, *Agrarian History*, pp. 757–60, 789; '17th century agriculture and social change', pp. 170–76; my *Reformation to Industrial Revolution*, p. 138.

30. B. G. Blackwood, 'The Lancashire Cavaliers and their Tenants', *Transactions of the Historical Soc. of Lancashire and Cheshire*, vol. 117; 'Agrarian Unrest and the Early Lancashire Quakers', *Journal of the Friends' Historical Soc.*, LI, pp. 72–6. I have had the advantage

of reading Mr Blackwood's Oxford B.Litt. thesis, 'Social and Religious Aspects of the History of Lancashire, 1635–1655'.

31. *The Moderate*, 22–9 May 1649; *C.S.P.D., 1649–50*, p. 385. I owe the first reference to Mr Blackwood's thesis.

32. G. Fox, *Journal* (1902), I, p. 301.

33. White, 'The Organization of the Particular Baptists, 1646–1660', pp. 209–13; cf. C. E. Whiting, *Studies in English Puritanism from the Restoration to the Revolution* (1931), pp. 98, 117, 255.

34. B. Capp, *The Fifth Monarchy Men: A Study in Seventeenth-Century Millenarianism* (1972), pp. 76–7, 79, 206–7.

35. See my 'Propagating the Gospel', p. 56; Howell, *Newcastle upon Tyne*, pp. 245–7; *V.C.H., Cumberland*, II, pp. 94–5.

36. Burton, *Parliamentary Diary*, I, p. 155.

37. S. Rutherford, *A Survey of the Spirituall Antichrist* (1648), p. 194. For Saltmarsh see A. L. Morton, *The World of the Ranters*, pp. 45–69.

38. R. C. Bald, *John Donne* (Oxford U.P., 1970), p. 22.

39. *I.O.E.R.*, p. 65.

40. C. Webster, 'Henry Power's Experimental Philosophy', *Ambix*, XV, pp. 157–9; 'Richard Towneley, the Towneley Group and Seventeenth-Century Science', *Transactions of the Historical Soc. of Lancashire and Cheshire*, vol. 118, pp. 51–76. We should add John Webster again.

41. Mr Charles Hobday, however, reminds me of the Plymouth Brethren.

42. R. Marchant, *The Puritans and the Church Courts in the Diocese of York* (1960), pp. 40–41, 46.

43. ibid., pp. 40–41, 127–8. Webster dedicated his *Examen Academiarum* to Lambert in 1654. See pp. 37 above, 57–8, 146 below for Webster.

44. op. cit., p. 91.

45. W. S. Weeks, *Clitheroe in the Seventeenth Century* (Clitheroe, n.d., ?1928), p. 176.

46. Ed. R. H. Tawney and E. Power, *Tudor Economic Documents* (1953) I, pp. 81–4.

47. Marchant, op. cit., p. 47; Thomas Sippell, *Zur Vorgeschichte des Quäkertums* (Giessen, 1920), pp. 24–30.

48. Sippell, op. cit., pp. 50–55.

49. 'Autobiography of Thomas Shepard', *Publications of the Colonial Soc. of Massachusetts*, XXVII (1927–30), pp. 362–3.

50. G. F. Nuttall, *The Holy Spirit in Puritan Faith and Experience* (Oxford, 1946), pp. 178–80.

51. Pagitt, *Heresiography* (1654), p. 87. For a definition of the Eternal Decrees see p. 126 below.

52. See p. 162 below.

53. Sippell, op. cit., p. 49; ed. G. F. Nuttall, *Early Quaker Letters from the Swarthmore MSS. to 1660* (duplicated, 1952), p. 229.

54. R. Brearley, *Poems,* p. 94, in *A Bundle of Soul convincing ... and Comforting Truths* (1677).

55. R. M. Jones, *Mysticism and Democracy in the English Commonwealth* (Harvard U.P., 1932), p. 79. See p. 36 above for support for Parliament from this area.

6 A NATION OF PROPHETS

1. A. Evans, *The Bloudy Vision of John Farley* (1653), p. 39.

2. A. Macfarlane, *Witchcraft in Tudor and Stuart England* (1970), pp. 201–6, 244–52; *The Family Life of Ralph Josselin* (Cambridge U.P., 1970), pp. 176–7, 193; Thomas, op. cit., esp. pp. 638–40. See p. 253 below.

3. *I.O.E.R.*, p. 149.

4. Aubrey, *Brief Lives*, I, p. 27.

5. Thomas, op. cit., esp. ch. 9.

6. S. Clarke, *Lives of Thirty-two English Divines* (1677), p. 76.

7. Ed. C. H. Josten, *Elias Ashmole, 1617–1692* (Oxford U.P., 1966) I, pp. 21–2.

8. H. F. Fletcher, *The Intellectual Development of John Milton* (Illinois U.P.) II (1961), p. 557; H. Rusche, 'Merlini Anglici: Astrology and Propaganda from 1644 to 1651', *E.H.R.*, LXXX, pp. 322–33.

9. Thomas, op. cit., pp. 294, 343.

10. See ch. 14 below.

11. T. Fuller, *Church History of Great Britain* (1655) II, p. 396; J. Hacket, *Scrinia Reserata* (1692) II, p. 226.

12. Ed. P. Toon, *Puritans, the Millennium and the Future of Israel* (Cambridge, 1970), p. 111.

13. W. Lilly, *A Collection of Ancient and Modern Prophecies* (1645).

14. Lilly, *Prophetical Merlin* (1644), p. 24; *Supernatural Sights and Apparitions* (1644), sig. Av, A 2.

15. Rusche, op. cit., pp. 325, 332.

16. A. Evans, *The Voice of King Charls* (1655), p. 41.

17. Lilly, *Supernatural Sights and Apparitions*, pp. 47–8; *A Prophecy of the White King*, p. 6; *The Starry Messenger* (1645), p. 23; *An Astrological Prediction of the Occurrences in England* (1648), p. 17.

NOTES

18. Lilly, *Annus Tenebrosus* (1652), p. 40.

19. J. Ridley, *John Knox* (Oxford U.P., 1968), pp. 409, 451, 519.

20. Selden, *Table Talk* (1847), p. 185.

21. Hobbes, *English Works*, VI, p. 399; cf. T. Sprat, *History of the Royal Society* (1667), pp. 364–5, quoted on p. 273 below.

22. G. Leff, 'The Mythology of a True Church', Papers presented to the *P. and P.* Conference on Popular Religion, July 1966, pp. 6–10.

23. This is suggested by Sir Francis Hubert, *Poems*, ed. B. Mellor (Hong Kong U.P., 1961), pp. 83–4.

24. cf. Peele's *Edward I*, in which Llewellyn is, in a very similar way, fooled by a prophecy (ed. A. Dyce, *Dramatic and Poetical Works of Robert Greene and George Peele*, 1861, p. 410).

25. E. L. Eisenstein, 'The Advent of Printing and the Problems of the Renaissance', *P. and P.*, 45, pp. 78–9.

26. See my *God's Englishman: Oliver Cromwell and the English Revolution* (1970), p. 223.

27. See my *Antichrist in Seventeenth-Century England, passim*. For Hobbes see Appendix I below.

28. cf. pp. 226–9 below.

29. Macfarlane, *Josselin*, p. 24; cf. J. Bunyan, *Works*, ed. G. Offor (1860) III, p. 711; *Mercurius Politicus*, No. 34, 1656, p. 7366.

30. A. Evans, *An Eccho to the Voice of Heaven* (1653), p. 17.

31. W. Y. Tindall, *John Bunyan, Mechanick Preacher* (New York, 1964), *passim*; A. Evans, *The Bloudy Vision of John Farley*, sig. A 8.

32. Dell, *Several Sermons*, p. 144: cf. Dell, *Power from on High* (1645), p. 18. I owe this reference to Mr Charles Webster.

33. A. Evans, *A Voice from Heaven to the Common-Wealth of England* (1652), pp. 27, 33, 45.

34. cf. pp. 286–7 below.

35. W. Lamont, *Godly Rule* (1969), *passim*; *P. and R.*, p. 313; Ralegh, *History of the World* (1820) I, p. 204; W. Chillingworth, *Works* (Oxford U.P., 1838) III, p. 300; cf. pp. 369–82.

36. R. Baillie, *Letters and Journals* (1775) II, p. 156. A translation of Joseph Mede's *The Key of the Revelation* was published in 1643, by order of a committee of the House of Commons, with Preface by the Prolocutor of the Westminster Assembly of Divines. The translation was made by an M.P. (see my *Antichrist in Seventeenth-Century England*, p. 28).

37. Milton, *Complete Prose Works* (Yale edn) I, p. 616.

38. See my *Antichrist in Seventeenth-Century England, passim*.

39. P. Toon, op. cit., p. 218.

40. J. Spittlehouse, *Rome Ruin'd by Whitehall* (1650), p. 339; A. Evans, *An Eccho to the Voice from Heaven* [n.d., ?1653], p. 115.

41. Underhill, *Church meeting in Broadmead, Bristol*, p. 60.

42. Macfarlane, *Josselin*, pp. 23–4, 185, 189–91; J. Tillinghast, *Generation-work*, Part III (1654), pp. 73, 156, 226–49. Tillinghast died in 1655.

43. Bunyan, *Works*, III, p. 722.

44. Quoted by B. S. Capp, in Toon, op. cit., p. 73; cf. p. 91 below.

45. Nuttall, *The Welsh Saints, 1640–1660* (Cardiff, 1957), pp. 46, 70–71.

46. Braithwaite, p. 147. See p. 184 below.

47. Edwards, *Gangraena*, I, pp. 153–4, 187–9; III, pp. 261–2, 267.

48. Ed. Sir C. Petrie, *Letters of Charles I* (1935), pp. 200–206; G. Goodman, *The Court of King James* (1839) I, p. 421; H. Peter, *Good Work for a Good Magistrate* (1651), p. 11.

49. cf. Dell, *Several Sermons*, pp. 264–6, 273–4.

50. S. Fisher, *Christianismus Redivivus* (1655), p. 201. For Fisher see ch. 11 below.

51. Dell, op. cit., pp. 20, 26–7, 33–5, 60, 64.

52. ibid., p. 142. It is hardly surprising that the House of Commons did not invite him to print this sermon. He printed it nevertheless.

53. Quoted by John Forster, *Historical and Biographical Essays* (1858) I, p. 34.

54. Lilburne, *Come out of her my people* (Amsterdam, 1639), p. 19.

55. See esp. W. K. Jordan, *History of Religious Toleration in England* (4 vols., 1932–40); Woodhouse, Wolfe, and Haller, *Liberty and Reformation in the Puritan Revolution* (Columbia U.P., 1955), *passim*.

56. T. Case, *Spiritual Whordome discovered in a sermon before the House of Commons* (1647), p. 34.

57. [Anon.] *The Poore-Mans admonition unto all the Plain People of London*, quoted by D. W. Petegorsky, *Left-Wing Democracy in the English Civil War* (1940), p. 113.

58. Ed. M. H. Lee, *Diaries and Letters of Philip Henry* (1882), p. 277.

59. Sabine, pp. 445–6; cf. pp. 94–5 below.

60. [Anon.] *The Ancient Bounds, or Liberty of Conscience* (1645) in Woodhouse, p. 258.

61. Roger Williams, *The Bloudy Tenent of Persecution* (Hanserd Knollys Soc., 1848), p. 46.

62. Dell, op. cit., pp. 185, 246.

63. See pp. 14–17 above.

64. [Anon.] *The Spiritual Courts Epitomized* (1641), p. 1.

65. Edwards, *Gangraena*, III, p. 173; *Portland MSS*. (H.M.C.) III, p. 156.

66. [Francis Cheynell] *An Account Given to the Parliament by the Ministers sent by them to Oxford* (1646[-7]), pp. 13, 18; J. G., *Independency Gods Verity* (1647) in Woodhouse, p. 186.

67. [Walwyn] *The Vanitie of the Present Churches* (1649) in H. and D., pp. 257, 263-4; Lilburne, *Legal Fundamental Liberties* (1649), p. 39.

68. Wolfe, pp. 140, 405, 408.

69. E. Pagitt, *Heresiography* (1654), p. 146.

70. Erbery, *Testimony*, pp. 42, 53, 90-91, 306-7. This last had been the view of the Grindletonians: see p. 56 above.

71. Underdown, op. cit., p. 275.

72. Jordan, *History of Religious Toleration in England*, IV, pp. 320-21, 330, 351, 360.

73. J. F. Maclear, 'Popular Anti-clericalism in the Puritan Revolution', *Journal of the History of Ideas*, XVI, p. 452.

74. Burrough, *Works*, pp. 515-16.

75. Baxter, *The Holy Commonwealth*, pp. 92-4, 226-9.

76. J. Saltmarsh, *The Smoke in the Temple* (1646), sig. xx 5.

77. Winstanley, *The Breaking of the Day of God* (1648), p. 58.

78. J. Spittlehouse, *The First Addresses* (1653), p. 13.

79. J. Nayler, *The old Serpents Voice, or Antichrist discovered* [n.d., ?1656], p. 5; cf. R[ichard] F[arnsworth], *An Easter-Reckoning: . . . the difference of the Ministry of Christ and the Ministry of the world or of Antichrist* (1656), *passim*.

80. J. Robinson, *The Peoples Plea for the Exercise of Prophecie* (1618) in *Works* (1851) III, pp. 290-98, 305-6, 325-35.

81. J. Cotton, *The True Constitution of a Particular Visible Church Proved by Scripture* (1642), quoted by L. Ziff, *The Career of John Cotton* (Princeton U.P., 1962), p. 185. The word prophesying reminds us of those exercises in the Elizabethan church to which the Queen took such strong exception that she suspended Archbishop Grindal. Her fear was of participation by the laity. How prescient she was!

82. Dell, op. cit., pp. 273-5.

83. Edwards, *Gangraena*, I, pp. 116-19, 126.

84. Barclay, *The Inner Life of the Religious Societies of the Commonwealth* (1876), pp. 296, 290.

85. Edwards, *Gangraena*, I, pp. 97-8. Ranters were also accused of interrupting church services (*Mercurius Politicus*, Nos. 245 and 246, 1654, pp. 5142, 5164).

86. *Extracts from State Papers relating to Friends*, p. 41 – a Quaker petition of 1658. See note 88 below.

87. Fox, *Journal*, I, pp. 160, 184–5; Barclay, *Inner Life*, pp. 281–7.

88. This was the Act of Parliament referred to in note 86 above. Quakers were normally prosecuted, for causing disturbances, under this Act or under the Vagrancy Act of 1656. There was no special legislation against them before 1660 (*State Papers relating to Friends*, p. 345).

7 LEVELLERS AND TRUE LEVELLERS

1. See p. 8 above.

2. W. G. Hoskins, 'Harvest Fluctuations and English Economic History, 1620–1759', *A. H. R.*, XVI, pp. 15–31; cf. Underdown, op. cit., pp. 90–97, 281–2.

3. *V.C.H., York*, p. 172.

4. Wolfe, pp. 71, 278.

5. [Anon.] *Salus Populi Solus Rex*, quoted by Brailsford, op. cit., pp. 345–6; cf. Wildman, quoted on p. 45 above.

6. [Anon.] *The Humble Representation of the Desires of the Soldiers and Officers of the Regiment of Horse for the County of Northumberland*. See p. 84 below for this pamphlet.

7. Chamberlen, *The Poore Mans Advocate*, p. 2.

8. Underdown, op. cit., p. 281; Wolfe, p. 371.

9. Sabine, pp. 627–40. See p. 84 below.

10. Petegorsky, op. cit., p. 160.

11. Ed. E. Hockliffe, *Diary of the Rev. Ralph Josselin, 1616–1683* (Camden Soc., XV, 1908), p. 70.

12. See pp. 156–9 below.

13. Walker, *History of Independency*, Part II, pp. 152–3. See p. 141 below.

14. Petegorsky, op. cit., p. 172.

15. cf. *S. and P.*, p. 213.

16. *The Kingdomes Faithfull and Impartiall Scout*, 20–27 April 1649, quoted by Petegorsky, op. cit., p. 164. Thorns and briars symbolized 'the wisdom and power of selfish flesh' (Sabine, p. 237) which Winstanley's *Fire in the Bush* would consume.

17. *Clarke Papers*, III, p. 211.

18. MS. Harley 164 f. 96v. I owe this reference to the kindness of Professor C. M. Williams.

19. W. Blith, *The English Improver Improved* (1652), sig. C 3; cf. *V.C.H.*, *Surrey*, III, p. 467, and Sabine, p. 260.

20. E. Arber, *An Introductory Sketch to the Martin Marprelate Controversy* (1895), pp. 81, 95; Collinson, *The Elizabethan Puritan Movement*, p. 492. When the press was driven from Kingston the printers withdrew to Fawsley in Northamptonshire, twenty-odd miles from Wellingborough, for which see p. 89 below.

21. Collinson, op. cit., pp. 353, 389.

22. D. Masson, *Life of John Milton*, I (1875), p. 150. cf. p. 8 above.

23. *C.S.P.D., 1635*, p. xliv.

24. H. Cary, *Memorials of the Civil War*, I, p. 120; *Portland MSS.* (H.M.C.) I, p. 480; Gardiner, *Great Civil War*, III, p. 350; Wolfe, p. 208; Abbott, op. cit., I, pp. 496, 561.

25. *Portland MSS.*, III, p. 201; C. H. Firth, *The House of Lords in the Civil War* (1910), p. 233.

26. Barclay, *Inner Life*, p. 343; ed. N. Penney, *The First Publishers of Truth* (1907), p. 167; J. Besse, *An Abstract of the Sufferings of . . . Quakers* (1733) I, pp. 252–4.

27. Burrough, *Works*, p. 234.

28. Sabine, p. 315; cf. pp. 92–3 below.

29. *A Modest Narrative*, 28 April 1649, quoted by Abbott, op. cit., II, p. 58. The journalist who reported the incident wrongly thought the Diggers had already 'left their new plantation'.

30. W. Style, *Reports* (1658), pp. 166, 360; Sabine, pp. 20–21, 360, 432.

31. L. Clarkson, *A General Charge* (1647). See pp. 160–62 below.

32. H. Denne, *The Levellers Designe Discovered* (1649), p. 8, quoted by R. Howell and D. E. Brewster, 'Reconsidering the Levellers', *P. and P.*, 46, p. 69. Denne's remark seems in fact to have been made about the New Model Army rather than about the Levellers.

33. By the Soviet historian, Professor M. A. Barg, *Lower-Class Popular Movements in the English Bourgeois Revolution of the 17th Century* (Moscow, 1967), in Russian.

34. See pp. 42–5 above.

35. E. Spenser, *The Fairie Queen*, Book II, canto 9, stanza 13; Book IV, canto 1, stanza 28; Book V, canto 2, stanzas 35–52; canto 11, stanzas 57–9; W. Shakespeare, *Coriolanus*, Act II, scene iii; *Henry VI, Part II*, Act IV, *passim*. For evidence of the continuity of this tradition, see my 'The Many-Headed Monster', pp. 297–303.

36. T. Cooper, *An Admonition to the People of England*, 1589, ed. E. Arber (1895), p. 118; cf. pp. 144–5, 148, 159, 168–9.

37. Edwards, *Gangraena*, I, p. 34; II, pp. 150–51; III, p. 16.

38. P. Chamberlen, *A Voice in Rhama* (1647), pp. 49–59.

39. Ed. J. A. F. Bekkers, *Correspondence of John Morris with Johannes de Laet* (Assen, 1970), pp. 122, 149; cf. p. 37 above.

40. W. K. Jordan, *Edward VI: The Young King* (1968), p. 433.

41. Gardiner, *Great Civil War*, III, p. 370.

42. [Anon.] *Tyranipocrit Discovered* (Rotterdam, 1649) in *British Pamphleteers*, I, ed. G. Orwell and R. Reynolds (1948), pp. 84–6, 96, 108.

43. A. Coppe, *A Fiery Flying Roll*, Part II (1649) in N. Cohn, *The Pursuit of the Millennium* (1957), p. 372. For Coppe see pp. 156–9 below.

44. C. H. Firth, *Cromwell's Army* (1902), p. 408. See pp. 155–6, 243 below.

45. K. V. Thomas, op. cit., pp. 403, 407; cf. Brailsford, op. cit., pp. 239, 265, and my 'The Many-Headed Monster', p. 300.

46. Fuller, *Church History of Britain* (1842) I, p. 451.

47. Verney Correspondence, cited by A. M. Johnson, 'Buckinghamshire 1640–1660: A Study in County Politics' (unpublished Welsh M.A. thesis, 1965), pp. 16, 261–3; cf. *Memoirs of the Verney Family in the Seventeenth Century*, ed. F. P. and M. M. Verney (1892–9), III, p. 221.

48. Sabine, p. 611.

49. See p. 77 above.

50. Quoted by Petegorsky, op. cit., p. 139. Note the order – soldiers first, officers following.

51. Petegorsky, op. cit., pp. 165, 170.

52. [Anon.] *The King of Scots Declaration* (1649).

53. [Anon.] *The Discoverer* (1649), pp. 9–15.

54. Lilburne, *A Whip for the Present House of Lords* (February, 1647–8); H. and D., p. 449. The Congregational Societies of London in 1647, John Cook and Henry Parker in 1648, also found it necessary to dissociate themselves from theories of communism (*A Declaration by Congregational Societies in and about the City of London*, November 1647; Petegorsky, op. cit., p. 150).

55. Wolfe, p. 288.

56. Quoted by Petegorsky, op. cit., pp. 161–2.

57. Wolfe, pp. 194–5. *The Case of the Armie* in October 1647 called for restoration to the 'ancient public use and service of the poor' of 'all the ancient rights and donations belonging to the poor, now embezzled and converted to other uses, as enclosed commons, almshouses, etc.' (H. and D., p. 113): repeated by John Coates, 'a present member of the navy', in *A Glasse of Truth* (1649), p. 27.

NOTES

58. *A Petition from the Agitators of Colonel Richs Regiment* (1648), p. 5.
59. H. and D., pp. 302–3; Wolfe, p. 178.
60. H. and D., p. 374; Haller, *Tracts on Liberty*, II, p. 275; cf. p. 230. Overton may refer to the anonymous *Short History of the Anabaptists of High and Low Germany* (1642), which made the statistically improbable statement that 'there was not one woman of 14 years of age but was violated' during the commune of Münster (p. 25). Walwyn certainly had read it (Haller, op. cit., III, p. 100).
61. *The Moderate*, 41, 17–24 April 1649, pp. 409, 416–21, 424, quoted by J. Frank, *The Beginnings of the English Newspaper, 1620–1660* (Harvard U.P., 1961), p. 179; Howell and Brewster, op. cit., pp. 75–86.
62. Ed. R. W. Blencowe, *Sydney Papers* (1825), pp. 78, 94.
63. This had been suggested by Don M. Wolfe in *Milton in the Puritan Revolution* (New York, 1941), p. 324.
64. Sabine, pp. 282, 348, 393, 434.
65. Brailsford, op. cit., pp. 355–6; *C.S.P.D., 1649–50*, p. 385.
66. [Anon.] *The Discoverer* (1649), pp. 9–15.
67. See pp. 90–91 below.
68. C. B. Macpherson, *The Political Theory of Possessive Individualism* (Oxford U.P., 1962), pp. 154–9. Professor Macpherson's critics have suggested that he depicts the Levellers as altogether too monolithic in outlook. Professor Barg's explanation could serve to reconcile the two positions.
69. J. D. Hughes, 'The Drainage Disputes in the Isle of Axholme', *The Lincolnshire Historian*, II, pp. 13–34.
70. Abbott, op. cit., III, pp. 184, 435–6.
71. *The unanimous declaration of Colonel Scroops and Commissary-General Iretons Regiments* (1649).
72. N. Homes, *A Sermon Preached Before ... Thomas Foote* (1650), p. 32; cf. p. 181 below.
73. W. Hartley, *The Prerogative Passing Bell* (1651), pp. 9–10.
74. Blith, *The English Improver Improved*, sig. C 3.
75. J. Harrington, *Works* (1737), p. 166; cf. pp. 264–5, 502.
76. R. Crab, *The English Hermit* (1655) in *Harleian Miscellany* (1744–6) IV, p. 462. See also p. 292 below.
77. Winstanley, *Englands Spirit Unfoulded* (1650), ed. G. E. Aylmer, in *P. and P.*, 40, pp. 3–15. Not in Sabine; cf. p. 262 below.
78. Orwell and Reynolds, op. cit., p. 56.
79. Sabine says Cox Hill, five miles north-west of Dover, but if there was a Digger community in Kent one would expect it to be in or near the

Weald. One possibility is Cox Heath, near Linton, on the road from Maidstone to the Weald. Cox Heath was not enclosed until the nineteenth century; cricket was played there in 1646. Another possibility is Cock Hill, between Maidstone and Chatham, close to a radical Brownist group at Boxley, and itself later known for its robbers and poachers. (I am indebted to Mr and Mrs Peter Clark for this suggestion.) It may even be worth considering whether Kent is not a slip, or a misprint, for Essex, where Coggeshall was a well-known radical centre, often spelt Cox Hall in the seventeenth century. The Iver pamphlet's reference to Cox Hall, Kent, may have been copied from Winstanley's one mention of Cox Hall in *An Appeale to all Englishmen* (Sabine, p. 411). The strongest argument for Kent is the pamphlet mentioned on p. 90 below, but this is not conclusive.

80. Thomas, 'Another Digger Broadside', *P. and P.*, 40, p. 59. The common lands at Dunstable had been noted by Walter Blith as ripe for improvement (*The English Improver*, 1649, pp. 90–91).

81. Strype, *Life of Whitgift* (Oxford U.P., 1822) II, p. 11; S. Palmer, *The Nonconformists' Memorial* (1775) II, p. 235; A. G. Mathews, *Calamy Revised* (Oxford U.P., 1934), pp. 11–12.

82. Edwards, *Gangraena*, I, p. 215; II, p. 173; [Ryves] *Angliae Ruina*, pp. 51–7.

83. Sabine, pp. 649–51; *C.S.P.D., 1650*, p. 106.

84. W. Deusbury, *The Discovery Of the great enmity of the Serpent against the seed of the Woman* (1655), pp. 9–10; *True Prophecie of the Mighty Day of the Lord* (1655); *First Publishers of Truth*, pp. 194, 197–9; *Sufferings of the Quakers*, I, pp. 176–9, 186–7, 190–91; Fox, *Journal*, I, p. 250; Barclay, *Inner Life*, p. 313; Braithwaite, p. 174.

85. Ed. Joan Wake, *Northamptonshire Quarter Sessions Records, 1630 and 1657–8* (Northamptonshire Record Soc., 1924), p. 136; *Sufferings of the Quakers*, I, pp. 446–8; cf. pp. 171, 180–81 below.

86. D. G. C. Allan, 'The Rising in the West, 1628–1631', *Economic History Review*, Second Series, V, pp. 82, 84; *C.S.P.D., 1650*, p. 218; J. Smyth, *A Description of the Hundred of Berkeley* (1785), p. 328. But then Smyth sighed nostalgically for the good old days of villeinage (ibid., p. 43).

87. K. V. Thomas, 'Another Digger Broadside'.

88. See p. 84 above.

89. V. F. Snow, *Essex the Rebel* (Nebraska U.P., 1970), p. 198; J. M. Patrick, 'William Covell and the troubles at Enfield in 1659; a sequel to the Digger movement', *University of Toronto Quarterly*, XIV

(1944–5), pp. 45–57. Colonel Joyce was among the intending purchasers at Enfield. See pp. 266–7 below.

90. Fox, *Journal*, II, p. 396, and *passim*.

91. Sabine, pp. 440–41; Petegorsky, op. cit., p. 163. Dunstable and Wycombe (also visited) were parishes in which the Feoffees for Impropriations had bought patronage; the curate whom they presented to Dunstable subsequently emigrated to New England (I. M. Calder, *Activities of the Puritan Faction of the Church of England, 1625–1633*, 1957, esp. pp. 45, 47, 56).

92. For Colnbrook, see Thomas, 'Another Digger Broadside', pp. 59–60. In September 1647 the Leveller William Thompson, subsequently killed near Wellingborough, was in trouble at Colnbrook (see pp. 15, 44–5 above). Connection with Harrow depends on a curious story which Morrison Davidson attributed to the Rev. Thomas Hancock of Harrow, to whose 'profound knowledge of the commonwealth' Berens also paid tribute. This says that in 1652 Winstanley 'started out from Harrow-on-the-Hill; got as far as Nottingham, where he was "run in" by the myrmidons of "law and order", and disappears' (M. Davidson, *The Wisdom of Winstanley*, 1904, p. 25; L. H. Berens, *The Digger Movement in the Days of the Commonwealth*, 1906, p. 148). The tale would fit the summer of 1650 better than 1652. Hancock, a Laudian socialist (cf. his *The Puritans and the Tithes*, 1905), may have had access to some source now missing. Confirmation is suggested by the existence of a Digger colony in Nottinghamshire, and by the allegation that Winstanley invaded the parish of Fenny Drayton (the birthplace of George Fox) at about this time and had discussions with the minister there, Nathaniel Stephens (Stephens, *A Plaine and Easie Calculation of . . . the Name of the Beast*, 1656, pp. 267–71; *D.N.B.*, Stephens). Stephens tells us that his pamphlet was 'finished certain years ago' (p. 295).

93. *Fenstanton Records*, p. 269. The name Warboys suggests a wooded district. There had been famous witches at Warboys in 1593. For Foster see pp. 167–9 below.

94. *Fenstanton Records*, p. v; P. Hardacre, 'Gerrard Winstanley in 1650', *Huntington Library Quarterly*, XXII, pp. 345–9. Lady Eleanor, an eccentric personality who regarded herself as a prophetess, deserves more space than she can be given here. See T. Spencer, 'The History of an Unfortunate Lady', *Harvard Studies and Notes in Philology and Literature*, X, pp. 43–59, and p. 212 below.

95. *The Perfect Diurnall*, 1–8 April 1650, quoted by Tindall, *John Bunyan, Mechanick Preacher*, p. 255; *Fenstanton Records*, pp. 269–71. For Fifth Monarchists see pp. 67–9 above.

96. W. S. Hudson, 'Gerrard Winstanley and the Early Quakers', *Church History*, XII, pp. 191–4.

97. Sabine, pp. 200, 304, 356; Thomas, 'Another Digger Broadside', p. 58.

98. Sabine, pp. 408, 414; Hoskins, 'Harvest Fluctuations in English Economic History, 1620–1759', p. 29.

99. R. Coster, *A Mite Cast into the Common Treasury* (1649) in Sabine, p. 657.

100. Sabine, pp. 307–8, 322–3; cf. p. 420. See pp. 34–5 above.

101. ibid., pp. 414, 507; cf. E. G., *Wast Lands Improvement* [n.d., ?1653], pp. 1–7.

102. Sabine, pp. 190, 194, 262. For visions see pp. 222–3 below.

103. Thomas, 'Another Digger Broadside', p. 58; Thirsk, 'Seventeenth Century Agriculture and Economic Change', p. 166.

104. E. Kerridge, *The Agricultural Revolution* (1967), chs. VII and VIII.

105. Sabine, pp. 428, 558.

106. ibid., pp. 433, 272–4.

107. ibid., pp. 363, 557–8, 560.

108. Lee, *A Vindication of regulated Enclosure*, pp. 27–8; cf. p. 71 above.

109. Sabine, pp. 390–91, 454, 471.

110. ibid., pp. 251–2, 269.

111. ibid., pp. 321, 519–20, 288.

112. ibid., pp. 303, 390. For the Norman Yoke, cf. *P. and R.*, pp. 50–122.

113. Sabine, pp. 357, 381–2; cf. pp. 484–6.

114. ibid., pp. 573–4.

115. ibid., p. 292; cf. p. 259, and pp. 105–6 below.

116. Sabine, pp. 316, 519–20, 595–6; cf. pp. 191–2 and epigraph to this chapter.

117. E. Dell, 'Gerrard Winstanley and the Diggers', *The Modern Quarterly*, IV, pp. 138–9.

118. Sabine, pp. 282, 512; cf. Walwyn, quoted on p. 205 below.

119. Sabine, pp. 283, 471–2, 512, 380, 197.

120. ibid., pp. 515, 527, 535–9, 562, 571–6.

121. ibid., pp. 539–40, 552–3, 572–3.

122. See pp. 173, 243–4 below.

123. Sabine, pp. 553–4, 591–9. Rape incurred the death penalty because it takes away the freedom of the body.

124. ibid., pp. 193, 197–8, 432.

125. ibid., pp. 515, 552.

126. ibid., pp. 536–42, 556–7, 599.

127. ibid., pp. 578–9, 526; cf. the attack on town oligarchies in *Light Shining in Buckinghamshire* (ibid., p. 620).

128. Sabine, pp. 564, 571, 580, 595.

129. ibid., pp. 541, 548–9; cf. pp. 190–91, 194–6, 261–2, 423.

130. Walwyn also favoured a polytechnic education (H. and D., p. 336).

131. Sabine, pp. 576–80.

132. ibid., pp. 570–71. The point was noted by that sensitive scholar Margaret James, *Social Problems and Policy during the Puritan Revolution*, p. 305.

133. Sabine, p. 473.

134. ibid., p. 333.

135. In Cohn, *The Pursuit of the Millennium*, p. 372.

136. Sabine, pp. 262, 253–4.

137. ibid., pp. 152, 157, 169, 186–7, 243, 260, 290, 534.

138. Winstanley, *The Saints Paradice* [n.d., ?1648], sig. B, E; pp. 54–7.

139. Winstanley, *Several Pieces gathered into one Volume* (1650), Introduction. In Manchester Free Reference Library.

140. Sabine, pp. 164–71, 451; cf. pp. 112, 130–32, 251, 445–6, 508–9.

141. ibid., pp. 224–5.

142. B. Spinoza, *Ethics*, Part V. Proposition XXIV, quoted by S. Hampshire, *Spinoza* (Penguin edn), p. 169; cf. p. 323 below.

143. Thomas Tymme, dedication to his translation of J. Duchesne's *The Practice of Chymicall and Hermeticall Physicke* (1605), quoted by A. G. Debus, *The English Paracelsians* (1965), pp. 88–90; cf. pp. 219–23 below.

144. Pierre Lefranc, *Sir Walter Ralegh, Ecrivain* (Paris, 1968), pp. 462–4.

145. Sabine, pp. 544, 331.

146. ibid., pp. 409, 569.

147. ibid., pp. 107–8; cf. *The Saints Paradice*, sig. A–B and p. 55; Sabine, p. 456.

148. ibid., p. 496.

149. ibid., pp. 105, 219–20.

150. ibid., p. 168; cf. pp. 383, 476.

151. ibid., pp. 222, 496.

152. ibid., p. 332; cf. pp. 137, 197, 327, 437, and K. V. Thomas, 'Another Digger Broadside', p. 61 – 'their God covetousness, the God of this world'. This is an argument for supposing either that Winstanley had a hand in writing this pamphlet or that it was written by someone closely associated with him; cf. the reference to Cain on the same page.

153. Sabine, pp. 385, 532. Here Winstanley is clearly speaking of the God of the Old Testament; cf. p. 569.

154. ibid., p. 434; cf. L. Clarkson, *A Single Eye* (1650), sig. A 1v.

155. Sabine, pp. 567–9, 471. See pp. 134–6 below.

156. ibid., p. 565; cf. R. O[verton], *Man Wholly Mortal* (2nd edn, 1655), pp. 23–4.

157. Perkins, *Works* (1617–18) III, p. 392; H. Clapham, *Errour on the Right Hand* (1608), p. 46.

158. Salmon, *Anti-Christ in Man* (1647), p. 27.

159. [Coppe] *Some Sweet Sips of some Spirituall Wine* (1649), pp. 10–11 and *passim*; cf. Richard Coppin, quoted on p. 166 below.

160. W. E., *The Mad Mans Plea* (1653), p. 1; Bauthumley, quoted on p. 165 below.

161. J. Canne, *Truth with Time* (1656), sig. B 3.

162. G. F. Nuttall, *James Nayler: A Fresh Approach* (Journal of the Friends' Historical Soc., Supplement 26), pp. 14–15.

163. Sabine, p. 210; cf. Walwyn, in H. and D., p. 298. Belief in a world before Adam was attributed to Elizabethan Familists by John Rogers (*The Displaying of the Family of Love*, 1578), and to Thomas Hariot, Ralegh's protégé, by Thomas Nashe (*Works*, ed. R. B. McKerrow, I, p. 171).

164. See pp. 195–203 below.

165. Sabine, pp. 462, 116, 128–9, 204; cf. p. 536.

166. ibid., p. 480.

167. ibid., pp. 113–17, 173, 215; cf. *The Saints Paradice*, pp. 21, 82–3.

168. Sabine, pp. 229–31, 234–5; cf. pp. 463, 484.

169. ibid., pp. 184, 260.

170. ibid., pp. 262, 161–4, 264; cf. pp. 107–8 below.

171. ibid., pp. 203, 210–18; cf. pp. 446, 457; *The Saints Paradice*, pp. 90–97, 126–34.

172. Sabine, pp. 176, 120, 457–9; cf. p. 251.

173. ibid., pp. 480–81, 176.

174. ibid., p. 259; cf. p. 96 above.

175. ibid., pp. 288–9; cf. pp. 253, 256, 323, 425, 490, 673–5.

176. Thomas, 'Another Digger Broadside', p. 61.

177. Sabine, pp. 149, 173, 176–9, 569; cf. pp. 189, 206, 228, 480. Winstanley does not emphasize the point that in the Bible Jacob blackmailed his elder brother into selling his birthright for a mess of pottage.

178. *Certain Queries Presented by Many Christian People* (1649) in Woodhouse, p. 244.

179. Coppe, *The Fiery Flying Roll*, Part I, pp. 1–5.

180. Fox, *The Lambs Officer* (1659), p. 19.

181. Bunyan, *Works*, II, p. 445; cf. Morton, op. cit., p. 139, who perceptively links Coppe and Bunyan. For Jacob and Esau see also G. Smith, *Englands Pressures, Or, The Peoples Complaint* (1645), pp. 4–5; R. Coppin, *Divine Teachings*, Part II (1653), p. 52; W. Sprigge, *A Modest Plea for an Equal Commonwealth* (1659), p. 54; for Cain and Abel see Sir H. Vane, *The Retired Mans Meditations* (1655), p. 173.

182. J. Thirsk, 'Younger Sons in the Seventeenth Century', *History*, LIV, pp. 358–77.

183. D. Veall, *The Popular Movement for Law Reform in England, 1640–1660* (Oxford U.P., 1970), pp. 217–19; Thirsk, 'Younger Sons', pp. 369–71; Covell, *A Declaration unto the Parliament* (1659), p. 17; [Anon.] *A Door of Hope* (1661).

184. R. T. Vann, 'Quakerism and the Social Structure in the Interregnum', *P. and P.*, 43, p. 91.

185. Bunyan, *Works*, I, pp. 22–4, 34–5; II, pp. 442–52; cf. J. Lindsay, *John Bunyan* (1937), ch. 9, and A. L. Morton, 'The World of Jonathan Swift', *Marxism To-day*, December 1967, p. 369 – Swift on the Irish peasantry selling itself.

186. Sabine, p. 530. See pp. 114–16 below.

187. Mr Morton found the doctrine of the Everlasting Gospel in the writings of Crisp, Saltmarsh, Collier and Coppe (*The Matter of Britain*, 1966, p. 103). We may add Henry Denne (Edwards, *Gangraena*, I, p. 23); John Warr (*Administrations Civil and Spiritual*, 1648, pp. 23, 42 – see pp. 206–9 below); Major-General Harrison (C. H. Simpkinson, *Thomas Harrison*, 1905, p. 132); William Dell (*Several Sermons*, pp. 26–7); Isaac Penington (*Works*, 3rd edn, 1784, III, pp. 494–500) and George Fox (*The Lambs Officer*, 1659, p. 13). Thomas Edwards identified the Everlasting Gospel with the doctrine of universal salvation (*Gangraena*, I, p. 22); cf. Blake, *The Everlasting Gospel* and pp. 301–3 below.

188. Sabine, pp. 100, 105, 122, 162–3, 169, 198, 453, 458. 'Light I take to be that pure spirit in man which we call Reason, which discusseth

things right and reflecteth, which we call conscience' (*Light Shining in Buckinghamshire*, in Sabine, p. 611, echoing Winstanley's *Truth Lifting up its Head*). This approaches the idea that God will ultimately abdicate (see W. Empson, *Milton's God*, 1961, pp. 130–46).

189. Sabine, pp. 385, 203; cf. pp. 248, 270, 334, 383.

190. ibid., pp. 230, 297; cf. p. 457.

191. ibid., pp. 385, 395, 472; cf. pp. 613, 631, 636–7. See my *Antichrist in Seventeenth-Century England*, pp. 116–18.

192. Sabine, pp. 458–9, 452; cf. pp. 454, 468, 477–8.

193. ibid., p. 165; cf. p. 251.

194. ibid., pp. 455, 485–6; cf. p. 399 and Appendix I below.

195. Sabine, pp. 169–70, 227, 145. My italics.

196. Ed. Firth, *Clarke Papers*, II, p. 224.

8 SIN AND HELL

1. E. Troeltsch, *The Social Teaching of the Christian Churches*, trans. O. Wyon (1931) I, p. 234; II, p. 922.

2. See pp. 127–9 below.

3. R. H. Tawney, *Religion and the Rise of Capitalism* (Penguin edn.), p. 109.

4. T. Hooker, *The Application of Redemption* (1659), p. 557. Written before 1647.

5. J. Marlowe. *The Puritan Tradition in English Life* (1956), pp. 130–31. The point was originally made by Marx (*Selected Essays*, translated by H. J. Stenning, 1926, p. 27).

6. cf. *The Reformation of the Ecclesiastical Laws*, ed. E. Cardwell (Oxford U.P., 1850), pp. 11, 14–16, 328.

7. *Selections from the Table Talk of Martin Luther*, trans. Captain Henry Bell (1892), pp. 136–7.

8. J. Calvin, *The Institutes of the Christian Religion*, trans. H. Beveridge (1949) I, p. 178.

9. Perkins, *Works*, III, p. 698.

10. Calvin, *Institutes*, II, p. 667.

11. Hooker, *The Laws of Ecclesiastical Polity* (Everyman edn) I, p. 188.

12. [H. Parker] *Observations upon some of his majesties late Answers and Expresses*, in Haller, *Tracts on Liberty*, II, p. 179.

13. *Patriarcha and Other Political Works of Sir Robert Filmer*, ed. P. Laslett (Oxford, 1949), pp. 289–90.

14. J. Rushworth, *Trial of Strafford* (1680), p. 662. My italics.

15. Sir John Davies, 'Nosce Teipsum', in *Silver Poets of the Sixteenth Century*, ed. G. Bullitt (Everyman edn.), pp. 368–9.

16. Perry Miller, *The New England Mind: The Seventeenth Century* (New York, 1939), 401–8.

17. T. Goodwin, *Works* (Edinburgh, 1861–3) II, pp. 130–33; A Burgesse, *The Doctrine of Original Sin* (1659), pp. 2, 38–9, 46, 165.

18. Erbery, *Testimony*, p. 25; cf. Milton, quoted on p. 313 below.

19. W. Crashaw, *A Sermon Preached in London* (1610), sig. F 2.

20. T. Hooker, *The Soules Preparation for Christ* (1632), p. 70.

21. Perkins, *Works*, II, p. 44. But contrast ibid., II, p. 537. See also V. Kiernan, 'Puritans and the Poor', *P. and P.*, 3, pp. 45–53.

22. J. Downame, *Christian Warfare* (1604), p. 120.

23. Ed. J. O. Halliwell, *The Autobiography and Correspondence of Sir Simonds D'Ewes* (1845) II, p. 278.

24. T. Goodwin, *Works*, II, p. 29; cf. p. 18 above.

25. See chs. 9 and 15 below. I am indebted to discussions with Mr A. L. Morton on this point; cf. *S. and P.*, p. 474, and references there cited.

26. G. Burnet, *History of the Reformation* (1825) III, p. 46.

27. Milton, *Complete Prose Works* (Yale edn) II, p. 28.

28. Chapman, *Comedies and Tragedies* (1873) II, p. 39.

29. *Bath MSS.* (H.M.C.) II, pp. 52–3; cf. pp. 124, 129 below. The lines quoted come in fact from the tragedy *Selimus*, attributed to Robert Greene. I owe this point to the kindness of Mr Charles Hobday.

30. Sabine, p. 381; cf. pp. 253–62, 452, 489–94.

31. ibid., pp. 156–9, 190–99, 305, 323, 423–4, 464, 491, 530; cf. p. 276.

32. *I.O.E.R.*, pp. 89–91, 200.

33. Ed. I. A. Poldauf, *Selections from the Works of J. A. Comenius* (Prague, 1964), pp. 98–9; Comenius, *Naturall Philosophie Reformed by Divine Light* (1651), sig. a 6, A 2v. See pp. 220, 229 below.

34. op. cit., p. 4. Variously attributed to Henry Marten, Richard Overton and John Lilburne.

35. Lilburne, *The Free-mans Freedom Vindicated* (1646), pp. 11–12.

36. Wolfe, p. 282.

37. Underdown, op. cit., p. 178.

38. H. and D., p. 231.

39. Woodhouse, p. 161.

40. See pp. 55–8 above.

41. Edwards, *Gangraena*, I, p. 23.

42. Haller, *Tracts on Liberty*, II, p. 322; cf. H. and D., p. 361.

43. Winstanley, *The Mysterie of God* (1648), pp. 17, 35–6, 56–8; *The Breaking of the Day of God*, p. 35. See p. 132 below.

44. Coppin, *Divine Teachings* (1653), Part II, pp. 50–51. First published 1649; *Truths Testimony* (1655), pp. 21, 31. See pp. 165–7 below. Lawrence Clarkson also preached universal salvation: see pp. 160–62 below.

45. In Orwell and Reynolds, op. cit., *passim*, esp. p. 82.

46. H. and D., p. 175.

47. *Harleian Miscellany*, VII, pp. 213–21; J. Owen, *Works* (1850–53) XII, pp. 3, 164; cf. X, p. 561; H. J. McLachlan, *Socinianism in Seventeenth-Century England* (Oxford U.P., 1951), ch. 10.

48. Clarkson, *The Lost Sheep Found*, *passim*; [Anon.] *The Routing of the Ranters* (1650), p. 2. See pp. 120–1 above.

49. R. Crab, *Dagons-Downfall* (1657), p. 12.

50. Fox, *Journal*, I, pp. 28, 34.

51. Quoted by Perry Miller, *Errand into the Wilderness* (Harvard U.P., 1956), p. 116.

52. Rushworth, *Historical Collections*, V, p. 345.

53. See p. 126 below.

54. [Anon.] *Sine Qua Non* (1647), p. 2, quoted by G. Huehns, *Antinomianism in English History* (1951), p. 80.

55. H. and D., p. 312.

56. G. Goodman, *The Two Great Mysteries of Christian Religion* (1653), p. 90.

57. *The Perfect Weekly Account*, 18–25 July 1649, p. 582; Petegorsky, op. cit., p. 172.

58. T. Fuller, *Church History of Britain* (1655) II, pp. 65–6.

59. Baxter, *The Holy Commonwealth*, p. 92.

60. Denne, *Grace, Mercy and Peace* (1645) in *Fenstanton Records*, p. 398.

61. Quoted by G. F. Nuttall, *The Welsh Saints, 1640–1660*, p. 59. Nayler spoke in 1654 of the preachers pleading for sin (G. F. and J. N., *Several Papers*, 1654, p. 25). Alexander Parker in 1656 applied the phrase to Vavasor Powell (*A Testimony of God*, quoted by Nuttall, loc. cit.). It became common form.

62. S. Fisher, *The Testimony of Truth Exalted* (1679), p. 650.

63. Fox, *Epistles* (1662) § 222, quoted by R. B. Schlatter, *The Social Ideas of Religious Leaders* (Oxford U.P., 1940), p. 242.

64. Bunyan, *Works*, II, p. 150.

65. W. Prynne, *Anti-Arminianism* (1630), pp. 72–5, in Woodhouse, pp. 232–3.

66. D. P. Walker, *The Decline of Hell* (Chicago U.P., 1964), p. 59; K. V. Thomas, *Religion and the Decline of Magic*, pp. 472, 479, 491–503.

67. H. Bullinger, *Decades* (Parker Soc., 1849–52) IV, p. 187.

68. Quoted by A. C. Underwood, *A History of the English Baptists* (1947), p. 134.

69. L. Babb, *The Elizabethan Malady* (Michigan, 1951), esp. pp. 51–2; H. C. White, *English Devotional Literature, 1600–1640* (University of Wisconsin Studies in Language and Literature, 29, 1931), pp. 54–5; K. V. Thomas, *Religion and the Decline of Magic*, pp. 474–5, 521; R. Burton, *Anatomy of Melancholy, passim*.

70. See p. 57 above.

71. W. Orme, *Remarkable Passages in the Life of William Kiffin* (1823), pp. 10–11.

72. E. Rogers, *Life and Opinions of a Fifth Monarchy Man* (1867), pp. 13–20.

73. J. Saltmarsh, *Free Grace* (10th edn, 1709), pp. 47–8. First published 1645.

74. H. Jessey, *The Exceeding Riches of Grace Adorned by the Spirit of Grace* (1647), p. 27.

75. [Anon.] *Pseudochristus* (1650), p. 6. For Franklin see p. 242 below.

76. I. Penington, *A Voice out of the Thick Darkness* (1650), pp. 19–20; L. V. Hodgkin, *Gulielma: Wife of William Penn* (1947), p. 32.

77. [A. Trapnel] *The Cry of a Stone* (1654), pp. 8–10.

78. Cohn, *The Pursuit of the Millennium*, p. 358; J. Bauthumley, *The Light and Dark Sides of God* (1650), pp. 46–8.

79. Ed. J. T. Wilkinson, *Richard Baxter and Margaret Charlton* (1928), p. 128; *Reliquiae Baxterianae*, I, pp. 21–2.

80. G. I. Wade, *Thomas Traherne* (Princeton U.P., 1944), pp. 43–6.

81. W. Deusbury, *The Discovery of the great enmity of the Serpent against the seed of the Woman* (1655), pp. 17–18; Burrough, *Works*, pp. 14–15, 49; cf. Jane Turner, *Choice Experiences* (1653), pp. 27–9.

82. *A Short History of the Life of John Crook*, in Theodor Sippell, *Werdendes Quäkertum* (Stüttgart, 1937), p. 238.

83. Ed. D. H. Fleming, *Diary of Sir Archibald Johnston of Wariston* (Scottish History Soc., 1911–40) II, pp. 259–60.

84. Ed. E. S. Morgan, *The Diary of Michael Wigglesworth, 1653–1657* (New York, 1965), pp. 49, 54, 59.

85. *The Weekly Intelligencer*, 18 March 1652, quoted by Jordan, op. cit., IV, p. 256.

86. H. and D., pp. 298–9.

87. Winstanley, *The Saints Paradice*, pp. 32–4.

88. Thomas, *Religion and the Decline of Magic*, p. 521; J. Stearne, *A Confirmation and Discovery of Witch Craft* (1648), p. 59.

89. E. Rogers, op. cit., p. 19.

90. T. Goodwin, *Works*, III, pp. 315–40; IV, p. 208; VI, pp. 157, 385–9.

91. Orwell and Reynolds, op. cit., p. 89.

92. Sabine, pp. 567–70.

93. Hobbes, *English Works*, VI, pp. 195–6.

94. L. Muggleton, *The Acts of the Witnesses* (1764), pp. 18, 24–36; cf. p. 62. First published 1699. Cf. *The Journal of Richard Norwood*, ed. W. F. Craven and W. B. Hayward (New York, 1956), p. 64.

95. Richard Harvey, *A Theological Discourse of the Lamb of God* (1590). I owe this reference to Professor D. B. Quinn.

96. Bunyan, *Works*, I, pp. 8–9, 13–19, 22–6, 34–5; III, p. 715; cf. pp. 646, 681, 711.

97. Fox, *Journal*, I, pp. 4, 22, 26; Braithwaite, p. 45.

98. G. C. Coulton, *Fourscore Years* (Cambridge U.P., 1945), p. 340.

99. Strype, *Annals*, II, part i, p. 563; J[ohn] R[ogers], *The Displaying of an horrible secte* (1578), sig. K.

100. Sir J. E. Neale, *Elizabeth I and her Parliaments, 1584–1601* (1957), p. 70.

101. Lefranc, *Sir Walter Ralegh*, p. 381.

102. Marlowe was also alleged to have said that Moses was but a juggler (ed. G. B. Harrison, *Willobie His Avisa, 1594*, 1926, p. 210); cf. Giovanni in John Ford's *'Tis Pity She's a Whore* (published 1633) who thought hell or heaven was a dream (Act V, scene 5).

103. Edwards, *Gangraena*, I, pp. 27, 35, 116–19, 218; II, pp. 8, 50–51; III, pp. 10, 26, 35–8, 110.

104. *I.O.E.R.*, pp. 50–51.

105. Edwards, *Gangraena*, II, p. 163; III, p. 251. 'Arse' is my insertion where Edwards coyly leaves a blank.

106. [Anon.] *A Discovery of the Most Dangerous and Damnable Tenets that have been spread within this few yeeres* (1647), single sheet.

107. J. Boehme, *Six Theosophic Points*, 1620 (Ann Arbor Paperback, 1958), p. 98; R. M. Jones, *Mysticism and Democracy*, p. 135.

108. See pp. 143, 169 below; Lilly, *Astrological Predictions* (1654), p. 25; *Astrological Judgments . . . for the Year 1655*, sig. B 7.

109. *Reliquiae Baxterianae*, I, p. 77.

110. Ed. J. Nickolls, *Original Letters and Papers of State Addressed to Oliver Cromwell* (1743), p. 99. Blake speaks enthusiastically of Boehme (*Poetry and Prose*, Nonesuch edn, p. 201).

111. *Walwins Wiles*, in H. and D., pp. 296–7. The Baptist Samuel Richardson asked the same question in 1660 (*A Discourse of the Torments of Hell*).

112. Winstanley, *The Mysterie of God*, p. 56; *The Breaking of the Day of God*, p. 110; *The Saints Paradice*, pp. 85–7, 97–8, 101–5; Sabine, pp. 216–19, 523.

113. D. P. Walker, *The Decline of Hell*, pp. 104–5; McLachlan, *Socinianism in Seventeenth-Century England*, pp. 186, 201–2; G. Foster, *The Sounding of the Last Trumpet* (1650), pp. 52–3: Reeve, *A Transcendent Spiritual Treatise* (1651), pp. 4–5, 38, 82–3; *The Form of an Excommunication made by Mr Sidrach Sympson ... against Captain Robert Norwood* (1651), pp. 2–3; G. Burnet, *History of My Own Time* (Oxford U.P., 1897) I, p. 285.

114. T. Hobbes, *Leviathan* (Penguin edn), pp. 646, 661.

115. See ch. 9 below.

116. J. Nayler, *Love to the Lost* (2nd edn, 1656), p. 32.

117. J. Owen, *Works*, X, pp. 538–9; XII, pp. 581–7.

118. F. Osborne, *Advice to a Son* (1656) in *Miscellaneous Works* (1722) I, pp. 98–9.

119. Bunyan, *Works*, II, p. 127; cf. my *Reformation to Industrial Revolution*, pp. 43, 204–6.

120. Walker, *Decline of Hell*, pp. 183, 262–3; cf. pp. 67–8 above.

121. Winstanley, *The Mysterie of God, passim*; *The Saints Paradice*, pp. 133–4; Sabine, pp. 381, 454. See p. 123 above. Theological universalism plays no very great part in Winstanley's thought after 1648; he had advanced beyond it

122. Sabine, p. 290.

123. See pp. 128–9 above.

124. Clarkson, *The Lost Sheep Found*, p. 32; cf. Humphrey Ellis, *Pseudochristus* (1650), p. 37: Henry Dixon, one of the 'destroying angels' who accepted William Franklin as the Messiah. See ch. 9 below.

125. Sabine, pp. 114, 117; cf. pp. 215–17.

126. Salmon, *Heights in Depths* (1651), pp. 37–8.

127. Quoted by D. Bush, *English Literature in the Earlier Seventeenth Century* (Oxford U.P., 2nd edn, 1962), p. 339.

128. Quoted by Underdown, op. cit., p. 330.

129. T. Fuller, *The Holy State* (Cambridge U.P., 1831), pp. 257–63; *The Works of the ... Author of The Whole Duty of Man* (1704) II, pp. 109–11.

130. Quoted by Bush, op. cit., p. 339.

131. Edward Stillingfleet, *Origines Sacrae* (1662), sig. Av; cf. b 2v.

132. Burnet, *History of My Own Time* (Oxford U.P., 1823) IV, p. 378; cf. pp. 321–2 below.

133. op. cit., II, p. 169; I, p. 269.

134. Johnston of Wariston, *Diary*, III, p. 71.

135. Haller, *Tracts on Liberty*, II, pp. 288–91; H. and D., pp. 259–60.

136. Sabine, p. 218.

137. ibid., p. 568; cf. p. 103 above.

138. See Appendix II below.

139. *P. and R.*, pp. 93–6; *I.O.E.R.*, pp. 181–5.

140. See p. 278 below.

9 SEEKERS AND RANTERS

1. Fuller, *Church History* (1655) IV, p. 53; William Penn's Preface to Fox's *Journal* (I, p. xxv),

2. I owe this information to Dr R. C. Richardson.

3. John Etherington, *The Defence of John Etherington against Steven Denison* (1641), pp. 9–10. Etherington said he was prevented from publishing this pamphlet earlier: he wrote it apparently in the late twenties or early thirties (ibid., pp. 46, 62).

4. S. R. Gardiner, *Reports of Cases in the Courts of Star Chamber and High Commission* (Camden Soc., 1886), pp. 188–94.

5. S. Rutherford, *A Survey of the Spirituall Antichrist* (1648), pp. 45, 194–297.

6. In 1641 a hostile *Description of the Sect called the Familie of Love* had been published.

7. Thomas, *Religion and the Decline of Magic*, pp. 270–71, 375; Muggleton, *Acts of the Witnesses*, p. 53. See p. 221 below.

8. *C.S.P.D., 1648–9*, p. 176. The words are those of Dr John Lambe, Dean of the Court of Arches and one of Laud's most active supporters.

9. Everard, *The Gospel Treasury Opened* (2nd edn, 1659) I, p. 221; II, pp. 103, 254, 340, sig. b 3; cf. p. 457. First published 1653. Cf. Haller, *The Rise of Puritanism* (Columbia U.P., 1938), pp. 207–12; *P. and R.*, p. 149.

10. Everard, *Gospel Treasury*, I, sig. a.

11. See pp. 55–8 above.

12. Erbery, *Testimony*, pp. 67–8.

13. R. Sibbes, *Beames of Divine Light* (1639), pp. 231–3, quoted by C. H. and K. George, *The Protestant Mind of the English Reformation* (Princeton U.P., 1961), p. 99.

14. Sibbes, *Works* (Edinburgh, 1862–4) II, p. 311; VI, p. 458; cf. p. 558.

15. Preston, *Life Eternal* (4th edn, 1634), p. 34; cf. *P. and R.*, p. 272.

16. R. Bolton, *Workes* (1631–41) IV, p. 25, quoted by the Georges, op. cit., pp. 99–100.

17. T. Crisp, *Christ Alone Exalted in Seventeene Sermons* (1643), pp. 87, 156–9; cf. pp. 276–7; *Complete Works* (1832) I, pp. 122, 130–33, 224–6; cf. pp. 137, 178–9; II, pp. 137, 173–4, 267. The 1646 edition of *Christ Alone Exalted* contains a Preface by the Antinomian Henry Pinnell. Erbery praised Crisp (*Testimony*, p. 68); Clarkson had heard and read him (*The Lost Sheep Found*, p. 9).

18. Baillie, *Letters and Journals*, I, pp. 408, 437.

19. Baillie, *A Dissuasive from the Errours of the Time* (2nd impression, 1645–6), pp. 26, 167.

20. Edwards, *Gangraena*, I, pp. 19, 26, 35–6, 110–13, 213; II, pp. 2–3.

21. J. Trapp, *Commentary on the New Testament* (Evansville, Indiana, 1958), p. 501. First published 1647.

22. Edwards, *Gangraena*, I, pp. 21, 116–19; II, p. 8; III, pp. 10, 26–7, 35–8, 88–92.

23. [Anon.] *A true and perfect Picture of our present Reformation* (1648), p. 13. Such ideas were not necessarily plebeian by origin. The fashionable Inns of Court poets under the first two Stuart kings had made a cult of adultery and promiscuity, equating marriage and enclosure, sentimentally regretting a lost Golden Age (John Carey, 'The Ovidian Love Elegy in England', unpublished Oxford D.Phil. thesis, 1960, esp. pp. 199, 376, 386–7, 419–21).

24. D. Brunton and D. H. Pennington, *Members of the Long Parliament* (1954), pp. 15–16; G. E. Aylmer, *The King's Servants* (1961), pp. 393–4.

25. Edwards, *Gangraena*, I, pp. 121, 124 and *passim*; III, p. 99.

26. *Reliquiae Baxterianae*, I, p. 26; Dell, *Several Sermons*, p. 79.

27. *A Short History of the Life of John Crook*, in Sippell, *Werdendes Quäkertum*, p. 238. For Lilburne see P. Gregg, *Free-Born John* (1961), p. 47.

28. Barclay, *Inner Life*, p. 331; see pp. 179–80 below.

29. See p. 183 below.

30. Walker, *History of Independency*, Part II, pp. 152–3. See p. 78 above.

31. R. Abbot, *The Young Mans Warning-piece*, sig. A 3v–4; cf. the well-known passage about the wickedness of the young in *The Continuation of the Life of Edward Earl of Clarendon* (1759) II, pp. 39–41.

32. William Grigge, *The Quakers Jesus* (1658), p. 47.

33. In Woodhouse, pp. 390–96.

34. R. M. Jones, *Mysticism and Democracy in the English Common-wealth* (Harvard U.P., 1932), pp. 87–8; Edwards, *Gangraena*, I, pp. 81–2. I am not sure that 'Seeker' is the right word for Writer.

35. J. Salmon, *A rout, a rout* (1649), pp. 9–13; R. Coppin, *Truths Testimony* (1655), pp. 10–15; A. L. Morton, *The World of the Ranters*, pp. 116–19; Cohn, *The Pursuit of the Millennium*, p. 353; F. Freeman, *Light Vanquishing Darknesse* (1650), pp. 5–6. Clarkson went on to become a Muggletonian. Coppin denied being a Ranter, but it is difficult to know how else to describe him.

36. W. Deusbury, *The Discovery of the great enmity of the Serpent against the seed of the Woman* (1655), *passim*; Francis Howgill, *The Inheritance of Jacob Discovered* (1655), *passim*; T. Sippell, *Zur Vorgeschichte des Quäkertums* (Giessen, 1920), p. 47.

37. C. Burrage, 'The Restoration of Immersion by the English Ana-baptists and Baptists (1640–1700)', *American Journal of Theology*, January 1912, esp. p. 76.

38. Edwards, *Gangraena*, I, p. 128; Haller, *Tracts on Liberty*, III, p. 330.

39. Burrage, *Early English Dissenters*, I, p. 367.

40. Edwards, *Gangraena*, II, pp. 7–8.

41. *Reliquiae Baxterianae*, I, p. 87.

42. [Anon.] *A Publike Conference Betwixt the Six Presbyterian Ministers, And Some Independent Commanders, Held at Oxford* (1646), p. 3.

43. Erbery, *Testimony*, p. 209.

44. ibid., p. 333.

45. Edwards, *Gangraena*, I, pp. 77–8, 109–10; III, pp. 89–92, 250. John Webster, also an admirer of Boehme, confirms that 'the Trinity was not perfectly owned' by Erbery (*Testimony*, p. 264; cf. pp. 278–9).

46. [F. Cheynell?] *Truth Triumphing over Errour and Heresie* (1646[-7]), p. 5; Erbery, *Nor Truth nor Error* (1646[-7]), pp. 2, 4, 8, 16–17, 20–21; cf. *Testimony*, p. 22; [Cheynell] *An Account Given to the Parliament by the Ministers sent by them to Oxford* (1646[-7]), pp. 13, 18–20.

47. Erbery, *Testimony*, pp. 24, 40, 207.

48. [Cheynell] *An Account Given to the Parliament*, pp. 13, 22, 38, 50.

49. Woodhouse, pp. 169–74; cf. Erbery's *Testimony*, pp. 26, 333–4, and *An Account Given to the Parliament*, p. 35, for Erbery's tolerance to Jews and Turks – though not to papists.

50. Erbery, *Testimony*, p. 205.

51. ibid., pp. 25, 30, 40–42, 73.

52. Ed. J. Nickolls, *Original Letters and Papers of State Addressed to Oliver Cromwell* (1743), pp. 88–9.

53. Erbery, *Testimony*, pp. 75, 59.

54. ibid., pp. 53, 90–91.

55. Saltmarsh, *Sparkles of Glory* (1648), pp. 215–17.

56. Erbery, *Testimony*, pp. 80, 231–3, 268–9, 336.

57. ibid., p. 73.

58. ibid., p. 100.

59. ibid., pp. 87, 167, 171–9.

60. ibid., pp. 52–3. See p. 72 above.

61. ibid., pp. 182–6; cf. pp. 232, 247–8.

62. ibid., p. 191.

63. ibid., sig. (a) 2, pp. 209–10.

64. ibid., pp. 260, 265.

65. ibid., pp. 232, 337–8.

66. ibid., p. 338

67. J. L., *A Small Mite in Memory of the late deceased ... Mr. William Erbery* (1654), title-page.

68. Erbery, *Testimony*, pp. 47, 259.

69. Christopher Fowler, *Daemonium Meridianum, Satan at Noon, or Antichristian Blasphemies* (1655), pp. 29, 132; cf. Erbery, *Nor Truth nor Error*, pp. 1–2.

70. Erbery, *Testimony*, p. 312.

71. ibid., pp. 312–16, 331; cf. pp. 124, 176.

72. ibid., p. 176, quoted on p. 146 above.

73. ibid., pp. 260, 266, 195–8, 275–6.

74. [Anon.] *Religions Enemies* (1641), p. 6. Attributed to John Taylor the Water-Poet.

75. Henry Wilkinson, *Miranda, Stupenda* (1646), p. 26.

76. John Heydon, *A New Method of Rosie Crucian physick* (1658), p. 49; ed. B. R. White, *Association Records of the Particular Baptists of England, Wales and Ireland to 1660*, Part I, *South Wales and the Midlands* (Baptist Historical Soc., 1971), p. 37; ed. Nuttall, *Early*

Quaker Letters from Swarthmore MSS. to 1660, pp. 258–9. Cf. V. L. Pearl, *London and the Outbreak of the Puritan Revolution* (Oxford U.P., 1961), pp. 233–4, for use of taverns for political purposes.

77. J. Eachard, *The Axe against Sin and Error* (1646), sig. (a)v. In *Good Newes for all Christian Souldiers* (1645) he had answered the question 'Should not a faithful soldier be content with his wages?' 'Yes, saith the soldier, if he could get it' (p. 31).

78. Sabine, pp. 141–3; cf. Edwards, *Gangraena*, III, p. 25 (Giles Randall).

79. Edwards, *Gangraena*, II, p. 146; III, p. 107; D. Underdown, *Somerset in the Civil War and Interregnum* (Newton Abbot, 1973), p. 146.

80. H. Maurice, *An Impartial Account of Mr John Mason of Water Stratford* (1695), p. 52.

81. Ed. W. E. Minchinton, *The Growth of English Overseas Trade in the Seventeenth Century* (1969), p. 21. On tobacco see Herrick's poems, 'The Tobacconist' and 'The Censure' (*Poetical Works*, ed. L. C. Martin, Oxford U.P., 1956, pp. 424–7).

82. R. M. Jones, *Studies in Mystical Religion*, p. 474.

83. F. Freeman, *Light Vanquishing Darknesse* (1650), p. 3; cf. p. 201 below.

84. Quoted by Masson, *Life of Milton*, III, p. 525.

85. Muggleton, *Acts of the Witnesses*, pp. 56–7.

86. Dell, *Several Sermons*, p. 607.

87. [Anon.] *Strange Newes From the Old-bayley* (1651), pp. 2–3.

88. Clarkson, *The Lost Sheep Found*, pp. 28–9.

89. E. Pagitt, *Heresiography* (5th edn, 1654), p. 144.

90. Freeman, *Light Vanquishing Darknesse*, p. 19.

91. Bunyan, *Works*, II, pp. 182–3.

92. Muggleton, *Acts of the Witnesses*, p. 5; *The Routing of the Ranters*, p. 4.

93. Fox, *Journal*, I, pp. 85, 199, 212.

94. Bunyan, *Works*, I, p. 85.

95. Braithwaite, p. 85.

96. Coppe, *A Fiery Flying Roll*, Part II, pp. 18–19.

97. I owe this to Mr J. F. McGregor's Oxford B.Litt. thesis, 'The Ranters: A Study of the Free Spirit in English Sectarian Religion, 1648–1660'.

98. [Anon.] *The Ranters Ranting* (1650), p. 5.

99. Coppe, *A Fiery Flying Roll*, Part I, ch. 2.

100. *Leyborne-Popham MSS.* (H.M.C.), p. 57; cf. pp. 163–4 below.

101. Bunyan, *Works*, III, p. 601; cf. Fox, *Journal*, I, pp. 47, 198.

102. *S and P.*, pp. 405–6.

103. Ed. J. Spedding, R. L. Ellis and D. D. Heath, *The Works of Francis Bacon* (1870–74) VII, p. 185. Wrongly attributed to Bacon.

104. cf. Trotsky on Bolshevik opposition to 'the swearing of masters and slaves' in the name of human dignity (Isaac Deutscher, *The Prophet Unarmed*, 1959, pp. 165–6).

105. Morton, *The World of the Ranters*, p. 90.

106. See pp. 169–70 below; cf. [Anon.] *All the Proceedings of the Sessions of the Peace holden at Westminster the 20th day of June, 1651*, pp. 3–9.

107. S. S[heppard], *The Joviall Crew, or The Devill turned Ranter* (1651), Prologue.

108. Robert Gell, *A Sermon touching God's Government of the World by Angels* (1650), pp. 39–40.

109. Ed. H. E. Rollins, *Cavalier and Puritan* (New York U.P., 1923), pp. 320–24.

110. Reeve, *A Transcendent Spiritual Treatise* (1711), An Epistle to a Quaker, p. 2; cf. pp. 1, 5–6. First published 1651; cf. Muggleton's *Acts of the Witnesses*, pp. 53–7.

111. Bunyan, *Works*, I, pp. 11, 25–6; III, p. 724; cf. I, pp. 49–50, 210, 217, 454; II, pp. 150, 182–3, 214, 664; III, pp. 383, 385, 724.

112. S. Fisher, *Christianismus Redivivus* (1655), pp. 466–7, 482, 492, 513.

113. Fox, *Journal*, I, p. 47.

114. [Anon.] *The Arraignment and Tryall, with a Declaration of the Ranters* (1650), p. 6.

115. Pagitt, *Heresiography* (1654), pp. 143–4.

116. *Reliquiae Baxterianae*, I, pp. 76–7.

117. J. Holland, *The Smoke of the bottomles pit* (1650[-51]), p. 2; J. Bauthumley, *The Light and Dark Sides of God* (1650), p. 4.

118. Edward Hide, *A Wonder, yet no Wonder* (1651), pp. 35–41. Hide was an opponent of the Ranters, yet so far as we can check him he seems to present their views with tolerable fairness.

119. L. Muggleton, *The Acts of the Witnesses*, p. 56.

120. Winstanley, *The Saints Paradice*, p. 123; cf. pp. 80 above, and 169 below.

121. [Coppe] *Some Sweet Sips of some Spirituall Wine*, p. 60 and *passim*; Salmon, *Heights in Depths*, pp. 37–8.

122. S. Fisher, *Baby Baptism meer Babyism* (1653), pp. 511–12. For Fisher see ch. 11 below.

123. J. Holland, op. cit., pp. 2–6; cf. R. Coppin, *Divine Teachings* (2nd edn, 1653), pp. 9–10.

124. Cohn, op. cit., p. 329. See p. 234 below.

NOTES

125. cf. Fox, *Journal*, I, p. 231; II, p. 7.
126. Peter Sterry, *A Discourse of the Freedom of the Will* (1675), p. 156.
127. Clarkson, *The Lost Sheep Found*, p. 28; Holland, loc. cit.; cf. Coppin, *Truths Testimony*, p. 31.
128. [Anna Trapnel] *The Cry of a Stone* (1654), pp. 8–10. See p. 127 above.
129. Hide, op. cit., pp. 36–8.
130. Clarkson, *A Single Eye*, in Cohn, op. cit., pp. 350–53.
131. See his own account of the very sympathetic attitude of Chief Baron Wilde, Serjeant Green, Judge Hutton and Serjeant Glynne in 1651–4 (*Truths Testimony*, pp. 31–71, 85–8). Major-General Kelsey was much tougher in 1655 (see p. 167 below).
132. W. Deusbury, *True Prophecie of the Mighty Day of the Lord* (1655), pp. 5–15: Judge Hale and Judge Windham very sympathetic.
133. A. L. Morton, *The World of the Ranters*, p. 104.
134. I owe this information to Mr McGregor's B.Litt. thesis.
135. *Mercurius Politicus*, 23 May–5 June 1651. I owe this reference to Mr McGregor's thesis.
136. Firth, *Cromwell's Army*, p. 408; cf. pp. 288–9, 400. William Franklin's disciple Henry Dixon held similar views (H. Ellis, *Pseudochristus*, 1650, pp. 32, 37); cf. *The Arraignment and Tryall, with a Declaration of the Ranters*, p. 6; *Theauraujohn his Theous Ori Apokolipikal* (1651), p. 35.
137. *Mercurius Politicus*, 3 July 1656, No. 316, pp. 7064–6.
138. See pp. 158–9 below.
139. See p. 123 above.
140. See *Reliquiae Baxterianae*, I, pp. 436–7.
141. Coppe, *A Fiery Flying Roll*, I, pp. 1–5, 11.
142. Coppe, I, pp. 1–5; Cohn, op. cit., pp. 362–3.
143. Cohn, op. cit., p. 365.
144. Coppe, *A Fiery Flying Roll*, Part II, pp. 18–19, 21; Cohn, op. cit., pp. 368, 372.
145. *Copps Return to the wayes of Truth* (1651), p. 4.
146. ibid., pp. 8–9, 14, 24–5.
147. ibid., pp. 19–21.
148. J. Tickell, *The Bottomles Pit Smoaking in Familisme* (1652), *passim*.
149. Fox, *Journal*, I, p. 212.
150. A. Coppe, *A Character of a true Christian* (1680), single sheet.
151. [Anon.] *The Routing of the Ranters*, sig. A 2.
152. Morton, *The World of the Ranters*, pp. 115–42.
153. Clarkson's first publication was dedicated to the Mayor, Aldermen and inhabitants of Preston (*Truth Released from Prison, to Its*

Former Libertie, 1646), as Winstanley had dedicated his to his beloved countrymen of Lancashire (*The Mysterie of God*, 1648).

154. Clarkson, *A Generall Charge*, pp. 10–14, 17–18, 27.

155. Clarkson, *A Single Eye*, sig. A 1 verso, pp. 7–8, 13, 15–16; *The Lost Sheep Found*, p. 33.

156. Clarkson, *A Single Eye*, pp. 8–12, 16.

157. M. Luther, *Thirty-four Sermons* (trans. William Gace, 1747), p. 281; H. Haydn, *The Counter-Renaissance* (New York, 1950), p. 485.

158. Calvin, *The Institutes of the Christian Religion*, II, pp. 135, 683.

159. Ed. E. F. Rimbault, *The Miscellaneous Works ... of Sir Thomas Overbury* (1890), p. 102. Overbury died in 1613 and his *Characters* were published posthumously.

160. Crisp, *Complete Works* (1832) I, pp. 224–6; cf. *Christ Alone Exalted* (1648) III, p. 326.

161. R. Towne, *The Assertion of Grace* (n.d. – ? before 1648), p. 73; Towne was attacked in Samuel Rutherford's *A Modest Survey of the Secrets of Antinomianism* (1648), p. 25.

162. Cohn, op. cit., pp. 345–6, 353; Morton, op. cit., pp. 131, 135. For Winstanley's measured and friendly scepticism about Clarkson's 'single eye' see Sabine, pp. 477–8, 485–6.

163. Morton, op. cit., pp. 98, 107, 133.

164. Clarkson, *Look about you* (1659), pp. 92–3.

165. Salmon, *Anti-Christ in Man*, sig. A 2v, pp. 10–16, 34.

166. cf. pp. 104 above, 197–203 below.

167. Salmon, op. cit., pp. 47–53, 58.

168. Salmon, *A rout, a rout*, pp. 4–5, 15–16, 21.

169. ibid., pp. 9–13. See p. 166 below. But cf. Clarkson, *A Single Eye*, sig. A 1 verso.

170. *A Perfect Diurnall*, 1–8 April 1650, p. 175; Walter Rosewell, *The Serpents Subtilty Discovered* (1656), p. 1.

171. *Leyborne-Popham MSS.* (H.M.C.), p. 57.

172. Salmon, *Heights in Depths and Depths in Heights*, Preface, p. 7.

173. ibid., p. 28.

174. R. S. Dunn, *Sugar and Slaves* (1973), p. 103. I owe Salmon's emigration to Mr McGregor's thesis.

175. Bauthumley, *The Light and Dark Sides of God*, pp. 4, 14.

176. ibid., pp. 33, 36, 39.

177. ibid., pp. 14, 28–31, 45–9, 52, 57, 71–84. See p. 199, Appendix II below.

178. Morton, op. cit., pp. 96–7.

179. Rosewell, *The Serpents Subtilty Discovered*, pp. 1, 16; Morton, op. cit., p. 98.

180. Coppin, *Divine Teachings* (2nd edn, 1653), pp. 8, 10; *Man's Righteousnesse Examined* (1652), pp. 9–11; cf. pp. 163–4 above.

181. *Divine Teachings*, pp. 3, 8–9, 23–4, 75–6, 99–101, 107; *The Exaltation of All Things in Christ* (1649), pp. 1, 33–7, 46.

182. John Osborne, *The World to Come . . . also . . . a Conference between him and Richard Coppin of Westwell* (1651), p. 68.

183. Coppin, *A Blow at the Serpent* (1656), pp. 87–8; *A Man-Child Born* (1654), p. 1; *The Exaltation of All Things*, pp. 17–18.

184. Coppin, *Man's Righteousnesse Examined*, pp. 9–10, 18; cf. *Saul Smitten for not Smiting Amalek* (1653), p. 18; cf. Coppe, quoted on p. 110 above.

185. Coppin, *Truths Testimony* (1655), pp. 15, 20–21, 81; *A Blow at the Serpent*, p. 18. Coppin was in fact accused of playing the Catholic and Jesuit game, but by allegorizing the Scriptures and so showing that they are no safe guide (Rosewell, *The Serpents Subtilty Discovered*, p. 16).

186. *A Blow at the Serpent*, p. 52.

187. *Thurloe State Papers* (1742) IV, p. 486; Rosewell, op. cit., sig. A 3, pp. 14–15; Morton, op. cit., p. 98.

188. Coppin, *Crux Christi* (1657), pp. 52, 57.

189. Muggleton, *A True Interpretation of All the Chief Texts . . . of the whole Book of the Revelation of St. John* (1665), p. 106.

190. *Fenstanton Records*, p. 269.

191. Foster, *The Sounding of the Last Trumpet* (1650), pp. 17–18, 42, 46, 50–52; cf. Captain Francis Freeman, *Light Vanquishing Darknesse* (1650), pp. 56–7.

192. Foster, *The Pouring Forth of the Seventh and Last Viall* (1650), sig. A 3, pp. 7, 11–12, 15, 26, 64–6. There seem to be several verbal reminiscences of Winstanley in Foster's writings.

193. ibid., sig. A 2, sig. a. For 'fellow-creatures' see *The Arraignment and Tryall, with a Declaration of the Ranters*, p. 6.

194. J. Pordage, *Innocence appearing Through the dark Mists of Pretended, Guilt* (1655), p. 25.

195. Pordage, op. cit., pp. 2, 19, 24, 71, 102; Nuttall, *James Nayler*, p. 5; D. Hirst, 'The Riddle of John Pordage', *Boehme Soc. Quarterly*, I, 6 (1953–4), p. 6.

196. *P. and R.*, p. 316.

197. See pp. 216–18 below.

198. *Reliquiae Baxterianae*, I, pp. 77–8. Dr Nuttall identifies this man as Thomas Bromley (*James Nayler*, pp. 3–6).

199. Christopher Fowler, *Daemonium Meridianum*, pp. 60–61; Pordage, op. cit., p. 73.

200. Fowler, op. cit., pp. 32, 41, 53–5; Pordage, op. cit., pp. 9, 11–12.

201. T. Tani, *The Nations Right in Magna Charta discussed with the thing Called Parliament* (1650[–51]), p. 8. See p. 215 below.

202. *Theauraujohn his Theous Ori Apokolipikal* (1651), pp. 5, 35; *Theauraiohn High Priest to the Jewes his Disputive challenge to the Universities of Oxford and Cambridge* (1651[–2]), p. 5.

203. Style, *Reports*, p. 312; cf. p. 131 above. *Theous Ori*, pp. 69–78; cf. *Thau Ram Tanjah* (1654) and *Theauraujohn his Aurora* (1655), Epistle Dedicatory.

204. Arise Evans, *To the Most High and Mighty Prince Charles II ... An Epistle* (1660), p. 51; Burton, *Parliamentary Diary*, I, p. cxxvi.

205. *Theauraiohn ... his Disputive challenge*, p. 8.

206. Muggleton, *A True Interpretation of the Eleventh Chapter of the Revelation of St. John* (1751), p. 180: first published 1662; *A True Interpretation of All the Chief Texts ... of the whole Book of the Revelation of St. John* (1665), p. 128; *The Acts of the Witnesses*, pp. 20–21, 44. See also *P. and R.*, pp. 84, 141–2, 316; my *Antichrist in Seventeenth-Century England*, pp. 115, 176.

207. E. Stokes, Esq., *The Wiltshire Rant* (1652), esp. pp. 12–14, 47, 56; *V.C.H.*, *Wiltshire*, III, p. 102; Pagitt, *Heresiography* (1654), p. 144.

208. Stokes, op. cit., pp. 4, 12–13, 21–2, 43, 53, 61, 66. Marlowe had thought Moses a conjurer (p. 130 above, and p. 359 n. 102). See also p. 215 below.

209. Morton, op. cit., p. 111.

210. [T. Collier] *A Looking-Glasse for the Quakers*, p. 16; for Joshua Garment, disciple of John Robins and 'prophet of the most high God', see Garment's *The Hebrews Deliverance at hand* (1651). See also Nuttall, *Early Quaker Letters*, p. 150; *V.C.H.*, *Wiltshire*, III, p. 102; A. R. Bayley, *The Great Civil War in Dorset* (Taunton, 1908), pp. 344–5; Thomas, *Religion and the Decline of Magic*, p. 126.

211. See pp. 89–90 above.

212. Ed. B. H. Cunnington, *Records of the County of Wilts: being extracts from the Quarter Sessions Great Rolls of the Seventeenth Century* (Devizes, 1932), p. 231.

213. Muggleton, *The Neck of the Quakers Broken* (1663), pp. 66–7; see p. 162 above.

214. Sabine, p. 441. See p. 91 above.

215. *Fenstanton Records*, pp. 2, 8, 33–4.

216. ibid., pp. 73–9, 88–93.

217. ibid., pp. 330–31.

218. Sabine, p. 364.

219. ibid., pp. 399–403; cf. *Englands Spirit Unfoulded*, ed. G. E. Aylmer, *P. and P.*, 40, pp. 14–15.

220. Sabine, pp. 526–7, 535–6, 539. See p. 98 above.

10 RANTERS AND QUAKERS

1. Pagitt, *Heresiography* (1654), pp. 135–6 (should be 137–8, wrongly numbered in original); [T. Collier] *A Looking-Glasse for the Quakers* (1657), p. 17; *Reliquiae Baxterianae*, I, p. 77.

2. Burton, *Parliamentary Diary*, I, p. 98.

3. Braithwaite, *The Second Period of Quakerism* (1919), p. 250.

4. cf. Nuttall, *James Nayler, passim*.

5. Fox, *Journal*, I, pp. 8, 34, 36; cf. p. 28; *Short Journal*, pp. 17, 32. See pp. 67–9 above.

6. His target was presumably the 'Proud Quakers': see p. 191 below.

7. Fox, *The Lambs Officer* (1659), pp. 3, 9–10 and *passim*.

8. Fox, *Journal*, I, p. 168. See pp. 182–6 below for the Quakers and politics.

9. Winstanley, *The Breaking of the Day of God*, sig. A 2v, p. 93; *The Saints Paradice*, p. 22.

10. Burrough, *Works*, p. 14.

11. Fox, *Gospel-Truth Demonstrated* (1706), p. 6.

12. Ed. A. H. Dodd, *History of Wrexham* (1957), p. 148.

13. Braithwaite, pp. 122, 169; Fox, *Journal*, I, pp. 81–3, 98, 106, 111, 113, 138, 143, 168, 189–90, 195, 227.

14. Fox, *Journal*, I, *passim* – Hotham, Fell, Pearson, Robinson, Benson; cf. Underdown, op. cit., pp. 36–7, 317, 321.

15. Fox, *Journal*, I, pp. 174, 178–9.

16. Braithwaite, pp. 208–9.

17. Burton, *Parliamentary Diary*, I, pp. 70, 96. Skippon, Nayler's main Army opponent, had been regarded as Parliament's man in the Army in 1647.

18. cf. p. 181 below.

19. [H. Stubbe] *Light Shining out of Darknes* (1659), p. 88.

20. Ed. J. Hall, *Memorials of the Civil War in Cheshire* (Lancashire and Cheshire Record Soc., 1889), pp. 229–30.

21. Fox, *Journal*, I, p. 95; W. Penn, *Judas and the Jews* (1673), p. 31; cf. Henry Marten's unpublished pamphlet, *Justice Would-bee that made himself a Ranter last week in opposition to those he calls Quakers* (see Appendix to Professor C. M. Williams's unpublished Oxford D.Phil. thesis, 'The Political Career of Henry Marten, with special reference to the origins of republicanism in the Long Parliament'). See pp. 193–4, 291 below.

22. [T. Collier] *A Looking-Glasse for the Quakers*, p. 7.

23. Bunyan, *Works*, II, pp. 182–3; *Reliquiae Baxterianae*, I, p. 77; cf. Pagitt, *Heresiography* (5th edn, 1654), pp. 143–4.

24. Bunyan, *Works*, I, p. 21; II, p. 664.

25. Clarkson, *The Lost Sheep Found*, p. 33.

26. Fox, *A Word from the Lord* (1654), p. 13; cf. John Audland, *The Innocent Delivered out of the Snare* (1658), pp. 13–14.

27. Fox, *Journal*, I, pp. 87, 212; *Short Journal*, p. 8.

28. A. E. Wallis, 'Anthony Pearson (1626–1666)', *Journal of the Friends' Historical Soc.*, LI, p. 85.

29. James Parnell, *A Shield of the Truth* (1655), p. 39.

30. J. Nayler, *Love to the Lost* (2nd edn, 1656), p. 48.

31. Burrough, *A Trumpet of the Lord Sounded out of Sion* (1656), pp. 26–8; *Works*, pp. 15, 108, 138, 279–80, 746.

32. Fox, *Journal*, I, pp. 85, 195, 199–200, 230–31.

33. Jonathan Clapham, *A Full Discovery and Confutation Of the wicked and damnable Doctrines of the Quakers* (1656), p. 62.

34. Stokes, *The Wiltshire Rant*, pp. 12–13, 61, 66; Bayley, *The Great Civil War in Dorset*, p. 344.

35. Ed. Nuttall, *Early Quaker Letters from the Swarthmore MSS. to 1660*, p. 150.

36. *The First Publishers of Truth*, p. 261.

37. S. Fisher, *The Testimony of Truth Exalted*, pp. 91–2.

38. William Jeffery, *The Deceived and deceiving Quakers discovered* (1656), pp. 29, 41, 55.

39. William Grigge, *The Quakers Jesus* (1658), pp. 51–2; Fox, *Journal*, I, pp. 69–70.

40. See p. 172 above.

41. [Anon.] *Folly and Madness made Manifest* (1659), pp. 1–3; Fox, *Journal*, II, p. 96; cf. Whiting, *Studies in English Puritanism*, p. 173.

42. F. H., *A Brief Relation of the Irreligion of the Northern Quakers* (1653), p. 10. The Quakers also 'hold that all things ought to be common'. The Rev. John Ward tells us that several Levellers settled

into Quakers (see his *Diary*, ed. C. Severn, 1839, p. 141); cf. A. Parker, *A Discovery of Satans Wiles* (1657), p. 39.

43. Fuller, *History of the University of Cambridge* (1840), p. 680.
44. Burton, *Parliamentary Diary*, I, p. 169; cf. pp. 24–5, 49, 128.
45. Fox, *A Word from the Lord* (1654), p. 13.
46. N. Homes, *A Sermon Preached Before the ... Lord Mayor* (1650), p. 32.
47. Fisher, *The Testimony of Truth Exalted*, pp. 48–9.
48. T. Comber, *Christianity no Enthusiasm* (1678), pp. 90–92, 181. See p. 236 above.
49. The opening paragraphs of this section owe a great deal to discussion of the Quakers with Professor W. A. Cole.
50. Deusbury, *Discovery of the great Enmity of the Serpent* (1655), p. 16; Fox, *Journal*, I, pp. 129, 256, 287; *An Account of the Convincement ... of ... Richard Davies* (1928), p. 30; *Sufferings of the Quakers*, I, pp. 273–4, 285, 310, 445, 490; I. Grubb, *Quakerism and Industry before 1800* (1930), p. 100; Brailsford, op. cit., p. 639; Barbour, *The Quakers in Puritan England*, p. 89; O. C. Watkins, *The Puritan Experience* (1972), p. 168.
51. Fox, *Journal*, I, pp. 189, 409; *Short Journal*, p. 53; *Thurloe State Papers*, VI, p. 241; ed. C. H. Firth, *Scotland and the Protectorate* (Scottish History Soc., 1899), pp. 350–51; T. Wright and J. Rutty, *A History of ... Quakers in Ireland* (1811), p. 105; *State Papers relating to Friends*, p. 116; [Anon.] 'George Watkinson of Scotton (d. 1670),' *Journal of the Friends' Historical Soc.*, L, p. 69.
52. *Thurloe State Papers*, IV, pp. 508, 642; VI, p. 162; *Leyborne-Popham MSS.* (H.M.C.), pp. 157, 168; Firth, *Scotland and the Protectorate*, pp. 362–3; Cole, 'The Quakers and the English Revolution', *P. and P.*, 10, pp. 46, 53; G. B. Burnet, *Quakers in Scotland* (1952), p. 141; R. Howell, *Newcastle upon Tyne and the Puritan Revolution*, p. 261; Barbour, op. cit., pp. 221–2.
53. F. R. Harris, *Life of Edward Montagu* (1912) I, p. 175.
54. M. R. Brailsford, *A Quaker from Cromwell's Army* (1917), pp. 23–5; Barbour, op. cit., pp. 192, 196; Braithwaite, p. 440; Nuttall, *The Holy Spirit*, pp. 131–2, 164.
55. cf. Fox, *Journal*, I, pp. 426, 448, 450.
56. Ed. Nuttall, *Early Quaker Letters*, p. 273.
57. Burrough, *Works*, pp. 537–40; Barbour, op. cit., p. 40.
58. *Bath MSS.* (H.M.C.) II, p. 134; ed. Sir G. F. Warner, *Nicholas Papers* (Camden Soc.) IV (1920), p. 265; Barbour, op. cit., pp. 221–2;

Braithwaite, p. 480; *Leyborne-Popham MSS.*, p. 161; V. A. Rowe, *Sir Henry Vane the Younger* (1970), p. 223.

59. Whiting, *Studies in English Puritanism*, p. 181.

60. Cole, 'The Quakers and the English Revolution', p. 42.

61. *Leyborne-Popham MSS.* (H.M.C.), p. 141; Burton, *Parliamentary Diary*, IV, pp. 357, 440–46; cf. Whiting, op. cit., p. 184; *State Papers relating to Friends*, pp. 6, 31–2; Braithwaite, p. 313; Fox, *Journal*, I, pp. 226–7.

62. Cole, 'The Quakers and the English Revolution', pp. 46–7; Barbour, op. cit., pp. 199–206.

63. Brailsford, op. cit., pp. 639–41.

64. Burrough, *A Trumpet of the Lord Sounded out of Sion* (1656), pp. 9–10; *Works*, pp. 671–3.

65. *A Collection of Sundry Books, Epistles and Papers written by James Nayler* (1716) I, p. 187; Fox, *Several Papers Given Forth* (1660), pp. 1–18; *Journal*, I, pp. 290, 292; F. Howgill, *One Warning more* (1660), pp. 4–7, 10–12.

66. F. G., *To the Council of Officers of the Armie* [n.d., ?1659]. I owe the attribution to Fox to Professor Cole; cf. G. P. Gooch, *The History of English Democratic Ideas in the Seventeenth Century* (Cambridge U.P., 1898), pp. 276–81.

67. Thomas Aldam and other Quakers, *A Brief Discovery Of a three-fold estate of Antichrist* (1653), pp. 4–5; cf. pp. 7–8.

68. Ed. J. Hall, *Memorials of the Civil War in Cheshire*, p. 229.

69. Burrough, *Works*, sig. c 2, pp. 157, 233.

70. A. Pearson, *The Great Case of Tithes* (1732), pp. 60, 66. First published 1657.

71. B. Nicholson, *A Blast from the Lord* (1653), quoted by J. F. Maclear, 'Quakerism and the End of the Interregnum', *Church History*, XIX, p. 245.

72. Burrough, *Works*, p. 500; *State Papers relating to Friends*, p. 42.

73. Nayler, *Wisdom from Beneath* (1653); Howgill, *A Woe to Magistrates* (1654), quoted by P. S. Belasco, *Authority in Church and State* (1928), pp. 77–8; cf. Fox, *Mans Coming up from the North*.

74. Fox, *To the Parliament of the Common-wealth of England* (1659), pp. 5, 8–9.

75. Fox, *Gospel-Truth*, p. 6; cf. pp. 27, 105, 129, 219. Fox's words are echoed in an anonymous Quaker pamphlet of 1655: *To all that would Know the Way to the Kingdom*, p. 9.

76. Audland, *The Innocent Delivered out of the Snare* (1658), p. 33.

77. Braithwaite, p. 147; Fisher, *Testimony*, pp. 554, 580–83, 588–92.
78. [Anon.] *The Glorie of the Lord Arising* (1654), p. 9.
79. Audland, *The Innocent Delivered out of the Snare*, p. 6.
80. Burton, *Parliamentary Diary*, I, pp. 170–71; Braithwaite, pp. 169, 268; *Thurloe State Papers*, III, pp. 94, 118.
81. Fox, *Several Papers* (1654), pp. 7, 9–10.
82. Nayler, *Love to the Lost* (2nd edn, 1656), pp. 26–7.
83. Burrough, *A Word of Reproof* (1659), pp. 71–7.
84. Burrough, *Works*, pp. 64–7 (1655), 538 (1659); *A Trumpet of the Lord Sounded out of Sion* (1656), p. 37.
85. See my *Antichrist in Seventeenth-Century England*, pp. 78–88.
86. Burrough, *Works*, p. 11.
87. Firth, *Scotland and the Protectorate*, pp. 381, 362–3; *Thurloe State Papers*, IV, p. 508; cf. pp. 122, 210, 222, 240 above.
88. Strype, *Annals*, IV, p. 97.
89. *The History of the Life of Thomas Ellwood* (1906), p. 60 and *passim*. First published 1714; cf. Fox, *Gospel-Truth*, p. 27.
90. Fuller, *Church History*, III, Dedication to Book VIII.
91. Barbour, op. cit., pp. 74, 164–5. A ballad of 1583 tells us of John Lewis, who was burnt for denying the divinity of Christ and who 'did thou each wight the which / With him had any talk', 'despising reverence to prince or any state' (ed. H. E. Rollins, *Old English Ballads, 1553–1625*, Cambridge U.P., 1920, p. 56). I owe this reference to Mr Charles Hobday.
92. J. Clapham, *A Full Discovery*, p. 81.
93. Ed. A. Soboul, *1789, Il'an 1 de la liberté* (Paris, 1939), p. 81; G. V. Plekhanov, *Art and Social Life* (1953), p. 160.
94. R. M. Jones, *Studies in Mystical Religion*, p. 479; cf. Nuttall, *James Nayler, passim*.
95. J. N., *A Few Words* (1654), pp. 21–2.
96. G. Fox and J. Nayler, *Several Papers*, p. 23.
97. Nayler, *A Collection of Sundry Books*, I, p. 187; II, pp. 755–6; cf. II, pp. 591–6.
98. Ellwood, *Life*, pp. 18–19. For free grace see Nayler, *Love to the Lost*, p. 32.
99. Fox and Nayler, *Several Papers*, p. 25.
100. Nayler, *A Second Answer to Thomas Moore* (1655), p. 29; *Love to the Lost*, pp. 22–3.
101. Nayler, *A Salutation to the Seed of God* (3rd edn, 1656), pp. 7–8.
102. See p. 242 below.

103. A. Evans, *An Eccho to the Voice from Heaven* (1652[–3]), pp. 62–7.
104. The irony of dating his letter to Parliament on Christmas Day can hardly have escaped him.
105. G. F., *Sauls Errant to Damascus* (1653), p. 30.
106. Braithwaite, pp. 255, 128.
107. Burrough, *Works*, p. 208; Fisher, *Testimony*, p. 621.
108. Nayler, *A Collection of Sundry Books*, I, pp. xlii, liii; II, pp. 495–6.
109. Nayler, *What the Possession of the Living Faith is* (1659), quoted by Nuttall, *James Nayler*, p. 17; cf. pp. 7–9, and *passim*.
110. Nayler, *A Collection of Sundry Books*, II, p. 689; cf. p. 694.
111. ibid., p. 696.
112. Burrough, *Works*, p. 541; cf. p. 441. See pp. 125, 187 above.
113. Ed. H. J. Cadbury, *George Fox's 'Book of Miracles'* (Cambridge U.P., 1948), p. ix, and *passim*.
114. J. F. Maclear, 'Quakerism and the End of the Interregnum', pp. 260–68.
115. Penn, Preface to Fox's *Journal*, I, pp. xlix, xxv.
116. Penn, *The Spirit of Alexander the Coppersmith lately revived* (1673), pp. 8–9.
117. Penn, *A Brief Examination* (1681), pp. 2–3.
118. R. M. Jones, in Braithwaite, *Second Period of Quakerism*, pp. xlii–xlvi. See pp. 351, 370–71 below.
119. Braithwaite, *Second Period*, pp. 45–6.
120. Fox, *Journal*, I, p. 519; Braithwaite, *Second Period*, pp. 233–42. Perrot went to Barbados in 1662, where he linked up with Robert Rich, one of Nayler's supporters whom orthodox Quakers had denounced as a Ranter. Perrot had been preceded by Joseph Salmon (K. L. Carroll, *John Perrot*, Supplement No. 33 to *Journal of the Friends' Historical Soc.*, 1970, *passim*); cf. p. 164 above. Barbados as centre of lower-class radicalism might be worth investigating. In 1643 there were 'divers sects of familists' among 'those of mean quality' on the island (C. Bridenbaugh, *Vexed and Troubled Englishmen*, Oxford U.P., 1967, p. 432).
121. Fox, *Journal*, II, pp. 347n., 424; *First Publishers of Truth*, pp. 256, 267–9; Braithwaite, *Second Period*, ch. XI and p. 307.
122. *Westminster Drollery* (1674) in *Choyce Drollery, 1656*, ed. J. W. Ebsworth (Boston, Lincolnshire, 1876), p. 191.
123. *Fenstanton Records*, p. 270.
124. Fox, *Journal*, I, p. 85.
125. See pp. 370–8 below.

126. cf. pp. 370–5 below.

127. 'As if the light were inconsistent with itself, or admitted of unity under . . . contrary practices in the one family and flock of God': the words are Penn's, the subject the Story–Wilkinson separation (Braithwaite, *Second Period*, p. 307); cf. Carroll, *John Perrot*, pp. 58–9, 92.

128. Fox, *Journal*, I, p. 195. It is fair to add that Nayler also had a following among upper-class ladies (Nuttall, *James Nayler*, pp. 11–13). Many of his humbler female followers transferred their support to Perrot (Carroll, op. cit., pp. 50, 86).

129. Fox, *Journal*, I, p. 95. See p. 178 above.

130. See pp. 376–8 below.

131. Fox, *Journal*, II, p. 512; I. Ross, *Margaret Fell* (1949), p. 11. She could have heard of it if she had read Winstanley: see p. 140 above.

132. Fox, *Journal*, I, p. 268. Nayler too had long hair – in order to look like Christ, M.P.s hinted in December 1656 (Burton, *Parliamentary Diary*, I, p. 153). Fox was reticent about the reason for wearing his hair long; cf. Thomas Webbe (p. 171 above). Perrot offended Fox by growing a beard like Nayler's. Contemporaries suggested that they were both imitating Christ's appearance (Carroll, op. cit., pp. 59–60).

133. Fox, *The Lambs Officer*, p. 21.

134. Nuttall, *James Nayler*, p. 20.

11 SAMUEL FISHER AND THE BIBLE

1. S. Fisher, *Christianismus Redivivus, Christendom Both unchrist'ned and new-christ'ned* (1655), pp. 269, 293, 307–9, 491, 525.

2. ibid., pp. 466, 482.

3. ibid., pp. 492, 513.

4. ibid., pp. 527, 627 and *passim*.

5. *An Additional Appendix to the Book Entituled Rusticus Ad Academicos* (1660), title-page; *The Testimony of Truth Exalted* (1679), pp. 590–92, 735.

6. ibid., p. 783; cf. p. 154 above.

7. ibid., pp. 851, 711.

8. ibid., pp. 36–8, 132; cf. pp. 653, 680.

9. ibid., pp. 625–39, 643.

10. Edwards, *Gangraena*, I, p. 21.

11. Everard, *The Gospel Treasury Opened* (2nd edn, 1659), p. 232; Sabine, pp. 212–13, 496; cf. pp. 65, 104, 172 above and p. 334 below.

12. Erbery, *Testimony*, p. 84.

13. Sabine, pp. 224, 289, 509.

14. ibid., pp. 99–102, 122–8, 523; cf. pp. 455–6.

15. Bunyan, *Works*, III, p. 646. Bunyan himself at one time thought the Scriptures only 'a dead letter, a little ink and paper' (ibid., III, p. 711).

16. Holland, op. cit., pp. 2–6; Carroll, op. cit., p. 85. For Walton-on-Thames and Tany see pp. 78, 141, 170 above.

17. H. and D., p. 298.

18. Clarkson, *A Single Eye*, p. 16; *The Lost Sheep Found*, pp. 32–3; cf. Holland, loc. cit., and pp. 104, 175–6 above.

19. *Leyborne-Popham MSS.* (H.M.C.), pp. 57, 59; cf. Edwards, *Gangraena*, III, p. 10.

20. Braithwaite, p. 170; R. Farnsworth, *The Ranters Principles and Deceits Discovered* (1655), p. 19.

21. Bauthumley, *The Light and Dark Sides of God*, pp. 71–84.

22. Ed. A. R. and M. B. Hall, *The Correspondence of Henry Oldenburg*, I, *1641–1662* (Wisconsin U.P., 1965), pp. 89–91.

23. Capp, *The Fifth Monarchy Men*, p. 166.

24. [H. Parker] *Jus Populi* (1644), p. 57.

25. Milton, *Complete Prose*, I, p. 699; II, pp. 8, 588, 623.

26. See pp. 191–4 above. For other links between Milton and the radicals see Appendix II below.

27. Milton, *Treatise of Christian Doctrine*, Book I, ch. 30.

28. Bauthumley, op. cit., pp. 76–7.

29. Quoted by C. Webster, 'English Medical Reformers of the Puritan Revolution', *Ambix*, XIV, pp. 26–7.

30. Sabine, p. 251; see p. 143 above.

31. Fox, *Journal*, I, p. 36; *Gospel-Truth*, pp. 131, 138; Burrough, *Works*, p. 541.

32. See pp. 172–3 above, p. 289 below.

33. *Fides Divina, passim*; *The Jus Divinum of Presbyterianism* (2nd edn, enlarged, 1655), pp. 66–9; *An Apologetical Narration* (2nd edn, 1658), pp. 62, 78.

34. Writer, *An Apologetical Narration*, pp. 75, 80, 11; Appendix and Supplement, pp. 8–9.

35. *Reliquiae Baxterianae*, I, p. 116.

36. Fisher, *Testimony*, pp. 14, 51–2, 272–97.

37. We recall that Bunyan had similar doubts. (See p. 129 above.) A translation of the Koran had been published in England in 1649, which no doubt explains the sudden awareness.

38. Fisher, *Testimony*, pp. 384, 389.
39. ibid., pp. 396, 400, 403, 420, 435.
40. ibid., pp. 440–41.
41. ibid., p. 555.
42. ibid., pp. 701–4.
43. Sir John Vanbrugh, *The Provok'd Wife*, Act I, scene i. See pp. 320–1 below.

12 JOHN WARR AND THE LAW

1. See my *Century of Revolution* (Sphere Books), pp. 48–9, 157–8; *S. and P.*, pp. 373–5; *Reformation to Industrial Revolution*, pp. 48–59; 'The Many-Headed Monster', pp. 302–3.
2. W. J. Jones, *The Elizabethan Court of Chancery* (Oxford U.P., 1967), p. 321; cf. pp. 382, 461–2.
3. Osborne, *A Miscellany of Sundry Essays* (1659), p. 35, in *Miscellaneous Works* (1722) I.
4. Veall, op. cit., p. 73; J. Jones, *The Judges Judged out of their own Mouths* (1650), pp. 93–4.
5. Veall, op. cit., *passim*; *I.O.E.R.*, pp. 69, 259–65; *H. and D.*, pp. 82, 109–10; cf. S. Butler, *Characters and Passages from Note-Books*, ed. A. R. Waller (Cambridge U.P., 1908), pp. 74–5.
6. Sabine, pp. 589, 468; cf. pp. 276, 557–9.
7. Erbery, *Testimony*, p. 42.
8. Howgill, *A Woe to Magistrates* (1654), quoted by Belasco, op. cit., p. 95.
9. Burrough, *Works*, p. 500; Belasco, op. cit., pp. 94–5; *State Papers relating to Friends*, pp. 39–44 – a petition of 1658. See also Fox, *Journal*, I, p. 54; Sabine, p. 201.
10. G. Fox, *A Few Plain Words* (1659), p. 2.
11. Ludlow, *Memoirs*, I, p. 246.
12. *Walwins Wiles* (1649) in H. and D., p. 303.
13. Winstanley, *The Law of Freedom* (1652) in Sabine, p. 512.
14. Capp, op. cit., p. 160.
15. J. Jones, *The Jurors Judges of Law and Fact* (1650), pp. 49–76. Jones was defending Lilburne. But see Veall, op. cit., p. 156, who suggests that the wealthy and the poor wanted the jury system to be restricted: and that it was the 'middle sort' who wanted it extended.
16. E. Rogers, op. cit., pp. 87–8.

17. *The Tryal of Lieutenant-Colonel John Lilburne* (2nd edn, 1710), p. 108n.; cf. pp. 106–7, and Brailsford, op. cit., p. 342.

18. P. Gregg, *Free-Born John* (1961), p. 299.

19. Fox, *Several Papers Given Forth* (1660), pp. 32–3.

20. C. G. Cocke, *Englands Compleat Law Judge and Lawyer* (1656), Introduction and p. 20.

21. Sabine, pp. 508, 587; cf. my *God's Englishman*, p. 141.

22. J. Warr, *The Corruption and Deficiency of the Laws of England* (1649) in *Harleian Miscellany* (1744–6) III, pp. 240, 245–7.

23. ibid., pp. 240–43, 248.

24. ibid., p. 246.

25. Warr, *Administrations Civil and Spiritual* (1648), pp. 3–5, 34.

26. ibid., pp. 6–10.

27. ibid., pp. 6–15, 36.

28. H. and D., p. 55; Wolfe, p. 362.

29. No. 354, 19–26 March 1653; Woodhouse, p. 36.

30. Cook, *Redintegratio Amoris* (1647), p. 24.

31. [Coppe] *Some Sweet Sips of some Spirituall Wine* (1649), p. 13.

32. Sprat, *History of the Royal Society of London*, p. 73; cf. p. 53. See my *God's Englishman*, p. 58.

33. Warr, *The Priviledges of the People* (1649), pp. 3–6, 10–11.

34. M. James, *Social Problems and Policy during the Puritan Revolution*, p. 359. For Wildman, see M. Ashley, *John Wildman* (1947), ch. VI.

13 THE ISLAND OF GREAT BEDLAM

1. cf. C. B. Macpherson, 'The University as Multiple Fool', *Bulletin of the Canadian Association of University Teachers*, Autumn 1970, p. 6. Professor Macpherson suggests that universities might play a similar role in contemporary society; cf. N. Z. Davis, 'The Reasons of Misrule', *P. and P.*, 50, esp. pp. 70–75.

2. Ed. L. H. Carlson, *Writings of Henry Barrow, 1590–91* (1966), pp. 200–201.

3. W. Andrews, *Curiosities of the Church* (1890), pp. 162–4; E. Welsford, *The Fool* (1935), pp. 192–3.

4. Ed. P. Toon, *The Oxford Orations of Dr John Owen* (n.d., ?1971), p. 26.

5. Aubrey, *Natural History of Wiltshire* (1847), p. 93; *Remaines of Gentilisme and Judaisme* (1881), pp. 205, 241.

6. Arise Evans, *The Voice of King Charls*, pp. 27–8, 44–6, 71–2; *The Bloudy Vision of John Farley*, sig. A 8; *To the Most High and Mighty Prince, Charles II ... An Epistle* (1660), pp. 18–19.

7. P. Heylyn, *Cyprianus Anglicus*, quoted by T. Spencer, 'The History of an Unfortunate Lady', *Harvard Studies and Notes in Philology and Literature*, XX, p. 52.

8. Contrast Thomas Brewer, who was imprisoned in 1626 for foretelling the destruction of England within three years by two kings; he remained in jail till the Long Parliament released him (Burrage, *The Early English Dissenters*, I, pp. 202–3).

9. Underdown, op. cit., p. 183.

10. See pp. 167–70 above.

11. Cohn, op. cit., pp. 368–9. '- - -' represents Coppe's punctuation; '. . .' as usual indicates omissions made by me.

12. Fox, *Journal*, I, pp. 77–8.

13. Thomas, *Religion and the Decline of Magic*, pp. 149–50.

14. J. Lilburne, *Coppy of a Letter* (1646), p. 14.

15. Sabine, pp. 205, 291; cf. *The Saints Paradice*, sig. D.

16. Sabine, pp. 484, 480; cf. p. 172.

17. See pp. 208–9 above.

18. Milton, *Complete Prose Works*, I, p. 808.

19. L. Clarkson, *Truth Released from Prison to its Former Libertie* (1646), sig. B 5v; cf. R. Coppin, *A History of the Glorious Mystery of Divine Teachings*, ch. II; Henry Pinnell, *A Word of Prophecy concerning The Parliament, Generall and Army* (1648), p. 75.

20. Salmon, *A rout, a rout*, p. 13; cf. *Heights in Depths*, pp. 18, 23.

21. Penington, *Light or Darknesse* (1650), sig. A 2v.

22. Covell, *The true Copy of a Letter sent To the Kings Most Excellent Majestie* (n.d., ?1660), single sheet. Covell addresses the King as 'thou'.

23. *A Short History of the Life of John Crook*, in Sippell, *Werdendes Quäkertum*.

24. W. E[rbery], *The Mad Mans Plea: Or, A Sober Defence of Captaine Chillintons Church* (1653), pp. 1–3, 7–8. The title is ironical: the pamphlet is as little a defence as it is sober: it attacks Chillenden and his Baptist church. The words quoted in the epigraph to this chapter, 'Come, let's all be mad together', Erbery attributes to 'a great man of the sea ... when he heard of the [Long] Parliament dissolved'. Would this be Blake? Or Deane? Hardly Monck or Montague, one feels.

25. T. Tani, *The Nations Right in Magna Charta, discussed with the thing Called Parliament*, p. 8. See p. 170 above.

26. *The Weekly Intelligencer*, 1–8 October 1650, quoted by Morton, op. cit., pp. 103–4; *The Routing of the Ranters*, p. 2.

27. Salmon, *Heights in Depths*, pp. 18, 23.

28. *A Lasting Almanack for the Raigne of the Fifth Monarchy* (1660). I owe this point to Mr W. A. Hunt. For Webbe see pp. 170–71 above.

29. See p. 169 above.

30. Penington, *Light or Darknesse*, sig. A 4.

31. cf. Huehns, *Antinomianism in English History*, pp. 171–2.

32. Sabine, p. 400. For Muggleton Reason was the Devil.

33. John Pordage, *Innocence appearing Through the dark Mists of Pretended Guilt* (1655), pp. 9–12, 26, 69–80; [Anon.] *A Most faithful relation of two wonderful passages which happened very lately . . . in the Parish of Bradfield* (1650), pp. 2–3; Christopher Fowler, *Daemonium Meridianum*, pp. 53–5, 59–61, 80; S. Hutin, *Les Disciples anglais de Jacob Boehme* (Paris, 1960), pp. 82–9.

34. *Clarke Papers*, II, pp. 210–12; Whitelocke, op. cit., p. 383; Petegorsky, op. cit., p. 135. Theaureaujohn too was 'of the race of the Jews'.

35. Sabine, p. 103.

36. Ed. I. G. Philip, *Journal of Sir Samuel Luke* (Oxfordshire Record Soc., 1950–53), pp. 16, 35, 38, 41, 61–2, etc.

37. Wolfe, p. 258; *Clarke Papers*, I, p. 414; *Englands Standard Advanced in Oxfordshire, or a Declaration from Mr Will. Thompson and the oppressed people of this nation now under his conduct* (1649). We should perhaps not make too much of the echoes of Digger titles – *The True Levellers Standard Advanced*, which William Everard signed and which went to the press on 20 April 1649, and *A Declaration from the Poor Oppressed People of England*, the next Digger pamphlet, which Thompson dated 1 June 1649.

38. Woodhouse, pp. 6–7, 23, 34–6, 42–4, 83–4; ed. C. H. Firth and G. Davies, *A Regimental History of Cromwell's Army* (Oxford U.P., 1940) II, p. 503; Nickolls, *Original Letters and Papers of State Addressed to Oliver Cromwell*, p. 81.

39. With the theme of this chapter, cf. H. Marcuse, *An Essay on Liberation* (Penguin edn), p. 68.

14 MECHANIC PREACHERS AND THE
MECHANICAL PHILOSOPHY

1. See pp. 90–98 above.

2. See pp. 221–4 below.

3. Fuller, *Abel Redivivus* (1651), p. 432; T. Ball, *The Life of the Renowned Dr Preston* (1885), pp. 14–16.

4. *I.O.E.R.*, p. 149.

5. Bacon, *Works*, III, p. 289; IV, pp. 32, 349, 366–7. See *I.O.E.R.*, ch. III.

6. Peter, *Gods Doings and Mans Duty* (1646); *Good Work for a Good Magistrate*, esp. pp. 74–8.

7. See p. 122 above.

8. J. A. Comenius, *Panegersia*, quoted in *The Teacher of the Nations* (ed. J. Needham, 1941), p. 6; cf. Winstanley, quoted on p. 239 below, and Webster, *Academiarum Examen*, sig. B 1v.

9. R. Boyle, *Works* (1744) I, p. 20.

10. S. Butler, *Hudibras*, ed. J. Wilders (Oxford U.P., 1967), p. 200; cf. Butler's Character of a Hermetic Philosopher in *Characters and Passages from Note-Books*, pp. 97–108.

11. Stokes, *The Wiltshire Rant*, p. 22.

12. Braithwaite, *Second Period of Quakerism* (1919), p. 39.

13. For the whole of this paragraph, see Thomas, *Religion and the Decline of Magic*, pp. 313, 359, 366–77 and *passim*; Fox, *Journal*, I, p. 41.

14. Thomas, *Religion and the Decline of Magic*, pp. 270–71.

15. *I.O.E.R.*, p. 58; T. Hall, *Vindiciae Literarum* (1655), p. 199.

16. Eyraeneus Philaletha Cosmopolita, *Secrets Reveal'd* (published by W. C. Esq., 1669), p. 48. See my *Antichrist in Seventeenth-Century England*, p. 119, for this pamphlet, and for a prediction by an English-woman, possibly Mary Cary, that 'gold would shortly be commonly made'.

17. Erbery, *Testimony*, p. 266; Osborne, op. cit., I, p. 91.

18. S. Fisher, *The Testimony of Truth Exalted*, pp. 51, 57; cf. Samuel Hartlib's reference to Richard Sibbes as 'one of the most experimental divines now living'. He attributed the opinion to John Pym (*Ephemerides*, 1634. I am grateful to Professor Trevor-Roper for giving me a transcript of this passage). The elevation of 'chemical divinity' seems to date from the 1640s. The Grindletonian Roger

Brearley spoke disparagingly of 'chemical theology' (T. Sippell, *Zur Vorgeschichte des Quäkertums*, p. 12).

19. *I.O.E.R.*, p. 121; Fox, *Journal*, I, pp. 430–31; *Gospel-Truth*, p. 1088.
20. Pinnell, *Philosophy Reformed and Improved in Four Profound Tractates* (1657), sig. A 7v, a 3.
21. J. T. Fowler, *Durham University* (1907), p. 18; Sprigge, *A Modest Plea for an Equal Common-wealth* (1659), p. 53. Tonge was later an associate of Titus Oates.
22. B. Bourne, *The Description and Confutation of Mysticall Anti-Christ, the Familists* (1646), sig. T 1, quoted by Thomas, op. cit., p. 376.
23. Thomas, op. cit., pp. 327, 332, 361.
24. Fox, *Journal*, I, p. 9. Manfred Weidhorn, *Dreams in Seventeenth Century English Literature* (The Hague, 1970) emphasizes the significance of the dreams of Adam and Eve in *Paradise Lost* and the dream framework to Bunyan's masterpiece (esp. pp. 82–8, 154–5).
25. Thomas, op. cit., pp. 125–8. See J. Aubrey, *Miscellanies* (1890), p. 137, for a Quaker of Kingston curing by astrology.
26. *George Fox's 'Book of Miracles'*, p. 44 and *passim*; cf. p. 190 above.
27. *I.O.E.R.*, p. 298.
28. Ed. I. B. Cohen, *Isaac Newton's Papers and Letters on Natural Philosophy* (Cambridge U.P., 1958), p. 436.
29. Lord Keynes, 'Newton the Man' in *Newton Tercentenary Celebrations* (Cambridge U.P., 1947), pp. 27, 31–2; cf. R. J. Forbes, 'Was Newton an Alchemist?', *Chymia*, II (1949), pp. 35–6.
30. cf. Thomas, op. cit., pp. 643–4.
31. Sabine, pp. 565–7.
32. cf. p. 130 above; S. F. Mason, *A History of the Sciences* (1953), pp. 282–90; 'The Scientific Revolution and the Protestant Reformation: II, Lutheranism in relation to Iatrochemistry and the German Nature-Philosophy', *Annals of Science*, vol. 9, pp. 154–75.
33. Sabine, pp. 42–3, 221; cf. p. 169.
34. N. Hodges, *Vindiciae Medicinae et Medicorum* (1665), *passim*; W. Johnson, *Brief Animadversions* (1665), *passim*; C. Goodall, *The Royal College of Physicians* (1684), sig. A 4. I owe the first two references to Mr I. A. McCalman; cf. Sir William Temple, quoted in *I.O.E.R.*, pp. 122–3.
35. I owe this point to Mr McCalman.
36. *I.O.E.R.*, pp. 127, 66.

37. J. Aubrey, *Brief Lives* (Oxford U.P., 1898) II, p. 318; cf. Sir T. Browne, *Religio Medici* (Everyman edn), p. 34; H. More, *An Antidote against Atheism* (1653), *passim*.

38. Thomas, op. cit., pp. 638–40; my *Reformation to Industrial Revolution*, p. 117.

39. Thomas, op. cit., pp. 377–8.

40. Plockhoy also wanted all economic information to be pooled (see pp. 266–7 below).

41. Haller, *Tracts on Liberty*, III, p. 294.

42. Culpeper, *A Physical Directory* (1649), sig. A.

43. C. Goodall, *The Royal College of Physicians*, sig. A 4; *The College of Physicians Vindicated* (1676), sig. A 4v–5v, pp. 1–2, 22–3, and *passim*.

44. J. J. Keevil, *Medicine and the Navy* (1957–8) II, p. 2.

45. Sabine, p. 598; ed. Nickolls, *Original Letters . . . addressed to Oliver Cromwell*, pp. 100–101, 129–30.

46. Petty, *The Advice of W. P. to Mr Samuel Hartlib* (1648).

47. J. Cook, *Unum Necessarium* (1648).

48. Dell, *Several Sermons*, p. 644.

49. Webster, *The Saints Guide* (1654), pp. 26–7 and *passim*. See pp. 230–32 below.

50. J. Heydon, *The Wise-mans Crown: or, the Glory of the Rosie-Cross* (1664), sig. C 3v, quoted by Thomas, op. cit., p. 375.

51. For Culpeper see *I.O.E.R.*, pp. 29, 72, 81–2, 120, 122; Thomas, op. cit., p. 343. For Lilburne see *I.O.E.R.*, p. 261.

52. The sub-title of Clarkson's *A Single Eye* was *All Light, No Darkness; or Light and Darkness One*; cf. Bauthumley's *The Light and Dark Sides of God* and Francis Freeman's *Light Vanquishing Darknesse* (1650); cf. Morton, op. cit., pp. 74–5, and Debus, *The English Paracelsians*, pp. 102, 104, 108, 112–18, 132.

53. Sabine, p. 565; Debus, op. cit., pp. 41, 61, 88–90, 138; G. H. Turnbull, *Samuel Hartlib* (1920), pp. 10–13; cf. pp. 139–40, 142 above. I am indebted to Mr Charles Webster for help in this matter.

54. Winstanley, *The Breaking of the Day of God*, pp. 17–18: 'the heart of man hath adjoining to it a bladder or stem of water which cools the heat of the blood – the pericardium'.

55. Fox, *Journal*, I, pp. 29–30; A. Everitt, *Change in the Provinces in the Seventeenth Century*, pp. 43–6.

56. Sabine, pp. 572–3.

57. Ed. R. F. Young, *Comenius in England* (Oxford U.P., 1932), p. 65; *Selections from Comenius*, pp. 19–21.

58. *I.O.E.R.*, pp. 108–9, 124; R. L. Greaves, *The Puritan Revolution and Educational Thought* (Rutgers U.P., 1969), pp. 55–6, 59–60. Note that ten of the twelve proposed new universities are in the North and West, or on the borders.

59. Stone, 'Literacy and Education in England, 1640–1900', *P. and P.*, 42, pp. 109–12.

60. *The Advice of W. P. to Mr. Samuel Hartlib.*

61. Dell, *Several Sermons*, pp. 642–8. Similar proposals were made by George Snell, *The Right Teaching of Useful Knowledge* (1649), pp. 311–27.

62. See epigraph to this chapter.

63. Dell, op. cit., p. 585; cf. p. 273. Samuel Fisher made the same point (*Testimony*, p. 336; cf. pp. 207, 331, 469).

64. Sabine, pp. 568–70, 236–40.

65. Ed. A. Peel and L. H. Carlson, *Writings of Robert Harrison and Robert Browne* (1953), pp. 530–31; ed. Carlson, *Writings of John Greenwood* (1962) I, pp. 268–9; *Writings of Henry Barrow* (1962–6) I, pp. 344–53, 534–41; II, pp. 191, 211–24.

66. [Anon.] *These Tradesmen are Preachers* (1647), single sheet.

67. Roger Williams, *The Hireling Ministry None of Christs* (1652), pp. 14–17; Erbery, *Testimony*, p. 86; Coppin, *Divine Teachings*, pp. 21–4; *Truths Testimony* (1655), p. 16; Norwood, *The Form of an Excommunication made by Mr Sydrach Sympson . . . against Captain Robert Norwood* (1651), pp. 33–4; Fox, *The Lambs Officer*, pp. 2–3, and *passim*; *Journal*, I, pp. 7, 11, 386; *Gospel-Truth*, p. 1016; Nayler, *The Old Serpents Voice*, p. 5; Thomas Adams, *An Easter-Reckoning* (1656), Preface by Richard Farnsworth; [R.F.] *Antichrists Man of War* (1655), pp. 53, 55; Fisher, *Testimony*, pp. 298, 589–90; Webster, *Academiarum Examen* (1654), *passim*.

68. *Mr Peters Last Report of the English Warres* (1646), p. 13.

69. Hobbes, *Leviathan* (Penguin edn), pp. 728, 324; *Behemoth*, in *English Works*, VI, p. 347; cf. pp. 184–5, 215–20, 230–34, 276–82.

70. Dell, *Several Sermons*, p. 398.

71. See my 'The Radical Critics of Oxford and Cambridge in the Sixteen-fifties', in *Universities in Politics*, ed. J. W. Baldwin and C. Goldthwaite (Johns Hopkins U.P., 1972).

72. Dell, *Several Sermons*, p. 403.

73. John Hall, *The Advancement of Learning* (1649), ed. A. K. Croston (Liverpool U.P., 1953), pp. 27–8; N. Biggs, *The Vanity of the Craft of Physick* (1651), sig. b, pp. 229–31. Biggs repeats Hall almost verbatim.

74. Webster, *Academiarum Examen*, sig. B iv, pp. 20, 51, 68–70, 106–8.

75. [John Wilkins and Seth Ward] *Vindiciae Academiarum* (1654), pp. 6, 23, 43, 48; T. Hall, *Vindiciae Literarum* (1655), p. 199.

76. Sabine, p. 271.

77. ibid., pp. 562–5. In Plattes's *Macaria* (1641) parsons were also to be physicians (see C. Webster, 'The authorship ... of *Macaria*', *P. and P.*, 56).

78. See pp. 226–9 above, 274 below. For the disuse of Latin in Chancery see W. J. Jones, *The Elizabethan Court of Chancery*, pp. 291, 298.

79. C. Webster, 'Science and the challenge to the scholastic curriculum, 1640–1660', in *The Changing Curriculum* (History of Education Soc., 1971), pp. 32–4.

15 BASE IMPUDENT KISSES

1. *The Ranters Last Sermon* (1654), p. 3.

2. J. Bale, *Select Works* (Parker Soc., 1849), p. 336; cf. Lucy Hutchinson's remark that Edward the Confessor was 'sainted for his ungodly chastity' (*Memoirs of the Life of Colonel Hutchinson*, 1846, p. 4).

3. C. Bridenbaugh, *Vexed and Troubled Englishmen* (Oxford U.P., 1968), p. 28.

4. A. Harbage, *Shakespeare and the Rival Traditions* (New York, 1952), *passim*.

5. *Verney Memoirs*, IV, p. 17.

6. C. S. Lewis, *The Allegory of Love* (Oxford U.P., 1936), *passim*.

7. W. Davenant, *The Dispensary*, Act I, scene i.

8. J. Harrington, *Works* (1737), pp. 109–10.

9. T. E. Thiselton-Dyer, *Church Lore Gleanings* (1891), p. 192.

10. Style, *Reports*, pp. 69–70, 100, 229, 326, 455; C. V. Wedgwood, *The King's Peace, 1637–1641* (1966), p. 40. Gouge wrote strongly against wife-beating in *Of Domesticall Duties*, pp. 223–6.

11. A. C. Carter, *The English Reformed Churches in Amsterdam in the Seventeenth Century* (Amsterdam, 1964), p. 162; P. Williams, *Life in*

Tudor England (1969), p. 70. For Yorkshire, see J. Addy, 'Ecclesiastical Discipline in the County of York, 1559–1714' (unpublished Leeds M.A. thesis), p. 96.

12. H. T. Buckle, *Miscellaneous and Posthumous Works* (1872) III, p. 577.

13. Smyth, *Lives of the Berkeleys* (Gloucester, 1883) II, p. 413.

14. Ed. Z. N. Roginsky, *London in 1645–6* (Yaroslavl, 1960), p. 13. In Russian.

15. W. and M. Haller, 'The Puritan Art of Love', *Huntington Library Quarterly* (cf. p. 350 n. 94; p. 391 n. 85; p. 393 n. 24), V (1942), *passim*; cf. *S. and P.*, ch. 13; *I.O.E.R.*, pp. 273–5.

16. H. Bullinger, *Decades* (Parker Soc., 1849–52) I, pp. 406, 411–12, [J. Dod and R. Cleaver] *A plain and familiar Exposition of the Ten Commandements* (19th edn, 1662), p. 262; John Hall of Richmond, *Of Government and Obedience* (1654), p. 27.

17. Gouge, op. cit., p. 128; D. Rogers, *Matrimoniall Honour* (1642), pp. 80–81; K. V. Thomas, 'The Double Standard', *Journal of the History of Ideas*, XX, p. 203.

18. T. Goodwin, *Works*, II, p. 422.

19. R. Sibbes, *Works* (Edinburgh, 1862–4) V, p. 349; cf. Gouge, op. cit., p. 273.

20. e.g. Calvin, *A Commentary on Genesis* (trans. J. King, 1965) II, p. 133.

21. J. Hooper, *Early Writings* (Parker Soc., 1843), pp. 378–85; *The Reformation of the Ecclesiastical Laws*, pp. 49–58.

22. S. E. Morison, *The Intellectual Life of New England* (Cornell U.P., 1963), p. 10.

23. H. Peter, *Good Work for a Good Magistrate*, p. 117; C. L. Powell, *English Domestic Relations* (New York, 1917), pp. 67–76.

24. Thomas, *Religion and the Decline of Magic*, pp. 656–7.

25. E. M. Williams, 'Women Preachers in the Civil War', *J.M.H.*, I, pp. 561–9; K. V. Thomas, 'Women and the Civil War Sects', *P. and P.*, 13, pp. 42–62; Nuttall, *The Holy Spirit in Puritan Faith and Experience*, pp. 87–8.

26. R. P. Stearns, *Congregationalism in the Dutch Netherlands, 1621–1635* (Chicago U.P., 1940), p. 56.

27. Edwards, *Gangraena*, I, pp. 116–19, 187; cf. pp. 34, 121, 138, 171; II, p. 8; III, pp. 14, 99.

28. S. Torshell, *The Womans Glorie* (1645), pp. 2, 10–11. Bolton had made the same point earlier (*Works*, 1631–41, IV, pp. 245–6, quoted by Walzer, op. cit., p. 193).

29. Fox, *Gospel-Truth*, p. 81 (1656); cf. pp. 331, 724.

30. Edwards, *Gangraena*, I, pp. 220–23; II, pp. 11, 141, 178–9.

31. Thomas, 'Women and the Civil War Sects', pp. 52–5; cf. *P. and R.*, p. 319: Roger Crab: 'They bargain and swop like horse-coursers.'

32. *S. and P.*, p. 443n.

33. E. Rogers, *Life and Opinions of a Fifth Monarchy Man*, p. 69.

34. Morton, *The World of the Ranters*, pp. 122–3; Sabine, p. 599.

35. I. Ross, *Margaret Fell*, pp. 214–15. Stephen Marshall, who also married a wife from a wealthier family, made similar arrangements (E. Vaughan, *Stephen Marshall*, 1907, pp. 26–7).

36. Sabine, p. 599. From the way Winstanley puts it, the woman would seem to be as free to propose marriage as the man. Do Winstanley's words echo those of Comenius, quoted on p. 220 above?

37. E. H[all], *A Scriptural Discourse of the Apostasie and the Antichrist* (1653), sig. b 4.

38. P. E. H. Hair, 'Bridal Pregnancy in Rural England', *Population Studies*, XX, pp. 233–43; P. Laslett, *The World We Have Lost* (1965), p. 136.

39. Veall, op. cit., p. 141. The point had been made in 1881 by John Stoughton, who described it as 'a considerable judicial and social revolution' (*History of Religion in England*, 1881, I, pp. 473–5); cf. *S. and P.*, p. 331.

40. Fuller, *Good Thoughts in Bad Times* (1830), pp. 174–5.

41. W. E., *The Mad Mans Plea* (1653), p. 4. Erbery, one imagines, would regret this less than did Fuller. See pp. 214–15 above.

42. Marchant, *The Church under the Law*, pp. 20–22, 80–82.

43. F. Osborne, op. cit., I, pp. 30, 34.

44. Burton, *Parliamentary Diary*, III, pp. 296–305.

45. Ed. Lansdowne, *Petty Papers* (1927), II, pp. 52–4.

46. J. Hall, *Paradoxes* (1650), ed. D. C. Allen (Gainsville, Florida, 1956), pp. 54–77; Burton, *The Anatomy of Melancholy* (Everyman edn), III, pp. 88–9; Bunyan, *Works*, III, p. 645.

47. Fox, *Journal*, I, p. 8.

48. *Divine Songs of the Muggletonians* (1829), p. 140.

49. R. Herrick, 'His Wish', in *Poetical Works* (1956), p. 294.

50. J. Reeve, *A Transcendent Spiritual Treatise*, p. 12.

51. Cohn, op. cit., pp. 364–71; Coppe, *A Fiery Flying Roll*, II, p. 9; *Some Sweet Sips of some Spirituall Wine*, p. 46. See pp. 213–14 above.

52. *Copps Return to the wayes of Truth*, pp. 1–13.

53. Clarkson, *A Single Eye*, in Cohn, op. cit., p. 351.

54. Clarkson, *The Lost Sheep Found* (1660), pp. 25–6; *Look about you* (1659), pp. 30, 92–3; cf. Holland, op. cit., p. 4; E. Hide, op. cit., p. 42, whose summaries are not unfair; and E. Stokes, *The Wiltshire Rant*, pp. 8–9, for an example.

55. Clark and Slack, *Crisis and Order in English Towns, 1500–1700*, p. 153; see ibid., pp. 135, 159–60, for earlier examples of unmarried itinerant couples.

56. H. Ellis, *Pseudochristus* (1650), pp. 45–53 and *passim*; cf. Cohn, op. cit., pp. 330–33, and D. M. Wolfe's Introduction to Vol. IV of Milton's *Complete Prose Works*, pp. 73–5. Mary Gadbury may have been an epileptic.

57. Bunyan, *Works*, III, p. 613.

58. Those interested will find references in Cohn, op. cit., pp. 328–9.

59. Morton, op. cit., p. 122.

60. Burton, *Parliamentary Diary*, I, p. 24.

61. *The Routing of the Ranters*, p. 3. For Coppe's indignant denial see his *Remonstrance Of The sincere and zealous Protestation* (1651), p. 6.

62. R. Abbott, *The Young Mans Warning-piece*, sig. A 3v–4. Abbott claimed to be describing the behaviour of Ranters.

63. See pp. 161–2 above.

64. Holland, *The Smoke of the bottomles pit*, p. 3.

65. Firth, *Cromwell's Army*, p. 408; cf. Fox, *Journal*, II, pp. 95–6.

66. Gardiner, *Commonwealth and Protectorate*, II, p. 95. For examples see pp. 162 (Ranter) and 180 (Quaker) above.

67. Nuttall, *James Nayler*, pp. 8–10; *George Fox's 'Book of Miracles'*, pp. 5, 32–4.

68. Pordage, *Innocence appearing*, pp. 9, 18–19, 30–34, 56–8, 77–80, 84–6, 91. See p. 169 above.

69. Ed. Nuttall, *Early Quaker Letters*, pp. 181, 277.

70. Winstanley, *A Vindication of those . . . called Diggers* (1649[–50]), in Sabine, pp. 399–403; cf. *Englands Spirit Unfoulded*, ed. G. E. Aylmer P. and P., 40, pp. 14–15. Clarkson in 1659 – rather late – made the same point (*Look About You*, pp. 94–6).

71. cf. p. 151 above.

72. R. Younge, *The Poores Advocate* (1654), p. 11, quoted by P. Slack in Clark and Slack, *Crisis and Order in English Towns*, p. 167.

73. Fuller, *History of the Worthies of England* (1840), I, p. 398.

74. Quoted in Thirsk, *Agrarian History*, IV, p. 411.

75. Penry Williams, *The Council in the Marches of Wales under Elizabeth I* (Cardiff, 1958), p. 101.

76. J. Knox, *The History of the Reformation . . . in Scotland* (Glasgow, 1832), pp. 232, 237.

77. Thomson, *The Later Lollards*, p. 127; see p. 238 above.

78. Clarkson, *A Single Eye*, p. 11; cf. Milton, quoted on pp. 120 above and 308 below.

79. op. cit., p. 6; cf. Winstanley, quoted on pp. 238–9 above.

80. Nuttall, *Early Quaker Letters*, p. 200.

81. M. Cary, *A Word in Season to the Kingdom of England* (1647), p. 9.

82. M. Cary, *The Resurrection of the Witnesses* (1648), title-page and pp. 82–9, 98–100, 156–62, 189–94. In my *Antichrist in Seventeenth-Century England*, p. 107, the date is misprinted as 4 April 1645.

83. M. Cary, *The Little Horns Doom and Downfall* (1651), pp. 133, 238, 285–317.

84. M. R[ande], *Twelve Proposals to the Supreme Governours of the Three Nations* (1653), pp. 5, 7–11.

85. [L. Magalotti] *Travels of Cosmo III, Grand Duke of Tuscany, through England* (1821), pp. 453–4. I have not been able to identify Mary Cary's husband. In 1650 Lady Eleanor Davies's agent was a John Rand (P. Hardacre, 'Gerrard Winstanley in 1650', *Huntington Library Quarterly*, XXII, p. 348). Daniel and Walter Rand signed a Fifth Monarchist tract in 1657 (Capp, *Fifth Monarchy Men*, p. 244). A Mary, wife of William Rand, appears in the State Papers, but there seems to have been more than one William Rand (*C.S.P.D., 1650*, p. 500; *1652–3*, pp. 333, 341, 445; *1653–4*, pp. 44–6, 117, 434). William, son of the apothecary James Rand, was an associate of Nicholas Culpeper, Samuel Hartlib and William Walwyn, a physician and translator of chemical works who originated the scheme for a College of Graduate Physicians (C. Webster, 'English Medical Reformers of the Puritan Revolution', *Ambix*, XIV, pp. 24, 31–2, 36–9; N. Culpeper, *Culpeper's School of Physick*, 1659, sig. A 6v, C; W. W., *Healths new Store-house Opened*, 1661, p. 25). Mary Cary's works seem to have been known in chemical circles (see my *Antichrist in Seventeenth-Century England*, p. 119n., and pp. 221–2 above).

86. Fox, *Gospel-Truth*, p. 1059; cf. p. 243 above.

87. S. Fisher, *Testimony*, p. 584.

88. R. H. West, *Milton and the Angels* (Georgia U.P., 1955), esp. pp. 170–74. See pp. 309–10 below.

89. A. L. Morton, *The Matter of Britain*, esp. pp. 104–21. See pp. 261, 295 below.

16 LIFE AGAINST DEATH

1. Baxter, *The Holy Commonwealth*, p. 94.
2. C. H. and K. George, *The Protestant Mind of the English Reformation* (Princeton U.P., 1961), pp. 48, 130–33; for Perkins, see *P. and R.*, pp. 225–35.
3. op. cit. (6th impression, 1632), pp. 27–9.
4. Roger Williams, *The Bloudy Tenent of Persecution* (Hanserd Knollys Soc., 1848), p. 357. First published 1644.
5. R. Sibbes, quoted in *S. and P.*, p. 128. See ibid., pp. 128–33, *passim*, for this theme.
6. Strype, *Annals*, II, part ii, pp. 288–9.
7. Ed. C. H. Hull, *Economic Writings of Sir William Petty* (1899) I, pp. 274–5.
8. T. Weld, *A Short Story of the Rise, raign and ruine of the Familists and Libertines* (1644), p. 32.
9. P. Miller, *The New England Mind: From Colony to Province* (Harvard U.P., 1953), p. 56.
10. Rutherford, *A Survey of Antinomianism*, p. 209, in *A Survey of the Spirituall Antichrist* (1648).
11. [Anon.] *The Ranters Religion* (1650),
12. Burton, *Parliamentary Diary*, I, p. 119.
13. Thirsk, *Agrarian History*, pp. xxxiv–xxxv. I have benefited by hearing Mrs Thirsk lecture on this subject.
14. Everard, *The Gospel Treasury Opened* (2nd edn, 1659), pp. 329–35.
15. *S. and P.*, ch. III and esp. p. 127.
16. A. C. Carter, *The English Reformed Church in Amsterdam in the Seventeenth Century* (Amsterdam, 1964), pp. 36, 114, 128, 141–2.
17. Ed. A. Peel, *Tracts Ascribed to Richard Bancroft* (Cambridge U.P., 1953), p. 72; ed. Carlson, *Writings of Henry Barrow, 1590–1591*, p. 244; Hobbes, *English Works*, VI, pp. 194–5; cf. *P. and R.*, pp. 230–31 (Perkins).
18. See pp. 127–30 above.
19. See my *Reformation to Industrial Revolution*, pp. 260–66.
20. cf. K. V. Thomas, 'Work and Leisure in Pre-industrial Society', *P. and P.*, 29, pp. 61–2.
21. Orwell and Reynolds, op. cit., p. 83; cf. pp. 257–8 below.
22. W. Ames, *The Marrow of Sacred Divinity* (1642), p. 378: English translation published by order of the House of Commons; cf. Perkins, quoted in *P. and R.*, pp. 229–30.

23. R. Sibbes, *Works*, VII, p. 62; W. Gouge, *A Commentary on ...
Hebrews* (1867) III, pp. 290–95; T. Taylor, *Works* (1653), p. 477.

24. E. F. Gay, 'The Temples of Stowe and their debts (1603–1653)', *Huntington Library Quarterly*, II, p. 408.

25. H. Peter, *Good Work for a Good Magistrate*; [Anon.] *The Vanity and Mischief of Making Earthly Treasures our Chief Treasure* (1655).

26. J. Lee, *A Vindication of regulated Enclosure*, p. 21.

27. R. Baxter, *A Christian Directory* (1825) II, pp. 585–6. First published 1673.

28. Fox, *Journal*, I, p. 186; cf. W. Penn, *Some Fruits of Solitude* (1693) (Everyman edn), p. 60.

29. Orwell and Reynolds, op. cit., p. 92.

30. See p. 61 above.

31. Baxter, *Chapters from a Christian Directory* (1925), pp. 69, 71; Abbott, op. cit., III, p. 438.

32. Shakespeare, *I Henry IV*, Act I, scene ii; C. H. George 'The Making of the English Bourgeoisie', *Science and Society*, 35 (Winter 1971).

33. Perkins, *Works*, III, pp. 63–4; cf. *P. and R.*, pp. 215–38, *S. and P.*, pp. 138–43.

34. Sabine, pp. 633–4. Winstanley made the same point (ibid., p. 432).

35. ibid., pp. 258, 511–12, 595, 580–81; cf. pp. 159, 190–98.

36. ibid., pp. 109, 496–7; cf. George Foster's justification of expropriation quoted on pp. 167–9 above. For Ireton see Woodhouse, p. 73; for Baxter, pp. 252–3 above.

37. Ed. H. E. Rollins, *Cavalier and Puritan* (New York U.P., 1923), pp. 322–4.

38. Bunyan, *Works*, III, p. 314; cf. p. 333.

39. Cohn, op. cit., p. 370.

40. Sabine, p. 139. For more evidence of hostility to family prayers, see *S. and P.*, pp. 461–2, and K. V. Thomas, 'Women and the Civil War Sects', p. 52.

41. Coppe, Preface to Richard Coppin's *Divine Teachings*.

42. The marginal comment on this delicate passage in the Geneva Bible is entertaining; it stresses that the rich whom the Apostle condemns to weep and howl are the wicked and profane rich.

43. Cohn, op. cit., pp. 365–8. 'A dialogue between a learned divine and a beggar', which John Everard translated, may have given Coppe a starting point (Everard, *The Gospel Treasury Opened*, 2nd edn, 1659, pp. 528–31).

44. Nayler, *The Old Serpents Voice* (n.d., ?1656), p. 6. That Nayler was not exaggerating may be gathered from the following passage from Henry Newcome's *Autobiography*: 'This is now my constant fear, lest I die and shall leave nothing for my wife and children; and so men will say, "This was his strictness, and this is Puritanism! See what it gets them! What it leaves to wife and children!"' (Ed. R. Parkinson, Chetham Soc., 1852, pp. 135–6). Even Milton thought that the duty of charity is owed first to oneself and only in the second place to others (*Complete Prose Works*, II, p. 750).

45. Nayler, *A Salutation to the Seed of God* (3rd edn, 1656), p. 20; cf. p. 187 above.

46. Orwell and Reynolds, op. cit., pp. 86–7.

47. Sabine, p. 193.

48. R. Crab, *Dagons-Downfall* (1657), pp. 5–6, 13. In *The English Hermit* (1655) Crab had been facetious at the expense of those who explain away the Biblical advice to the rich man to sell all he had and give to the poor (*Harleian Miscellany*, IV, p. 461).

49. Dell, *Several Sermons*, p. 132.

50. Edwards, *Gangraena*, III, pp. 23, 227, 237–9; II, p. 27; H. and D., pp. 288–9, 310, 315; cf. Wolfe, p. 318, T. Prince, *The Silken Independents Snare Broken* (1649), pp. 6–7.

51. Rutherford, *A Modest Survey of the Secrets of the Antinomians*, pp. 176–7.

52. Orwell and Reynolds, op. cit., pp. 105, 90–91.

53. Sabine, pp. 277, 525; Burrough, *Works*, p. 500.

54. Wolfe, pp. 167, 171, 176, 180–81, 271, 369–70.

55. Ross, *Margaret Fell*, p. 59; ef. Troeltsch, *Social Teaching of the Christian Churches*, II, pp. 841, 920.

56. W. Penn, *No Cross, No Crown* (1669), ch. II, § 6. My italics.

57. See pp. 257–8 above, pp. 308, 317 below.

58. Sabine, pp. 315, 290, 475, 579, 457; cf. pp. 395, 409, 567; cf. Blake: 'He who desires but acts not breeds pestilence.'

59. Clarkson, *The Lost Sheep Found* (1660), p. 28; cf. Sabine, p. 565.

60. See pp. 150, 241 above.

61. I have benefited greatly from discussing this subject with Mr W. A. Hunt.

62. Clarkson, *A Single Eye*, in Cohn, pp. 352–3.

63. [Coppe] *Some Sweet Sips of some Spirituall Wine*, title-page and p. 52.

64. See p. 246 above.

65. See pp. 151, 249–50 above, 275–6 below.
66. P. W. Thomas, *Sir John Berkenhead, 1617–1679* (Oxford U.P., 1969), p. 57.
67. I owe this suggestion to Mr C. Russell's *The Crisis of Parliaments* (1971), p. 374.
68. *S. and P.*, p. 179.
69. See pp. 319–20 below.
70. See p. 88 above.
71. Ed. G. E. Alymer, 'Englands Spirit Unfoulded', pp. 14–15; cf. Sabine, pp. 241, 312–13, 399–403.
72. Sabine, pp. 468–9; cf. Milton's reference to 'scarecrow sins' quoted on p. 120 above, and Clarkson quoted on p. 245 above.
73. Sabine, p. 593. For the idea of a counter-culture, see the pioneering book by Jack Lindsay, *Civil War in England* (1954), pp. 313–24.
74. Haller, *The Rise of Puritanism*, p. 193; cf. pp. 193–205 *passim*; cf. p. 38 above.

17 THE WORLD RESTORED

1. In Orwell and Reynolds, *British Pamphleteers*, I, p. 106.
2. Gardiner, *Great Civil War*, IV, pp. 302–3; cf. G. Foster, *The Pouring Forth of the Seventh and Last Viall* (1650), p. 12.
3. Sabine, p. 198.
4. Milton, *Complete Prose Works*, IV, part i, p. 681; cf. Sabine, pp. 336, 513, 527, 574.
5. Hockliffe, *Diary of the Rev. Ralph Josselin*, p. 65.
6. J. Price, *The Cloudie Clergy* (1650), p. 14. I owe this reference to the kindness of Mr David Kirby. See Underdown, *Pride's Purge*, ch. IX, esp. pp. 262–4.
7. See pp. 87–8, 240–41 above; Abbott, op. cit., III, pp. 435–6; [Wilkins and Ward] *Vindiciae Academiarum*, p. 6; T. Hall, *Histrio-Mastix* (1654), pp. 198–9; Underdown, *Pride's Purge*, pp. 323, 356; *The Whole Duty of Man*, I, pp. 314, 423, 441.
8. W. Covell, *A Declaration unto the Parliament* (1659), pp. 8–11, 18, 21. See p. 90 above.
9. P. Cornelius, *The Way to the Peace and Settlement of these Nations* (April 1659), esp. pp. 8–27; *A Way propounded* (May 1659), *passim*; L. and M. Harder, *Plockhoy from Zurick-zee* (Newton, Kansas, 1952), esp. pp. 101–2.

10. [W. Sprigge] *A Modest Plea for an Equal Common-Wealth* (1659), pp. 36–42, 75–86.

11. [Anon.] *The Armies Vindication of This Last Change* (1659), pp. 4–6, 20–21.

12. op. cit., Milton, *Complete Works* (Columbia U.P.) XVIII, p. 6. First published 1938.

13. Ed. F. J. Routledge, *Clarendon State Papers*, IV (1932), pp. 191 (4 April 1659), 210 (23 May), 628 (30 March 1660), 640 (4 April); A. Evans, *A Rule from Heaven* (1659), p. 50; Burton, *Parliamentary Diary*, IV, pp. 458–9 (April 1659), rumours; ed. W. L. Sachse, *Diurnal of Thomas Rugg* (Camden Soc., 1961), pp. 66, 74 (March–April 1660); *Leyborne-Popham MSS.*, pp. 168 (February 1660), 176 (20 April); Gooch, *English Democratic Ideas*, p. 259.

14. *Clarendon State Papers*, IV, pp. 220, 228, 235–6, 330, 381, 405, 440, and *passim*.

15. Ed. J. A. Atkinson, *Tracts relating to the Civil War in Cheshire (1641–1659)* (Chetham Soc., 1909), p. 186.

16. Capp, *The Fifth Monarchy Men*, p. 142; cf. p. 19 above.

17. *A Door of Hope* (1661), Venner's Manifesto.

18. Ed. R. Parkinson, *Autobiography of Henry Newcome* (Chetham Soc., 1852), pp. 118–19.

19. Baxter, *The Holy Commonwealth*, p. 93.

20. *A Coffin for the Good Old Cause*, in *The Posthumous Works of Mr Samuel Butler* (6th edn, 1754), p. 300. The attribution to Butler is almost certainly incorrect.

21. Sir T. Aston, *A Remonstrance against Presbytery* (1641), sig. M 4v.

22. *Thurloe State Papers*, VII, p. 387.

23. [Anon.] *The Cause of God and of these Nations* (1659), quoted by A. H. Woolrych, Introduction to Vol. VII of Milton's *Complete Prose*, Yale edn.

24. Trotter, *Seventeenth Century Life in the Country Parish*, p. 36.

25. The Diggers had in fact been moved on to another parish, after consuming a good deal of timber in Walton-on-Thames, leaving their children on the parish, even though many of them were householders (Thomas, 'Another Digger Broadside', pp. 59, 65; Sabine, pp. 348, 434). The principle of settlement had been in operation in some areas for many years.

26. R. North, *Lives of the Norths* (1826) I, pp. 34–6. The speaker is Lord Keeper Guilford.

27. Trotter, op. cit., p. 169. For forests as a refuge from post-restoration persecution, see A. Everitt, *The Pattern of Rural Dissent: The Nineteenth Century* (Leicester U.P., 1972), pp. 44–6, 50; Capp, *The Fifth Monarchy Men*, p. 79.

28. Sabine, pp. 367–8, 436; *Fenstanton Records*, p. 82; Bunyan, *Works*, III, pp. 699, 712, 714.

29. *Reliquiae Baxterianae*, I, p. 297 (1663).

30. Woodhouse, p. 244.

31. Erbery, *Testimony*, pp. 184–5; see pp. 145–7 above.

32. See pp. 182–5 above.

33. Burrough, *Works*, pp. 659, 669–73, 684, 687, 706, 783–5.

34. I. Barrow, *The Duty and Reward of Bounty to the Poor* (1671), pp. 120–22.

35. *The Works of the . . . Author of The Whole Duty of Man* (1704) I, pp. 62–3. First published 1658.

36. A. Marvell, *The Rehearsal Transpros'd*, ed. D. I. B. Smith (Oxford U.P., 1971), p. 139. First published 1672.

37. See pp. 321–2 below; cf. *Petty Papers*, I, pp. 116–18, for some reflections on the social functions of religion.

38. Roger North, *Lives of the Norths*, III, p. 344. The dual standard still remains with us. See a book entitled *Trousered Apes* by Duncan Williams, free copies of which were distributed in 1971 to a number of academics. The author claims to object not to the theological views of Bishop John Robinson but to their popularization among the 'immature' (pp. 13–14). Thomas Edwards would have approved of that line of argument no less than John North. The 'apes' of the title are of course other people.

39. J. Locke, *The Reasonableness of Christianity* (1695), p. 285.

40. Edmund Gayton, *Charity Triumphant* (1655), quoted in Fairholt, *Lord Mayors' Pageants*, i, p. 171.

41. *Mercurius Elencticus*, 7 February 1649; J. Frank, *The Beginnings of the English Newspaper, 1620–1660* (Harvard U.P., 1961), p. 166, quoting *Mercurius Militaris*, 17–24 October 1648, p. 9.

42. Sir James Frazer, *The Golden Bough* (abridged edn, 1963), p. 118; Sir G. Keynes, *The Life of William Harvey* (Oxford U.P., 1966), p. 268.

43. Ed. J. C. Jeaffreson, *Middlesex County Records* (Middlesex County Record Soc., 1886–92), III, pp. 303, 326–7; ed. D. L. Powell and H. Jenkinson, *Surrey Quarter Sessions Order Book and Sessions Rolls, 1661–1663* (Surrey Record Soc., 1935), p. 307; J. Lindsay, *Civil War in England* (1954), pp. 340–41.

44. E. Chamberlayne, *Angliae Notitia* (1669), pp. 389, 400–401; [Magalotti] *Travels of Cosmo III, Grand Duke of Tuscany, through England*, p. 428.

45. S. Pepys, *Diary* (ed. H. B. Wheatley, 1946) I, pp. 314–15; S. Butler, *Characters and Passages from Note-Books*, p. 318.

46. I. Barrow, *Theological Works* (ed. A. Napier, 1859) IX, p. 577.

47. Contemporary MS. comment on the Bodleian copy of *Mirabilis Annus* (1661).

48. e.g. John Spencer, *Discourse Concerning Prodigies* (1663) and *Discourse Concerning Vulgar Prophecies* (1665).

49. Sprat, *History of the Royal Society*, pp. 362–5.

50. See my *Antichrist in Seventeenth-Century England*, pp. 138–9; cf. Fox, *The Lambs Officer*, p. 2; Burrough, *Works*, p. 189; Bunyan, quoted on p. 316 below.

51. H. Kearney, *Scholars and Gentlemen* (1970), p. 76. See pp. 226–9 above.

52. P. W. Thomas, *Sir John Berkenhead, 1617–1649*, pp. 100–103, 120, 133–6, 143, 168–70, 193, 208–9. It was of course a European movement, though I am here concerned only with England.

53. See pp. 202, 339–41 above.

54. Blake, *Complete Poetry and Prose* (Nonesuch edn.), p. 767.

55. See *S. and P.*, pp. 249–50, where other examples of emphasis on the virtues of hypocrisy are given.

56. [Anon.] *Salus Populi Solus Rex* (1648), quoted by Brailsford, op. cit., p. 346; Thomas Hall, *Funebria Florae* (2nd edn, 1661), title-page and p. 19; *Reliquiae Baxterianae*, I, pp. 32–3, 44.

57. Baxter, *A Sermon of Repentance* (1660), p. 43.

58. G. V. Bennett, 'Conflict in the Church', in *Britain after the Glorious Revolution, 1689–1714* (ed. G. Holmes, 1969), pp. 156–63.

59. *S. and P.*, pp. 331–2, 363–5.

60. See Thomas, *Religion and the Decline of Magic*, p. 161, and C. W. Chalklin, *Seventeenth-Century Kent* (1965), p. 244, for examples.

61. *S. and P.*, pp. 458, 469, 484; my *Economic Problems of the Church*, pp. 175–82; J. Waddington, *Congregational History* (1874), pp. 615–16.

62. *The Spectator*, 112 (9 July 1711).

63. Capp, *The Fifth Monarchy Men*, p. 195.

64. [R. Overton] *The Araignement of Mr Persecution* (1645) in Haller, *Tracts on Liberty*, II, p. 213.

65. See my *Reformation to Industrial Revolution*, pp. 196, 279; *P. and R.*, p. 382. See p. 27 above.

66. S. S., Gent., *The Joviall Crew, or the Devill turned Ranter* (1651). His Ranters are a mere caricature. They drink excessively, smoke (including the ladies) and fornicate. See pp. 320–21 below.

67. R. A. J. Walling, *The Story of Plymouth* (1952), pp. 138–9. For other examples, see Sir John Reresby's *Memoirs, passim.*

68. Bunyan, *Works*, III, p. 351.

69. Quoted by M. Ashley, *John Wildman* (1947), pp. 268–9.

70. P. Styles, 'The Evolution of the Law of Settlement', *University of Birmingham Historical Journal*, IX (1963), pp. 33–63.

71. J. Evelyn, *Sylva* (1664), sig. A4–B, pp. 1–2, 111–12.

72. Quoted by W. Tate, 'The Agrarian Problem and the Puritans', *Church Militant*, 8 June 1937, p. 5; cf. J. Aubrey, *Remaines of Gentilisme and Judaisme* (1881), pp. 247–8.

73. Hull, *Economic Writings of Sir William Petty*, I, pp. 302–3.

74. Kerridge, *The Agricultural Revolution*, p. 24.

75. Moses Wall to John Milton, May 1659, quoted in Masson, *Life of Milton*, V, p. 602.

18 CONCLUSION

1. Hobbes, quoted by A. Wolf, *A History of Science, Technology and Philosophy in the Sixteenth and Seventeenth Centuries* (1935), p. 565.

2. R. Nevo, *The Dial of Virtue: A Study of Poems on Affairs of State in the Seventeenth Century* (Princeton U.P., 1963), pp. 136–46. See pp. 135–6 above.

3. *Leyborne-Popham MSS.* (H.M.C.), p. 57.

4. Milton, *Areopagitica*, in *Complete Prose Works*, II, pp. 558, 551; cf. Hobbes, quoted on p. 300 below.

5. H. Power, *Experimental Philosophy* (1664), p. 192. Power began writing his book in 1653. Is the sentence beginning 'Methinks I see . . .' a conscious echo of Milton's similar sentence in *Areopagitica*?

6. Woodhouse, pp. 128, 143, 161.

7. Burton, *Parliamentary Diary*, I, pp. 69, 86, 158; cf. p. 76. The intention of the last clause was no doubt to prevent Cromwell releasing Nayler. He was freed by the restored Long Parliament in September 1659.

8. ibid., I, pp. 55–6.

9. Walker, *History of Independency*, Part I, pp. 140–41. See p. 48 above.

10. Burton, *Parliamentary Diary*, I, pp. 218, 272. Skippon had been one of Nayler's fiercest enemies: Robinson on the whole favoured mercy.

11. See pp. 140–41 above.

12. Brailsford, op. cit., ch. X.

13. J. Robinson, *Works* (1851) I, p. xliv.

14. J. Goodwin, *Imputatio Fidei* (1642), Preface.

15. T. Goodwin, *Works*, IV, p. 237.

16. Haller, *Tracts on Liberty*, II, pp. 160, 318–19, 331.

17. Nuttall, *The Holy Spirit*, pp. 104–7, 115–17, 126–30.

18. Woodhouse, p. 247.

19. Milton, *Christian Doctrine*, in *Works* (Columbia edn) XIV, p. 9.

20. J. Goodwin, *Hagiomastix* (1646), Preface.

21. Hobbes, *English Works*, V, pp. 397–8; cf. Ralegh, quoted in *I.O.E.R.*, p. 182.

22. Bunyan, *Works*, I, p. 392; Woodhouse, p. 390.

23. See p. 167 above.

24. Quoted by Huehns, op. cit., p. 49.

25. Winstanley, *Several pieces gathered into one volume*, Introduction; cf. *The Saints Paradice*, p. 102.

26. Sabine, pp. 125, 185, 289; cf. 315, 564, 579.

27. ibid., pp. 564–6; *I.O.E.R.*, p. 110.

28. W. Tyndale, *Doctrinal Treatises* (Parker Soc., 1848), pp. 55–6; *An Answer to Sir Thomas More* (Parker Soc., 1850), pp. 51–2, 55.

29. T. Taylor, *Works* (1653), p. 411.

30. W. Gilbert, *De Magnete* (1600), Preface; cf. Lynn Thorndike, 'Newness in Seventeenth Century Science', *Journal of the History of Ideas*, XII, pp. 585–98.

31. *I.O.E.R.*, pp. 114–15; cf. Bacon, *Works*, IV, p. 14.

32. J. Hall, *An Humble Motion ... Concerning the Advancement of Learning* (1649), p. 34. In *I.O.E.R.*, I have collected a number of examples of the convergence of the religious emphasis on experience with the scientists' and alchemists' emphasis on experiment (pp. 112–15, 121, 295–7); cf. C. Webster, 'English Medical Reformers of the Puritan Revolution', *Ambix*, XIV, pp. 26–7.

33. Stubbe, *The Lord Bacons Relation of the Sweating Sickness Examined* (1671), Preface.

34. Dell, *Several Sermons*, pp. 298, 428. Descartes and Locke, in their different ways, brought about a similar openness of mind in philosophy. For the Everlasting Gospel see pp. 141–8 above.

35. cf. John Lewis, who in 1656 urged the religious radicals in Wales not to go too fast or too far in inveighing against old customs and against

the superstitious Welsh regard for church buildings (*Some seasonable and modest thoughts*, 1656, pp. 11–17); cf. pp. 250–57 above.

36. See pp. 288–92 below.
37. Ed. D. F. Gladish, *Sir William Davenant's Gondibert* (Oxford U.P., 1971), p. 22; cf. p. 49.
38. *I.O.E.R.*, pp. 81–2, 261–3; cf. pp. 66–7, 228 above.
39. Burrough, *Works*, sig. b 2v–b 3.
40. Sabine, pp. 223–4; Erbery, *Testimony*, pp. 263–5, 337–8; Fox, *Journal*, I, p. 425.
41. Sabine, pp. 231–2; for Salmon see pp. 163–4 above.
42. Winstanley, *The Breaking of the Day of God*, sig. A 4v; Sabine, pp. 445–6; cf. Erbery, quoted on p. 145 above.
43. See p. 154 above.
44. S. Fisher, *Testimony*, p. 548.
45. T. Hall, *Vindiciae Literarum*, p. 215.
46. Morton, op. cit., pp. 98, 106, 132–3; Ashley, *John Wildman*, pp. 194–5. I do not think this last fact justifies Professor Cohn in referring to Calvert as himself a Ranter (op. cit., p. 464).
47. Morton, op. cit., pp. 138–42.
48. See p. 256 above.
49. See pp. 86–7 above.
50. See pp. 46, 172–3 above.
51. cf. *S. and P.*, pp. 286–7, 428.
52. *Fenstanton Records*, pp. 17–19, 85.
53. ibid., pp. 156, 210. The husband accepted the ruling; his wife did not.
54. Ed. G. B. Harrison, *The Church Book of Bunyan Meeting, 1650–1821* (1928), p. x; Bunyan, *Works*, II, pp. 582–3; cf. Walzer, op. cit., p. 305.
55. *The Ranters Declaration, . . . published by M. Stubs, a late fellow-Ranter* (1650) in Cohn, op. cit., p. 334.
56. Sabine, pp. 223–4; Erbery, *Testimony*, p. 137.
57. See pp. 119–23, 157, 167, 181, 245–7, 250–51, 304 above; J. Spittlehouse, *An Answer To one part of The Lord Protectors Speech: Or, A Vindication of the Fifth-Monarchy men* (1654), p. 1. As late as 1691 Richard Baxter felt he had to disavow levelling when he criticized the extravagance of the rich (*The Poor Husbandman's Advocate to Rich Racking Landlords*, 1691, in *The Rev. Richard Baxter's Last Treatise*, ed. F. J. Powicke, 1926, p. 46).
58. See Burrough, *Works*, p. 615.

59. See pp. 252–7 above; Carrol, op. cit., pp. 58–9, 92.

60. Pepys, *Diary*, III, p. 315.

61. See pp. 146–7, 164 above.

62. Sabine, p. 600. 'The Four' are the four elements.

63. Morton, op. cit., p. 36.

64. See *P. and R.*, pp. 105–7, and references there cited. The English Saint-Simonian J. E. Smith in 1833 said the true Christian was 'one who turns the world upside down' (W. H. G. Armytage, *Heavens Below*, 1961, p. 134).

65. E. D. Andrews, *The People Called Shakers* (New York, 1953), esp. pp. 13–20, 27–8. Like the Muggletonians the Shakers believed the Two Witnesses had come (p. 23). The name Shaker had been given to some sectaries in 1648 (*A Scottish Mist Dispel'd*, p. 17) and was later used for Quakers.

66. R. W. Ketton-Cremer, *Norfolk Assembly* (1957), p. 85.

67. J. Wesley, *Journal* (1864), pp. 10–11. I owe this reference to the kindness of Mr John Walsh.

68. See ch. 11 above.

69. Ed. J. Ashton, *Humour, Wit and Satire of the Seventeenth Century* (1883), p. 37.

70. D. Defoe, *Jure Divino* (1706), pp. 206–17. 'They' in the second line are the Saxon invaders.

71. Morton, *The Matter of Britain*, esp. pp. 104–21; see my *Century of Revolution*, p. 168.

72. The quotations are from Love and Liberty, Why should we idly waste our prime?, Epistle to a young friend; see also Third Epistle to J. Lapraik, To James Tennant of Glenconner, Holy Willie's Prayer, Elegy on Willie Nicol's Mare, Is there for honest poverty?, Look up and see!, The Tree of Liberty, The Author's Earnest Cry and Prayer. For all his sentimental Jacobitism Burns's poem The Solemn League and Covenant shows sound historical sense; Ye Jacobites by Name could be sung to the same tune as The Diggers' Song.

73. Mrs Gaskell, *Life of Charlotte Brontë* (World's Classics), p. 12.

74. Thomas, *Religion and the Decline of Magic*, p. 661.

75. This is suggested by Mr Arthur Clegg, in his poem *Fire in the Bush* (Breakthru Broadsheet, 1971); cf. Thomas, op. cit., pp. 656–7, and p. 237 above.

76. See Appendix II below.

77. See pp. 135–6, 223–5, 245, 289 above.

78. 'Music is almost as dangerous as gunpowder, and it may be requires looking after no less than the press or the Mint.' The words are those of Jeremy Collier, at almost the opposite pole in politics and religious views from Locke (*A Short View of the Immorality and Profaneness of the Stage*, 4th edn, 1699, p. 278).

79. See N. O. Brown, *Life against Death* (1959), ch. XIII and *passim*.

80. See my ' "Reason" and "reasonableness" in seventeenth-century England', *British Journal of Sociology*, XX, pp. 248–9, and references there cited.

81. Marx, *Capital*, I (ed. Dona Torr, 1946), p. xxx; Marx-Engels *Gesamtausgabe*, I, i, p. 563.

82. Sabine, pp. 493, 520.

83. Burrough, *Works*, p. 677.

84. See p. 317 below.

APPENDIX I

1. Hobbes, *English Works*, VI, p. 165.

2. Clarendon, *A Brief View and Survey of . . . Mr Hobbes's Book Entitled Leviathan* (Oxford U.P., 1676), pp. 181–2.

3. Sabine, pp. 513, 581.

4. Evidence for statements about Hobbes made here will be found (unless otherwise documented) in *P. and R.*, pp. 275–98. For Winstanley see ch. 7 above.

5. Hobbes, *Leviathan* (Penguin edn.), pp. 234, 18, 28; *English Works*, I, p. viii; Sabine, pp. 565, 567.

6. See p. 118 above.

7. Q. Skinner, 'The Ideological Context of Hobbes's Political Thought', *Historical Journal*, IX, pp. 286–317.

8. Sabine, pp. 456–7, 452, 529.

9. See pp. 147–8 above.

10. Sabine, pp. 105, 111–12.

11. ibid., p. 493; *The Saints Paradice*, pp. 123–4; cf. Sabine, pp. 111, 125, 197, 235, 261–2; Marcuse, *An Essay on Liberation*, p. 19.

12. Sabine, pp. 105, 206, 222, 261; *The Saints Paradice*, p. 72.

13. See pp. 410–13 below.

14. Skinner, 'The Ideological Context of Hobbes's Political Thought', *passim*.

15. Hobbes, *The Elements of Law* (ed. F. Tönnies, Cambridge U.P., 1928), p. 150.

16. K. Marx and F. Engels, *The Holy Family* (1844) in *Marx and Engels on Religion* (Moscow, 1957), pp. 64–5; Hobbes, *Leviathan* (Penguin edn), p. 111.

17. Sir W. Davenant, *Gondibert* (ed. Gladish), p. 235.

APPENDIX II

1. Milton, *Complete Prose Works*, I, p. 788; cf. II, p. 278. For Brooke see Haller, *Tracts on Liberty*, II, p. 134. D. M. Wolfe's *Milton in the Puritan Revolution* (1941) is the best discussion of Milton's dialogue with the radicals.

2. Edwards, *Gangraena*, I, p. 34; Writer, *The Jus Divinum of Presbyterianism*, pp. 80–84; cf. pp. 128–9, 283–4 above.

3. Milton, *Complete Prose Works*, II, pp. 366–7, 512, 670; cf. p. 120 above.

4. Milton, *Works* (Columbia edn) XVII, pp. 7–9; cf. XVI, pp. 112–63.

5. See p. 165 above.

6. Milton, *Complete Prose Works*, II, p. 750; cf. pp. 259–60 above.

7. Milton, *Works* (Columbia edn) VI, p. 98.

8. See p. 120 above.

9. See p. 267 above.

10. Milton, *Complete Prose Works*, III, pp. 198–9, 204.

11. cf. ibid., V, p. 421, for positions shared with the Levellers.

12. ibid., IV, p. 555.

13. A. J. A. Waldock, *Paradise Lost and Its Critics* (Cambridge U.P., 1947), pp. 23–4.

14. cf. the opening and close of *Paradise Regained* – 'Eden raised in the vast wilderness': 'A fairer Paradise is founded now.' For Coppin see pp. 166–7 above.

15. For the tendencies towards pantheism in Milton's *Christian Doctrine* see Saurat, *Blake and Milton*, pp. 145–8.

16. cf. Winstanley's view that exploitation rather than labour is the curse – p. 121 above. But see K. V. Thomas, 'Work and Leisure in Pre-industrial Society', pp. 56–7, on the long medieval tradition behind this idea of Milton's.

17. cf. p. 270 above.

18. Marvell, *Poems and Letters*, ed. H. M. Margoliouth (Oxford U.P., 1927) I, pp. 300–303; Rochester, *Poems* (ed. Pinto, 1953), p. 111.

19. This is of course only one small aspect of *Paradise Regained*. Another is the rejection of a worldly foreign policy, alliances with great powers – clearly a criticism of the Protector's government.

20. cf. p. 251 above.

21. D. Saurat, *Milton, Man and Thinker* (1944), Part IV; cf. pp. 164–5 above.

22. See p. 117 above.

23. See pp. 265–6 above. I am reluctant to accept the argument that *Samson Agonistes* was written before the restoration. So many of the allusions so aptly fit England after 1660 that it is difficult not to think it was at least redrafted then. But by the late 1650s Milton would see little difference between the ruling generals and royalists. Cf. Ants Oras, 'Milton's Blank Verse and the Chronology of His Major Poems', in *Essays on John Milton* (ed. J. M. Patrick, Florida U.P., 1953), pp. 128–95.

24. Dryden's is a more technical argument.

25. See pp. 174, 201, 204–5, 237 above. Cf. Jack Lindsay's pioneering *John Bunyan* (1937).

26. Tindall, *John Bunyan*, p. 138.

27. Bunyan, *Works*, I, p. 600.

28. ibid., III, p. 282.

29. ibid., III, p. 160. Bunyan presumably wrote this about ten years after the restoration.

30. ibid., I, pp. 51–6; cf. Underdown, op. cit., p. 353.

31. Bunyan, *Works*, III, pp. 394, 676, 695–6.

32. ibid., III, p. 130.

33. ibid., III, pp. 89–167 *passim*, 311, 322, 348. They might of course have been Ranters – see p. 238 above.

34. ibid., III, p. 591; cf. p. 166, and p. 106 above. In part this attitude is traditional: Richard Bernard in *The Isle of Man* (1627) made the enemies of religion gentlemen, including Sir Worldlywise, Sir Luke Warm, Sir Plausible-Civil and many more (pp. 70–71, 77–8, 128–9, 150).

35. Bunyan, *Works*, I, p. 362.

36. Tindall, *John Bunyan, Mechanick Preacher*, pp. 105–6.

37. Bunyan, *Works*, III, pp. 593, 695. See p. xv above.

38. ibid., III, p. 89.

39. See p. 257 above.

40. Bunyan, *Works*, III, p. 123. See p. 299 above.

41. S. Hieron, *Sermons* (1624), p. 373.

42. Bunyan, *Works*, III, p. 122.

43. H. Talon, *John Bunyan* (1951), p. 276.

44. Bunyan, *Works*, III, pp. 618–21, 654–5.

45. See *P. and R.*, pp. 381–2, where I give other examples.

46. See p. 240 above.

47. See p. 370n. above for Locke; cf. my ' "Reason" and "reasonableness" in seventeenth century England', *British Journal of Sociology*, XX, p. 244.

48. See pp. 123, 202, 340, 357–8, 375 above.

49. Butler, *Characters and Passages from Note-Books*, pp. 74–5, 168, 308, 310, 318–22, 341, 479; *Poetical Works* (Edinburgh, 1854) II, pp. 259–61.

50. See p. 133 above.

51. T. Otway, *Alcibiades*, Act III, scene ii.

52. *The Works of Mrs Aphra Behn*, ed. M. Summers (1915) I, p. xxv; IV, pp. 288–90, 303. Yet Mrs Behn was an admirer of the Behmenist vegetarian, Thomas Tryon (ibid., VI, pp. 379–81). For acute comments on Mrs Behn, linking her with Quakers and Diggers, see G. Woodcock, *The Incomparable Aphra* (1948), pp. 150–52, 229 and Part Six, *passim*.

53. G. Villiers, Duke of Buckingham, *Works* (1775) II, p. 134.

54. See ch. 11 above.

55. J. Collier, *A Short View . . . of the English Stage*, pp. 175, 101; cf. ibid., pp. 95–6, 129, 143–5, 190.

56. Rochester, *Poems*, pp. 49, 72, 121.

57. G. Burnet, *Some Passages of the Life and Death Of . . . John, Earl of Rochester*, in *The Lives of . . . Hale, . . . Rochester and Queen Mary* (1774), pp. 18, 22, 35, 47, 58.

58. cf. Rochester's defence of 'the commoners and cottagers' of Kingswood Chase, Gloucestershire, in 1670 (V. de Sola Pinto, *Enthusiast in Wit*, 1962, p. 146).

59. Rochester, *Poems*, pp. 107–13, 137; cf. p. 117. The reference to 'new rants' on p. 131 is in a poem doubtfully ascribed to Rochester.

60. See p. 127 above.

61. See p. 101 above.

62. T. Traherne, *Poems, Centuries and Three Thanksgivings*, ed. A. Ridler (Oxford U.P., 1966), pp. 284, 244.

63. ibid., pp. 10, 224, 267–71, 284, 327, 363.

64. Traherne, *Poems, Centuries and Three Thanksgivings*, p. 8. 'Proprieties' = properties.

65. Marcuse, *An Essay on Liberation*, p. 37.

Index